Mentoring and Diversity

NATIONAL UNIVERSITY
LIBRARY   SAN DIEGO

D0949103

Mentoring and Diversity
An international perspective

*David Clutterbuck
and Belle Rose Ragins*

OXFORD   AUCKLAND   BOSTON   JOHANNESBURG   MELBOURNE   NEW DELHI

Butterworth-Heinemann
Linacre House, Jordan Hill, Oxford OX2 8DP
225 Wildwood Avenue, Woburn, MA 01801-2041
A division of Reed Educational and Professional Publishing Ltd

A member of the Reed Elsevier plc group

First published 2002

© David Clutterbuck and Belle Rose Ragins 2002

All rights reserved. No part of this publication may be reproduced in
any material form (including photocopying or storing in any medium by
electronic means and whether or not transiently or incidentally to some
other use of this publication) without the written permission of the
copyright holder except in accordance with the provisions of the Copyright,
Designs and Patents Act 1988 or under the terms of a licence issued by the
Copyright Licensing Agency Ltd, 90 Tottenham Court Road, London,
England W1P 0LP. Applications for the copyright holder's written
permission to reproduce any part of this publication should be addressed
to the publishers

British Library Cataloguing in Publication Data

Library of Congress Cataloguing in Publication Data
[copy to come]

ISBN 0 7506 4836 8

For information on all Butterworth-Heinemann publications visit
our website at www.bh.com

Composition by Genesis Typesetting, Rochester, Kent
Printed and bound in Great Britain by Biddles Ltd, *www.biddles.co.uk*

FOR EVERY TITLE THAT WE PUBLISH, BUTTERWORTH-HEINEMANN
WILL PAY FOR BTCV TO PLANT AND CARE FOR A TREE.

Contents

Preface: how to read this book

Mentoring for Diversity: an international perspective is a collaborative venture, bringing together new and emerging perspectives on mentoring and diversity from both sides of the Atlantic and beyond. The purpose of this book is to link academic research and applied practice within an international context. This integration is essential: research and theory inform our practice, but our practice must also guide our research. If there is one topic that calls for the marriage of academic research and practical applications, it is the topic of mentoring and diversity in organizations! This sense of diversity is even reflected in the lead authors of this book: David Clutterbuck and Belle Rose Ragins, a male practitioner and a female academic who represent leading edges of mentoring practice and research in Europe and the USA.

A strength of this book lies in the diverse voices, perspectives and frameworks that are used to describe diversity in mentoring relationships in a host of international settings. We take a broad and inclusive view of diversity, because these differences in perceptions and experiences enrich our understanding of this complex and critical developmental relationship. In the pages that follow, you will hear diverse views from mentors and mentees/protégés who are:

- men and women
- heterosexual and gay
- disabled and able-bodied
- academics and practitioners
- formal and informal
- of different races, ethnicities, religions and socioeconomic backgrounds
- from different organizations, cultures and countries.

These voices may have much in common, but also they also point to distinct differences in the nature and functioning of mentoring relationships. Together they represent a rich symphony that can best be appreciated by understanding its unique parts.

Another strength of this book is that it provides an international perspective on diversity in mentoring relationships. This perspective furnishes unique insights into cross-cultural differences in mentoring, and shatters some assumptions in the process. In fact, we were surprised to learn at the very start of this project that Europeans and Americans do not even share the same language with respect to mentoring relationships! For example, the word 'protégé' is commonly used in the USA, but this term is considered unacceptable by Europeans as it suggests a somewhat patronizing, hierarchical, and one-way relationship. Europeans prefer the term 'mentee', but American researchers view this as a trendy term that is not actually a word. Do not be surprised, therefore, if you see both terms used in this book. But these language differences also reflect deeper differences and assumptions regarding the very nature of the mentoring relationship. Americans view mentoring as helping the protégé advance up the corporate ladder, while Europeans see this function as nepotism and favouritism. Europeans tend to use a more holistic concept of mentoring that is related to the life cycles and overall personal development of the mentee, irrespective of his or her rank or advancement patterns. Of course we do not want to give away the end of the book in the beginning, so you will need to read our book in order to capture fully the other international intricacies embedded in diverse mentoring relationships.

We would like to point out that *Mentoring for Diversity* is intended to be read as a series of reflections, empirical insights and signposts, not as a treatise or manual. Expect insights and informed opinions that are based on emerging research and theory, rather than a uniform set of 'cookbook' guidelines that can be used in every situation.

This book contains solid, practical advice grounded in empirical research, but please do not be surprised if you find seemingly conflicting views in different chapters. After all, diversity is the child of context and complexity, and 'right' answers sometimes become 'wrong' in specific circumstances.

That said, this book does have a structure and framework that evolved from the idea that theory and research informs practice, which in turn guide future research and theory. Accordingly, the book falls naturally into three sections that reflect this reciprocal impact of theory, research and practice:

- An overview of the theory and research on diversified mentoring relationships, followed by an applied model of diversity in mentoring relationships.
- Some empirically based and pragmatic observations of 'best practices' that are used by diversified mentoring programmes in various international contexts.
- A collection of case studies of diversity in both mentoring programmes and individual mentoring relationships that illustrate diversity in action, followed by an analysis of some of the recurring themes that are supported by existing research but also chart new ground for emerging research.

In our first chapter, Regina M. O'Neill reviews the extensive and often conflicting empirical research on diversity in mentoring relationships. Her comprehensive chapter lays the foundation for the book by summarizing what we know about diversified mentoring relationships and, more importantly, what is yet to be discovered.

In Chapter 2, Belle Rose Ragins builds on this academic foundation by providing an overview of the key challenges faced by members of diversified mentoring relationships. In the first part of this chapter, she examines how diversity affects the processes and outcomes of mentoring relationships and draws upon existing theories and research to develop a conceptual model of perceived diversity in mentoring relationships. In the second part of the chapter, she blends research with practice to present practical, empirically based strategies for developing effective diversified mentoring relationships in organizations.

In Chapter 3, David Clutterbuck draws on his extensive international consulting experience to present a broad framework for the design and management of diversified mentoring programmes. In Chapter 4, he takes a similar view of the practicalities of managing the diversity mentoring relationship – from the perspective of both mentor and mentee. Chapter 5 takes a deeper and more reflective journey into the nature and influence of stereotyping in mentoring – a somewhat different but largely complementary view with that expressed by Ragins in Chapter 2.

Chapter 6 presents a variety of first-hand reports of diversity in mentoring relationships, and reflects the real-world experiences of mentors and mentees in academia, business and the community at large. Chapter 7 is a brief reflection on the diversity mentoring process by a mentor, who has taken the time to look beneath the surface of her own motivations. Chapter 8 provides an overview of some of the recurrent themes underlying the individual cases, such as the discovery of deep diversity in diversified mentoring relationships, the importance of understanding the organizational context, and the potential for inflated expectations in diversified mentoring relationships. Chapter 9 takes an organizational perspective, featuring mentoring programmes for the disabled, teen parents, young ex-offenders, entrepreneurs and Pakistani students.

Finally, Chapter 10 gives a broader perspective of some of the recurrent themes from the cases, including the topics of power, culture change, training, acknowledging difference and matching of mentors and mentees. This chapter, by David Clutterbuck, illustrates that mentoring may occur with different individuals in different settings, but these relationships still share some common processes and themes reflecting the diversity in the relationship. This chapter, as well as the cases that precede it, provides rich qualitative data for mentoring researchers and practitioners.

In the end, our challenge to you, the reader, is to establish your own personally grounded understanding of the nature of diversity in mentoring relationships, and how this diversity can be applied to the benefit of your organization and the people in it. We hope and expect that you will select your own unique mixture of concepts and approaches to diversity in mentoring relationships – a mixture that can be used to build a mentoring programme that enriches the learning and sharing culture of your organization, a mixture that enables members of diversified relationships to give their very best to their relationship and a mixture that allows them to excel in an organization that values, recognizes and rewards their exceptional contributions. We believe passionately that mentoring is a key element in the effective management of diversity in organizations, and that diversity is an integral part of every successful mentoring relationship.

Vive la difference!

David Clutterbuck and Belle Rose Ragins

1

Gender and race in mentoring relationships: a review of the literature

Regina M. O'Neill

The role of mentoring for women and people of colour has become an increasingly important one. For example, as noted by Ragins, Townsend and Mattis (1998), the majority of women executives that responded to a recent survey by Catalyst identified mentoring as an important strategy used to break through the glass ceiling. In addition, scholars have pointed to the importance of mentoring relationships for people of colour (e.g. Ragins, 1997a).

Despite the recognized importance of mentoring for women and people of colour (Burke and McKeen, 1990; Noe, 1988b; O'Neill, Horton and Crosby, 1999; Ragins, 1989; 1997a; 1997b; 1999; Thomas, 1990; 1993; 1999), research on the role of gender and race in mentoring relationships has only recently begun to evolve, and it is only in the past decade that increasing attention has been paid to these issues.

The purpose of this chapter is to review the literature on gender and race in mentoring relationships. In particular, this chapter is organized as follows. First, I review the role of gender and race on the likelihood of a person becoming either a protégé or a mentor. I follow this by reviewing the role of gender and race on the type of mentoring received by protégés and provided by mentors. Next, I review how gender and race influence the outcomes of mentoring. Then, I consider the gender and race composition of mentoring relationships. I conclude the chapter with some directions for further research on race and gender, as well as on other dimensions of diversity in mentoring relationships.

Protégé gender and race in the formation of mentoring relationships

Given the extent of documented gender and racial prejudice and discrimination in the workplace, women and people of colour might have a harder time finding mentors than white men. The expectation of unequal access to mentors was certainly one of the guiding principles of early work (Collins and Scott, 1978; Cook, 1979; Fitt and Newton, 1981) including the pioneering work of Kram (1985) and Collins (1983). Scholars with similar expectations have offered a variety of conceptualizations (e.g. Auster, 1984; Bowen, 1986; Farylo and Paludi, 1985; Gilbert and Rossman, 1992; Hetherington and Barcelo, 1985; Nichols, Carter and Golden, 1985; Noe, 1988a; Ragins, 1997a), reviewed the existing literatures (e.g. Burke and McKeen, 1990; O'Neill, Horton and Crosby, 1999; Paludi et al., 1990; Ragins, 1989; 1999) or conducted qualitative studies (e.g. Clawson and Kram, 1984; Maack and Passet, 1993; Thomas, 1993).

Despite these expectations, in the simplest terms, the gender of a junior person does *not* influence the person's probability of becoming a protégé. Across a number of studies using a variety of conceptual and operational definitions, no pattern emerges regarding the sheer likelihood of having had a mentor for men versus women. However, the research that compares whites versus non-whites is inconclusive about the effects of race in mentoring relationships.

The first study to use quantitative data to compare the probability of women and men receiving mentoring was published by Fagenson (1988; see also 1989). Fagenson distributed a questionnaire to a stratified random sample of women and men in high- and low-level jobs in a large health-care company. Respondents were asked to indicate whether or not they 'have a mentor', and a mentor was defined as 'someone in a position of power who looks out for you, or gives you advice, or brings your accomplishments to the attention of other people who have power in the company' (Fagenson, 1988, p. 186). Thirty-seven per cent of the respondents claimed to have a mentor. Although high-level workers were much more likely than low-level ones to have a mentor, there were no gender differences at either level.

Similarly, studying three research and development firms, Ragins and Cotton (1991) found no differences in the percentages of women and men who could be characterized as having been protégés in a mentoring relationship. Fifty-five per cent of the men and 50 per cent of the women had had at least one mentor. Virtually identical percentages of women and men – slightly under 18 per cent in both cases – had had extensive mentoring. These similarities in actual percentages were especially striking because more women than men in the survey said they needed to have a mentor and because women perceived more barriers to obtaining a mentor than did men.

The studies by Fagenson (1988, 1989) and Ragins and Cotton (1991) are not isolated examples. A number of other studies in the workplace have substantiated these findings. Swerdlik and Bardon (1988), Dreher and Ash (1990), Cox and Nkomo (1991), Whitely, Dougherty and Dreher (1992), Turban and Dougherty (1994), Baugh, Lankau and Scandura (1996) and McGuire (1999) all report that men and women acknowledge in equal measure having been protégés. A number of other studies have included gender as a variable and found no gender effects, implying that women and men are equally likely to receive help (Chao, Walz and Gardner, 1992; Corzine, Buntzman and Busch, 1994; Whitely, Dougherty and Dreher, 1992; Dreher and Cox, 1996; Hill et al., 1989).

In fact, two recent studies – one of managers (Thomas, 1990) and the other of lawyers (Mobley et al., 1994) – found that women were more likely than men to have been someone's protégé. In the study of lawyers, however, the apparent gender difference was due to the fact that women in the sample were more likely to be at the associate level whereas men were more likely to be partners.

In addition to the vast number of studies that consider career development in corporate and professional settings, research in academic settings also provides insights into gender differences in mentoring relationships. Interestingly, a number of researchers like Tidball (e.g. 1986) assume that women students have a more difficult time than men finding mentors. Indeed, part of the rationale for the continued existence of women's colleges is to provide women with greater access to mentors (Conway, 1989). By implication then, coeducational environments are seen as difficult places for women to find mentors.

Although the empirical research is scant, it suggests little gender difference. Busch (1985) conducted a study of mentoring during graduate education among 432 education department faculty. She found that those who had been mentored were significantly more likely to mentor others and that the percentages of men and women who had been mentored were approximately equal. When Keith and Moore (1995) questioned over 300 doctoral students in forty different departments of sociology, they found no differences in the degree to which women and men students acknowledged having had access to mentors.

Only one study in the last two decades has found women who reported having been mentored less than men (Wilson and Reschly, 1995). In that study, however, the measure of mentoring was a single item in a long inventory of items, and the sample was relatively small (eighty-seven men and eighty-nine women with doctorates in school psychology). There were no gender differences in responses to a similar question about role models.

Over the last decade, concerns have also been raised about the accessibility of mentoring relationships for people of colour (e.g. Ragins, 1997a; 1997b; Thomas and Alderfer, 1989). However, there has been very little research that explores the sheer likelihood of people of colour becoming protégés.

Several studies have examined the effects of protégé race on the presence of a mentor. In one study of managers at a public utility company, Thomas (1990) found that blacks and whites had the same average number of mentoring relationships. Similarly, in a study of a large financial services company, McGuire (1999) found that, contrary to some popular claims, people of colour were as likely to form mentoring relationships as whites. While Dreher and

Cox (1996) found no race differences in the sheer presence of a mentor, they did find, however, that protégés of colour were less likely to have white mentors than white protégés were. Most recently, in a study of 116 black and 756 white accountants, Viator (2001) found that blacks reported greater barriers to mentoring and that they are less likely to obtain an informal mentor.

While scholars have expected that workplace discrimination may have limited the likelihood of women and people of colour to obtain mentors, the empirical evidence has generally shown few differences in the presence of a mentor for women and men or for whites and non-whites. In contrast, however, there have been reported differences in access to mentoring. For example, in their matched sample of male and female managers, Ragins and Cotton (1991) found that women reported significantly greater barriers to obtaining a mentor than men. Despite these barriers, the women reported that they were as likely as men to obtain a mentor, suggesting that they overcame the barriers to access. Similarly, in his study of black and white managers, Thomas's (1990) finding that black managers build relationships outside the formal organizational hierarchy suggest they overcome barriers to obtaining a mentor.

The role of gender and race in mentoring functions

Kram (1985) suggests two broad categories of mentoring functions: career and psychosocial. Career functions include exposure and visibility, coaching, sponsorship, protection and challenging assignments; these functions facilitate protégés' professional advancement in the organization. Psychosocial functions include role modelling, counselling, acceptance and confirmation, and friendship; these functions enhance protégés' sense of competence, confidence, effectiveness and esteem.

There are different views on the generalizability of Kram's (1985) functions. In fact, as discussed in Chapter 3 of this book, these functions depend in part on a specific definition and context of mentoring. While research on the differing views of mentoring functions is emerging, existing studies have primarily focused on Kram's (1985) perspective. Moreover, although many studies have examined mentoring, most have considered protégés reports of mentoring functions; thus, these perceptions of mentoring from a protégé's perspective may or may not be accurate.

The effects of protégé gender and race on reported mentoring functions

While some research has suggested that women and people of colour receive different amounts and types of mentoring functions than white males, other research has not supported this perspective. In short, studies have yielded mixed results with respect to gender and race differences in amount and type of mentoring functions received.

Studies have found inconsistent results for the effect of gender on the amount of mentoring functions received. Dreher and Ash (1990) and Turban and Dougherty (1994) found no gender differences in protégés' reports of generalized mentoring functions. Interestingly, while Ragins and Cotton (1999) found no gender differences in mentoring functions received in informal relationships, they found that women reported receiving less mentoring functions than men in formal relationships.

Research on the effects of race on the amount of mentoring received has yielded mixed results. For example, Cox and Nkomo (1991) found that black masters of business Administration (MBAs) reported less mentoring than their white counterparts. Similarly, Viator (2001) found that black accountants reported receiving fewer mentoring functions than white accountants did. In contrast, Blake-Beard's (1999) study told a different story. Among MBA graduates, she found no difference in the amount of mentoring reported by black and white respondents. In fact, the findings, while not statistically significant, indicated that black women reported receiving more mentoring than white women.

Researchers have also suggested that gender may influence the type of mentoring received. In an early review, Ragins (1989) proposed that women may look for socioemotional support in a mentor while men look for instrumental help. In one study of graduate students, Gilbert (1985) found that the female students cared more about the lifestyles and values of their role models. Although the findings show that men were as likely as women to seek out mentors, their criteria for selection may have been more instrumental. In addition, Burke and his colleagues have suggested that mentors give psychosocial help to junior women and instrumental help to junior men (Burke, 1984; Burke and McKeen, 1990; 1995; Burke, McKeen and McKenna, 1990; 1993; Burke, McKenna and McKeen, 1991).

Some studies have shown differences in the type of mentoring received by men and women. For example, Koberg et al.'s (1994) study found that men reported receiving more career development functions than women, regardless of rank. In addition, McGuire (1999) found that men reportedly received more instrumental help from their mentors while women received more psychosocial help from their mentors.

Many studies show, however, that women and men receive equal amounts of instrumental and psychosocial help. Ragins and McFarlin (1990) asked men and women employees in three research and development firms about the kinds of help they have received from their men and women mentors. Using their Mentor Role Instrument (MRI), they defined a mentor as 'a high-ranking, influential member of your organization who has advanced experience and knowledge and who is committed to providing upward mobility and support to your career' (Ragins and McFarlin, 1990, pp. 326–7). In a series of analyses looking at instrumental help, socioemotional help, friendship and role-modelling, they obtained no effects for the gender of the protégé: The help women received was of the same nature as the help men received.

Other studies provide further confirmation of no differences in the type of help men and women are likely to receive. Tepper, Shaffer and Tepper (1996) studied five different samples of people from diverse backgrounds using a sixteen-item scale developed from Noe's (1988b) work; they confirmed the empirical distinction between instrumental and socioemotional help and found no gender differences in the type of help protégés received. In addition, Thomas (1990) administered a career experience questionnaire in a north-east utility company in which he measured eleven types of support junior managers received from a person who 'took an active interest in and concerted action to advance' their careers (Thomas, 1990, p. 483); the findings show no gender differences in the amount of instrumental or psychosocial help received by men and women.

Race may also influence the type of mentoring that protégés report receiving. However, studies have produced mixed results. On the one hand, Thomas (1990) found no differences in the amount of career and psychosocial support received by black versus white protégés. In contrast to these findings, McGuire (1999) found that white employees received more instrumental help from their mentors than did protégés of colour, and that people of colour received more psychosocial help than did white protégés.

The effects of mentor gender and race on reported mentoring functions

When considering the type of mentoring provided by the mentor, the typical expectation is that women and minorities provide different types of mentoring than white men. Most research has shown that protégés report that male and female mentors provide the same types of mentoring functions. Interestingly, despite the similarity in functions mentors provide, as shown later in this chapter, mentor gender affects outcomes.

Typically, studies have found no effects of mentor gender on functions reported by protégés. In Ragins and McFarlin's (1990) industry study, for example, there were no gender differences in reports of the kinds or amounts of help that male and female mentors gave to their protégés. Similarly, in a mailed survey to women working in retail stores, Gaskill (1991) found that of the over 200 women who responded, 135, or 65 per cent, acknowledged that they had been helped by at least one more senior retail executive. In response to items about socioemotional and instrumental help (which Gaskill developed from Kram's [1985] work), there were no differences between the kind of help men and women gave. And, Burke and McKeen's (1997) study of 196 women protégés showed no differences in protégé reports of functions received from male and female mentors. Finally, Ragins and Cotton (1999) found no support for the hypothesis that the presence of male mentors would be associated with greater reports of career development functions.

The same story emerged with a sample from the educational field. Looking at the experiences of 165 women professors who acknowledged that they had been mentored at some point in their careers, Struthers (1995) could uncover no differences in the types of help reportedly received from their male and female guides. But Struthers did find that the higher the rank of the more senior person, the more likely the woman was to report having received instrumental help from that person and the less likely she was to report having received psychosocial help. This finding suggests how what appear to be stereotypical gender differences may be misleading when mentors' gender is confounded with other factors, such as rank. If men tend to occupy senior ranks, and those in senior ranks are more likely to dispense instrumental help, it could appear that male mentors are more likely than female mentors to provide instrumental help. The untrained observer might then erroneously conclude that gender differences are real and robust.

Several studies have examined the effects of both mentor gender and race on the type of mentoring received. In a small interview study of twenty-eight African-American summer research assistants, Frierson, Hargrove and Lewis (1994) found that although white male teachers established somewhat less rapport with their protégés than did white female teachers or teachers of colour, there were no main effects for mentor gender. Similarly, Ensher and Murphy (1997), in a study that paired 104 protégés of colour with mentors of the same gender found no differences in the amount of psychosocial support provide by female and male mentors. They did find some race differences. Specifically, they found that protégés in same-race mentoring relationships reported receiving more instrumental support from their mentors than did protégés in cross-race mentoring relationships. However, protégés in same-race mentoring relationships did not report receiving significantly more psychosocial support than protégés in cross-race mentoring relationships. Finally, McGuire (1999) found that the type of help a mentor gives depends on his or her gender and race as well as the gender and race of the protégé; these findings support her suspicion that the gender and race differences she found derive from differences in rank.

The role of gender and race in mentoring outcomes

There are a large number of mentoring outcomes for the mentor, the protégé and the organization. Protégé outcomes include career advancement, success and satisfaction (Chao, Walz and Gardner, 1992; Dreher and Ash, 1990; Dreher and Cox, 1996; Fagenson, 1988; 1989; Koberg et al., 1994; Ragins and Cotton, 1999; Scandura, 1992; Scandura and Schriesheim, 1994; Turban and Dougherty, 1994; Whitely, Dougherty and Dreher, 1991; 1992). Mentors can benefit from increased promotion rates, rejuvenation and the acquisition of useful information (Hunt and Michael, 1983; Kram, 1985; Mullen, 1994). Organizational outcomes include increased employee motivation, better job performance and increased competitive advantage (Kram and Hall, 1989; Shea, 1994; Wilson and Elman, 1990).

Research on gender and race in studies of mentoring and its outcomes has tended to focus on protégé outcomes. Although men and women tend to report equivalent mentoring received, the outcomes of that mentoring are significantly different. Specifically, some studies have examined the effects of protégé and mentor gender on career outcomes such as promotion rate, compensation and work attitudes.

One theory is that men may benefit more from having a mentor than women. Certainly, if men are mentored by men and if senior men are more highly placed than senior women, then these relationships may serve to exaggerate rather than to eliminate gender (Nichols, Carter and Golden, 1985). Such was the reasoning of an early and much cited study in which Goldstein (1979) looked at the number of publications from young men and women scholars who had had male and female dissertation advisers. Goldstein found that same-gender pairs led to greater productivity than cross-gender pairs.

Nevertheless, over the 1980s and 1990s, the hypothesis that mentoring relationships might differentially benefit women and men has not received empirical support. Fagenson's meticulous study of managers in a large firm showed mentoring relationships to benefit protégés by providing access to important people and resources (Fagenson, 1988), greater career mobility and greater opportunity (Fagenson, 1989). These very same benefits were obtained equally for women and for men.

Other studies show the same pattern. Whitely, Dougherty and Dreher (1991) mailed surveys to recent MBAs from three universities, about a quarter of whom were female. They measured a notion that they called 'secondary mentoring' and which corresponds to Kram's (1985) variable of career functions. Respondents who received career help had earned more promotions and higher salaries than others. The association remained statistically significant even after the researchers controlled for demographic and motivational variables. Although women earned less than comparable men, the positive impact of mentoring was the same for both. The lack of gender differences is especially noteworthy because the detailed analysis was sensitive to other differences that could have seemed less important initially than gender. For example, they showed that mentoring aided only those people whose family of origin was middle class or upper middle class.

A number of other studies provide further confirmation that mentoring benefits women as much as men. In a study of business school graduates, Dreher and Ash (1990) found that gender did not moderate the relationship between mentoring and promotion, income and pay satisfaction. Chao, Walz and Gardner (1992) conducted an alumni survey and found that while informal (freely chosen) mentoring experiences are associated with higher job satisfaction and higher salaries than are formal mentoring programmes, there were no gender effects. Among bankers, Corzine, Buntzman and Busch (1994) found that women and men who have been protégés express greater job satisfaction and escape more from career plateauing than other women and men, and that the effects are equally visible in the two sexes. Mobley et al. (1994) report the same strong impact of mentoring on job satisfaction among women as among men.

Only one study showed clearly the mediating effects of gender on the relationship between protégé versus non-protégé status and job attitudes – but these were in the opposite direction of what researchers have hypothesized. In a comparison of executive men and women, Baugh, Lankau and Scandura (1996) found that while non-mentored men reported lower organizational commitment, lower job satisfaction and lower career expectations compared with mentored men, non-mentored women reported only lower career expectations compared with mentored women. In other words, failure to have a mentor proved more detrimental for men than for women.

Similar to the effects that protégé gender has on outcomes of mentoring, it might be expected that protégé race will influence the outcomes of mentoring. Few studies, however, have examined the effects of protégé race on career outcomes such as promotion rate, compensation and work attitudes. Moreover, despite the expectation of differences, Blake-Beard's (1999) results show that protégé race did not influence four different career outcomes of mentoring.

While the *protégé's* gender and race does not seem to influence the career outcomes associated with mentoring, the *mentor's* gender and race has been found to exert a very powerful effect on outcomes. Dreher and Cox (1996) sent questionnaires to MBAs from nine schools in a consortium. Slightly over a quarter of the MBAs responded to the questionnaire, yielding a sample of 742 men and 276 women. They asked all respondents if they had had a mentor in their careers and defined a mentor as 'an individual who holds a position senior to yours, who takes an active interest in developing your career' and who typically is not the direct supervisor. Participants in the study provided information about their mentors and about themselves. Salary was one of the self-referential pieces of information. They found that MBAs who had had a mentor earned substantially higher salaries than other MBAs – but *only* if the mentor were a white male. Female mentors and male mentors of colour brought no additions to income. The income advantage of the protégés of white males, relative to all others in the sample, amounted to somewhere between $16 840 and $22 454 per annum depending on the other factors considered in the calculations.

Similar findings have emerged from other studies. In Dreher and Chargois's (1998) study of graduates of a historically black college, they replicated the findings reported by Dreher and Cox (1996). Specifically, they found that a mentoring relationship with a white man accounted for an income advantage of almost $9800, while a mentoring relationship with a non-white woman provided no income advantage over those reporting no mentoring relationship.

Ragins and Cotton (1999) found support for increased career outcomes provided by male mentors. Specifically, they found that protégés with a history of male mentors reported more compensation and more promotions than protégés with a history of female mentors, even after controlling for career interruptions, length of relationship, type of mentor, position tenure and occupation. In addition, they found that male protégés with male mentors earned more than any other gender combinations.

The dynamics behind these findings have some interesting implications. For example, senior white men in the Dreher and Cox (1996) study tended to give instrumental help. This suggests that if senior white men in corporations are involved in formal mentoring programmes in which they are expected to provide instrumental help to women and people of colour, but are not expected to develop instant friendships and close emotional ties, some progress toward gender and race equity might be made.

The gender and race composition of mentoring relationships

Gender composition of mentoring relationships

Although research has tested for the effects of gender on mentoring, existing studies have considered mentor gender and protégé gender separately. Very little research has considered the interaction of mentor and protégé gender (Ragins, 1999). However, it is possible that the gender composition of the relationship might have the greatest effect on mentoring (Ragins, 1997a; 1997b).

As discussed earlier, research has shown that women and men appear equally likely to be a protégé in a mentoring relationship. However, there might be differences in the gender composition of relationships. More specifically, it is likely that men will have more same-gender mentoring relationships than will women.

There is clear evidence that men are more likely than women to have a mentor at work who is of their own gender. The men participants in Swerdlik and Bardon's (1988) study named 294 senior men as mentors and only 76 senior women. The women participants in the study named 187 senior women and 278 senior men. In the study by Hill et al. (1989) of faculty at two universities, 96 per cent of the men and 70 per cent of the women claimed to have had male mentors. Ragins and McFarlin (1990) also found that a greater proportion of women protégés was in cross-gender mentoring relationships (48 out of 66) compared to men (11 out of 115). Similarly, the survey conducted by Ragins and Cotton (1991) revealed 77 cross-gender mentoring relationships for the women and 19 for the men, whereas same-gender relationships numbered 40 for the women and 114 for the men. Hale's (1995) review of research conducted in government organizations showed that women were divided equally as protégés of men and women, whereas men worked almost exclusively as the protégés of other men. Independently, Javidan et al. (1995) found the very same result in their study of three governmental organizations. Most recently, Ragins and Cotton (1999) designed their study to yield a larger number of female mentors. Nevertheless, the gender composition of their final sample of 614 protégés supports previous research: while 5 protégés did not report their gender, 233 male protégés reported having male mentors, 237 female protégés reported having male mentors, 115 female protégés reported having female mentors and only 24 male protégés reported having female mentors.

In addition to the research findings of few female-mentor–male-protégé relationships in corporate settings, the scarcity of men who are guided by senior women is apparent in educational settings as well. Four separate studies (Basow and Howe, 1985; Erkut and Mokros, 1984; Farylo and Paludi, 1985; Gilbert, 1985) have shown that men students cite men teachers and family members as influential people or role models but do not cite women teachers or family members. Two studies (Basow and Howe, 1985; Gilbert, 1985) have shown that women students also seek mentors of their own sex; one study (Erkut and Mokros, 1984) showed no particular preference among women in this respect.

There are many possible explanations for why male protégés are more likely to have same-gender mentoring relationships than female protégés. One reason is the shortage of women at higher ranks. Another reason may be that senior women are less willing to serve in mentor roles. It is conceivable that senior women may be reluctant to pair with junior men as protégés, or perhaps they are so overburdened in their workplaces that they seek to escape altogether from the role of being anyone's mentor. After all, if senior women resist these roles, then junior women who seek a mentor would have no one to turn to except a senior man. However, in Collins' (1983) classic study, 315 out of 387 professional women considered mentoring important enough to go out of their way to do it. No woman in Collins' (1983) study declared herself unwilling to mentor.

Studies that compare men and women show that they are equally likely to mentor at executive levels. While women at mid-level positions are less likely to serve as mentors (Ragins and Cotton, 1993), that distinction disappeared above the glass ceiling (Ragins and Scandura, 1994). Although women anticipate more drawbacks to mentoring relationships than do men, senior women are as likely as senior men to want to be mentors (Ragins and Cotton, 1993). Senior women guide and promote junior members of their organizations as frequently as do men (Ragins and Scandura, 1994). At least one study (Ragins and McFarlin, 1990) has shown that women mentor men and women equally whereas men mentor men more frequently than they mentor women.

The relative scarcity of mentoring pairs including a senior woman and a junior man, therefore, is likely the result of small numbers of senior women rather than their attitudes or preferences. In academia, for example, faculties, especially at the senior levels, are still inhabited largely by white males (Clark and Corcoran, 1986). This is particularly true in the sciences. As recently as 1992, for example, most major academic chemistry departments had their first female faculty member on tenure track (Amato, 1992), and in 1990–91 the top ten mathematics departments had fifty tenure-track men and only three tenure-track women. Even in psychology, where women were being awarded nearly half of the doctorates by 1980, the proportion of women full professors in graduate departments of psychology for that year was 182 out of 2073 or 8.8

per cent (Russo et al. 1981). The greater number of men in senior faculty positions means that there are more men than women in positions to mentor both graduate students and junior faculty members.

In a study of 90 graduate students in psychology, Cronan-Hillix et al. (1986) found that, although about half (53 per cent) reported having mentors, only 13 per cent had women mentors. (Although the term 'mentor' was not defined, it was clear to students that a mentor did not necessarily include their advisers since both mentored and non-mentored students had advisers.) This appeared to be a function of the small number of women faculty. Of sixty-one full-time faculty in the psychology department, only twelve were women, four of whom were full professors, compared with forty-nine men faculty, thirty-four of whom were full professors. No men students had women mentors, while women students had women mentors in the proportion that women faculty were available for mentoring.

Of course, in business, women are even more scarce at the upper reaches than in academia. Catalyst's (1996) census of women in corporate leadership positions shows that only 3 per cent of officers of Fortune 500 companies are women. In one in-depth analysis of mentoring relationships in a corporate setting, McCambley (1999) found that although women were ready to mentor, they held so few of the positions in senior management that men tended more often to serve in those roles instead.

Despite the absence of gender differences in the studies reviewed, it seems plausible that the greater frequency of cross-gender relationships for women may nevertheless provide women with a different set of mentoring experiences than men. Some have suggested, for example, that in a cross-gender mentoring relationship both parties may assume stereotypical behaviors (Clawson and Kram, 1984; Kram, 1985). Uncertain and ambiguous situations seem to call for familiar or traditional behaviour (Kram, 1985). In the case of a male mentor and a female protégé, the mentor may act as a protector and helper, indicating that he is powerful and dominant (Kram, 1985), while the female protégé may come to rely excessively on him for guidance and advice, thus implying that she cannot act autonomously. In this way, this relationship may elicit stereotypical behaviours that imply a more powerful and knowing male and a more supplicant female, thus reinforcing the power dynamics that are inherent in the hierarchical relationship (Kram, 1985). At the same time, the woman-mentor–woman-protégé dyad may unconsciously remind the junior woman of her experiences with her mother, arousing childlike expectations and frustrations (Heinrich, 1995), which in turn may influence her mentor's reactions to her.

Some data suggest that the gender composition of the mentor–protégé dyad affects the quality and nature of the relationship. Ragins and McFarlin (1990) found that the gender composition of the mentoring relationship influenced neither the type nor the amount of help the mentor gave. There were, however, two important interaction effects that suggest how the gender composition of the dyad did matter. First, the women in their study were more likely to perceive role models among their female mentors than among their male mentors (e.g. 'this person represents who I want to be'), whereas men in the sample appeared to identify slightly more with their male mentors than with their female mentors. Second, both the women and men in the study reported that they avoided socializing with their cross-gender mentors after work hours.

More recently, Ragins and Cotton (1999) specifically explored the effects of gender composition on the functions and outcomes of mentoring in their study of 352 female and 257 male protégés in formal and informal mentoring relationships. While there were only 24 female mentor–male protégé dyads in this study, male protégés with female mentors reported fewer functions and less satisfaction with their mentor than any other gender combinations. In addition, replicating the findings of Ragins and McFarlin (1990), female protégés were more likely to report that they engage in after-work social activities when paired with a female mentor than when paired with a male mentor.

The empirical findings about the avoidance of women socializing with their male mentors means that women do not have as much access as men have to the information that is exchanged during informal after-hours gatherings. However, the findings are not surprising in view of the problem of sexuality in the workplace. Where cross-gender relationships might be especially detri-mental is in their potential to lead to sexual involvement or the perception by others of sexual involvement (Clawson and Kram, 1984; Devine and Markiewicz, 1990; Fitt and Newton, 1981; Ragins, 1989; Ragins and Cotton, 1991). Since the beginning of scholarship on the topic, observers have worried about sexual involvement between mentor and protégé. Fitt and Newton (1981) noted that 10 per cent of their cross-gender mentoring pairs had been romantically involved. Among the professional women in Collins's (1983) study, a quarter admitted to having had affairs with their male mentors. Approaching matters from the other side, Fitzgerald et al. (1988) found that 25 per cent of male faculty in their study reported having had sexual relationships with students (though, interestingly, only one thought he might be guilty of sexual harassment).

Sexual involvement can produce anxiety and confusion for both members of the relationship. Special harm may await the junior woman in the romance. Looking back on their situations, many of the women in Collins's study felt that the sexual liaisons had been harmful to them, and none felt they had been helpful.

Sexual liaisons between mentors and protégés can also create problems for organizations. As Clawson and Kram (1984) note, every mentoring relationship has two aspects: an internal one and an external one. The internal relationship is what transpires between the two individuals, and the external relationship is the relationship between the two individuals and the rest of the organization (Clawson and Kram, 1984; Kram, 1985). Even a false appearance of sexual intimacies can stir up unproductive feelings among those outside the relationship.

Women and men are equally likely to acknowledge that they have been someone's protégé, but women are more likely than men to have been in a cross-gender mentoring relationship. Research suggests that for most mentoring relationships, gender matching or mismatching may not matter. But for some proportion, it does – especially because of sexual tensions. In other ways not yet measured by researchers, differences in the quality of the mentoring experience may exist. For example, perhaps women have access to senior guides who are older or younger, more or less experienced, or more or less powerful than the senior guides to whom men have access. The extent to which women play into gender-typed roles may also influence the nature and quality of the mentoring relationship and create gender interaction effects. Specifically, women may feel more comfortable than men asking for and receiving help; conversely, women may worry more than men about appearing anything less than perfectly competent and therefore avoid asking for help.

Race composition of mentoring relationships

The racial composition of a mentor-protégé relationship is also certain to have an influence on mentoring (e.g. Ragins, 1997a). For example, Thomas (1990) found some interesting results on career and psychosocial support provided in cross-race versus same-race mentoring relationships. Specifically, he found more psychosocial support in same-race relationships than in cross-race relationships. Thomas observes that the difficulty of developing the psychosocial aspect of cross-race mentoring relationships lies in the discomfort that white and black managers feel with each other. In addition, Turner, Blake-Beard, and Crosby's (2001) study of engineers in a Silicon Valley company compared the mentoring experiences of Asian and Asian-American employees with those of white employees. Their results showed that although access to a mentor did not vary with protégé ethnicity, Asian protégés were significantly more likely to be in a cross-race mentoring relationship.

There are different reasons why people may not either initiate or feel comfortable in cross-race mentoring relationships. For example, racial taboos might lead to constrained interactions in cross-race mentoring relationships (Thomas, 1989). Moreover, research has shown that people tend to form relationships with others from the same identity group (see Tsui, Egan and O'Reilly [1992] for a review of the literature). Perhaps this partially explains Thomas's (1990) finding that 91 per cent of white males enter mentoring relationships with other white males.

Despite the issues that would suggest otherwise, studies have shown that people of colour are more likely to form mentoring relationships with whites than with other people of colour (Thomas, 1990; 1993; 1999). There are two explanations for this. First, because there are more whites in managerial ranks, people of colour have little other choice than to form cross-race mentoring relationships (e.g. Thomas, 1999). Indeed, in addition to the lack of women mentors in organizations, there are also few people of colour available to serve as mentors. Moreover, people of colour may face barriers similar to those faced by women, such as job and performance demands which leave little time to serve as a mentor. For example, Thomas's (1990) study found that white males were the most common mentors used by both minority and majority protégés. In addition, Blake's (1999) research uncovered a theme among respondents that there was a general lack of black role models who might become mentors to the women in her study. Second, because whites have more power in organizations, people of colour are at a disadvantage unless they have a mentoring relationship with a white senior person (e.g. Ragins, 1997a). Expanding these two explanations, Thomas (1999) offers an analysis of the formation of cross-race relationships including the motivations of whites to mentor people of colour and the influence of non-whites in positions of power and authority.

Directions for future research

Ragins (1989) suggests that organizations that want to become or remain competitive may wish to increase the pool of skilled managers. Such an increase will come if they remove barriers that keep women and people of colour artificially excluded from power. Involving women and minorities in mentoring relationships certainly seems to be a prime way to effect such change.

In response to the recognized benefits that mentoring provides, many organizations have created formal mentoring programmes. However, relatively little is known about gender or race effects in formal mentoring relationships as most of the research to date has looked at informal mentoring only. Two recent studies have found interesting gender effects in formal mentoring relationships. First, Ragins and Cotton (1999) found that protégés in formal cross-gender relationships reported that their mentors provided fewer challenging assignments than those in informal relationships, while protégés in same-gender relationships reported that their mentors provided more challenging assignments when in a formal mentoring relationship. In another study, although Ragins, Cotton and Miller (2000) found that men and women reported equal attitudinal benefits from having an informal mentor, women with formal mentors reported significantly less career commitment than men with formal mentors, and even less than both men and women who were not mentored. Moreover, in this study, female protégés with male mentors reported less satisfaction with the formal mentoring programme than did male protégés who were paired with either male or female mentors. Given the findings to date, future research directions should include the effects of gender and race in formal mentoring relationships.

Research also started to consider the negative sides of mentoring (e.g. Eby et al., 2000; O'Neill and Sankowsky, 2001; Scandura, 1998). However, this recent research has not considered the influence of gender and race on dysfunctional mentoring relationships. For example, there may be differences in the types and amount of abuse between same-gender and cross-gender mentoring relationships or between cross-race and same-race mentoring relationships. Therefore, future theoretical and empirical research on negative mentoring experiences would be well served to consider the role of gender and race in these relationships.

Related, additional potential pitfalls must be considered. Olson and Ashton-Jones (1992) and Nichols, Carter and Golden (1985) warn us that the hierarchical nature of mentoring relationships may simply reinforce the patriarchy of the larger society. More specifically, the prevalence of unhelpful sexual or romantic feelings in cross-gender relationships has prompted some scholars and activists to advocate developmental relationships that differ from the old-fashioned mentoring ones that Kram (1985) and others (e.g. Zey, 1984) describe. For example, some organizations are instituting 'mentoring circles' or groups in which several senior people share responsibility for several junior people (Catalyst, 1993; McCambley, 1999).

As diversity gains more of a foothold in various organizations, some interesting questions arise. For example, would female-dominated or sex-balanced organizations look the same as the traditional, male-dominated ones in terms of mentoring relationships? Or, will women be more likely to mentor male protégés of colour because of a sharing of minority status in their organizations and an understanding of the associated challenges? Following the observations of different researchers, it will be imperative in future research to track the effects of various dimensions of diversity such as gender, race, social class, sexual orientation, religion, age and physical ability on mentoring relationships (Hoyt, 1999; Ibarra, 1993; Ibarra and Andrews, 1993; Nkomo, 1992; Ragins, 1997a). Future research that incorporates the many aspects of diversity will help provide answers to these and similar questions, and will deepen our knowledge of the basic social psychology of organizational life while making positive and practical change in the world.

References

Amato, I. (1992). Profile of a field: Chemistry. Women have extra hoops to jump through. *Science*, **255**, 1372–8.

Auster, D. (1984). Mentors and protégés: power-dependent dyads. *Sociological Inquiry*, **54**, 142–53.

Basow, S. and Howe, K. (1985). Role-model influence: effects of sex and sex-role attitude in college students. *Psychology of Women Quarterly*, **4**, 558–72.

Baugh, S. G., Lankau, M. J. and Scandura, T. A. (1996). An investigation of the effects of protégé gender on responses to mentoring. *Journal of Vocational Behavior*, **49**, 309–23.

Blake, S. (1999). At the crossroads of race and gender: lessons from the mentoring experiences of professional black women. In *Mentoring Dilemmas: Developmental Relationships within Multicultural Organizations* (A. J. Murrell, F. J. Crosby and R. J. Ely, eds) pp. 83–104, Lawrence Erlbaum.

Blake-Beard, S. D. (1999). The costs of living as an outsider within: an analysis of the mentoring relationships and career success of black and white women in the corporate sector. *Journal of Career Development*, **26**(1), 21–36.

Bowen, D. D. (1986). The role of identification in mentoring female protégés. *Group and Organization Studies*, **11**(1–2), 61–74.

Burke, R. J. (1984). Mentors in organizations. *Group and Organization Studies*, **9**, 353–72.

Burke, R. J. and McKeen, C. A. (1990). Mentoring in organizations: implications for women. *Journal of Business Ethics*, **9**, 317–32.

Burke, R. J. and McKeen, C. A. (1995). Do managerial women prefer mentors? *Psychological Reports*, **76**, 688–90.

Burke, R. J. and McKeen, C. A. (1997). Benefits of mentoring relationships among managerial and professional women: a cautionary tale. *Journal of Vocational Behavior*, **51**, 43–57.

Burke, R. J., McKeen, C. A. and McKenna, C. S. (1990). Sex differences and cross-sex effects on mentoring: some preliminary data. *Psychological Reports*, **67**, 1011–23.

Burke, R. J., McKeen, C. A. and McKenna, C. S. (1993). Correlates of mentoring in organizations: The mentor's perspective. *Psychological Reports*, **72**, 883–896.

Burke, R. J., McKenna, C. S. and McKeen, C. A. (1991). How do mentorships differ from typical supervisory relationships? *Psychological Reports*, **68**, 459–66.

Busch, J. W. (1985). Mentoring in graduate schools of education: Mentor's perceptions. *American Educational Research Journal*, **22**(2), 257–65.

Catalyst (1993). *Mentoring: A Guide to Corporate Programs and Practices*. Catalyst.

Catalyst (1996). *The 1996 Census of Women Corporate Officers and Top Earners*. Catalyst.

Chao, G. T., Walz, P. M. and Gardner, P. D. (1992). Formal and informal mentorships: a comparison of mentoring functions and contrast with nonmentored counterparts. *Personnel Psychology*, **45**(3), 619[en36.

Clark, S. M. and Corcoran, M. (1986). Perspectives in the professional socialization of women faculty: a case of accumulative disadvantage? *Journal of Higher Education*, **57**(1), 20–43.

Clawson, J. G. and Kram, K. E. (1984). Managing cross-gender mentoring. *Business Horizons*, **27**(3), 22–31.

Collins, E. G. C. and Scott, P. (1978). Everyone who makes it has a mentor. *Harvard Business Review*, August-September, 89–100.

Collins, N. (1983). *Professional Women and their Mentors*. Prentice-Hall.

Conway, J. J. (1989). Higher education for women. *American Behavioral Scientist*, **32**, 633–9.

Cook, M. F. (1979). Is the mentor relationship primarily a male experience? *Personnel Administrator*, **24**(11), 82–6.

Corzine, J., Buntzman, G. and Busch, E. (1994). Mentoring, downsizing, gender and career outcomes. *Journal of Social Behavior and Personality*, **9**, 517–28.

Cox, T. H. and Nkomo, S. M. (1991). A race and gender group analysis of the early career experience of MBAs. *Work and Occupations*, **18**(4), 431–46.

Cronan-Hillix, T. Gensheimer, L. K., Cronan-Hillix, W.A. and Davidson, W. S. (1986). Students' views of mentors in psychology graduate training. *Teaching of Psychology*, **13**(3), 123–7.

Devine, I. and Markiewicz, D. (1990). Cross-sex relationships at work and the impact of gender stereotypes. *Journal of Business Ethics*, **9**, 333–8.

Dreher, G. F. and Ash, R. A. (1990). A comparative study among men and women in managerial, professional, and technical positions. *Journal of Applied Psychology*, **75**(5), 1–8.

Dreher, G. F. and Chargois, J. A. (1998). Gender, mentoring experiences, and salary attainment among graduates of an historically black university. *Journal of Vocational Behavior*, **53**, 401–16.

Dreher, G. F. and Cox, T. H. (1996). Race, gender, and opportunity: a study of compensation attainment and the establishment of mentoring relationships. *Journal of Applied Psychology*, **81**(3), 297–308.

Eby, L. T., McManus, S., Simon, S. A. and Russell, J. E. A. (2000). The protégé's perspective regarding negative mentoring experiences: the development of a taxonomy. *Journal of Vocational Behavior*, **57**(1), 1–21.

Ensher, E. A. and Murphy, S. E. (1997). Effects of race, gender, perceived similarity, and contact on mentor relationships. *Journal of Vocational Behavior*, **50**, 460–481.

Erkut, S. and Mokros, J. R. (1984). Professors as models and mentors for college students. *American Educational Research Journal*, **21**, 399–417.

Fagenson, E. A. (1988). The power of a mentor: protégés' and nonprotégés' perceptions of their own power in organizations. *Group and Organization Studies*, **13**(2), 182–94.

Fagenson, E. A. (1989). The mentor advantage: perceived career/job experiences of protégés versus non-protégés. *Journal of Organizational Behavior*, **10**(4), 309–20.

Farylo, B. and Paludi, M. (1985). Developmental discontinuities in mentor choice by male students. *Journal of Social Psychology*, **125**, 521–2.

Fitt, L. W. and Newton, D. A. (1981). When the mentor is a man and the protégé a woman. *Harvard Business Review*, **58**(2), 56–60.

Fitzgerald, L., Weitzman, L., Gold, Y. and Ormerod, M., (1988). Academic harassment: sex and denial in scholarly garb. *Psychology of Women Quarterly*, **12**, 329–40.

Frierson, H. T. Jr, Hargrove, B. and Lewis, N. R. (1994). Black summer research students' perceptions related to research mentors' race and gender. *Journal of College Student Development*, **35**, 475–80.

Gaskill, L. R. (1991). Same-sex and cross-sex mentoring of female protégés: a comparative analysis. *Career Development Quarterly*, **40**, 48–63.

Gilbert, L. and Rossman, K. (1992). Gender and the mentoring process for women: implications for professional development. *Professional Psychology: Research and Practice*, **23**, 233–8.

Gilbert, L. A. (1985). Dimensions of same-gender student-faculty role-model relationships. *Sex Roles*, **12**, 111–23.

Goldstein, E. (1979). Effect of same-sex and cross-sex role models on the subsequent academic productivity of scholars. *American Psychologist*, **34**, 407–10.

Hale, M. (1995). Mentoring women in organizations: practice in search of theory. *American Review of Public Administration*, **25**, 327–39.

Heinrich, K. T. (1995). Doctoral advisement relationships between women. *Journal of Higher Education*, **66**, 447–69.

Hetherington, C. and Barcelo, R. (1985). Womentoring: a cross-cultural perspective. *Journal of NAWDAC*, Fall, 12–15.

Hill, S. K., Bahniuk, M. H., Dobos, J. and Rouner, D. (1989). Mentoring and other communication support in the academic setting. *Group and Organization Studies*, **14**(3), 355–68.

Hoyt, S. (1999). Mentoring with class: connections between social class and developmental relationships in the academy. In *Mentoring Dilemmas: Developmental Relationships within Multicultural Organizations* (A. J. Murrell, F. J. Crosby and R. J. Ely, eds) pp. 189–210, Lawrence Erlbaum.

Hunt, D. M. and Michael, C. (1983). Mentorship: A career training and development tool. *Academy of Management Review*, **8**(3), 475–85.

Ibarra, H. (1993). Personal networks of women and minorities in management: a conceptual framework. *Academy of Management Review*, **18**, 56–87.

Ibarra, H. and Andrews, S. (1993). Power, social influence, and sense making: effects of network centrality and proximity on employee perceptions. *Administrative Science Quarterly*, **38**, 277–303.

Javidan, M., Bemmels, B., Devine, K. and Dastmalchian, A. (1995). Superior and subordinate gender and the acceptance of superiors as role models. *Human Relations*, **48**, 1271–84.

Keith, B. and Moore, H. A. (1995). Training sociologists: an assessment of professional socialization and the emergence of career aspirations. *Teaching Sociology*, **23**, 199–214.

Koberg, C. S., Boss, R. W., Chappell, D. and Ringer, R. C. (1994). Correlates and consequences of protégé mentoring in a large hospital. *Group and Organization Management*, **19**(2), 219–39.

Kram, K. E. (1985). *Mentoring at Work: Developmental Relationships in Organizational Life*. Scott, Foresman and Co.

Kram, K. E. and Hall, D. T. (1989). Mentoring as an antidote to stress during corporate trauma. *Human Resources Management*, **28**(4), 493–510.

Maack, M. and Passet, J. (1993). Unwritten rules: mentoring women faculty. *Library and Information Science Research*, **15**, 117–41.

McCambley, E. (1999). Testing theory by practice. In *Mentoring Dilemmas: Developmental Relationships within Multicultural Organizations* (A. J. Murrell, F. J. Crosby and R. J. Ely, eds) pp. 173–88, Lawrence Erlbaum.

McGuire, G. M. (1999). Do race and gender affect employees' access to and help from mentors? Insights from the study of a large corporation. In *Mentoring Dilemmas: Developmental Relationships within Multicultural Organizations* (A. J. Murrell, F. J. Crosby and R. J. Ely, eds) pp. 105–20, Lawrence Erlbaum.

Mobley, M., Jaret, C., Marsh, K. and Lim, Y. (1994). Mentoring, job satisfaction, gender and the legal profession. *Sex Roles*, **31**, 79–98.

Mullen, E. J. (1994). Framing the mentoring relationship as an information exchange. *Human Resource Management Review*, **4**, 257–81.

Nichols, I., Carter, H. and Golden, M. (1985). The patron system in academia: alternative strategies for empowering academic women. *Women's Studies International Forum*, **8**, 383–90.

Nkomo, S. (1992). The emperor has no clothes: Rewriting 'race organizations'. *Academy of Management Review*, **17**, 487–513.

Noe, R. (1988a). Women and mentoring: a review and research agenda. *Academy of Management Review*, **13**(1), 65–78.

Noe, R. (1988b). An investigation of the determinants of successful assigned mentoring relationships. *Personnel Psychology*, **41**, 457–79.

O'Neill, R. M. and Sankowsky, D. (2001). The Caligula phenomenon: Mentoring relationships and theoretical abuse. *Journal of Management Inquiry*, **10**(3), 206–16.

O'Neill, R. M., Horton, S. and Crosby, F. J. (1999). Gender issues in developmental relationships. In *Mentoring Dilemmas: Developmental Relationships within Multicultural Organizations* (A. J. Murrell, F. J. Crosby and R. J. Ely, eds) pp. 69–80, Lawrence Erlbaum.

Olson, G. and Ashton-Jones, E. (1992). Doing gender: (en)gendering academic mentoring. *Journal of Education*, **174**, 114–27.

Paludi, M. A., Meyers, D., Kindermann, J., Speicher, H. and Haring-Hidore, M. (1990). Mentoring and being mentored: issues of sex, power, and politics for older women. *Journal of Women and Aging*, **2**, 81–92.

Ragins, B. R. (1989). Barriers to mentoring: the female manager's dilemma. *Human Relations*, **42**(1), 1–22.

Ragins, B. R. (1997a). Diversified mentoring relationships in organizations: a power perspective. *Academy of Management Review*, **22**(2), 482–521.

Ragins, B. R. (1997b). Antecedents of diversified mentoring relationships. *Journal of Vocational Behavior*, **51**, 90–109.

Ragins, B. R. (1999). Gender and mentoring relationships: a review and research agenda for the next decade. In *Handbook of Gender in Organizations* (G. N. Powell, ed.) pp. 347–70, Sage.

Ragins, B. R. and Cotton, J. L. (1991). Easier said than done: gender differences in perceived barriers to gaining a mentor. *Academy of Management Journal*, **34**(4), 939–51.

Ragins, B. R. and Cotton, J. L. (1993). Gender and willingness to mentor in organizations. *Journal of Management*, **19**(1), 97–111.

Ragins, B. R. and Cotton, J. L. (1999). Mentor functions and outcomes: a comparison of men and women in formal and informal mentoring relationships. *Journal of Applied Psychology*, **84**(4), 529–50.

Ragins, B. R. and McFarlin, D. B. (1990). Perceptions of mentor roles in cross-gender mentoring relationships. *Journal of Vocational Behavior*, **37**, 3231–339.

Ragins, B. R. and Scandura, T. A. (1994). Gender differences in expected outcomes of mentoring relationships. *Academy of Management Journal*, **37**(4), 957–71.

Ragins, B. R., Cotton, J. L. and Miller, J. S. (2000). Marginal mentoring: the effects of type of mentor, quality of relationship, and program design on work and career attitudes. *Academy of Management Journal*, **43**(6), 1177–94.

Ragins, B. R., Townsend, B. and Mattis, M. (1998). Gender gap in the executive suite: CEOs and female executives report on breaking the glass ceiling. *Academy of Management Executive*, **12**, 28–42.

Russo, N. F., Olmedo, E. L., Stapp, J. and Fulcher, R. (1981). Women and minorities in psychology. *American Psychologist*, **36**, 1315–63.

Scandura, T. A. (1992). Mentorship and career mobility: An empirical investigation. *Journal of Organizational Behavior*, **13**, 169–74.

Scandura, T. A. (1998). Dysfunctional mentoring relationships and outcomes. *Journal of Management*, **24**(3), 449–67.

Scandura, T. A. and Schriesheim, C. A. (1994). Leader–member exchange and supervisor career mentoring as complementary constructs in leadership research. *Academy of Management Journal*, **37**(6), 1588–602.

Shea, G. F. (1994). *Mentoring: Helping Employees Reach their Full Potential*. AMA Membership Publications Division.

Struthers, N. J. (1995). Differences in mentoring: a function of gender or organizational rank? *Journal of Social Behavior and Personality*, **10**, 265–72.

Swerdlik, M. and Bardon, J. (1988). A survey of mentoring experiences in school psychology. *Journal of School Psychology*, **26**, 213–24.

Tepper, K., Shaffer, B. C. and Tepper, B. J. (1996). Latent structure of mentoring function scales. *Educational and Psychological Measurement*, **56**, 848–57.

Thomas, D. A. (1989). Mentoring and irrationality: the role of racial taboos. *Human Resource Management*, **28**, 279–90.

Thomas, D. A. (1990). The impact of race on managers' experiences of developmental relationships. *Journal of Organizational Behavior*, **11**, 479–92.

Thomas, D. A. (1993). Racial dynamics in cross-race developmental relationships. *Administrative Science Quarterly*, **38**, 169–194.

Thomas, D. A. (1999). Beyond the simple demography-power hypothesis: how blacks in power influence white-mentor – black-protégé developmental relationships. In *Mentoring Dilemmas: Developmental Relationships within Multicultural Organizations* (A. J. Murrell, F. J. Crosby and R. J. Ely, eds) pp. 157–70, Lawrence Erlbaum.

Thomas, D. A. and Alderfer, C. P. (1989). The influence of race on career dynamics: theory and research on minority career experiences. In *Handbook of Career Theory* (M. B. Arthur, D. T. Hall and B. S. Lawrence, eds) pp. 133–58, Cambridge University Press.

Tidball, M. E. (1986). Baccalaureate origins of recent natural science doctorates. *Journal of Higher Education*, **57**, 606–20.

Tsui, A. S., Egan, T. D. and O'Reilly, C. A. (1992). Being different: relational demography and organizational attachment. *Administrative Science Quarterly*, **37**, 549–79.

Turban, D. B. and Dougherty, T. W. (1994). Role of protégé personality in receipt of mentoring and career success. *Academy of Management Journal*, **37**(3), 688–702.

Turner, E., Blake-Beard, D. S. and Crosby, F. J. (2001). The role of mentoring in Silicon Valley. Manuscript submitted for publication.

Viator, R. (2001). An examination of African-Americans access to public accounting mentors: perceived barriers and intentions to leave. Manuscript submitted for publication.

Whitely, W., Dougherty, T. W. and Dreher, G. F. (1991). Relationship of career mentoring and socioeconomic origin to managers' and professionals' early career progress. *Academy of Management Journal*, **34**(2), 331–51.

Whitely, W., Dougherty, T. W. and Dreher, G. F. (1992). Correlates of career-oriented mentoring for early career managers and professionals. *Journal of Organizational Behavior*, **13**(2), 141–54.

Wilson, J. A. and Elman, N. S. (1990). Organizational benefits of mentoring. *Academy of Management Executive*, **4**(4), 88–94.

Wilson, M. S. and Reschly, D. J. (1995). Gender and school psychology: issues, questions, and answers. *School Psychology Review*, **24**, 45–61.

Zey, M. G. (1984). *The Mentor Connection*. Irwin.

Regina M. O'Neill is an Assistant Professor at Management at the Sawyer School of Management at Suffolk University in Boston. She received her PhD from the University of Michigan Business School. Her research interests include the role of professional and personal relationships at work in mentoring and social support, and the ways these relationships shape and are shaped by factors such as gender and diversity. Her research has been published in *Academy of Management Journal, Strategic Management Journal, Journal of Management Inquiry, Educational and Psychological Measurement, Human Resource Management Journal* and other journals.

2

Understanding diversified mentoring relationships: definitions, challenges and strategies

Belle Rose Ragins

Diversity has become a fact of life for most organizations. Increasingly, organizations are composed of a virtual mosaic of employees who differ on race, ethnicity, gender, sexual orientation, class, religion, disability and other group memberships that influence their view of the world, the workplace and each other. This diversity extends into mentoring relationships, which are also increasingly diverse. Consequently, mentoring researchers and practitioners are confronted with a number of challenging questions about diverse mentoring relationships. What does it mean to talk about diversity in mentoring relationships? How does diversity affect the development and functioning of mentoring relationships? How can we capitalize on the strengths of diversity within these relationships? What are the challenges faced by members of diversified relationships and what strategies can be employed to meet these challenges?

The purpose of this chapter is to answer these questions and to provide a lens for viewing the unique processes and outcomes involved with diversified mentoring relationships. The cases in this book illustrate these processes in action. What I seek to provide here is a framework or cognitive map for viewing and integrating these cases.

This chapter first examines the complexities involved with defining diversified mentoring relationships. I then delve into how diversity affects the initiation, development and functioning of mentoring relationships. Using existing theory and research, I then present some practical strategies for developing effective diversified mentoring relationships in organizations. I will conclude with an assessment of formal mentoring programmes as a strategy for developing diverse mentoring relationships in organizations.

What are diversified mentoring relationships?

Diversified mentoring relationships are defined as relationships comprising mentors and protégés who differ on the basis of race, ethnicity, gender, sexual orientation, class, religion, disability or other group memberships associated with power in organizations (Ragins, 1997a). For example, a diversified mentoring relationship may involve a male mentor and female protégé, a Latino mentor and Caucasian protégé, a lesbian mentor and heterosexual protégé, or any combination of these various group memberships.

I use a power perspective in defining diversity in organizations and diversity in mentoring relationships. There are two basic premises underlying this perspective (Ragins, 1995; 1997a; 1997b). The first premise is that individuals are members of groups that have varying degrees of power or influence in organizations. These group memberships impact employees' access to power and resources in organizations, define their roles in the organization, and elicit stereotypes and attributions about their competence and abilities. A group's power is affected by its control over power resources, which involve control over persons, information, and other organizational resources (Ragins, 1997a). The power of a group may or may not reflect its numbers; black Africans in South Africa during apartheid, for example, were in the majority in terms of numbers, but the minority in terms of power.

The second premise of this power perspective is that mentors and protégés do not leave their group memberships behind when they enter a mentoring relationship, but bring these group memberships with them into the relationship. These group memberships influence the mentoring relationship's development and effectiveness. An example may help clarify these processes. Specifically, gender may influence whether individuals are selected for a mentoring relationship, how they are viewed in the relationship by their partners or others in the organization, and even the overall effectiveness of the relationship (cf. Burke and McKeen, 1990; O'Neill, Horton and Crosby, 1999; Ragins, 1989; 1999b; Sosik and Godshalk, 2000). Women have less power in organizations (Ragins and Sundstrom, 1989), face greater barriers to advancement (Lyness and Thompson, 1997; Schneer and Reitman, 1995; Stroh, Brett and Reilly, 1992), and need to develop different strategies for advancement than their male counterparts (Ragins, Townsend and Mattis, 1998). These group differences in power influence the female protégée's career and her developmental needs in the mentoring relationship. Some key questions come to mind when viewing these gender effects. Will her male mentor recognize her specific needs and the fact that the organization she faces as a woman may be quite different than the organization he faces as a man? Will he recognize that his female protégée may not have the power associated with her position because of her gender, or that she may face a daily battle to be perceived as competent as her male peers? The male mentor may pride himself on being 'gender-blind' in his relationship with her, but he may be performing her a disservice if he is blind to the fact that advancement strategies that may work for his male protégés may actually backfire for his female protégées. For example, 'showcasing your talent' may be viewed as an assertive and confident act for men, but an immodest and bragging act for women (Schein, Mueller and Jacobson, 1989). This example begins to illustrate some of the issues and complexities involved with diversity in mentoring relationships. We now turn to a more in-depth examination of the complexities involved with defining and understanding diversified mentoring relationships.

What are the issues involved with defining and understanding diversified mentoring relationships?

There are a number of complexities involved with defining diversity in mentoring relationships. As a start, it is important to understand that diversity in mentoring relationships involves multiple group memberships that are not equally weighted or visible, and that the effects of these group memberships may vary over time. As discussed below, we need to examine and consider these issues before we can gain a clearer picture of the processes and challenges involved in diversified mentoring relationships.

The importance of multiple group memberships

Individuals hold multiple group memberships and vary on multiple dimensions of diversity. Therefore, the first basic issue to consider when examining diversified mentoring relationships is the number of shared group memberships held by the mentor and the protégé.

Mentoring relationships that vary on multiple group memberships face greater challenges and demands than relationships that vary on just a single group membership (Ragins, 1999a). Consider, for example, mentoring relationship 'A' that involves a white, heterosexual, Christian male mentor paired with a white, heterosexual, Christian female protégée. Compare this relationship with relationship 'B', that involves a white, middle-class, heterosexual, male mentor who is Christian paired with a protégée who is black, working class, lesbian and a Muslim. In terms of group membership, members of the 'A' relationship vary only on the basis of one group membership: their gender. In contrast, the members of the 'B' relationship vary on race, class, sexual orientation, gender and religion. The members of the 'A' relationship share more group memberships than the members of the 'B' relationship, and may therefore share common backgrounds, values and ways of viewing the world and work relationships. As is discussed later in this chapter, shared group memberships may affect the selection of the partner in the mentoring relationship, and the expectations, perceptions and communication patterns in the relationship.

All group memberships are not created equal

While it is important to consider multiple group memberships, we also need to understand that group memberships are not equivalent. Group memberships vary with respect to visibility, the group's history with respect to hate crimes and discrimination, the current discrimination faced by the group, the saliency of group membership to the individual and the work group, and the larger context of the group's interaction with the organization and geographic region.

These differences within group membership affect mentoring relationships. For example, we often talk about 'race and gender' as if membership in these groups is independent (i.e. one has a race or a gender but not both), and also interchangeable (i.e. race or gender). As a point in fact, research on race and gender effects in mentoring relationships reveals that race and gender may not have the same impact on mentoring relationships (cf. Blake, 1999; McGuire, 1999; Murrell, Crosby and Ely, 1999). For example, women have been found to be as likely as white men to have mentors and receive equivalent benefits from the relationship (cf. review by Ragins, 1999b), but the findings on race are mixed; some studies have found no race differences in sponsorship or supervisory support (Dreher and Cox, 1996; Greenhaus, Parasuraman and Wormley, 1990), while other studies have race effects in the presence (Cox and Nkomo, 1991) or type of mentoring (Thomas, 1990; 1999; 2001; McGuire, 1999) and supervisory (Jeanquart-Barone, 1996) relationship. It is therefore important to consider not only the ways in which mentors and protégés differ, but also the salience and significance of those differences.

Another related issue is that majority members sometimes combine individuals from different races and ethnicities into the global category of 'minority' without considering the fact that different ethnic and racial groups have very different workplace experiences. In support of this idea, a recent report by the not-for-profit research firm Catalyst concluded that race is not monolithic in mentoring relationships. Their study of 1735 women from thirty companies in the USA found that Asian-American women were less likely than Latina-Americans to have mentors and that African-American women received job advice relating to their race from their mentors to a greater extent than did other women of colour (Catalyst, 1999). This suggests that it is important to understand the specific racial and ethnic differences involved with both members of the mentoring relationship. For example, a mentoring programme may intend to link up two individuals who share a common ethnicity, but the matching of a Korean protégé with a Japanese or African mentor may not accomplish the goal of having a common racial or ethnic bond in the relationship. Both individuals may have the experience of being an ethnic minority in the organization, but the differences in their cultural backgrounds and group histories may be greater than their shared experiences of being in the minority in the organization (cf. Goto, 1999).

The organizational and regional context also affects diversity in mentoring relationships. The impact of a group membership on a mentoring relationship may be influenced by how that membership is viewed in the organization or the locality (Ragins, 1997a). For example, religious differences among members of mentoring relationships are not significant in some countries, but are a defining point of difference and potential conflict in other countries. As an illustration, matching a Catholic mentor with a Protestant protégé is not an issue in the USA but may certainly become an issue in Northern Ireland.

Along similar lines, the organization's demographics are important contextual factors influencing diversified mentoring relationships. A female protégée with a male mentor may be very visible in a primarily male organization, but may go unnoticed in an organization that is gender balanced. Another example is that socioeconomic class differences in the mentor–protégé pair may be more of an issue in unionized or blue-collar organizations than in organizations where class is less of an issue. It is therefore important to examine diversity in mentoring relationships from the perspective of the specific group membership: the history of the group, the political issues faced by the group, and the organizational and regional contexts in which the mentoring relationship exists.

What you see may not be what you get

Mentoring relationships may also be affected by the visibility of group memberships; some group memberships are easily visible, whereas others are not easily observable or even are invisible. Examples of invisible group memberships include sexual orientation, religion, socioeconomic class, mental disability and some forms of physical disability.

Invisibility of group memberships may lead to a number of potential complications in the initiation and development of mentoring relationships. One of the issues faced in diversified mentoring relationships is whether members of the relationship feel comfortable disclosing non-visible group memberships that are stigmatized in their organization or region. As illustrated in some of the individual cases presented later in this book, gay employees may be reluctant to disclose their sexual orientation at work for fear of discrimination and reprisal (cf. Ragins and Cornwell, in press). Trust and acceptance are critical elements of effective mentoring relationships, yet gay protégés may feel that heterosexual mentors may not accept their sexual orientation or may think less of them because they are gay. As a consequence, gay protégés may feel the need to hide their sexual orientation from their heterosexual mentors or even fabricate a heterosexual identity (Woods, 1994). This may create social distance, role conflict and stress in the relationship. To make matters worse, the mentor may feel betrayed if he or she finds out about the protégé's sexual orientation from someone else in the organization. Of course, there is always the possibility that the mentor harbours negative attitudes towards gays, is uncomfortable developing close working relationships with gay protégés, or holds anti-gay religious views that create conflict in the relationship. In this case, a gay protégé's disclosure of his or her sexual orientation may meet with disastrous results in the relationship.

Individuals who are members of non-observable, stigmatized groups face different organizational climates than other employees, and it may be very difficult for a mentor or a protégé who is not a member of this group to understand these 'micro climates' and the daily challenges faced by members of stigmatized groups. Individuals who enjoy majority status in the organization are often unaware of the privilege associated with their majority status, and may not understand the experience of being a member of a group that faces discrimination, or even termination, if their group membership is revealed. To make matters worse, majority members frequently assume that others share their group membership, and thus the burden of disclosure shifts to the 'invisible minority' to reveal his or her minority status, and risk the potential for rejection or discrimination in the mentoring relationship.

Timing is everything

Another important issue to consider when viewing diversified mentoring relationships is that the effects of diversity on mentoring relationships may vary over the course of the relationship. Visible group differences between members may be highly salient and have a strong impact on the development of the relationship in early phases of the relationship, but may become less of an issue with time. This may be because mentors and protégés may lack other information early in the relationship, and therefore may rely on readily available stereotypes to guide their perceptions and interactions with their partners. However, as time goes by and the members get to know each other on a deeper level, they may discover other similarities or differences that transcend group memberships. In essence, mentoring relationships may move from 'group' or 'surface' diversity to an 'individual' diversity that reflects deeper differences and similarities in values, attitudes and backgrounds (cf. Harrison, Price and Bell, 1998). This idea is supported by emerging research on the effects of work group diversity, which indicates that diversity among teams initially dampens team performance, but over time diverse teams end up outperforming homogeneous teams (Harrison, Price and Bell, 1998). These findings indicate that as group members interact, stereotypes may be replaced with more accurate knowledge of co-workers and the discovery of deeper levels of connection.

We can certainly apply these research findings to the mentoring arena. Although there has not been much research in this area, it is reasonable to expect that mentors and protégés may initially connect on the basis of perceived similarities or 'group diversity', but over time may find other, perhaps even more important, individual similarities that cement their relationship. Some diversified mentoring relationships may get off to a rocky start, but with proper training, support, communication and patience, may outperform homogeneous relationships by optimizing the diversity in the relationship while finding a common ground in values, interests, hobbies, families or background. Of course, the opposite may also be true; mentors and protégés may develop relationships based on similarity of group membership, but with time they may find that they have little else in common. This line of thought has important implications for mentoring programmes. Programmes that pair mentors and protégés solely on the basis of gender or race may find that members connect on the basis of these group memberships and the important experiences associated with being a minority in the organization and society, but they may or may not connect on other, deeper levels of diversity that define their inner values and sense of self.

This discussion really touches on a larger issue that is grappled with by diversity scholars. Some scholars observe that demographic group memberships shape world experiences and views in profound ways, while others contend that we are more similar than different. Another view is that demographic group memberships for minority members have a stronger impact on their sense of self and their world experience than group membership for majority members. For example, given societal discrimination, the identity of race has a stronger meaning and a greater impact on one's sense of self and social identity for people of colour than for white people. In mentoring relationships, minority group membership becomes the tip of the iceberg for a host of other value differences, world experiences and backgrounds that are associated with being a minority in society. In this sense, group diversity really taps individual diversity. An opposing view is that individuals are more similar than different, and that two individuals who share a common racial or ethnic heritage may be more different than two individuals who differ on the basis of their race. Although this debate may not be resolved soon, it is useful to keep these issues in mind while assessing the assumptions that underlie our views of diversity in mentoring relationships.

Who defines diversity in the relationship?

A final issue to consider when examining diverse mentoring relationships is who defines the diversity in the relationship. Is the degree of diversity in the mentoring relationship established by the members of the relationship, or some external third party?

This issue becomes salient in formally assigned mentoring relationships. A mentoring programme co-ordinator may match a mentor and protégé on the basis of shared group memberships, but the group memberships chosen by the co-ordinator may or may not be important to the individuals in the relationship. According to social identity theory, individuals classify themselves into social categories that shape their personal identities and allow them to define themselves in relation to their social environment (Ashforth and Mael, 1989; Tajfel and Turner, 1986). In essence, these social identities help us answer the personal identity question: 'Who am I?' Mentors and protégés have multiple social identities, and some identities may be more important than other identities in developing a sense of self and establishing the common basis for the mentoring relationship. Informal mentoring relationships may develop naturally on the basis of shared social identities and group memberships, but formal relationships are typically matched by third parties (Ragins, Cotton and Miller, 2000). A mentoring programme co-ordinator does not know automatically which social identities are salient and important to the members of the relationship, and may therefore match members based on his or her perceptions of shared group memberships rather than the perceptions of the members of the relationship. It may therefore be advisable to ask the members of the formal relationship about their social identities, needs and preferences before making the match.

Summary

The relationships among the key constructs discussed in this section are displayed in Figure 2.1. According to this model, perceived diversity in mentoring relationships is affected by differences based on group memberships as well deeper, individually based differences. Individual diversity is influenced by group diversity since the values, beliefs and attitudes of mentors and protégés are affected by their group memberships. The length of the relationship plays a key role in perceptions of diversity in the mentoring relationship; over time individual diversity may become more apparent and differences based on group memberships may play less of a role in perceived

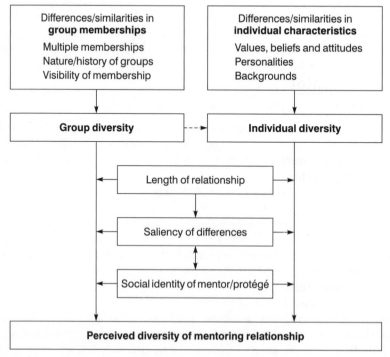

Figure 2.1 Dyadic perceptions of diversity in mentoring relationships

diversity. The length of the relationship also impacts the saliency of the differences; longer relationships may reach a level of 'diversity saturation' in which group or individual differences that were salient in the beginning of the relationship become less noticeable or important with time. While mentors and protégés may objectively differ on group memberships or individual characteristics, these differences may or may not be viewed as important by the members of the relationship. The saliency or importance of the differences therefore becomes another key factor in the perception of diversity in the mentoring relationship. Although not depicted in Figure 2.1, the organizational context plays a key role in saliency perceptions. For example, race differences in a mentoring relationship may be less salient to the members of the relationship when they work within groups or organizations that are racially and ethnically diverse, compared with those who work in homogeneous settings. Finally, the social identity of the members affects the importance they place on their group memberships and their perceptions of group-based diversity in the relationship. Length of relationship, saliency of differences and social identity of members therefore moderates the relationship between objective and perceived differences. This perceptual model helps to explain why, for example, gender may be a key issue in one diversified mentoring relationship but an extraneous issue in another.

Now that we have explored some of the complexities involved with defining diversity within mentoring relationships, let us now turn to examining how diversity affects the development and functioning the relationship.

How does diversity affect the development of informal mentoring relationships?

In this section I examine the processes that affect the development of informal, spontaneously developed mentoring relationships and then propose some interventions that may increase the effectiveness of the diversified mentoring relationship. Three interrelated factors impact the development of diversified mentoring relationships: identification, stereotypes and comfort zones.

Identification and role-modelling

Identification is a key process that guides the mentor's selection of the protégé, and vice versa. For the mentor, the development of the relationship serves an intrinsic and developmental need that is guided, in part, by their identification with the protégé (Erickson, 1963; Kram, 1985; Levinson et al., 1978). The relationship provides the mentor with a sense of generativity, or contribution to future generations (Erickson, 1963). Mentors often view their protégés as a younger version of themselves and a representative of the mentor's past. In support of this view, existing research indicates that mentors choose protégés who are viewed as being similar to themselves (Allen, Poteet and Burroughs,

1997) and that satisfaction with the relationship increases with perceived similarity (Ensher and Murphy, 1997).

To the extent that protégés select mentors, identification may also guide the protégé's selection of the mentor. Protégés may choose mentors who are viewed as competent role models; the mentor represents who the protégé wants to become (Ragins, 1997b). In this sense, the protégé represents the mentor's past, and the mentor represents the protégé's future.

Given the mutual identification processes underlying the development of mentoring relationships, diverse mentoring relationships face a clear challenge. For example, how likely is it that, holding other similarities constant, a white male mentor will identify with a black female protégée as a younger version of himself and choose her as his protégée? Of course, the white male mentor may make a conscious decision to overcome his natural tendency to select someone who is similar to him and seek out a diverse mentoring relationship. However, if identification based on group membership is the driving factor in the selection of protégés, this mentor could be expected to choose a white male protégé over a black female protégée. Given the lack of similarities in visible group memberships, members of diverse mentoring relationships may need to find other common ground. In essence, identification may still occur in diverse relationships, but this identification may be based on similarities in values, backgrounds, personalities and interests. As discussed earlier, mentors and protégés in diverse relationships may find they have much in common, but this discovery takes time and a deeper level of interaction. Therefore, mentoring relationships that are homogeneous may be easier to initiate than those that are diverse.

Existing research supports the idea that diversity represents an initial barrier to the development of mentoring relationships. In a study of 229 female and 281 male middle-level managers, we found that women reported greater barriers to gaining a mentor than men, and that they were more likely to report that potential male mentors were unwilling to mentor them because of their gender (Ragins and Cotton, 1991). However, in spite of this, the women in that study were as likely as the men to get a mentor, suggesting that they overcame these barriers and actively sought out these important developmental relationships.

Although mutual identification guides the development of mentoring relationships, the development of diversified relationships is also affected by the availability and sheer number of minority mentors. In most corporations, the higher the rank the fewer the number of women and employees of colour. Since mentors are generally found at higher ranks in organizations, this situation results in a restricted pool of female and minority mentors. Moreover, the few female and minority mentors that are available may be deluged with requests for mentoring from female and minority protégés seeking role models. Given the shortage of female and minority mentors, female and minority protégés often end up in mentoring relationships with white male mentors. This results in a situation in which majority protégés are in same-gender or same-race relationships, whereas female and minority protégés are in cross-race and cross-gender relationships. Existing research indicates that relationships that are cross-race and cross-gender usually involve majority mentors with minority protégés, rather than minority mentors with majority protégés (Dreher and Cox, 1996; McGuire, 1999; Ragins and Cotton, 1999; Ragins and McFarlin, 1990). In fact, the minority mentor–majority protégé is a relatively rare relationship. The rarity of this relationship is reflected in our recent study of mentoring relationships. We explicitly sought to increase the number of relationships involving female mentors and male protégés by using a balanced sample of men and women in female-typed, male-typed and gender-balanced fields (social work, journalism and engineering) in our recent study of gender and mentoring relationships (Ragins and Cotton, 1999). In spite of our sampling strategy, the 1162 respondents in our study yielded only twenty-four male protégés with female mentors. Accessibility could not fully account for this finding, since we used female-typed and gender-balanced occupations that were likely to have a relatively large pool of female mentors. An alternative explanation for the scarcity of the female mentor–male protégé relationship is that male protégés may not identify with female mentors and may perceive them as having less power and organizational resources than their male counterparts.

Therefore, it is clear that the development of mentoring relationships is guided not just by identification, but also by stereotypes, attitudes, attributions and perceptions about what the other party brings to the relationship.

Stereotypes: the lens used to view others

Stereotyping is defined as 'a cognitive structure that contains the perceiver's knowledge, beliefs and expectancies about some human group' (Hamilton and Trolier, 1986, p. 133). It is a basic human tendency to use stereotypes to process the vast amount of information we receive about individuals, and we use stereotypes to categorize individuals into easily defined groups (Tajfel and Turner, 1986). Stereotyping helps us gain a sense of control over our environment; instead of having to process a broad array of information about an individual, we use stereotypes to typecast a person into a limited set of behaviours and expectations, and we respond to that individual based on a relatively narrow set of expectations and preconceptions. While stereotypes reduce our workload in processing information about others, they also limit our ability to accurately assess the competencies and behaviours of others. In fact, stereotypes often result in distorted perceptions and misattributions regarding the behaviours of others.

These restrictions have important implications for diversified mentoring relationships. Perceptions of competence are central to the development of mentoring relationships, and these perceptions are also are highly susceptible to stereotyping (Ilgen and Youtz, 1986; Pettigrew and Martin, 1987; Ragins and Sundstrom, 1989). Stereotyping may cloud the mentor's perceptions, and may result in female and minority protégés being perceived as less competent than their white male counterparts. This process is not limited to white male mentors. Female and minority mentors may also internalize these stereotypes and use them in perceptions of their minority protégés; in this case they may not view female and minority protégés as less competent than white male protégés as much as they may view white male protégés as more competent in general. In this sense, perceptions of mentor and protégé competence may be 'gendered' in the same way that perceptions of leadership and power are 'gendered' (cf. Bohan, 1993; Hare-Mustin and Marecek, 1990). This refers to the idea that power and leadership are viewed as male constructs (Ragins, 1995); in other words, when one thinks of 'powerful leader' one thinks of men. This line of thinking can also be extended to race, ethnicity, disability, sexual orientation and other dimensions of diversity in mentoring relationships. The perception or visual image of a 'competent mentor' or a 'high-achieving protégé' may therefore be a white, male, heterosexual and able-bodied individual. Protégés who are both competent and in the minority defy existing stereotypes and require the perceiver to move from an automatic stereotyping to an individualized cognitive process.

Looking at the other side of the relationship, majority protégés may view female and minority mentors as less competent than majority mentors. Since stereotypes affect perceptions of power (Ragins and Sundstrom, 1989), female mentors and mentors of colour may not be perceived as having as much power or organizational resources as their white male counterparts (Ragins, 1989). This may affect both the development and functioning of the mentoring relationship.

Even if female and minority mentors and protégés perform exceptionally well, the cause of successful performance may be attributed to external, rather than internal causes. Greenhaus and Parasuraman (1993), for example, found that performance of highly successful black managers was attributed to help from others, rather than ability and effort. Attributing successful performance to external factors, such as luck or help from others, not only discounts the individual's competence, but also calls into question their future performance. On the other hand, if the attribution for a protégé's exceptional performance is intelligence or competence, a mentor could expect that performance to occur consistently in the future. These stereotyping and attributional processes are pervasive and often unconscious, but may have a tremendous impact on the development and functioning of the mentoring relationship.

Individuals in diversified mentoring relationships may reduce their reliance on stereotypes by employing a cognitive differentiation approach to dealing with others. According to Miller and Brewer (1986), we respond to individuals who are members of other groups, or 'out-groups' in one of three ways:

- category-based responding
- differentiated responding
- personalized responding.

These responses fall on a continuum of differentiation. Category-based responding employs the most rigid stereotyping system. In this case the individual views the out-group members as different from in-group members, but very similar to each other. Differentiated responding also involves stereotyping but is less rigid; the in-group is still viewed as different from the out-group, but members of the in-group can be viewed as distinct from one another. Personalized responding involves the greatest degree of differentiation and the least stereotyping. In this case, individuals view each out-group member as distinct and complex, and uses individual interaction rather than group stereotypes in perceptions and reactions. Mentors and protégés can view each other on the basis of their actual differences, rather than group stereotypes, by consciously employing a cognitive differentiation approach that is personalized and individualized. Stereotypes may further be broken down by constant reality testing and by increasing interactions and contact with minority group members (Allport, 1954; Pettigrew and Martin, 1987). Contact may not only dispel stereotypes, but may also increase mentors' and protégés' comfort with interacting with those who are different from them.

Moving out of the comfort zone

The comfort zone reflects the individual's level of comfort interacting with those who are different from them on one or more group memberships. Comfort zones are based on the 'similarity-attraction' paradigm, which essentially holds that we are attracted to and tend to like people who are like ourselves (Byrne, 1971). Those who are similar to us affirm our existence and also increase our belief that we can control the situation because we can predict the other person's behaviours. Individuals who are similar to us become a 'known quantity' in our social interactions and affect the degree to which they are included in work decisions and processes. A recent study found that individuals who differed from their work group in terms or race or gender reported less workplace exclusion than those who were demographically similar to their work group (Pelled, Ledford and Mohrman, 1999). In particular, members who were in the minority reported less job security, less access to sensitive information and less decision-making influence than those who were similar to other group members.

Interpersonal similarity also increases the ease of communication in relationships (Lincoln and Miller, 1979). Individuals who share group memberships also share common verbal and non-verbal communication patterns, perceptions and assumptions. The 'rules of the game' in homogeneous relationships are also more straightforward because both members of the relationship share them. The rules extend not only to the norms of the social relationship, but also to how members address conflict or disagreements within their relationship.

Comfort zones vary across individuals

Some individuals have very narrow comfort zones, and are only comfortable with those who are very similar to them on key social identities or group memberships. Other individuals relish pushing the envelope of their comfort zone, and may seek diverse relationships that challenge them to examine their beliefs, values and assumptions. A key factor that may determine individuals' comfort zones is their ability to tolerate ambiguity, their attitudes towards cultural differences (cf. Mendenhall and Oddou, 1985; Tung, 1981), and their overall dexterity in negotiating unchartered relational waters. Prior positive experiences interacting in diverse work and non-work relationships may extend comfort zones and provide the individual with insights, strategies, and skills that will help them work effectively in future diverse relationships.

By their very nature, diversified mentoring relationships involve less of a comfort zone than homogeneous relationships. Mentoring those who are different may lead to discomfort, a sense of lack of control and self-censorship. Mentors and protégés may be afraid that they will say or do the wrong thing, will be insensitive, or will unintentionally insult the other member of the relationship. While many mentoring relationships involve some degree of closeness and friendship, self-censorship and discomfort with diversity may lead to emotional and relational distance in the mentoring relationship. This represents a significant barrier to the development of effective diversified mentoring relationships, that may be overcome with honest and open communication, as discussed in the next section.

Having discussed the complexities of diversified mentoring relationships and the particular challenges faced by individuals in these relationships, I now provide some general strategies for developing and maintaining effective diversified mentoring relationships.

Strategies for developing effective diversified mentoring relationships

There are a number of practical strategies that mentors and protégés can use to develop effective diversified mentoring relationships. Inherent in these interventions is the broader issue of understanding how diversity affects personal and work relationships. Since mentoring relationships are embedded in the larger context of intergroup relations and diversity in organizations (cf. Ragins, 1997a; Thomas, 1999; 2001), the members of the mentoring relationship need to understand, both cognitively and emotionally, the 'big picture' with respect to group differences in power, privilege and diversity in their organizations before they can understand the impact of diversity on their own individual mentoring relationships.

Consciousness-raising: Understanding the nature and privilege of being the 'other'

One of the more difficult consciousness-raising tasks in diversified mentoring relationships is coming to terms with the nature of privilege. Privilege refers to the fact that some group memberships give individuals privileges and advantages that they may not ask for or even recognize, but certainly enjoy. There are multiple sources of privilege, based on race, ethnicity, gender, sexual orientation, class, age, religion and other group memberships. Nearly all organizational employees enjoy some form of privilege associated with a group membership; even if individuals are in the minority on the basis of one group membership (i.e. race), they may simultaneously enjoy the privilege and benefits associated with being in the majority in another group membership (i.e. sexual orientation or physical ability). Since privilege is usually unac-knowledged by its recipient, insights into the nature of privilege is one of the most daunting tasks faced by members of diversified mentoring relationships. As an example, a mentor who is physically able needs to understand the privilege and benefits that are accrued simply by the nature of that group membership, and that these benefits are not extended to his or her physically disabled protégé. Inherent in the understanding of privilege is the recognition that the organization faced by one group is not necessarily the same organization as faced by another.

For example, while heterosexual employees are able to talk openly at work about their spouses and partners, and bring these partners to work-related social functions, most gay and lesbian employees do not enjoy this privilege (Ragins and Cornwell, in press), and may in fact face negative reactions if they behaved in the same way as their heterosexual counterparts.

Along with privilege, members of diversified mentoring relationships also need to understand the experience of being 'the other' in their organization. Being 'the other' is sometimes referred to as being in the numerical minority (Kanter, 1977) or being an 'outsider within' (Collins, 1999).

Kanter (1977) observes that being in the numerical minority results in increased performance pressures, heightened visibility, increased stereotyping, exaggeration of group differences, increased vulnerability and fear of retalia-tion. In a broader sense, being 'the other' can also be viewed in terms of exclusion, isolation and marginalization. The culture, rules, norms and reward structure of the organization are developed by and for the majority group. As a consequence, groups in the minority often feel that they are 'a stranger in a strange land': they may not understand the rules of the game, or even that a game is being played.

How do mentors and protégés understand the experience of privilege and being the 'other' in organizations? One way is to place oneself in the position of being a minority, and process the feelings and reactions to that experience. This could be accomplished in work or non-work settings. Many individuals who are in the majority on multiple group memberships (i.e. race, gender or sexual orientation) have not had the experience of being the 'other' in an organizational setting. Individuals who are in the minority on one group membership (i.e. sexual orientation) may be sensitized to the general experience of otherness, but still do not automatically understand the specific experiences associated with other group memberships (i.e. race).

Another way of understanding privilege and being the 'other' is to seek out and expose oneself to the specific experiences of diverse groups. What is the experience of being a racial minority employee, a gay employee or an employee with a disability in the organization? What are the stereotypes and barriers faced by these groups? Diversity training, focus groups and one-on-one discussions can help sensitize mentors and protégés to different group experiences in the organization. Seeking out experiences by interacting with other groups outside the work setting may also be a method of raising consciousness and understanding group differences. Even exposure to different books, music, food and films may be a first small step towards understanding various group differences and cultures.

Stretching the comfort zone: cognitive restructuring

Members of diversified mentoring relationships need to first understand the dimensions of their comfort zones before they can systemically work towards increasing their level of comfort interacting with those who are different. A wide and inclusive comfort zone will not only help them be more effective in their current diversified mentoring relationship, but may also make them become more open to initiating future diversified relationships.

One way to stretch our comfort zones is to increase the amount of positive contact and interactions with individuals who are different from us. However, while positive contact is an important first step, it must also be accompanied by cognitive restructuring. Cognitive restructuring involves a critical assessment and confrontation of one's deep-seated fears, attitudes and stereotypes about other groups.

These deep-seated fears and attitudes go deep, are often denied, and are sometimes unconscious. Dovidio and Gaertner (1991; 1998) contend that these fears and feelings, which they call 'aversive racism,' have replaced 'old-fashioned' racism. Old-fashioned racism involves overt acts of hatred, while aversive or modern racism is quite covert (cf. Brief et al., 1997; Eberhardt and Fiske, 1998). Aversive racists may not believe they are racists and may deny their racist feelings, even as they behave in discriminatory and racist ways. These negative feelings do not involve hate as much as discomfort, uneasiness and fear. Comparable analogies can be found with homophobia, which is the fear of homosexuality (Herek, 1984), and fears associated with individuals with disabilities. While contact with other groups provides information and an opportunity for cognitive restructuring, it may also trigger negative reactions, discomfort, aversion and fear. These feelings should not be suppressed, but rather should be confronted, examined, tested and then consciously relinquished.

Dealing with diversity in the relationship: a continuum of strategies

Mentors and proteges in diversified mentoring relationships face a decision continuum on the strategies they may use to address diversity in their relationship.

On the one end of the continuum, they may choose to avoid the issue entirely and pretend to each other and themselves that there are no group-based differences between them. This 'blind to differences' strategy may provide some degree of comfort and a sense of control over the relationship; the members may feel that if they pretend there are no differences, the existing differences will simply go away. However, there are a number of problems with this avoidance strategy. The first is that conflicts and issues that will naturally arise in the relationship because of differences will not be identified as diversity issues, and may be misattributed to individual characteristics or shortcomings. For example, a female Asian protégée who is collectivist in orientation may avoid taking credit for individual achievements because of her cultural background (Goto, 1999). In the meantime, her white male mentor, who has an individualistic orientation, may perceive his protégée as lacking self-confidence, rather than adhering to the collectivist values of her cultural group. The second problem with this strategy is that it does not capitalize on the diversity in the relationship: by ignoring differences the members of the relationship do not learn from their differences or from each other. Finally, the strategy of ignoring differences places the burden of 'making the differences disappear' on the minority member in the relationship, who already holds the role of 'the other' in the organization. In this case, the minority member may try to assimilate, be a clone to the mentor, or deny his or her social identity or group background.

On the other end of the continuum, members of the relationship consciously and actively articulate and discuss all of the possible diversity differences in their relationship. In this 'constant examination' case, members of the relationship may confront, examine and scrutinize every perception, behaviour and interaction for diversity underpinnings. This strategy avoids the limitations of the avoidance strategy, and capitalizes on the diversity in the relationship: the relationship essentially becomes a 'learning lab' for understanding differences and raising the consciousness of its members. However, when used in its most extreme sense, all differences may become viewed as group differences, even those that are based on individual differences. Diversity becomes the central and overriding theme in the relationship; resulting in everything becoming a 'race thing' or a 'gender thing'. The paradox of this strategy is that group memberships overshadow the individuals in the relationships; individuals are viewed as group members first and individuals second. The personal identity of the individual becomes preempted by his or her group membership.

The third strategy falls midway on this continuum, and perhaps represents an optimal approach to dealing with differences in mentoring relationships. In this strategy, group differences are discussed and acknowledged, but do not overshadow the relationship. Individual differences are also examined and are distinguished from group differences. This 'acknowledgement' strategy involves members actively processing the relationship and their interactions from both a group as well as an individual differences perspective. Trust and open communication are critical prerequisites for this 'acknowledgement' strategy. The acknowledgement strategy also requires substantial introspection by both members of the mentoring relationship. Members need to ask themselves the 'Who am I?' question and understand the differences between their individual personal identities (i.e. 'I am an extrovert') and their group-based social identities ('I am an African-American'), as well as the situations in which these different identities become salient or important to the individual. This information should be shared among members of the relationship, so both understand the complexities of their partner's identities.

While it is important to select an optimal strategy for addressing diversity in mentoring relationships, it may be even more important to ensure that the strategy selected is shared by both members of the relationship. In his interview study of twenty-two cross-race mentoring relationships, Thomas (1993) found that the most effective mentoring relationships involved members who had complementary strategies: either both agreed to deny the effect of race on the relationship or both agreed to deal with it openly. Mentoring relationships involving one member who denied the effects of race and another member who wanted to talk openly about race reported less psychosocial support and friendship in their relationship than those who approached their racial differences in the same way.

Since it is unlikely that both members of the mentoring relationship will be at the exact same point in the strategy continuum, direct and honest communication on this issue becomes imperative. Members should identify where they are on the continuum with respect to their comfort level, as well as their aspirations for where they would like to be by the end of the relationship. For example, a heterosexual male mentor may not feel totally comfortable talking to his gay male protégé about sexual orientation issues in the workplace. Instead of pretending that the differences do not exist, and that the gay protégé is really a heterosexual, the members should discuss this issue and their relative comfort zones on this dimension of diversity. This may be part of the 'ground rules' process in which members of the relationship are forthcoming about topics that should be discussed and dealt with, as well as topics that are 'off limits' for discussion. The gay protégé, for example, may feel uncomfortable talking about what it is like being gay in their organization and may not feel that it is his responsibility to educate the mentor on this issue. The members of this relationship may agree that it is up to the mentor to gain insights about this issue through other means. This discussion illustrates the importance of establishing clear ground rules and expectations in the mentoring relationship.

Diversity ground rules

Ground rules are established and agreed upon expectations, standards and methods for interacting in the mentoring relationship. Ground rules may address such issues as the frequency and mode of interaction, the topics that are open for discussion and 'off limits' in the relationship, confidentiality in the relationship, and any other topics that may influence the communication, trust and effectiveness of the relationship. While ground rules are important for all mentoring relationships, they are particularly important for diversified mentoring relationships. As discussed earlier in this chapter, these relationships may be particularly susceptible to miscommunication and misperceptions.

Although ground rules may vary from one mentoring relationship to the next, diversified relationships often share some common themes springing from the diversity in the relationship. As discussed earlier, the members may agree to identify their individual and group differences and discuss the impact of those differences on their relationship and other work relationships. The first two ground rules might be very basic, but essential to the relationship. The first might be: 'We identify and celebrate our differences.' This ground rule not only starts a dialogue about differences in the relationship, but also pushes the members of the relationship to examine factors that may suppress and subvert diversity in the relationship. For example, members may discuss the signs of 'cloning' and assimilation in the mentoring relationship, processes that may naturally occur but may be detrimental to the effective functioning of diversified relationships. The members of the relationship may also agree to be non-judgemental of their differences. The second basic ground rule may be: 'Differences are not good or bad, they're just different.' In discussing this ground rule, members may share the behavioural outcomes of their group differences, and the underlying assumptions, values and beliefs that are reflected in these behaviours.

Another issue faced by members of diversified mentoring relationships is that majority members may have difficulty accepting the fact that discrimination exists in their organization. Minority members may come to their majority partners with stories and experiences of being discriminated against in their organization, and the first reaction of the majority member may be to deny that such injustice exists and attribute the experience to causes other than discrimination. This denial is tied directly to privilege; by recognizing that minority members face discrimination on the basis of their group membership, the majority member needs to also recognize that he or she is immune from this discrimination and may even benefit from it in the non-level organizational playing field. Promotions may be granted not only the basis of 'what you know', but also on the basis of 'who you know', 'who you are' and 'how you are perceived.' A third ground rule might therefore be: 'Just because an experience is unbelievable does not mean that it should not be believed.'

Other ground rules may be developed based on specific questions or situations. For example, what happens when one partner says something that the other finds racist, sexist, heterosexist or otherwise offensive? How do the members talk about differences without worrying about self-censorship or unintentional offences? What topics related to diversity should be addressed in the relationship, and what topics are off limits? What are the signs and symptoms of cloning in the relationship, and what should the members of the relationship do in this situation? How do members of the relationship handle diversity-related situations involving others in the organization? This final question leads us to the next strategy, which involves other members of the workplace.

Navigating the perceptions of others

Mentoring relationships do not exist in a vacuum, but exist within the larger context of the organization. The effectiveness of mentoring relationships is often dependent on interactions with others in the organization, and it is therefore important to understand how others in the organization view the members of the mentoring relationship. In particular, supervisors' and co-workers' perceptions of members of diversified relationships might be influenced by discriminatory stereotypes and attributions (Ragins, 1997b). As an example, minority protégés may be perceived as needing a mentor for 'remedial' purposes, and the protégé's career success may be attributed to the mentor's intervention, rather than the protégé's skills and abilities. Similar processes regarding misattributions and devaluations may occur with minority mentors. Minority mentor's work with protégés may be unrecognized or undervalued, particularly if their protégés are members of the majority (Ragins and Cotton, 1993). Minority mentors with minority protégés may be threatening to others, and may be viewed as 'planning a revolution' in the organization (Ragins, 1989). Majority mentors with minority protégés may face a backlash from peers if they are perceived as helping minority members at the expense of majority members.

Another challenge faced by members of diversified relationships is that they are particularly vulnerable to charges of favouritism. These charges of favouritism often stem from jealous co-workers and peers, and are somewhat common in mentoring relationships (Myers and Humphreys, 1985). However, the visibility of diversified relationships makes them even more susceptible to negative reactions from co-workers and supervisors. In support of this idea, in our study of 229 female and 281 male managers, we found that women were more likely than men to report that supervisors and co-workers would disapprove of their initiation of a relationship with a potential mentor (Ragins and Cotton, 1991).

Members of cross-gender relationships face the additional burden of navigating through perceptions of romantic involvement (Hurley and Fagenson-Eland, 1996; Ragins, 1989). In his study of thirty-five cross-gender mentoring relationships, Bowen (1985) found that female protégées reported being the target of discrediting sexual innuendoes and rumours circulated by jealous co-workers. We also found that women were more likely than men to report that they were reluctant to develop a relationship with a male mentor for fear that the mentor or others in the organization would misconstrue such initiation as sexual in nature (Ragins and Cotton, 1991).

These perceptions and attributions cannot be ignored, but must be confronted and promptly defused. Image management, buttressed with assertive interventions when needed, is an important strategy for managing diversified mentoring relationships. For example, the majority mentor may need to make the minority protégé's independent achievements and contributions in the relationship clear and salient to others in the organization. Misperceptions regarding romance in cross-gender relationships must be dealt with directly and immediately. Whispered speculations about the nature or intentions of diverse mentoring relationships should be confronted directly by members of the relationship as well as others in the organization. In fact, interventions by objective third parties are probably more effective in changing attitudes and stereotypes than interventions by the members of the relationship. This leads to the broader issue of developing an organizational climate that supports diversity and diversified mentoring relationships.

Creating organizational change

It is clear that diversified mentoring relationships are most likely to flourish in environments that accept and nurture diversity in all of its forms and relationships. Organizations that have problems with diversity are also likely to create challenges and barriers to members of diversified mentoring relationships (cf. Thomas, 2001). Organizational change therefore represents a long-term and optimal strategy for promoting the development of diversified relationships. The ideal organization for diversified mentoring relationships is one in which these relationships are so commonplace, natural and accepted that they do not even warrant a second glance. Unfortunately, this is not the case for most organizations.

Although it is beyond the scope of this chapter to provide a lengthy discussion on how to create an organization that values diversity, there are two fundamental prerequisites. First, the leaders of the organization must recognize the importance of diversity and the impact of both diversity and discrimination on individual performance, work relationships, and the organization's 'bottom line' (Ragins, Townsend and Mattis, 1998; Robinson and Dechant, 1997). These leaders must be absolutely committed to creating a culture that is inclusive, equitable and open (Cox, 1991; 1993), and to equalizing power relationships among groups in their organization (Linnehan and Konrad, 1999; Ragins, 1997a; Ragins and Sundstrom, 1989). Organizations that represent 'best practices' with respect to diversity go beyond discrimination and access issues; they are organizations that value all of their employees, and promote openness, growth and lifelong learning among its members (Thomas and Ely, 1996). These types of organizations also have a culture that naturally promotes the development of all types of mentoring relationships.

Second, organizations must dissolve the glass ceiling and obtain diversity in the executive suite (Ragins, Townsend and Mattis, 1998). Since the organization's culture embodies the values of its leaders, diversity in leadership ensures diversity in organizational values. A diverse leadership also encourages diverse mentoring relationships and provides effective role models for those seeking such relationships (Athey, Avery and Zemsky, 2000; Ragins, 1995). There are a number of strategies that can be used for ensuring representative leadership, such as succession planning, performance appraisals tied to diversity objectives, leadership development and formal mentoring pro-grammes (cf. Catalyst, 1998). Although formal mentoring programmes are included in many diversity programmes in organizations (Catalyst, 1993), some caveats about the use of formal mentoring programmes for women and people of colour are warranted.

Formal mentoring: the good, the bad and the marginal

Formal mentoring has been used as a strategy to promote the development of diversified mentoring relationships and is included in many diversity initiatives aimed at promoting the advancement of women and people of colour in organizations (Catalyst, 1993). However, while the popularity of these programmes has skyrocketed, there has been increasing debate as to their value, use and effectiveness.

Limitations and considerations in formal mentoring programmes

Most formal mentoring programmes in the USA are designed to replicate the benefits of informal mentoring (Burke and McKeen, 1989). The benefits of informal mentoring are clear: a number of studies have found that employees with informal mentors advance faster and farther in organizations than those lacking mentors (Dreher and Ash, 1990; Ragins and Cotton, 1999; Scandura, 1992). Informal mentors are an important tool for the advancement of women and employees of colour. For example, our study of 461 top-ranking female executives in Fortune 1000 companies revealed that a full 91 per cent had one or more informal mentors during the course of their careers, and they identified mentoring as a specific strategy that they employed to break through the glass ceiling (Ragins, Townsend and Mattis, 1998). It is clear that mentoring may be the 'ice pick' for breaking through the glass ceiling.

Although mentoring is critical for women and people of colour, these groups also report greater barriers to developing informal mentoring relationships than their majority counterparts (Ragins and Cotton, 1991; Thomas, 1990). In recognition of these barriers, many organizations in the USA offer formal mentors as a substitute for informal mentors. However, existing research suggests that these organizations may be doing their employees a disservice; a number of studies conducted in the USA have found that formal relationships are less effective than informal relationships (Chao, Walz and Gardner, 1992; Fagenson-Eland, Marks and Amendola, 1997; Ragins and Cotton, 1999; Viator, 2001). In a national study of 510 protégés with informal mentors, 104 protégés with formal mentors and 548 non-mentored individuals, we found that employees with informal mentors were more likely to advance in organiza-tions than non-mentored individuals, but employees with formal mentors did not advance further than those lacking mentors (Ragins and Cotton, 1999). A particularly disturbing finding in our study was that while protégés with formal mentors reported less mentoring functions and less satisfaction with their mentor than protégés with informal mentors, this effect was stronger for women than for men, indicating that formal mentors were less effective for women than for men. In a subsequent report, using the same data, we also found that women were less satisfied with their formal mentoring programmes than men were (Ragins, Cotton and Miller, 2000).

This is not to say that formal mentoring programmes are bad or that they should not be used. Quite the contrary: formal programmes can be highly effective for promoting diversity initiatives, as discussed below. However, there are at least three important considerations that can be gleaned from the research that has been conducted in this area. First, it is clear that formal mentoring must be distinguished from informal mentoring. Studies in the USA have found that compared with informal mentors, formal mentors are more limited with respect to role-modelling, counselling and other mentoring functions (Fagenson-Eland, Marks and Amendola, 1997; Ragins and Cotton, 1999), and are focused more on helping the protégé meet job or role demands than life demands. In essence, formal mentors help protégés 'deal with their jobs', whereas informal mentors help protégés 'deal with their lives'.

The second consideration is that formal mentors should not be offered as a substitute for informal mentors, particularly for women and employees of colour. As discussed above, while informal mentoring is critical for helping women and people of colour break through the glass ceiling, the presence of a formal mentor had no effect on promotion or compensation (Ragins and Cotton, 1999). However, given the barriers to informal mentoring faced by women and minorities, formal mentoring cannot be dismissed. It may be best to promote a strategy of obtaining multiple formal and informal mentors. Some informal mentoring relationships may provide critical role modelling and counselling functions, whereas formal relationships may provide female and minority protégés with the 'rules of the road' and other inside information that is usually provided in the 'old boys club'.

Finally, it is important to consider the quality of the mentoring relationship. While informal relationships are, on average, more effective than formal relationships, all mentoring relationships are not created equal, and not all informal mentoring relationships are better than all formal relationships. Mentoring relationships fall along a continuum from high-quality, effective relationships, to marginal or even dysfunctional relationships (Eby et al., 2000; Ragins, Cotton and Miller, 2000; Ragins and Scandura, 1997). There is a 'dark side' of mentoring, and it is important to select high-quality mentors for mentoring programmes, particularly those aimed at women and employees of colour. In our follow-up comparison of formal and informal mentoring relationships, we found that the quality of the relationship had a greater impact on protégés' work and career attitudes than the presence of a mentor, the type of relationship or even the design of the mentoring programme (Ragins, Cotton and Miller, 2000). An important finding of that study was that the quality of the relationship was more important than whether the relationship was formal or informal. In fact, protégés with high-quality formal mentors had more positive work and career attitudes than protégés with marginal informal mentors. Even the presence of a mentor was not as important as the quality of the relationship.

Protégés in high-quality mentoring relationships reported more positive job attitudes than non-mentored individuals, but the attitudes of those in dissatisfying or marginally satisfying relationships were equivalent to those of non-mentored individuals. In some cases, non-mentored individuals had more positive attitudes than protégés in marginal mentoring relationships. Finally, even the design features of the mentoring programme were not as important as the quality of the relationship. In essence, the best-designed programmes did not compensate for a pool of marginal mentors. We concluded that a formal mentoring programme is only as good as the mentor it produces. This study underscored the fact that selection and training are critical components of effective mentoring programmes. Formal programmes first need to recruit skilled and motivated mentors who seek and appreciate diversity in relationships, and then need to provide mentoring and diversity training to all programme participants.

Diversity benefits of formal mentoring programmes

Although formal mentors are generally less effective than informal mentors, formal mentoring programmes can be used as a strategy for developing diverse mentoring relationships and for promoting the broader goals related to diversity in organizations. There are three diversity benefits associated with formal mentoring programmes. First, formal mentoring programmes not only provide women and minorities access to mentors, but they also increase the future pool of diverse mentors. We found that one of the best predictors of being a mentor was prior experience as a protégé (Ragins and Cotton, 1993). Protégés seek to become mentors because they recognize the importance of the relationship in their own careers. Many of the female executives we surveyed noted that they became mentors because they wanted to 'give back' to future generations of women (Ragins, Townsend and Mattis, 1998). Therefore, formal mentoring programmes may be pipelines to a diverse pool of future formal and informal mentors.

The second diversity benefit of formal mentoring programmes is that they sanctify cross-gender mentoring relationships and help dispel discrediting sexual innuendoes and destructive rumours about cross-gender mentoring relationships. This advantage extends to both formal and informal cross-gender relationships. The more commonplace these relationships are, the greater the probability that they will be accepted and valued, as opposed to being targeted for discrediting rumours.

The third benefit is that more diversity may be obtained in formal as compared to informal mentoring relationship. As discussed earlier in this chapter, this diversity not only fuels the effectiveness of the relationship, but it also raises the awareness and consciousness of its members. Pairing a majority mentor with a minority protégé may have the effect of helping the majority mentor understand the issues faced by minorities in their organization. This long-term and personal interaction may be even more effective than diversity training for dispelling stereotypes and changing attitudes. In a larger sense, diversified mentoring relationships involving majority mentors and minority protégés may be a powerful tool for changing the organization's culture (Ragins, 1995). The culture of the organization reflects the values of its power-holders. Diversified relationships may change and expand those values, and in so doing may make the organization more inclusive for all of its members.

Summary

A summary of the factors, interventions and outcomes associated with diversified mentoring programmes is presented in Figure 2.2. As illustrated in this figure, diversified mentoring relationships face a number of challenges that are not faced in homogeneous relationships. In particular, diversified relationships must address such factors as restricted identification and role-modelling, the use of stereotypes in perceptions and attributions, and restricted comfort zones among members of the relationship. There are a number of interventions that can be used to help increase the effectiveness of diversified relationships, such as cognitive differentiation, cognitive restructuring, diversity training, consciousness-raising, increasing positive contact and discovering deep-level diversity. The approach to dealing with diversity in the relationship falls along a continuum, ranging from absolute avoidance at one end to active confrontation at the other. The optimal strategy for dealing with diversity depends on the members of the relationship, but avoidance is

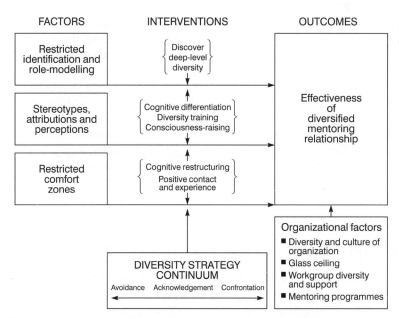

Figure 2.2 Factors and interventions in diversified mentoring relationships

generally viewed as an ineffective strategy for dealing with diversity in the mentoring relationship. Although it is not depicted in Figure 2.2, a key strategy that promotes success in any type of mentoring relationship, but is critical in diversified relationships, is the strategy of clarifying ground rules and expectations in the relationship. Another key point is that mentoring relationships do not exist in a vacuum, and it is important to consider the influence of the work group and organizational factors on the diversified mentoring relationship. A central issue here is whether the relationship was formally assigned as part of a formal mentoring programme or whether the relationship developed informally based on the mutual chemistry and developmental needs of the members. The debate involving formal and informal mentoring relationships will not be resolved in the near future, and takes on another level of complexity as formal relationships may vary by culture and region. The quality of the mentoring relationship is a critical factor for both formal and informal relationships.

Finally, recent conceptualizations of mentoring hold that traditional mentors are just one element in an entire constellation of developmental relationships (Higgins and Kram, 2001). In essence, this view holds that protégés may receive developmental support from supportive individuals representing a range of social systems (i.e. school, community, family, religious affiliations). We need more research that investigates how diversity affects the formation, development and effectiveness of these developmental networks.

Conclusion

In conclusion, diversity affects nearly every aspect of the mentoring relationship: its development, its processes and its outcomes. While it is clear that those in diverse mentoring relationships face more challenges than those in homogeneous relationships, those who take this challenge also stand to gain so much more from the relationship than those who retreat to the comfort of similarity and sameness in relationships. At its very core, diversity sparks creativity, questions prevailing and limiting assumptions, and opens the door to innovation and fresh ideas. Diverse mentoring relationships can be expansive and enriching, they can raise our consciousness and provide a true 'learning lab' for understanding our differences and similarities. Diverse relationships give us the opportunity that few other relationships offer – the opportunity to understand diversity in action.

References

Allen, T. D., Poteet, M. L. and Burroughs, S. M., (1997). The mentor's perspective: A qualitative inquiry and future research agenda. *Journal of Vocational Behavior*, **51**, 70–89.

Allport, G. W. (1954). *The Nature of Prejudice*. Addison-Wesley.

Ashforth, B. E. and Mael, F. (1989). Social identity theory and the organization. *Academy of Management Review*, **14**, 20–39.

Athey, S., Avery, C. and Zemsky, P. (2000). Mentoring and diversity. *American Economic Review*, **90**, 765–86.

Blake, S. (1999). At the crossroads of race and gender: lessons from the mentoring experiences of professional black women. In *Mentoring Dilemmas: Developmental Relationships within Multicultural Organizations* (A. Murrell, F. J. Cosby and R. Ely, eds) pp. 83–104, Lawrence Erlbaum.

Bohan, J. S. (1993). Regarding gender: essentialism, constructionism, and feminist psychology. *Psychology of Women Quarterly*, **17**, 5–21.

Bowen, D. D. (1985). Were men meant to mentor women? *Training and Development Journal*, **39**(2), 31–4.

Brief, A. P., Buttram, R. T., Reizenstein, R. M., Pugh, et al. (1997). Beyond good intentions: the next steps toward racial equality in the American workplace. *Academy of Management Executive*, **11**, 59–72.

Burke, R. J. and McKeen, C. A. (1989). Developing formal mentoring programs in organizations. *Business Quarterly*, **53**(3), 76–99.

Burke, R. J. and McKeen, C. A. (1990). Mentoring in organizations: implications for women. *Journal of Business Ethics*, **9**, 317–32.

Byrne, D. (1971). *The Attraction Paradigm*. Academic Press.

Catalyst (1993). *Mentoring: A Guide to Corporate Programs and Practices*. Catalyst.

Catalyst (1998). *Advancing Women in Business – the Catalyst Guide: Best Practices from the Corporate Leaders*. Jossey-Bass.

Catalyst (1999). *Women of Color in Corporate Management: Opportunities and Barriers*. Catalyst.

Chao, G. T., Walz, P. M. and Gardner, P. D. (1992). Formal and informal mentorships: a comparison on mentoring functions and contrast with nonmentored counterparts. *Personnel Psychology*, **45**, 619–36.

Collins, P. H. (1999). Reflections on the outsider within. *Journal of Career Development*, **26**, 85–8.

Cox, T. (1991). The multicultural organization. *Academy of Management Executive*, **5**(2), 34–47.

Cox, T. (1993). *Cultural Diversity in Organizations: Theory, Research and Practice*. Berret-Koehler.

Cox, T. H. and Nkomo, S. M. (1991). A race and gender-group analysis of the early career experience of MBA's. *Work and Occupations*, **18**, 431–46.

Dovidio, J. F. and Gaertner, S. L. (1991). Changes in the nature and expression of racial prejudice. In *Opening Doors: An Appraisal of Race Relations in Contemporary America* (H. Knopke, J. Norrell and R. Rogers, eds) pp. 201–41, University of Alabama Press.

Dovidio, J. F. and Gaertner, S. L. (1998). On the nature of contemporary prejudice: the causes, consequences, and challenges of aversive racism. In *Confronting Racism: The Problem and the Response* (J. Eberhardt and S. Fiske, eds) pp. 3–32, Sage.

Dreher, G. F. and Ash, R. A. (1990). A comparative study of mentoring among men and women in managerial, professional, and technical positions. *Journal of Applied Psychology*, **75**, 539–46.

Dreher, G. F. and Cox, T. H. (1996). Race, gender, and opportunity: a study of compensation attainment and the establishment of mentoring relationships. *Journal of Applied Psychology*, **81**, 297–308.

Eberhardt, J. L. and Fiske, S. T. (eds) (1998). *Confronting Racism: The Problem and the Response*. Sage.

Eby, L. T., McManus, S., Simon, S. A. and Russell, J. E. A. (2000). Does every silver lining have a cloud? A study of dysfunctional mentoring experiences. *Journal of Vocational Behavior*, **57**, 1–21.

Ensher, E. A. and Murphy, S. E. (1997). Effects of race, gender, perceived similarity, and contact on mentor relationships. *Journal of Vocational Behavior*, **50**, 460–81.

Erickson, E. (1963). *Childhood and Society.* W. W. Norton.

Fagenson-Eland, E. A., Marks, M. A. and Amendola, K. L. (1997). Perceptions of mentoring relationships. *Journal of Vocational Behavior*, **51**, 29–42.

Goto, S. (1999). Asian Americans and developmental relationships. In *Mentoring Dilemmas: Developmental Relationships within Multicultural Organizations* (A. Murrell, F. J. Cosby and R. Ely, eds) pp. 47–62, Lawrence Erlbaum.

Greenhaus, J. H. and Parasuraman, S. (1993). Job performance attributions and career advancement prospects: an examination of race and gender effects. *Organizational Behavior and Human Decision Processes*, **55**, 273–97.

Greenhaus, J. H., Parasuraman, S. and Wormley, W. M. (1990). Effects of race on organizational experiences, job performance evaluations, and career outcomes. *Academy of Management Journal*, **33**, 64–86.

Hamilton, D. L. and Trolier, T. K. (1986). Stereotypes and stereotyping: an overview of the cognitive approach. In *Prejudice, Discrimination, and Racism* (J. F. Dovidio and S. L. Gaertner, eds) pp. 127–58, Academic Press.

Hare-Mustin, R. T and Marecek, J. (1990). Gender and the meaning of difference: postmodernism and psychology. In *Making a Difference: Psychology and the Construction of Gender* (R. T. Hare-Mustin and J. Marecek, eds) pp. 22–64, Yale University Press.

Harrison, D. A., Price, K. H. and Bell, M. P. (1998). Beyond relational demography: time and the effects of surface- and deep-level diversity on work group cohesion. *Academy of Management Journal*, **41**, 96–107.

Herek, G. M. (1984). Beyond 'homophobia': a social psychological perspective on attitudes towards lesbians and gay men. *Journal of Homosexuality*, **10**, 1–21.

Higgins, M. C. and Kram, K. E. (2001). Reconceptualizing mentoring at work: a developmental nework perspective. *Academy of Management Review*, **26**, 264–88.

Hurley, A. E. and Fagenson-Eland, E. A. (1996). Challenges in cross-gender mentoring relationships: psychological intimacy, myths, rumours, innuendoes and sexual harassment. *Leadership and Organization Development Journal*, **17**, 42–9.

Ilgen, D. R. and Youtz, M. A. (1986). Factors affecting the evaluation, and development of minorities in organizations. In *Research in Personnel and Human Resources Management: A Research Annual* (K. M. Rowland and G. R. Ferris, eds) vol. 4, pp. 307–37), JAI Press.

Jeanquart-Barone, S. (1996). Implications of racial diversity in the supervisor–subordinate relationship. *Journal of Applied Social Psychology*, **26**, 935–44.

Kanter, R. M. (1977). *Men and Women of the Corporation*. Basic Books.

Kram, K. E. (1985). *Mentoring at Work*. Scott, Foresman and Co.

Levinson, D. J., Darrow, C. N., Klein, E. B., Levinson, M. H., et al. (1978). *The Seasons of a Man's Life*. Alfred A. Knopf.

Lincoln, J. R. and Miller, J. (1979). Work and friendship ties in organizations: a comparative analysis of relational networks. *Administrative Science Quarterly*, **24**, 181–98.

Linnehan, F. and Konrad, A. M. (1999). Diluting diversity: implications for intergroup inequality in organizations. *Journal of Management Inquiry*, **8**, 399–414.

Lyness, K. S. and Thompson, D. E. (1997). Above the glass ceiling? A comparison of matched samples of female and male executives. *Journal of Applied Psychology*, **82**, 359–75.

McGuire, G. M. (1999). Do race and sex affect employees' access to and help from mentors? In *Mentoring Dilemmas: Developmental Relationships within Multicultural Organizations* (A. Murrell, F. J. Cosby and R. Ely, eds) pp. 105–20, Lawrence Erlbaum.

Mendenhall, M. and Oddou, G. (1985). The dimensions of expatriate acculturation: a review. *Academy of Management Review*, **10**, 39–47.

Miller, N. and Brewer, M. B. (1986). Categorization effects on ingroup and outgroup perception. In *Prejudice, Discrimination, and Racism* (J. F. Dovidio and S. L. Gaertner, eds) pp. 209–29, Academic Press.

Murrell, A. J., Crosby, F. J. and Ely, R. J. (eds) (1999). *Mentoring Dilemmas: Developmental Relationships within Multicultural Organizations*. Lawrence Erlbaum.

Myers, D. W. and Humphreys, N. J. (1985). The caveats in mentorship. *Business Horizons*, **28**(4), 9–14.

O'Neill, R. M., Horton, S. and Crosby, F. J. (1999). Gender issues in developmental relationships. In *Mentoring Dilemmas: Developmental Relationships within Multicultural Organizations* (A. Murrell, F. J. Cosby and R. Ely, eds) pp. 63–80, Lawrence Erlbaum.

Pelled, L. H., Ledford, G. E. Jr and Mohrman, S. A. (1999). Demographic dissimilarity and workplace inclusion. *Journal of Management Studies*, **36**, 1013–31.

Pettigrew, T. F. and Martin, J. (1987). Shaping the organizational context for Black American inclusion. *Journal of Social Issues*, **43**, 41–78.

Ragins, B. R. (1989). Barriers to mentoring: the female manager's dilemma. *Human Relations*, **42**, 1–22.

Ragins, B. R. (1995). Diversity, power and mentoring in organizations: a cultural, structural and behavioral perspective. In *Diversity in Organizations* (M. Chemers, M. Costanzo and S. Oskamp, eds) pp. 91–132, Sage.

Ragins, B. R. (1997a). Diversified mentoring relationships in organizations: a power perspective. *Academy of Management Review*, **22**, 482–521.

Ragins, B. R. (1997b). Antecedents of diversified mentoring relationships. *Journal of Vocational Behavior*, **51**, 90–109.

Ragins, B. R. (1999a). Where do we go from here and how do we get there? Methodological issues in conducting research on diversity and mentoring relationships. In *Mentoring Dilemmas: Developmental Relationships within Multicultural Organizations* (A. Murrell, F. J. Cosby and R. Ely, eds) pp. 227–47, Lawrence Erlbaum.

Ragins, B. R. (1999b). Gender and mentoring relationships: a review and research agenda. In *Handbook of Gender and Work* (G. Powell, ed.) pp. 347–70, Sage.

Ragins, B. R. and Cornwell, J. C. (in press). Pink triangles: antecedents and consequences of workplace discrimination against gay and lesbian employees. *Journal of Applied Psychology*.

Ragins, B. R. and Cotton, J. (1991). Easier said than done: gender differences in perceived barriers to gaining a mentor. *Academy of Management Journal*, **34**, 939–51.

Ragins, B. R. and Cotton, J. (1993). Gender and willingness to mentor in organizations. *Journal of Management*, **19**, 97–111.

Ragins, B. R. and Cotton, J. (1999). Mentor functions and outcomes: a comparison of men and women in formal and informal mentoring relationships. *Journal of Applied Psychology*, **84**, 529–50.

Ragins, B. R. and McFarlin, D. (1990). Perception of mentor roles in cross-gender mentoring relationships. *Journal of Vocational Behavior*, **37**, 321–39.

Ragins, B. R. and Scandura, T. A. (1997). The way we were: gender and the termination of mentoring relationships. *Journal of Applied Psychology*, **82**, 945–53.

Ragins, B. R. and Sundstrom, E. (1989). Gender and power in organizations: a longitudinal perspective. *Psychological Bulletin*, **105**, 51–88.

Ragins, B. R., Cotton, J. and Miller, J. (2000). Marginal mentoring: an examination of the effects of type of mentor and program design on work and career attitudes. *Academy of Management Journal*, **47**, 1177–94.

Ragins, B. R., Townsend, B. and Mattis, M. (1998). Gender gap in the executive suite: CEOs and female executives report on breaking the glass ceiling. *Academy of Management Executive*, **12**, 28–42.

Robinson, G. and Dechant, K. (1997). Building a business case for diversity. *Academy of Management Executive*, **11**, 21–30.

Scandura, T. A. A. (1992). Mentorship and career mobility: an empirical investigation. *Journal of Organizational Behavior*, **13**, 169–74.

Schein, V. E., Mueller, R. and Jacobson, C. (1989). The relationship between sex role stereotypes and requisite management characteristics among college students. *Sex Roles*, **20**, 103–10.

Schneer, J. A. and Reitman, F. (1995). The impact of gender as managerial careers unfold. *Journal of Vocational Behavior, 47*, 290–315.

Sosik, J. J. and Godshalk, V. M. (2000). The role of gender in mentoring: implications for diversified and homogeneous mentoring relationships. *Journal of Vocational Behavior, 57*, 102–22.

Stroh, L. K., Brett, J. M. and Reilly, A. H. (1992). All the right stuff: a comparison of female and male managers' career progression. *Journal of Applied Psychology, 77*, 251–60.

Tajfel, H. and Turner, J. C. (1986). The social identity theory of intergroup behavior. In *Psychology of Intergroup Relations* (S. Worchel and W. G. Austin, eds) 2nd edn, pp. 7–24, Nelson-Hall.

Thomas, D. A. (1990). The impact of race on managers' experiences of developmental relationships (mentoring and sponsorship): an intra-organizational study. *Journal of Organizational Behavior, 11*, 479–91.

Thomas, D. A. (1993). Racial dynamics in cross-race developmental relationships. *Administrative Science Quarterly, 38*, 169–94.

Thomas, D. A. (1999). Beyond the simple demography-power hypothesis: how blacks in power influence white-mentor–black-protégé developmental relationships. In *Mentoring Dilemmas: Developmental Relationships within Multicultural Organizations* (A. Murrell, F. J. Cosby and R. Ely, eds.) pp: 157–70, Lawrence Erlbaum.

Thomas, D. A. (2001). The truth about mentoring minorities: race matters. *Harvard Business Review, 79*(4), 98–111.

Thomas, D. A. and Ely, R. J. (1996). Making differences matter: a new paradigm for managing diversity. *Harvard Business Review, 77*, 79–90.

Tung, R. L. (1981). Selection and training of personnel for overseas assignments. *Columbia Journal of World Business, 16*(1), 68–78.

Viator, R. E. (2001). The association of formal and informal public accounting mentoring with role stress and related job outcomes. *Accounting, Organizations and Society, 26*, 73–93.

Woods, J. D. (1994). *The Corporate Closet: The Professional Lives of Gay Men in America*. Free Press.

3

Establishing and sustaining a formal mentoring programme for working with diversified groups

David Clutterbuck

The extensive literature on both mentoring and diversity and the emerging literature on diversity mentoring might be expected to have provided a solid base for discussion of good practice, in terms of both individual relationships and the management of structured programmes. In practice, this does not seem to be the case. Both anecdote and academic analysis are often contradictory, confusing and sometimes plain unhelpful, whether they deal with individual informal relationships or with structured schemes (programmes).

One of the main reasons for this is the problem of definition. There is little real consensus about the definition of either mentoring or diversity. There are at least 100 definitions of mentoring in the literature, ranging from very hands-on to very hands-off descriptions. Case studies and research studies tend to make different assumptions about:

- whether the relationship is in-line or off-line (i.e. within or outside the direct reporting relationship)
- the appropriate gap in hierarchy level or experience between mentor and mentee
- the level of formality/informality in the relationship and in the programme
- the purpose of the relationship

- roles and responsibilities of mentor and mentee
- the use of power and influence by the mentor on the mentee's behalf
- distinctions between coaching, mentoring, counselling, tutoring and facilitating
- whether the mentor is internal or external to the mentee's organization.

Where these assumptions are clearly articulated, research can provide useful insights into the dynamics of relationships and programme management. Unfortunately, the vast majority of research on both sides of the Atlantic fails to define precisely what kind of relationship is being measured. For example, studies that lump together mentoring between line managers and direct reports and between dyads out of the reporting line are mixing two very different types of relationship, with very different dynamics. Leaving aside whether in-line mentoring is really coaching, there is likely to be less openness of dialogue between manager and direct report, no matter how good a relationship they have. The perspective of the line manager is likely to be very different from that of an off-line mentor. And other employees in the same team may are more likely to see the relationship as favouritism.

The situation is similar for diversity. Is it a narrowly defined issue, relating only to inequality of power for specific groups, based on gender, race or disability? Does it refer more broadly to the management task of building upon and using – to the maximum benefit of the organization and its members – the talents of all employees? Or does it mean valuing and exploiting differences in culture, background and personality? At one extreme, diversity can be seen as a means of overcoming injustice – righting wrongs – and at the other as a means of enhancing individual and group contribution to the organization's goals.

Even within the narrowest definitions, there are problems in drawing conclusions from research that focuses on a small number of potential or actual disempowering factors. To take a simple example, research that examines issues of gender discrimination without looking closely at other contextual factors is unlikely to provide more than half a story. Is the sample of both men and women coherent in the sense that they are all at the same hierarchical level? Do they have similar levels of education? Are they from a similar class? Is race a factor? The reality of diversity is that people differ on a multitude of characteristics and the more narrowly one examines one differentiating factor, without taking into account others, the less useful the research may sometimes be.

This chapter is not about resolving the definition issues, or dissecting research. It *is* about drawing on perceived good practice and providing guidelines on the issues programme co-ordinators need to address. In many cases, there is no right answer or best practice – but reflecting on the critical issues and on the experience of others will at least help to design initiatives that deliver results both in the short and long term.

However, it is relevant to define precisely what we are talking about with regard to both diversity and mentoring. In both cases, a pragmatic approach to definition divides the various attributes into *fundamentals* and *variables*. For mentoring, our expectation of fundamentals is that the programme should:

- be formally co-ordinated and supported by the organization
- be voluntary (at least to the extent that people can opt out)
- involve some form of training for both mentors and mentees
- be off-line relationships
- be concerned with developing the whole individual, rather than just focused on one or two aspects of performance.

Variables might include:

- the level of formality imposed on the relationship in terms of record-keeping, reporting back and so on
- the gap in age, experience and/or status between mentor and mentee
- expectations about the number of mentees per mentor
- expectations about the frequency and length of meetings
- the specific ground rules (e.g. how confidential is confidential?).

For diversity programmes, our expectation is that they should:

- be formally recognized and encouraged by the organization
- address a specific issue of disempowerment or inability of a defined group (or groups) of people to achieve their potential
- be voluntary
- be measured, at least in terms of statistical outcomes.

Variables might include:

- the homogeneity of the group targeted
- whether some form of affirmative action is built into the process
- the degree of consultation with and control by people from the target group.

The programme designer for a diversified mentoring initiative will need to begin by affirming the key fundamentals and some of the key variables, before proceeding any further. The authors' experience of large corporate programmes, in particular, is that failure to align all the senior decision-makers and influencers behind a common definition and set of expectations inevitably leads to conflict in implementation. This is particularly the case, where programmes span countries or continents.

The experiences of three multinationals introducing mentoring programmes – one French, one Anglo-Dutch and one from the USA – illustrate the point. The French company simply issued an edict on how things should be run, even though its Scandinavian, Dutch and British subsidiaries all said the approach was culturally inappropriate. Although some relationships did get off the ground, there was minimal support from local decision-makers and immense suspicion about the whole process from the intended beneficiaries. The company soon moved on to a new fad, rather than face up to the issues underlying the failure to implement. The Anglo-Dutch company adopted a laissez-faire approach, agreeing to very broad outlines with its international human resources (HR) community and country chief executives, and leaving it to them to determine how and when to introduce programmes. Where the programme was embraced with enthusiasm, it was done well, even though the approaches varied. However, many countries did not introduce programmes at all and the multinational is still grappling with how to encourage them to do so.

The US company rushed into a mentoring scheme, putting pressure on local top management around the world to implement programmes before anyone had really thought through what they wanted to achieve. There was a naïve assumption that everyone would interpret the requirement in the same way as the people in the Midwest headquarters had, and that therefore there would be a high degree of consistency. When this was found not to be the case, the company panicked, issuing instructions for how mentoring should be organized, in a belated effort to re-establish control. While a few subsidiaries welcomed this intervention, having been looking for some leadership, others greatly resented having to unpick what they regarded as best practice within their own context. Even had the imposed processes genuinely been better than those created locally, the HR professionals in the divisions now had little enthusiasm for them. Several thriving mentoring schemes in European countries simply died away because they no longer had enthusiastic champions.

The lesson of these three experiences is that programme design must be a participative activity that recognizes and values cultural diversity as an important element in gaining support for the programme and making it work. Getting the balance right between the fundamentals (what all cultures and groups can sign up to) and the variables (those elements that can be left to local decision-making) is critical.

A basic structure for planning diversity-mentoring programmes

Although every organization and programme has different needs, the same basic principles seem to apply in designing a mentoring initiative. The co-ordinators need to progressively design the programme taking into account the following headings:

- the *purpose* behind it – i.e. what exactly do you want to achieve and why? Our rough estimate is that 30 per cent of company programmes and 50 per cent of community schemes fail right here.
- the *audiences* – i.e. who specifically is the programme trying to help? Who are the intended mentors?)
- *key processes* such as selecting, matching and training
- the *leadership* issues – i.e. who will champion the programme?

- the *resource* issues – i.e. how will we fund the training and administration activities?
- the need for *continued support* – i.e. how will we ensure the continuation of relationships and the gradual development of the mentors' skills?
- *measurement* – i.e. how will we know how we are doing?

Clarifying the purpose

It is easy to assume that the purpose of a diversity-mentoring programme is obvious and therefore does not need stating. In practice, however, if mentor and mentee do not have a clear, shared vision of what they are trying to achieve, the relationship is restricted from the beginning. Expecting people to 'work it out as they go' is highly optimistic.

Some of the highly focused glass-ceiling programmes, such as that at Aer Rianta in Ireland, are very specific in their statements of purpose – in this case, to redress the imbalance of women to men in middle and senior management. Against such an objective, the mentor can work with the mentee to establish the level of her ambition, to help her develop a realistic perspective on her capability to manage a higher-level job, to help her create a development and career plan that will lead there, and to provide guidance and advice along the way. One of the reasons this programme worked was that it was very simple, both in terms of structure and objectives. Moreover, mentor and mentee could see clearly how the relationship contributed, or could contribute, directly to the intended outcomes.

Take another example, the UK government's New Deal programme, aimed at helping disadvantaged young people into work. Initially, the mentoring purpose was defined in the same terms as the programme as a whole – get them into a job. However, the mentor was only one of a number of supporting resources for the young person, over a relatively short period of six months, and arguably the person least able to help them into a specific job. A more realistic definition of the purpose of the mentoring therefore encompassed motivating and encouraging the young person to complete the training courses assigned, to extract the maximum learning from the working experiences they were exposed to and to develop the confidence (lacking in many of them to begin with) that they could contribute to society and earn their own way.

Four fundamental questions we have found useful in exploring the question of purpose with programme co-ordinators are the following:

1 What is going to change as a result of this programme?
2 Is this objective truly deliverable?
3 Is it what the target audience wants?
4 What is the intended timescale?

Being precise about the nature of the intended change often opens up debate. For example, a gender-based glass-ceiling programme defined its mentoring element in terms of helping women understand how to think and behave at a more senior level. Considering what would change brought about the realization that cloning the male executives would not necessarily be a positive change. Indeed, the company had a problem that there were insufficient role models at the top who exemplified some of the more people-oriented corporate values. In many cases, the women targeted for the programme were better exemplars of those values than the men who were to be their mentors. Redefining the purpose of the programme so that it focused on helping the advancement of the mentees without losing or compromising these values gave both parties in the dyad a very different focus, and one that was much more in line with the company's needs. (The Procter & Gamble case study – see Chapter 9 – has strong echoes of this.)

'Is the objective truly deliverable?' opens up a range of resourcing issues. A New England based financial service company recently decreed that its divisions should all ensure that everyone had a mentor – and particularly those in various minority groups (race, gender and disability). Unfortunately, the rapid growth in that organization and the high rate of labour turnover in the sector meant that 60 per cent of staff had been there less than two years. There were only just enough mentors to go round, by assigning every available experienced manager. However, many of these managers had neither the aptitude nor the interest to be effective in the role. The failed relationships infected those that were still struggling to find direction, threatening to discredit the whole diversity-mentoring process.

Grandiose objectives have a habit of proving unachievable. They may also be more difficult for people to relate directly to their personal needs and ambitions. The more straightforward and pragmatic the programme goals, the more likely they are to be achieved.

Checking what the audience itself wants is also very useful. An engineering subsidiary of an oil multinational decided to introduce a glass-ceiling programme some time ago. It assumed that this would receive a very positive response from women in the organization. Sensibly, it set up some listening sessions, where it could explore with a group of fifty women what their expectations of a programme would be. To the organizers' surprise, the women were almost unanimous in rejecting the idea of a specific glass-ceiling programme. They would much prefer to be encouraged to join a broader based programme that did not emphasize their minority status. A broader programme, they argued, would be taken much more seriously than one targeted just at one group of people. Moreover, they felt that a targeted programme would be regarded as remedial rather than developmental.

Similarly, a mentoring scheme designed to advance racial minorities within a government department initially attracted an array of mentors, but very few mentees. Again, people were reluctant to be categorized into a stereotypical group, even though the objective was to help them.

A trainer colleague, who worked some year's ago within the UK's Department of Health and Social Security (DHSS), recalls how diversity (Equal Opportunities) changed views on the advisability of publicly identifying target groups a decade ago. She explains: 'We did not call it diversity training; the concept was unknown. The concern at the time was the under representation of women in senior management. The solution was deemed to be management training for women and the introduction of equal opportunities sessions on all management courses.' She goes on:

> As part of the process of preparing the trainers, the DHSS introduced trainer training, which taught us to listen to one another as individuals, rather than as 'men' or 'women'. Many of us formed the view that separate training for women was not the answer. We felt it important not to highlight differences, which seemed to contribute to stereotyping, but rather to explore the similarities between men and women and the uniqueness of individuals irrespective of gender. We saw women-only courses as potentially divisive and decided that training should be provided on the basis of individual need, not on whether you were male or female.

Support for this broad view comes from recent developments in science. A number of studies suggest that stereotypes are so deeply ingrained in both the observer and the observed that they have a deep and lasting effect on behaviour (Gollwitzer and Bargh, 1996). The context, in which a mentoring relationship is formed, determines which stereotypes people will respond to. So defining a scheme as aimed at helping black people, for example, unconsciously stimulates black participants to behave according to stereotype when faced with a white mentor. Experiments by Claude Steele at Stanford University found that

> black college students score lower than white students on standardised tests of school achievement, aptitude and IQ, but only if they're told the tests are measuring intelligence, or if race is raised in some other way. Steele has found that he can completely erase the black-white differences on such tests by convincing students that the particular test they will take is not related to intelligence. Conversely, he can recreate the racial gap by an intervention as minor as having students indicate their race on a questionnaire. (Adler, 2000, pp. 38–41])

Similar experiments by Paul Davies of the University of Waterloo in Ontario have demonstrated that reminders of negative stereotypes before an interview causes intelligent, purposeful women to lower their achievement horizons dramatically.

Designating a mentoring programme for a specific group, then, may actually reduce the value they are able to extract from the relationship. This poses a dilemma for programme organizers – if funds are most readily available for programmes that address the needs of a definable, disadvantaged group, how do you make the case for a broader initiative?

Whose purpose?

It is important in this context to separate corporate objectives from those of the individuals taking part in the mentoring programme. The company may wish to use mentoring to improve retention of key talent. The employee may be more interested in building his or her competence and track record, with a view to moving on in due course. Such potentially conflicting goals can often be reconciled, but the time to consider such issues is in the planning stages of the programme, rather than once it is under way.

It is also important to separate objectives (desired outcomes) from behaviours and processes. One of the most influential analyses of the mentoring phenomenon was that by Kathy Kram (1985). In the years since, the eleven functions she identifies, grouped under the headings 'career development' and 'psychosocial', have been used in dozens of studies. In many of these studies, the functions have been used as a measure of output, rather than of mentor behaviour. The receipt of, for example, coaching or protection is regarded as proof of a successful relationship.

This assumption is, in my view, inaccurate and misleading, for a number of reasons:

1 Most of the functions are *enablers* not outcomes. Generally outcomes relate to a specific transition – an advancement of capability, confidence, etc. where the mentor is involved.
2 It fails to take account of the *expectation* of the mentee about the kind of relationship required. For example, while one mentee may value sponsorship, another may find it oppressive and interfering. The context in which mentoring occurs is important in defining which functions and outcomes are relevant.
3 It fails to address the interaction between mentor and mentee.
4 It is possible to receive all these kinds of help without any achievement by the mentee.

Kram's functions were based on a very specific model of mentoring, in which the mentor is relatively hands-on and his or her power and influence are crucial to the relationship. Career advancement therefore tends to be the dominant set of functions – as most of the studies using Kram's analysis confirm.

However, there is a very different model of mentoring, which typifies programmes in Europe and more recently in some US organizations. Here, the emphasis is on achieving self-reliance and on the *avoidance* of most of Kram's career development functions. Sponsoring, protection and furthering visibility of the mentee are exercises of power, which are seen as inappropriate in this context. Nor is the mentor normally in a position to provide challenging assignments – this being a responsibility of the line manager.

The failure to distinguish between these two models (and the range of alternatives in between) invalidates much – if not most – of the research

Table 3.1 Kram's eleven functions of a mentor – only some apply to developmental mentoring

Function	Mentoring as career oversight	Mentoring as personal empowerment
Career development:		
Coaching	X	X
Sponsorship	X	
Challenging assignments	X	
Protecting	X	
Fostering visibility	X	
Psychosocial support:		
Personal support		
Friendship	X	X
Acceptance	X	X
Counselling	X	X
Role-modelling	X	X
	X	X

derived from Kram's basic analysis. Kram herself, it appears, has never claimed that her functions were relevant for *all* models of mentoring.

Kram was also working from a relatively small pool of previously published literature on mentoring. We now have the advantage of much more extensive literature. As a result it is possible to obtain a much wider picture of mentor functions and to explore different kinds of groupings.

Such an analysis, combined with fieldwork has led to a set of four functions as shown in Table 3.1.

From an analysis of more than thirty sources referring to benefits of mentoring for individuals, very different categorisation emerges, as follows:

- development outcomes, which may include knowledge, technical competence and behavioural competence
- career outcomes, which may include the achievement (in part or whole) of career goals
- enabling outcomes, such as having a career plan, a (self)-development plan, a wider network of influencers or learning resources
- emotional outcomes – less tangible, but often powerful changes in emotional state, including increased confidence, altruistic satisfaction, reflective space, status and the pleasure of a different kind of intellectual challenge.

In general, these seem to be received by participants in mentoring programmes as an accurate and relevant way of focusing on measurable outcomes. As yet, very little research has been carried out using this categorization, measured outcomes, but the probability is high that this will in due course lead to a re-evaluation of some of the conclusions revealed in studies based on Kram's functions.

Another useful way of looking at outcomes is that proposed by Kirkpatrick:

- reaction – how the mentor and mentee perceive the relationship
- learning outcomes
- behaviour change
- results (e.g. effort and labour intensiveness or productivity).

This approach has the benefit that it measures programme outcomes as well as relationship outcomes.

The mentors' objectives should also be considered. Simply relying on mentors' perception that they are doing something useful for the company is not a firm foundation for success. Although there is some discussion in the literature about what mentors gain from the relationship, there is little concerning their perception of either their personal goals from it, or what they expect to achieve with the mentee. Among the exceptions are Ragins and Scandura (1994; 1999). First meetings between mentor and mentee are often awkward affairs, as the two people try to come to terms with why each of them is there.

Mentors in diversity-mentoring programmes may easily sign up to the corporate objectives and to those of the mentee. But acknowledging their own objectives requires either a high level of self-awareness, or some external stimulus to reflection. Based on interviews and group sessions with mentors, it appears that one useful (but often unexpected) outcome is the opportunity to learn how to see issues from alternative perspectives. Simple inquisitiveness is perhaps one driver here, but perhaps more important in many cases is being able to build better relationships with people, from the same diversity background as the mentee, who form part of the mentor's immediate working group. In addition, the mentor may have the objective of building new networks beyond the immediate working group, by accessing the mentee's networks.

Having a plethora of objectives for the programme can be a problem of itself, however. Will people be confused as to where the priorities lie? Quite probably, unless they are able to work within some form of hierarchy of purpose. A pragmatic approach is to treat the key objective of the company as an umbrella purpose and other objectives as enablers. This helps overcome the problem that key objectives are typically influenced by many other factors than mentoring. For example:

Our mentoring programme is aimed at retaining the talent within our business. Our aim is always to be at least three points below the employee turnover rate of our best competitor.

To achieve that goal, we expect the mentoring relationship to:

- provide a safe environment for employees to plan a fulfilling career within this business

- reinforce the value we place on talent from all backgrounds and cultures
- stretch and challenge mentors, so that they become better and better developers of their own teams
- ensure that talented people who do leave us to take up opportunities elsewhere, do so with sufficient goodwill to be pleased to return, should the right opportunity arise.

Note that the key purpose here is SMART (specific, measurable, etc.) while the others can be more aspirational and less readily measurable. In principal, of course, the more measurable the objectives are, the more useful they are in establishing the impact of the programme.

Thinking about the timescale raises questions of what is achievable over the lifetime of the relationship. Short timescales do not always mean lesser outcomes – indeed, the contrary can be true. An experiment with Shell in Brunei (Clutterbuck, 1995) involved a cross-cultural mentoring programme in which most of the mentors were English or Dutch expatriates and the mentees young local engineers and managers. The corporate objective was to speed the pace of indigenization – i.e. to develop local people more rapidly, so they could take over jobs currently filled by expatriates. Because the expatriates were generally only in the country for two to four years, some relationships had a relatively short time frame to operate in. This sense of urgency motivated mentor and mentee alike, to the extent that the quality and quantity or reported learning in the shorter-term relationships in all cases exceeded that of those where the time frames were more relaxed.

Clarity of purpose in the programme encourages clarity of purpose in the relationship. This assertion, based as yet primarily on observation rather than measurement, appears to be true across the broad spectrum of mentoring. Of course, the purpose has to be shared. An early mistake by one of the authors was to encourage participants in mentor/mentee training to identify the benefits for themselves, for the organization and for key third parties, such as line managers. But we did not establish firmly what were the priority outcomes the business was looking for – it was just generally assumed that mentoring was 'a good thing'. As a result, although mentors and mentees were clear about what they were supposed to do, subsequent review meetings showed that they were unclear about why.

The financial services division of a health-care multinational provides a somewhat different example. Here the group identified as a priority for mentoring help was made up of relatively senior staff, for whom the glass ceiling was not professional competence, but their lack of personal profile in the organization. They simply did not have enough presence to be noticed, or they had few networking skills, and were destined to be passed over again and again in favour of people with more obvious leadership behaviours. As one senior manager put it, they were 'too boring to go any further'. The purpose of the mentoring programme was to help them either change their behaviour and career management approach, or reconcile them to a role where they contributed to their vast experience, accepting that any ambitions for more senior management responsibility were unrealistic.

Mentor and mentee training was designed to allow people to decide at a later date whether they wanted to be a mentor or a mentee. Explaining the corporate purpose clearly helped many of those who had come with the expectation that their experience qualified them to be mentors, to recognize the value of becoming mentees instead. It helped that they also recognized that one of the best ways to become a good mentor is to be a good mentee.

In establishing clarity of purpose, it often helps to consult widely, both with senior managers and with other interested parties. If nothing else, this helps to establish a common foundation of expectations about the programme.

Who are the audiences?

In theory, the audiences for a mentoring programme are defined by the objectives. In practice, the selection of the audiences will often influence the objectives. So it is important to consider both issues in parallel.

The majority of diversity-mentoring programmes will have started with the recognition that there is a specific problem. It may be that retention is relatively low for a specific group of people, or that the proportion achieving promotion is below average or, as is frequently the case, there is a general concern at senior management levels that the company needs to be seen to be taking positive action to support a particular group.

However, the existence of an inequality of reward or influence is not of itself necessarily a reason for selecting a group for special attention. For example, it is usually deemed reasonable that younger people in an organization are on average paid less and have less senior positions than older people. The nature of the disadvantage needs to be articulated, along with the degree to which it applies across a specific group. For example, one organization stepped back from a planned programme to support black and Asian employees generally, when it was recognized that those with a university education were as well represented in job level and pay as their white peers. Two programmes resulted, neither of them focused solely on people of colour: one targeted people with poor literacy and numeracy, the other targeted young people of high potential. In both programmes, managers were asked to encourage their reports from minority backgrounds to take part.

An alternative approach here is to establish the source of disenfranchisement – be it low education, language issues, low self-confidence or problems with career-pathing – and to construct a mentoring programme specifically to deal with those issues. This has the advantage that it does not target people directly through their membership of a particular group.

A useful way of defining the audience is through the question: what transition do these people want/need to make? All effective mentoring involves some form of change of state in the mentee (and often in the mentor, too): for example, from low self-confidence to high, or from one job level to the next, from having only a vague career plan to having a very clear set of goals and steps towards them. People, for whom this transition is irrelevant or of only marginal interest, fall outside the programme's target audience.

Defining the mentee audience should lead automatically to defining the mentor group. This is not always what happens in practice – some of the most spectacular programme failures have occurred when the top management group decides it should become mentors, then looks for a deserving group, on which to dispense its goodwill! We will look at matching mentor and mentee later in this chapter, but some ground rules are of immediate relevance. First, the mentors must be sufficiently removed from the mentee's situation to offer a different and usually broader perspective, yet close enough to understand or at least empathize with the issues the mentee faces. Second, the mentor should come from a group that has some genuine interest, beyond the altruistic, in the success of the programme. Third, the mentor group should be made up of people, who are respected by the organization for their values and their achievements.

A difficult issue here is whether the mentor group should be from the same background as the mentees. Aside from the practical issues – the lack of role models of the same gender, race, or culture at higher levels in the organization – there are strong arguments, both rational and emotional, for and against a blanket expectation that mentor and mentee should be from the same group. These can be summarized under the following headings.

Perspective

Same-group mentors may have greater empathy with the issues the mentee faces. So, for example, Prudential UK's (the Pru's) programme to help mothers returning from maternity leave back into the organization used previous returnees, because they understood the emotional trauma and practical problems of this difficult transition. Interestingly, the Pru found that the more senior the returnees were, the more valuable mentoring was for them. An explanation for this is that those re-entering the organization, when colleagues have learned to cope without them, often have to rebuild networks and re-establish the value of their contribution. So their transition back into work is even more emotionally draining than at lower levels in the organization.

In so far as race is concerned, research (Thomas, 1990) suggests strongly that same-race mentoring relationships provide more psychosocial support than cross-race relationships.

However, same group mentors may have much greater difficulty in helping the mentee view their issues from a different or broader perspective. Empathy and insight can sometimes be in conflict. Sometimes it is important to examine barriers and opportunities through others' eyes. For example, managers in a multinational company had a view of potential high-flyers as people who made their ambitions clear, were prepared to question and challenge the way things were done, and were constantly taking initiative. To young Malay graduate employees, however, these behaviours were contrary to social norms – especially in a woman, they would appear presumptuous, if not offensive.

Those assigned mentors from the same culture generally had greater problems understanding and adapting to these different cultural expectations, than those who developed successful relationships with expatriate mentors. The expatriates became role models for the younger people and were less concerned, both about bringing up such topics for discussion and about losing face when the mentee exercised the art of challenge. Of course, not all the relationships with expatriate mentors worked; establishing rapport was much more difficult across the cultural barrier if one or both parties were reluctant to accept and work with a different perspective.

Networking

Much of the impact of mentoring comes from the interface between the mentor's networks and those of the mentee. Same-group mentors' networks can often be too similar to the mentee's to add much value. On the other hand, same-group networks may be more readily open to the mentee. Some mentees are clever enough to achieve the best of both worlds – a young man of Chinese origin, for example, explained proudly how he had developed mentoring relationships (and hence network contacts) both within the Chinese business community and within the North American company, for which he worked.

Power

If a group in an organization is relatively disempowered, it is likely to be under represented in senior positions of influence. So mentees choosing same-group mentors have to settle for people with less power in the organization. While this is of less significance in the European model of mentoring, with its emphasis on personal development as the relationship outcome, it is very significant in the traditional US approach, which relies heavily on sponsorship. Even in developmental mentoring, however, there may be disadvantages to having a mentor with low influence in the organization, because this person is likely to have less insight into the workings of the power systems.

Relationship purpose

The question 'who can best help the mentee achieve his or her goals?' is fundamental here. For example, a group of finance department employees in a UK company were found to have very divergent needs. Some, who were relatively young and inexperienced, needed a mentor from within the finance function, to help them develop their overall competence and visibility. Others, who were highly competent already, had a need to develop a broader understanding of the company and greater commercial awareness. Their mentors were found in other functions, such as sales and merchandising.

The same principle applies to other groups. If the goal is advancement and breaking the glass ceiling, it may be best to pair the mentee with a white male. If the goal is building self-esteem and self-efficacy, perhaps a homogeneous pairing would be optimal.

Role-modelling

It may be easier for the mentee to use the mentor as a role model in a same-group relationship. There is some evidence of this from studies of same and cross-gender mentoring (Ragins and McFarlin, 1990).

Table 3.2 summarizes these points.

Table 3.2 The arguments for and against same group mentoring

Issue	For	Against
Perspective	Greater empathy with mentee's issues and experiences Research suggests higher levels of psychosocial support in same-race mentoring than cross race More role-modelling occurs between same-gender pairs than cross-gender	More difficult to help mentee take different or broader perspective Research suggests career outcomes for mentees are less satisfactory than in cross-race mentoring
Networking	Same race/gender networks can be more close knit and sociable	Mentee's and mentor's networks may be too similar to add value to the relationship
Power (where same group mentors are not well represented in the higher levels of the hierarchy)	Easier to establish rapport when the authority/ hierarchy gap is relatively small	Mentors are likely to have less insight into politics and prospects
Relationship purpose	Favours relatively new developmental objectives	Favours relatively broad development objectives
Role modelling	Occurs more easily	May enlarge mentee's range of responses

Best practice seems to be to design programmes that have sufficient flexibility to meet a range of individual requirements. Where people have a choice and are well informed about the implications of the options, they are likely to opt for the solution that best meets their needs.

A case in point is the HR director of a quasi-governmental organization in the UK (Clutterbuck and Megginson, 1999). Several years ago, Tricia set her sights on achieving this top job. However, she was already the most senior woman in the organization. How could she learn to think and behave like a director, without the risk of losing some of the key feminine qualities that made her effective in her senior management role? Her solution was to seek a female mentor, who had extensive experience on boards and as a chief executive. This relationship ended shortly after Tricia achieved her goal. Once in post, however, she recognized that she needed a new kind of mentor – one with immense experience in the HR role – and that gender was no longer an issue. In the event, her new mentor was an older man who had held HR director roles in several organizations.

The key processes

The issues of selecting and matching fall from the definition of the target audience. The selection of mentors should depend on the specific needs of the mentees. The nature and experience of both mentors and mentees predicates the style and content of training required.

Selecting the mentees

Defining a mentee group is merely the starting point. Among key questions to consider thereafter are:

1 Do we want to provide mentors for everyone in this group, or just some? If everyone, what do we do about people who do not want to have a mentor?
2 What are their expectations from a mentor? Are those expectations realistic? If not, how will we manage their expectations?
3 Do we want them to have mentors all at the same time, or should the programme be staggered over a period?
4 How long do we expect these relationships to last? (Or, how long is the organization prepared to provide formal support for them?)
5 How will we persuade mentees to commit to the programme?

Most of these questions have resource implications, which we address later in this chapter. The answers to these questions will vary widely, according to scheme purpose and organizational circumstances. However, the last question demands particular attention here. If you adopt an approach that asks for volunteers, how sure can you be that people will come forward? We have already seen that closely targeted programmes can suffer from a dearth of volunteers, because people are unwilling to be labelled. On the other hand, if you coerce or oblige people to take part, they may be equally reluctant to participate.

Developing enthusiasm among the mentee group demands a planned campaign of iterative development – communicating to members of the target group the thinking of the steering committee and listening to their ideas about how the programme should be structured and presented, both to them and to the rest of the organization. This also provides an opportunity to understand and mould expectations.

Piloting the programme rather than going for a 'big bang' launch helps to identify any major barriers to success. If the pilot is low key, it allows for adjustments to the programme before cynicism can set in. Launch of the programme is often best achieved as a collaborative venture between the organization and representatives of the target group, who lend credibility to the process.

Among the many mentoring disasters observed by the authors over the years was the health-care company which invited volunteers, with some fanfare, to apply for the launch of its glass-ceiling mentoring scheme, aimed particularly at women and people of colour. The invited audience comprised all in junior management. Almost forty people applied. However, the company could only provide twenty mentors and was unwilling – given that this was their first experience of mentoring – to assign more than one mentee per mentor. The corporate HR department wrote back to those who were not selected to tell them they had been unsuccessful, and to recommend that they discuss alternative development routes with their local HR department.

What the company had not bargained for was the depth of disappointment – to the extent of feeling betrayed – among those rejected. Having built up their hopes of at last being able to compete on equal terms, they were not easily mollified and at least one quit immediately as a result. Worse still, perhaps, because those who were chosen did not know what the criteria were, some of them felt guilty about being given the opportunity and this became a barrier to openness in the relationship. The moral? Never promise, even by inference, what you cannot fulfil.

A factor often overlooked in the selection of mentees is how effective they are likely to be in the role. The literature on mentee behaviours is somewhat thin, but there is sufficient to suggest that certain types of people benefit more from mentoring than others. Engstrom (1997–8), for example, determines that proactive mentees get more out of their relationships than passive ones. This is borne out by one of the author's experience working in cultures with high power distance. (Power distance is a dimension of culture and refers to how comfortable they are with inequalities of power distribution. For further reading refer to Hofstede [1980].) Those mentees, who saw career advancement in terms of finding a sponsor and waiting for promotion to occur as a reward for loyalty, were far less demanding of their mentors and learned relatively little, compared with peers who were far more proactive (inner-directed people tend to be self-confident and to believe that they are to a large extent in control of their environment and future; outer-directed people tend to view the outside world as beyond their control). In general, it seems from observation that more reactive people are simply less well equipped to use mentoring to best advantage. It may well be, however, that in a high power-distance culture, where both mentor and mentee are from the same group, that the expectation of behaviour on both sides would favour a mentee who was not highly proactive. (The mentors in the example above were from European cultures or were Westernized locals.) We are not aware of any research into this phenomenon.

Another observed and related differentiating factor is educational experi- ence. Education systems that encourage students to develop the skills of enquiry and questioning appear to produce more people suited to mentoring than those that emphasize learning by rote and deference to academic authority. This is a particular issue for multinationals operating in strongly Muslim countries. Their inability to absorb and/or promote graduates of Koranic universities, on the rational grounds that they do not have the appropriate behaviours or thinking skills, can be a source of local resentment and may ignore other, unmeasured but valuable, skills.

Should we, then, focus mentoring only on those who exhibit strong positive traits? One argument against is that these are the people who are most likely to succeed on their own, and most likely to find a mentor informally. Another is that people who lack confidence in their own ability are a valuable resource whose talent the organization needs to release. Moreover, people who demonstrate an outer-directed world view may simply be reflecting the reality of their experience so far, and may think and behave very differently if they are exposed to new and contrary experiences.

A pragmatic answer is that it depends. People who by personality are highly outer directed and unwilling to challenge may benefit first from some form of counselling, to enable them to make the most of mentoring later. A mentor role-modelling radically different behaviours is unlikely to induce change, and may actually force the mentee more firmly back into learned defensive behaviours. On the other hand, people whose behaviour is primarily cultural in origin may benefit from insights into cultural alternatives.

Again, a critical factor here is programme purpose. If the programme is aimed solely at retaining and supporting high-flyers, the audience is by definition going to be largely composed of people who are self-motivated, inner directed and comfortable with both being challenged and giving challenge. If the goal is about large-scale indigenization, then a much wider spectrum of personalities and world views will be encompassed.

In the latter case, considerable attention will be needed to a number of factors:

1 The organization's expectations of the relationship: it may be appropriate to settle for less stretching initial outcomes, in relatively short time frames, in order to build up the mentees' self-confidence and demonstrate the value of the relationship
2 The participants' expectations of the relationships: in training workshops with mainly expatriate mentors and local mentees, sharing expectations of mentor behaviours and functions has proven a revelation to both parties. On one occasion, when the mentor group was exposed to a graph showing what mentees expected of them, there was almost two minutes silence as they absorbed the data (see Figure 3.1). While the mentors expected the mentees to take charge of the relationship and its agenda, to be self-resourceful and to use them as a sounding board, the mentees expected to have a sponsor, who would tell them what to do, create promotion opportunities for them and decide what they needed to learn next. The first mentor to break the silence said: 'Suddenly, I understand why I can't get my direct reports to learn, either.'

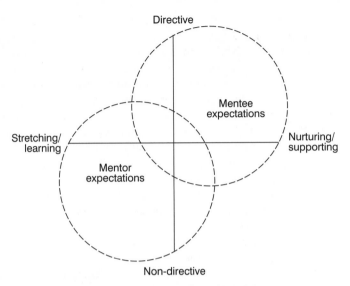

Figure 3.1 Mentor versus mentee expectations in South East Asia

3 The need to compromise on expectations: in the case above, mentors and mentees were encouraged to work out a comprise set of functions and behaviours that both they and the company could sign up to. A lesson from this experience was that neither the traditional US model of mentoring, nor the European developmental model was fully appropriate in this context. Programme designers therefore need to consider carefully what the appropriate emphasis needs to be on directive–non-directive behaviours and on stretching–nurturing behaviours.

These same principles appear to apply equally well to other areas of diversity. Young ex-offenders, for example, typically suffer from low self-esteem and an inability to envision a realistic future for themselves. At least to begin with, they are unlikely to be in the driving seat in the relationship. However, many of them can learn, with the mentor's help, to take on greater responsibility for their own development and for managing the relationship – especially if this is part of the initial expectations established between them.

If the organization decides that everyone in a group should be offered the chance to have a mentor and is able to resource that offer, there are still some practical steps that must be undertaken before they can be matched with a mentor. Training is one of these, which we will deal with shortly. However, it is also important to ensure that mentees are committed to the programme and have thought through what they want out of it. An example of good practice is to hold short lunchtime or breakfast briefings, at which the importance of clarity of relationship purpose is emphasized. Then intended mentees complete a registration from that explores their expectations in more detail. This information can be particularly useful in establishing appropriate matches.

Selecting the mentors

If selecting mentees is a potential minefield, so too is selecting mentors. Although the 'right' mentor will be different for every mentee, in practice, the programme co-ordinator will need to establish broad groupings to identify a sufficiency of volunteers.

Several ground rules apply here, from practitioner experience. The experience/status gap has to be one in which both parties can feel comfortable. One of the most common mistakes of early formal mentoring programmes in general was to select the most senior people in an organization to mentor the most junior. The status gap meant that the junior partner in the dyad tended to be deferential and very reserved about what they said, so the mentor ended up doing most of the talking. When the mentees did bring up issues important to them, mentors often either dismissed it as whinging or, worse still, intervened from on high, causing resentment by the mentee's line manager. Another problem was that the issues faced by the mentee and those faced by the mentor were so far removed that there was little point of contact between them.

In cultures with relatively high or even moderate power distance, this issue needs to be handled particularly carefully. The mentee's status may be highly influenced by that of their mentee (so there will be an instinct to go for the most senior person they can). In the presence of a much more senior person, however, the mentee's range of learning styles will be much truncated – effectively limited to sitting and listening.

At the other extreme, too small an experience/status gap can be just as dysfunctional (see Figure 3.2)

The rapport versus learning dimension is a related issue, illustrated in Figure 3.3. If the mentees have relatively low self-confidence and are relatively immature in their exposure to uncomfortable learning situations, they may

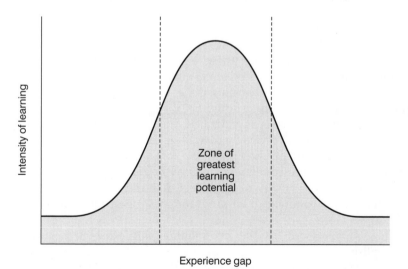

Figure 3.2 The experience gap versus learning intensity

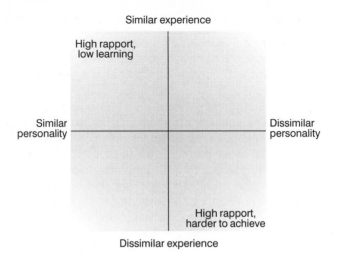

Figure 3.3 Rapport versus learning

need a relationship that places emphasis on rapport. So similarity of background and experience is important in making the match. Typically, the mentor may be two to five years ahead of the mentee in experience.

If, at the other extreme, the individual has high learning maturity and self-confidence, a more stretching match – one where building rapport will demand effort by both parties and will be part of the intended learning – may be more appropriate. One match that comes to mind is the chief executive officer (CEO) of a town council in the UK and an Indian pharmacist. Although they have very little in common, the relationship works because they both value the learning they acquire – about Asian cultures on the CEO's part and about management processes for the pharmacist. Interviews with programme co-ordinators indicate that they often take the stretching–nurturing spectrum into account instinctively when making specific matches. However, it is less common for them to consider these issues in the overall design of the programme, although it would be logical for them to do so.

Clearly, the rapport versus learning dimension this has implications for the discussion of whether mentors should be of the same group or from another group. Where the emphasis is primarily on rapport-building, same-group matches are likely to work best; where the emphasis is on learning, particularly taking the mentee out of their comfort zone and challenging their basic assumptions, a cross-group relationship may be more appropriate.

Mentors are no more likely to be perfect than mentees, but there are some basic requirements common to all programmes. The mentors must be:

- volunteers, interested in the programme and what it is intended to accomplish
- still interested and active in their own learning – and expecting to extract useful learning from the relationship

- effective one-on-one communicators – able to express ideas, help the mentee articulate half-formed thoughts and listen actively (as a rule of thumb, effective mentors spend less than 20 per cent of time in mentoring sessions talking).

In a business context, mentors need at least some ability in five key pairs of competencies, as follows:

- self-awareness (understanding self) and behavioural awareness (understanding others) – concepts from emotional intelligence
- business or professional shrewdness and a good sense of proportion
- communication ability and conceptual modelling (having a portfolio of models they can draw upon to help the mentee understand the issues they face, and being able to help structure issues into mental models)
- commitment to their own learning and a strong interest in developing others
- relationship management skills (in particular rapport building) and the ability to set and pursue clear goals.

This is not necessarily an exhaustive list, but represents the perceptions of large numbers of mentors and mentees as expressed in programme review interviews. While diversity awareness does not often arise naturally in these interviews, there are, we believe, strong grounds for its inclusion. Even in a relatively homogenous environment, people work better together when they are aware of and respect differences in perspective, background and personality. Effective mentors demonstrate acceptance by legitimizing the mentee's experience.

Defining the minimum skills requirements of mentors is an early and often difficult task for the programme co-ordinator – difficult because there is often insufficient data to go on. While it is clearly unreasonable to expect all mentors to be good at all these competencies, it is equally unreasonable to accept as a mentor someone who is poor at many of them. Training often acts as a filter to identify those mentors, who you will avoid using. (However, some companies deliberately work with some inadequate mentors with a view gradually to building up their overall competence as developers of others. Our view is that it would be better to provide them with some coaching in people development first, before letting them loose on mentees!) It is also important that the mentor has reached a sufficient level of personal commitment to the mentoring process. This is not necessarily a matter of age – we have observed very effective mentoring behaviours by teenagers – but of personal confidence and accumulation of experience.

Within the context of diversity mentoring, a willingness to accept and value alternative cultures and perspectives is likely to be core requirement. It may be necessary to address the issues of diversity separately, ahead of the mentoring programme, in order to establish sufficient understanding, although it is also common simply to make this an element of mentor training. Another core competence may be the ability to translate experiences from one background to another. For example, in trying to explain to a West African the notion of balanced scorecard, as it applied to relationships with small suppliers, a European mentor drew comparisons with the extended family responsibilities of the mentee's homeland. Even if the mentor does not have sufficient knowledge of the other culture to make such comparisons, he or she can help the mentee find suitable analogies, by identifying the underlying issues and assumptions.

Another way of looking at mentor selection is to define the characteristics you do *not* want to see in the diversity mentor and screen for the most important of these. There is a small but useful literature on toxic mentors, but most of the criteria are common sense. One that may not be immediately obvious, but which is important to recognize, is what I call Diana Syndrome, after Princess Diana. People with this behaviour set spend a great deal of effort getting involved with other people's problems in order to avoid confronting their own. As a result, their behaviour may range from patronizing to transference (seeing the mentee's issues only in terms of their own). Within the context of a diversity programme, this kind of behaviour can be especially damaging. Another form of toxic mentor is the executive who has his or her own agenda, manipulating the mentee for political purposes.

However you define the selection criteria, you will need some kind of registration form, which includes biographical data and some information on the mentor competencies you feel are essential – at the very least, the mentor's self-assessment on these. (Simply filling in the form helps to focus their attention on the behaviours required when it comes to putting them into practice.) A useful additional source of information is to ask mentors to write a few paragraphs about their own learning journey.

Matching

We have already covered some of the issues on matching in the discussion on mentor selection, but again, there seem to be some basic ground rules for good practice. In particular:

1 The more the mentee can feel ownership of the choice of mentor, the more committed he or she is likely to be to the relationship. This sounds obvious, but it is not always easy to put into practice. People who have just joined an organization at a junior level, for example, may not have the contextual knowledge to make their own selection. At the very least, mentees should be consulted about the characteristics of the mentor they feel would best be able to help them.
2 Free choice may be just as bad as no choice. Left to their own devices, mentees may choose as mentors people who they know and like (but who are too close to them for any real learning to take place) or senior high-flyers, in the hope that they will be able to hang on to the mentor's coat-tails. Neither choice is likely to achieve the potential of an effective mentoring

relationship. A pragmatic compromise is for the programme co-ordinator to guide the mentee's selection, perhaps by providing a short list of three suitable candidates. Some organizations, especially where the numbers of mentoring pairs are relatively few, encourage the mentees to meet with and discuss their needs with each of the potential mentors. A side-benefit of this is that it promotes cross-departmental networking. In large-scale programmes, all these meetings may create chaos, so mentees select from the descriptions given in the mentor database. (Software for matching mentor and mentee is available, for example, through the European Mentoring Centre.)

3 People make more adventurous choices when there is a 'get-out clause'. Sometimes called the no-fault divorce, many mentoring programmes now plan for the first few meetings to be on a probationary basis. Once mentor and mentee have got to know each other, they are expected to review the relationship objectively together. Key questions include:

(a) Is the relationship meeting each of our expectations?
(b) Would a different mentor be better able to meet the mentee's needs?
(c) Is mentoring the most appropriate approach for the mentee's needs?
   If it seems appropriate to transfer the mentee to another mentor, the initial mentor may help in thinking through who might be suitable.

Training

One of the big problems with informal mentoring – and with many formal programmes launched with inadequate preparation – is that neither mentors nor mentees are quite sure why they are there, nor how they should behave to get the best out of the relationship. Well-designed training aims to achieve main three objectives:

● to establish clarity of purpose and role
● to develop confidence in mentor and mentee that can fulfil their respective roles
● to provide an introduction to mentoring skills.

In addition, developmental mentoring often has a fourth objective – enabling the mentor to extract substantial learning from the relationship as well as the mentee. An additional benefit is that it equips the participants for future relationships, whether formal or informal.

As with almost any kind of training in a business or community context, mentoring training has to cope with a range of starting points and abilities among the participants. It is not just that some people will have more experience in one-to-one developmental situations than others. Participants may also vary considerably in their innate skills of, say, empathizing, listening and communicating, in their commitment to developing others and in the level of confidence they feel about how they could make a difference to someone else. In diversity mentoring, people will also vary considerably in their exposure to other cultures and their ability to respect/understand those cultures. Simply having worked overseas in developing countries, or having worked in a group where women were in the majority, is no guarantee that the individual will have gained any real understanding of alternative perspectives.

Initial training, then, can only achieve a certain amount, especially if it is limited to a short period of time. While two days (or more) initial training for mentors is widely recommended in practitioner literature as a minimum, in practice it is rare, especially in a business environment, for anything like so much time to be made available. In some exceptional cases, such as a trading floor, mentoring training sessions have had to be broken down into short 75-minute modules, spread over several days, to fit in with the demands of the job. Training should therefore not be seen as just a one-off-event, even if the initial training is the most significant educational input mentors and mentees will receive.

Practitioners seem largely agreed that no one should be allowed to become a mentor in a formal programme unless they have completed at least a minimal training course. In diversity mentoring this is probably an even more stringent requirement – the potential for a well-intentioned but uninformed mentor to do more harm than good is high. In particular, they may be prone to assessing issues solely in their own context, or to spending far too much time giving advice rather than helping the mentee explore their own alternative solutions.

Good practice also suggests that it is important to train mentees as well as mentors. Mentees who understand the nature of the mentoring relationship and their responsibilities within it are far more likely to establish and sustain effective relationships. A useful ground rule is that, left to their own devices (i.e. without training) mentors will initiate successful relationships – ones where at least one partner records significant learning from the relationship – up to 33 per cent of the time. If mentors are well trained and supported, this proportion rises to about 60 per cent. If both mentor and mentee are trained, the proportion rises to 90 per cent or more. (One programme facilitated by one of the authors recorded a 98 per cent success rate.) If the mentee is sufficiently senior or experienced, it often makes sense to train both together, on the grounds that understanding each other's perspective helps cement the relationship. In addition, the mentee may well be able to use mentoring behaviours informally within their own day-to-day work.

Training content will vary according to the programme objectives and the audience's starting point. However, in every case mentors and mentees will need to know what their responsibilities are, how to manage the relationship, what skills they will need to use and develop, and – most practical of all – how to get started. The shorter the time allocated to training, the less opportunity for skills practice – hence the need for additional support mechanisms, of which more later.

In the diversity context, it is important to enhance participants' under- standing of and respect for the other person's perspectives. One simple tool for doing so is to encourage both mentors and mentees to define what success means for them, and what they think it means for the other partner. At a more detailed level, participants will also benefit from focused diversity training that addresses the nature of group disempowerment, how stereotyping occurs and basic differences between how different cultures or genders may approach the same issues. To fit all this within a short mentor training session may not be practical – many diversity-mentoring programmes separate the two themes into sequential seminars.

The leadership issues

Any initiative that aims to change people's behaviours requires a champion, or a group of champions. Within an organization, the active endorsement and encouragement of top management – particularly where they emphasize the importance of the mentoring programme to achieving business goals – can have a major impact on success. In a few organizations, the CEO or another top team member has attended every training session, for both mentors and mentees, to talk about how their own mentoring relationships have and still do benefit them.

The most powerful message the champion of a diversity programme can give is publicly to accept the role of mentee. If the champion is from the same group as the programme is aimed at, he or she is effectively saying, 'Yes, I have much to learn still, too'. If the champion is from a different, dominant group, then selecting a mentor from the target group (either at peer level or upward) reinforces the message of mutuality of learning and the value they attach to understanding the diversity issues and bringing about positive change.

Perhaps the most difficult issue around leadership, for the programme co-ordinator, is how to sustain the level of visible commitment. At the very least, it is important to discuss with the champions what they will do to sponsor the programme once it has been up and running for a year or more. Ensuring that there are clear measures of programme success, linked to business goals, provides a platform for top management to reiterate their support for mentoring.

The resource issues

Although mentoring is often seen as a low-cost alternative to conventional training, done properly, it requires a substantial resource, both at the start of a programme and to maintain it. In particular, the organization needs to resource:

- the time of senior people to plan and promote the concept
- sources of further information
- the time and energy of a programme co-ordinator – planning, managing and troubleshooting

- provision of training (for the co-ordinator, for mentors, mentees and often for some third parties)
- time of participants – for initial training, review sessions and carrying out the mentoring process.

The role of the programme co-ordinator is critical to the success of the diversity-mentoring programme.

Just how much work is entailed on the part of the co-ordinator depends on the size and scope of the programme, how hands-on the organization wishes to be and the level of continuing support required. ABB in Sweden has a whole department, largely devoted to mentoring programme management; other companies make do with one or two days a week from a part-time employee. Figure 3.4 is an extrapolation from a wide range of programmes, indicating the likely investment of person-days in managing a mentoring programme. Diversity mentoring may require more resource, because it will normally be linked into a number of other initiatives, such as women's networks, which create a need for liaison and alignment.

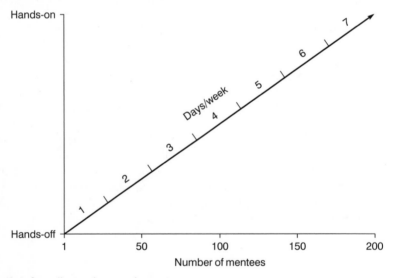

Figure 3.4 Co-ordinator time requirement

At the very minimum, the role of the co-ordinator is likely to include:

- recruiting mentors and mentees
- managing the matching process
- recruiting and overseeing trainers and specialist advisers
- sustaining the interest of mentors, mentees and top management champions

- troubleshooting and reassigning, where relationships fail to gel
- managing the processes of review and measurement/evaluation.

The role therefore requires someone who is resilient and resourceful. Among the other basic requirements are:

- a good general knowledge of mentoring and diversity issues – and a strong interest in them
- good organizational skills – able to cope with peaks of workload and to ensure that the programme mechanics work
- good innate skills of empathizing, influencing and communicating.

Finding suitable training for co-ordinators is not easy in most parts of the world, although it is available, for example, through the European Mentoring Centre. An option used by many co-ordinators is to find their own coach or mentor, in the form of someone who has been through the learning curve already. While this may not always lead to the passing on of best practice, it has the advantage of providing personal support in what can be a very lonely role.

Continuing support

One of the most frequent problems with both diversity-mentoring programmes and mentoring programmes in general is that they run out of steam. It is depressingly common to see organizations, which assume they can 'do' mentoring in one big campaign, after which it will be self-sustaining. In practice, it takes a continuing and well-planned effort to maintain the cycle of interest, action and outcomes over the medium to longer term.

Given that, for many mentors (and mentees) this is a new style of learning and a new area of learning, it is unreasonable to expect people to have the confidence and competence to be really effective after a short period of initial training. It helps, if mentors also have an opportunity to use the skills and approaches they have learned in other environments – for example, in coaching peers and direct reports. But enthusiasm is likely to wane quite rapidly, if mentors encounter barriers they cannot overcome.

One of the most powerful support mechanisms is therefore the opportunity for mentors (and sometimes mentees) to meet as a group to share their successes and concerns. Typical of the kind of issues that surface at such gatherings are:

- How do I deal with a mentee who always says, yes, he'll do what we've discussed but never actually does so?
- How can I encourage my mentee to challenge me more?
- How can I get my mentee to understand the impact of her own behaviour?
- How can I improve my skills at asking the right question?

Organizational realities will define how often these peer review sessions occur, but the minimum recommended, from the authors' experience, is twice a year. It helps if a trainer with good knowledge of mentoring best practice facilitates the sessions. If it is possible to feed into the discussion some general feedback from the mentees, about where they think the mentors are proving most and least effective, this helps target issues which will have most effect on the quality of the relationships.

Procter & Gamble's discussion notes are a useful means of stimulating dialogue between mentor and mentee, in such a way that both extract useful learning. Some observers might perceive this as being a formal intrusion into an informal relationship. However, some relationships, and particularly cross-group relationships where it is difficult to develop a great depth of rapport, may well find this a valuable prop until the dyad is able to identify its own discussion themes more readily.

Another concept, less well explored, is that of 'senior mentor' – a highly experienced mentor, who acts as coach to less experienced mentors. While not everyone is comfortable with the term, the concept is usually regarded favourably. In most organizations, however, finding people with sufficient mentoring experience and behavioural skills to take on the role is difficult. In general, this is an approach that probably fits best within organizations, which have a long history of effective mentoring.

Linking mentor development to some form of vocational or academic accreditation has only become possible recently. Draft standards for mentor competencies were published in the UK in early 2000. If mentors can be convinced that their efforts will help them achieve a diploma or certificate, to which they attach value, this is likely to influence their motivation positively.

Experience of formally linking mentoring programmes to HR systems such as appraisal or performance management is surprisingly limited. However, many companies do suggest to mentees that they share their appraisals and any other relevant developmental data with their mentor. The danger here is that the relationship is dragged into too much detail and that the mentor starts to duplicate the line manager's role.

Experience of linking mentoring programmes with succession planning is variable. One organization recently abandoned a programme because it found that only 20 per cent of the targeted individuals actually achieved promotion. In part, this was a result of poor selection of participants. A downside of this kind of initiative is that it raises expectations among participants, which may not be fulfilled.

A few organizations have also publicly recognized mentors by inviting them to become members of an elite group of people developers, with whom top management meet once or twice a year to discuss development issues and strategies. Becoming involved in senior-level strategic thinking seems to be a strong motivational factor, particularly for career-ambitious managers.

Again, what works and does not work may vary from culture to culture. Individual recognition (e.g. 'Mentor of the Month') may work in a North

American environment (though not in Canada) and to some extent in South America. In Europe and Asia-Pacific, however, it is likely to have a distinct demotivational effect, because the mentors selected will feel acutely embarrassed. Indeed, there is evidence that potential mentors will decline to take part. (One European mentor compared this individual limelight to telling other people how much money you give to charity.)

An organization, which used an article in its in-house magazine to fete a number of managers, who had each collected a number of mentees, found it backfired badly. One reason was that other mentors did not perceive the chosen peers as good role models – quantity was no substitute for quality. If an organization does elect to use individual reward, it had best be very sure that the measurement criteria it uses are well understood and accepted by mentors and mentees alike.

An additional form of support needs mention here. One of the skills of an effective mentor is to recognize where the boundaries of the relationship lie. When the mentee's issues extend into areas where counselling or professional advice is required – for example, if they have a finance problem, a mental health problem or an addiction problem – it is the mentor's responsibility to help them access this external resource, rather than try to sort the problem out themselves. (Even if they have the counselling skills, the mentor is likely to create a confusion of roles in crossing the boundary.) It is therefore important that the company provides some form of referral service, such as an Employee Assistance Programme, and ensures the mentors know how to access it.

Measurement

Defining what should be measured and when is frequently done too late and with insufficient thought. First, it is important to decide what purposes the results of measurement are intended to serve. Is it to enable rapid trouble-shooting and amendments to the pairings? Is it to facilitate quality control from tranche to tranche of participants? Or is it to demonstrate to top management that the investment is having an effect on specific business problems, such as retention? Or is it all of these?

Each measurement purpose requires a different set of timings and different types of question. A useful form of categorization is shown in Figure 3.5.

The degree, to which measurement will emphasize process rather than outcomes, or vice versa, is one of the first decisions that must be made and will depend on the pressure from above to measure. It does not help – as is so often the case – if top management fails to think through what evidence it actually needs. The fact that X proportion of the target group has been assigned a mentor may be an indicative measure of the process, but it gives no clues as to outcomes. Dragooned mentors and mentees may simply be going through the motions, without identifying or dealing with the mentee's developmental issues. More relevant questions to identify outcomes include, for example:

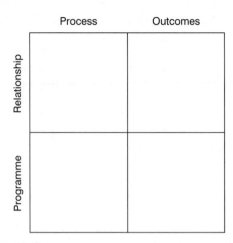

Figure 3.5 Measuring mentoring

- How much learning is taking place, by mentors as well as mentees?
- Are the dyads meeting as frequently as intended?
- Are people with mentors less likely to be looking for another job than those who do not have one?

Measuring the wrong things can be more destructive than not measuring at all

The best times to measure will vary as well. However, key points to measure are the following:

1 Before the programme begins, to establish a benchmark – for example, how do people feel about their potential to progress in the organization? What are the current retention levels for target groups?
2 During and immediately after training, to ensure that they have understood their role and are confident they can tackle it.
3 After two meetings, when mentor and mentee should assess whether the relationship is 'right' for them. This information may or may not be shared with the co-ordinator, but it seems to be good practice at least to check informally that this discussion has taken place. Dyads, who avoid discussing compatibility, are often those that run into most difficulties later, because they cannot develop sufficient depth of trust.
4 After four to six months, when the relationship should have begun to motor and some early outcomes will be apparent. At this point, there should be useful data to adapt some facets of programme management. It also becomes practical to introduce further development opportunities for mentors, to focus on particular, common skills needs.

5 After twelve months, when there should be sufficient outcomes to assess the business value of the programme, in terms of both soft and hard outcomes.

A useful approach to measuring the effectiveness of training, and seems to apply well to mentoring, comes from Kirkpatrick (1979), who suggests four basic evaluation steps:

1 Reaction – how the audience liked the training event in general.
2 Learning – what each participant specifically took away from the sessions, using standardized tests for skills wherever appropriate.
3 Behaviour – how each participant has changed in what they do/how they do it.
4 Results – organizational impact of the programme.

This seems to mesh quite well with our own measurement model.

A problem for the diversity-mentoring co-ordinator is to manage all this measurement without intruding on the relationships. There has been so little study of this area of mentoring management that it is difficult to provide grounded advice. However, experienced co-ordinators tend to agree that the key is to ensure that mentor and mentee perceive the information-gathering process as there to help them improve the effectiveness of their relationship.

What goes wrong? Perils and pitfalls

We have already referred to most of the common pitfalls, but it does no harm to reiterate them. Most diversity-mentoring programmes that fail, do so for one or more of the following twelve reasons:

1 They do not achieve a common understanding of what is fundamental to the concept of mentoring and what can be left to be defined by local culture and local needs.
2 They do not have a clearly defined purpose, linked to both individual and organizational goals.
3 They do not consult the participants sufficiently, nor design the programme with participants.
4 They do not have sufficient championship at the top and middle of the organization.
5 They fail to measure, or measure the wrong things.
6 They give insufficient thought to selection of mentors and mentees.
7 They fail to train mentors and mentees sufficiently to fulfil the role well.
8 They err on the side of too much or too little formality.
9 They (over)emphasize group differences and stereotypes to the extent that they may reinforce them.
10 They expect the programme to be carried out on a shoestring; resources are inadequate to the task.

11 They do not plan how to support the programme and the mentors/mentees over the medium and long term.
12 They try to do too much, too soon.

In short, if *any* of these elements describes your programme, you are limiting its potential to achieve great outcomes for both the participants and the organization. There is, of course, no substitute for preparation, preparation and yet more preparation.

References

Adler, R. (2000). Pigeon-holed. *New Scientist*, 30 September, 38–41

Clutterbuck, D. (1995). Mentoring in a multicultural environment. Proceedings of Second European Mentoring Centre Conference, Sheffield Business School, 10 November.

Clutterbuck, D. and Megginson, D. (1999). *Mentoring Executives and Directors*. Butterworth-Heinemann.

Engstrom, M. (1997/98). Personality factors' influence on success in the mentor–protégé relationship. MSc thesis, Norwegian School of Hotel Management.

Gollwitzer, P. M. and Bargh, J. A. (1996). *The Psychology of Action: Linking Cognition and Motivation to Behaviour*. Guildford Press.

Hofstede, G. (1980). *Culture's Consequences*. Sage.

Kirkpatrick, D. L. (1979). Techniques for evaluating training programs. *Training and Development Journal*, June, 78–92.

Kram, K. E. (1985). *Mentoring at Work: Developmental Relationships in Organizational Life*. Scott, Foresman and Co.

Ragins, B. and McFarlin, D. (1990). Perceptions of mentor roles in cross-gender mentoring relationships. *Journal of Vocational Behavior*, **37**.

Ragins, B. R. and Scandura, T. A. (1994). Gender differences in expected outcomes of mentoring relationships. *Academy of Management Journal*, **37**, 957–971.

Ragins, B. R. and Scandura, T. A. (1999). Burden or blessing? Expected costs and benefits of being a mentor. *Journal of Organizational Behavior*, **20**, 493–509

Thomas, D. A. (1990).The impact of race on manager's experience of developmental relationships (mentoring and sponsorship): an intra-organizational study. *Journal of Organizational Behaviour*, **11**, 470–92.

4

Building and sustaining the diversity–mentoring relationship

David Clutterbuck

Whether the mentoring dyad comes together informally or is arranged by others, the same general principles apply in making the relationship work. Both parties have to commit, to share and to develop understanding. Both parties share responsibility for managing the relationship and ensuring that it succeeds.

Before we examine what is involved in managing the relationship, however, we need to establish what we mean by success. Although this was discussed briefly in the previous chapter, with regard to the programme objectives, success in terms of the relationship is a much more diverse and individual entity. In a previous attempt, by one of the authors, to create a widely acceptable measure, relationship success was defined as when:

- both parties experience significant learning as a result of their dialogue *and*
- both parties feel that the quality of the relationship was high, particularly in terms of supportiveness (by the mentor) and thoughtfulness (in all meanings of the term, by the mentee).

The emphasis on both elements of the definition is deliberate. If the two people get on well together but do not extract much in the way of learning, then all that has been established is a friendship. If, on the other hand, there is learning but low quality of interpersonal behaviours, then the relationship is more akin to that of tutor. To be a genuine mentoring relationship demands both quality of relationship and depth of learning.

It is also appropriate to re-emphasize what we mean by diversity. As several of our case studies (for example, SAS in Chapter 9) indicate, diversity is about much more than race or gender. It encompasses everything that makes people feel they are part of a group and everything that makes one person perceive someone else as different – size, shape, accent, personality and a myriad other factors.

It would not be surprising if some observers disagreed with this definition. It is, however, the best we have so far!

Because both parties have an interest and responsibility to manage the diversity-mentoring relationship effectively, it helps to have a mutual understanding of what is required. Fortunately, some of the earliest work on mentoring, by Kathy Kram (1983), identified four basic phases of mentoring relationships. Although these phases were based primarily on informally established relationships, they have been modified over the years (Clutterbuck, 1985) to allow for a wider variety of relationship types. Thus every relationship that works is expected to work through the four phases of:

- rapport-building – getting to know each other, deciding if the relationship will work
- direction-setting – creating a sense of purpose for meeting, often something that begins to happen during the rapport-building stage and is subsequently refined
- progress-making – working together to achieve the relationship goals
- winding down – recognizing that the formal relationship needs to come to an end at some point; the mentor helps the mentee 'fly' on their own.

This chapter examines the diversity-mentoring relationship in its evolution through these phases. It explores both good practice and some of the behaviours that can undermine the effectiveness of the relationship.

The four phases have no set lengths. However, the first two are typically quite short in organized mentoring programmes and may run into each other (establishing rapport usually involves some discussion of relationship objectives).

Rapport-building

Both parties in a diversity mentoring relationship need to approach it with a willingness to learn from each other and to develop a *professional friendship*. By professional friendship, we mean a mutual respect and acceptance, built around mutual commitment to a set of goals. We find professional friendships everywhere in business life – everywhere, indeed, where small teams develop an energy and joy in working together. Professional friendship does not mean that mentor and mentee become part of each other's social circle (though there is usually little or no harm should they do so). By retaining a degree of personal detachment from the mentee's issues, the mentor is able to adopt a different perspective and is often better able to help the mentee see issues in alternative ways than someone who is very close to them.

The mentor and mentee need to develop a high degree of rapport for several reasons. First, it is very difficult without rapport for the mentee to open up about their deeper concerns. Second, the mentor may from time to time need to play the role of *critical friend* – the person who tells the mentee difficult and discomforting home truths. Without rapport, the mentee may be highly resentful of such negative insights. Third, if mentor and mentee do not both enjoy their meetings, they are less likely to be committed to making them happen.

So what is rapport? Again, a working definition used by one of the authors is: 'the state of being relaxed with and responsive to another person'. In interviews and discussions with individuals and groups of mentors and mentees, a handful of common factors have emerged, which appear to be important to creating and maintaining rapport in mentoring. These are consistent with the descriptions of rapport by Carl Rogers (1994), but provide in addition a practical context for analysing why rapport does and does not occur. They are:

1 *Trust* has two main aspects. Do you perceive the other person as reliable (i.e. will they do what they promise?) And, will they keep confidences? Trust is about knowing where you stand with someone else, being able to believe what they say and being able to speak your own mind without fear that your comments will be repeated outside the relationship. In diversity mentoring, trust between people of different race or gender can be affected negatively by either party's stereotypes and/or by specific past experiences.
2 *Focus* refers to how each party perceives the other's level of interest and involvement. Is the mentee's attention fully with the mentee, and vice versa, or are they thinking about the next meeting? Another aspect of focus concerns its intent. Does the mentor give the impression of listening without evaluating, or is he or she constantly assessing, judging or pigeon-holing the mentee against some pre-existing criteria (which may or may not be shared with the mentee). It is not easy, for example, to establish rapport with an examiner. In diversity mentoring, it is important for the mentor, in particular, to be aware of how culture can affect the appearance of whether someone is attending. For example, in some cultures people show they are listening by locking eyes; in others, people will look away, to show they are thinking about what has been said.
3 *Empathy* concerns the degree, to which each person demonstrates will-ingness to understand and respect the other's feelings, viewpoints and drives. It does not necessarily mean that the mentor has to feel what the mentee feels – their background of experience may simply be too different to do that other than by analogy. For example, it is very difficult for someone, who has never suffered a close bereavement, to understand fully the feelings

of someone going through such an experience. Similarly, the mentor from a privileged background may have few reference points for the experience of being discriminated against. In diversity mentoring, the development of empathy requires a high willingness by both parties to accept the other person for who/what they are.

4 *Congruence* refers to compatibility of objectives. It is hard to achieve positive outcomes from negotiations, for example, if one or both parties are not prepared to seek win-win outcomes. Whereas empathy concerns who the person *is*, congruence encompasses what the mentee wants to *become*. In essence, rapport demands a consensus between the diversity mentoring pair about what they are trying to achieve and why. Of course, there may be several subsidiary objectives – indeed, as we have seen earlier, these may be essential in maintaining the mentor's interest – but these must be accepted as legitimate by both parties, even if they involve some element of conflict. Another aspect of congruence is the willingness of the mentor to make opening moves, which expose him or her to some risk. So, for example, the mentor may talk about some of his or her own mistakes in order to draw out the mentee. This process of confidence-building can only occur where there is a mutual acceptance of the purpose of the dialogue.

5 *Empowerment.* Here the issue revolves around whether each of the parties feels that the relationship is confining and stifling, or liberating and opening up options. If the mentor feels put upon, or that the mentee is demanding too much of them (e.g. constantly calling on their time) then they will be reluctant to engage fully. Equally, if the mentee feels the mentor is trying to exert too much influence over his or her thinking and career choices, he or she is also likely to feel uncomfortable. In diversity mentoring, the mentor needs to be especially sensitive to these issues, establishing early on clear ground rules about how hands-on the relationship should be and checking from time to time that the balance is right for the mentee.

Stereotyping and rapport

A common and powerful barrier to developing rapport is stereotyping, already discussed to some extent in Chapter 2. To stand a chance of creating rapport in a mentoring relationship where there is a high level of cultural diversity, for example, both parties must accept that:

- they do have stereotypes
- even benevolent stereotypes can limit potential to achieve (e.g. the myth that women are better at 'soft' management tasks)
- recognizing and being open about stereotypes is the most effective way of dealing with them.

We have already seen the pervasive power of stereotypes, even in the target person, to reduce aspiration levels and performance. But how can mentors in particular develop the necessary sensitivity to their stereotypes? One approach –

useful both within diversity training and in dialogue with the mentee – is to develop a series of statements that compare perspectives. Against each statement is recorded the mentor's view, the mentee's view and – if available – any 'reality tests', i.e. any measured and valid data. Mentor and mentee indicate on a ten-point scale, the degree, to which they feel this statement is accurate. Hence, the statement 'Women are better at people management; men at taking the tough decisions' might be seen as broadly true by both a male mentor and a female mentee, but to different degrees. (In fact, there is little evidence to suggest that this apparent distinction is anything but a convenient myth, reinforced by the roles, into which women managers become typecast.)

These lists of statements can be generated by the mentoring pair itself, or suggested as topics of discussion by the programme co-ordinator.

When a potential stereotype is identified, mentor and mentee can work together to try to understand it, as a precursor to managing it. A useful approach is to test the stereotype by re-expressing it. For example, 'Hispanics are more likely to put family considerations ahead of work commitments' has at least some validity, but the statement has strong negative undertones. (Even more negative would be 'Hispanics show less commitment to the job than other groups of employees'.) Re-stating the issue as 'Hispanics tend to place more emphasis than other groups on maintaining a balance between family and work commitments' is both more accurate and more useful.

Another approach is recognizing the cultural bias of the organization, and the fact that the values of the organization reflect the values of the power holders – in this case that work comes before all else. Individuals who do not conform to that ideal are viewed as deficient – but the 'ideal' is never questioned! Companies are beginning to question these organizational values in discussions of the creation of family-friendly workplaces.

Equally important is considering whether the stereotype – even if generally true – applies to *this* individual, or to what degree it applies. This may not be obvious, or easy to assess. A highly intelligent minority employee, for example, may unconsciously perceive himself as less intelligent than his white colleagues, as a result of internalized beliefs or stereotypes, and this may influence his ability to put forward ideas or rely upon his own judgement. The mentor can help the mentee establish the strength of stereotype influences by encouraging him to review a variety of situations and to develop the skills of *intrinsic observation* – listening to and analysing interactions as they occur. The more the mentee can accurately identify stereotypes at work in themselves and in other people, the more useful their dialogue with the mentor will be.

Managing stereotypes, therefore, requires both parties to:

● respect and try to understand the differences
● identify the positive factors behind a different behaviour or viewpoint
● recognize the underlying common values, which the different behaviours address (most cultural differences are the result of variations in strategy for dealing with a common problem, rather than arising from a different set of basic values) (Hampden-Turner and Trompenaars, 2000).

Recent writers on diversity, such as Kandola and Fullerton (1998), emphasize the problems associated with focusing on differences, rather than on similarities. The individual, who is encouraged to see his or her career and achievement issues primarily in terms of their group disadvantage, is likely to take a narrower or even distorted perspective on opportunities and on their own development needs. People differ from each other genetically by less than 0.1 per cent; we are genetically more than 97 per cent the same as rats. At the level of underlying values, very few national cultures have significant differences from others – and those differences there are tend to be on a spectrum. For example, all cultures accept that it is important to balance the needs of the individual against the needs of society as a whole, but Asian cultures and African cultures are more likely to weight the scales towards the societal end of the spectrum, while Anglo-Saxon cultures weight it more strongly towards the individual. Nonetheless, the human potential to exaggerate differences is remarkable – witness the myriad of schisms in organized religion!

It is also important to recognize that values are dynamic, changing within each individual and each society all the time. It is doubtful whether any reader of this book has the same set of values today that they did ten years ago.

Mentors faced with a wide gap in experience or culture compared with their mentee have to find areas of similarity before they can progress the relationship. Very often, this is more difficult across social contexts than those of race or gender. Take the example of a middle-class, well-educated mentor and a young mentee from a deprived background – a combination commonly occurring in schools mentoring or programmes, such as that by FAS in Eire, to bring difficult to employ young people into the workforce. A simple list of what they both like doing in their spare time may not provide many obvious common experiences. For example, 'spending time with my kids' or 'hiking across the Alps' as pastimes for the mentor may produce no resonance in the mentee, if he or she has no children and has never left the home town. But the fact that one plays football and the other plays squash and tennis provides a basis for getting beneath the behaviour to the common values. What they can share is the feeling of elation when they are winning at their sport, the disappointments they feel when they lose by a narrow margin, the poor eyesight of all referees, and so on. Finding points of common reference is fundamental to building rapport.

Rapport-building is likely to be much more difficult if the programme structure allows or encourages communication between the mentor and the mentee's line manager or supervisor. Equally, any form of assessment of the mentee by the mentor is likely to make the mentee more circumspect in what he or she says (or, worse, encourage them to play to the gallery). This is an issue of great debate. If the mentee feels that the mentor will not maintain absolute confidentiality with respect to what is said in the mentoring sessions he or she is likely to be much more restrained in what he or she says. The triangular relationship typically works best, in practice, when:

- the mentee takes responsibility for keeping both manager and mentor informed
- the mentor is careful not to tread on the line manager's toes by 'second guessing' the line manager
- the line manager actively suggests issues the mentee could discuss with the mentor.

In this way, none of the three parties feels threatened by the relationship.

In a handful of cases, it will be obvious to one or both parties that there is a mismatch, either on personality grounds, or because the mentor's experience is not sufficiently relevant to the mentee's needs or for some other equal valid reason. In our view, mentor and mentee share the responsibility for reviewing the relationship from time to time, with the first and most important review occurring after the initial two or three meetings. The 'no-fault divorce' clause – an increasingly common element in programme design – encourages a pragmatic check for compatibility. Should one or both parties decide the relationship is not going to work, then the mentor has the responsibility to offer the mentee help in thinking through what kind of mentor they do need at this time. (When this is done well, it sometimes happens that the mentee returns to the original mentor some time later, when circumstances and learning requirements change.)

Clarifying purpose and rapport

In the earlier chapter on establishing and sustaining formal programmes, we discussed the importance of clarity of purpose. Observation in the field leads strongly to the view that clarity of purpose within the relationship has a

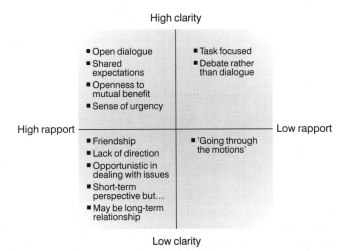

Figure 4.1 Clarity versus rapport – some observed dynamics

significant impact on whether the mentee (let alone the mentor) receives any real benefits from the association. One way of looking at the issues is represented in Figure 4.1.

Relationships with low clarity of purpose and low rapport are not likely to last long, even if the two people are under some pressure from the organization to try to make it work. High clarity/high rapport relationships have a much better chance of succeeding, but they may require more initial effort on behalf of both mentor and mentee.

Setting direction

In the previous chapter we touched on the importance of a clear sense of purpose in any mentoring relationship. It is particularly important in diversity mentoring, because the focus of the relationship can so easily be diverted into issues over which neither mentor nor mentee has significant influence. It is not uncommon, particularly where mentor and mentee are from the same disadvantaged group, for the discussion to centre on the unfairness of the system and how to change it from without, rather than on how to work within it and change it from within.

The greatest value from the relationship appears to occur when the mentor helps the mentee identify clear long-term career and personal development objectives and short-term steps that will take the mentee towards those goals. The more measurable those goals are and the more easily they can be converted into a flexible route map, the easier it is to focus the mentoring discussions and to assess progress. Specific issues of diversity may well arise as barriers along the way, but dealing with these should be seen as part of the process, not the goal of the relationship. 'What do you want to become?' is a much more important question than 'How do you want to be treated?', although one may encompass the other.

In general terms, diversity issues will only become part of the mentoring dialogue when:

- the mentee perceives they are being treated unfairly, by virtue of stereotyping on the part of a third party
- either mentor or mentee feel the mentee's inner stereotypes are limiting their capability
- either party perceives that negative (or overpositive) stereotypes are occurring within the relationship.

We will deal with each of these three situations in turn in the next section, on progress-making. Before we do so, however, there are some other issues that need to be dealt with in the direction-setting phase. In particular, this is the time to ensure that both mentor and mentee are working to the same set of expectations about behaviours, as well as outcomes.

Time allocation and frequency of meeting are also important issues to clarify. As basic ground rules, if mentor and mentee meet less than once a quarter, they do not have a relationship – they are just professional acquaintances. If they meet more than once a month, there is a serious danger that the mentor will end up doing the line manager's job. A practical approach, to ensure that meetings do not slip, is to have a rolling series, three meetings ahead in the diary. It is good practice to allow an extra half-hour on the intended session length, to permit the dyad to explore major issues that arise towards the end of the allotted time.

Testing the realism of the mentee's aspirations. One of the most difficult situations to manage is when the mentee comes with goals that seem to the mentor to be hopelessly unrealistic. Is it the mentor's role to help them focus on more achievable goals, or to go along with it (hopefully doing more than just humouring them)? On the one hand, it is important for the mentor's motivation to work on a project that has meaning and is achievable; on the other, there are all too many cases of people, who have achieved the impossible because they did not know it could not be done.

Experienced mentors try to achieve the best of both worlds by:

- accepting the mentee's goal at face value, but helping them to explore why they want to achieve it and what they are prepared to sacrifice to that end. They are quite open about saying 'That's an enormous challenge you've set yourself', but they also say 'My job is to help you think through how you can make it happen'
- building the mentee's understanding of what capabilities and experience will be needed to achieve the goal
- helping the mentee be realistic about where they are starting from
- helping them fill in the steps in between
- focusing attention on the short-term, instrumental steps and leaving the bigger aspirations as a background framework to inform future choices and decisions
- helping them build their self-confidence and self-esteem, to tackle the goal more vigorously.

The latter is perhaps the most difficult element. Any logic tree that attempts to trace the route to the top is likely to get hopelessly complicated somewhere in the middle (for a very forceful description of this phenomenon – which originates in scientific reductionism – see Stewart and Cohen [1997]), if the goal is really challenging – and it is this realization on the part of the mentee that often brings a healthy dose of realism to the discussion. Whether the mentee decides to set a lesser long-term goal or to continue with the more challenging ambition, creating the logic tree – with or without some big question marks in the middle – reinforces the need to open out options at each career step. At every point of choice in developing track record or taking on new responsibilities the mentee needs to consider: 'How will this help me achieve my long-term goal?'

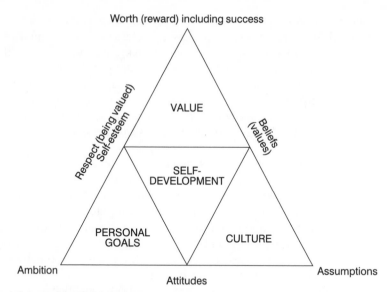

Figure 4.2 Intrinsic self-development

Exploring choices

People's values do not arise or exist in a vacuum. They are a consequence of personal experience, group culture, personality and many other factors. They do, however, exert a great influence on the choices we make, particularly the goals we set ourselves. Figure 4.2 attempts to place some of these influences in context.

If the core of mentoring is to enable and empower the mentee to manage their own self-development more effectively, it helps if they and the mentor have at least some understanding of the influences on their future choices. Let us take each of the elements in turn.

Self-development

Self-development is about taking personal responsibility for one's own growth and career. If the mentee is unable to make this mental commitment, then the mentor either has to adopt a sponsoring role, or help them build commitment, or give up. Hence a discussion of the mentee's willingness and desire to be the proactive partner in the relationship is a critical first step in setting direction.

Value

Values drive our notion of success – indeed, a useful working definition of success is 'achieving what you value'. What each individual values may change radically with time and circumstances. When offered four streams of things they might value (money, status, job satisfaction and work/life balance) most middle career individuals can trace an evolution in the relative importance to them of these factors, over the years. What motivates the mentor (i.e. what he or she values) may not be the same as for the mentee, especially if there is a significant generation gap.

What is more, we use the word 'value' to mean different things. In the psychological contract between employer and employee, there is (at least in theory) a social exchange on at least three levels of meaning. Where 'value' means worth (as in 'adding value') the employee is expected to contribute to the viability of the organization. In return, the organization provides tangible rewards, such as pay and bonuses, and intangible, such as training, development and other opportunities to gain experience, which enhance the employee's worth on the employment market.

Where 'value' means beliefs (as in 'we have a set of values') there is often an assumption by the organization that these are or should be shared by the employees. Leaving aside the vexing question of whether these beliefs are stated, as in a formal vision and values, or demonstrated – the two are often very different – people tend to gravitate towards and stay with organizations where the values are similar to their own. Shared values are seen as an important factor in achieving organizational cohesion around business goals. The mass exodus of people after a takeover or merger is often a consequence of a perception that the dominant organization does not reflect the values that originally attracted people to that workplace. When mentor and mentee explore their common beliefs, they are able to gain a greater understanding of each other and of how each relates to the organization at an emotional level.

Where 'value' means respect (as in 'I really value your contributions'), there is an assumed exchange between the organization giving praise and recognition to the individual, raising their self-esteem, and the individual gaining a sense of pride in belonging to the organization. Again, this is an emotional issue and one which mentor and mentee can usefully explore in seeking wider understanding of each other.

Culture

Culture and climate are notoriously difficult to define – and to measure – but the combination of beliefs, attitudes and assumptions is a close approximation to a working description. Useful areas for mentors and mentees to explore include assumptions about how the organization works, what senior managers do, how they view the employees and what really counts when people are being assessed for promotion or allocation to areas of learning opportunity.

Personal goals

Personal goals emerge from a similar mixture of influences. The higher the mentee's self-esteem and confidence, the more ambitious they are likely to be and, to a considerable degree, vice versa. A moderating factor is their attitude towards themselves, towards others and to the payoffs from investment in self-development.

Figure 4.2 is not intended to be a catch-all explanation of the psychology of self-development. It is simply a convenient means of capturing some of the critical, mainly intrinsic influences on how the individual approaches self-development. As such, it provides something between a checklist and a process model, which the mentor can use to delve into issues of learning motivation in a linked-up manner.

Progress-making

Once the relationship becomes established, mentor and mentee can start to focus on mutual learning and on how to achieve the relationship goals. It will still be important to reaffirm the rapport, both when they meet again informally and, if appropriate and possible, between planned meetings. Brief encounters in other work situations, or occasional e-mails, can be useful reinforcements for rapport.

The range of issues mentor and mentee may discuss is very wide, ranging from immediate and practical (where the mentor must be careful not to intrude on the line manager's role and responsibilities) to the long term and personal. This aspect of mentoring has been covered widely in the literature and in some of our own books (Clutterbuck, 1985; Clutterbuck and Megginson, 1999; Megginson and Clutterbuck, 1995), so we do not intend to explore it in detail here. However, there are some additional issues that may arise within diversity mentoring.

Earlier in this chapter, we referred to how the mentor (and mentee) should deal specifically with diversity issues when they arise. Each of the three main routes for initiating a discussion around a diversity issue has its own context. Taking them in turn:

When the mentee perceives they are being unfairly discriminated against

Discrimination at work occurs in many, often very subtle ways. The most common overt forms are probably:
  (a) pay
  (b) recruitment and promotion
  (c) sexual harassment.
More covert discrimination occurs in:
  (a) performance appraisals
  (b) access to projects/experience with high learning potential
  (c) level of supervision and/or control
  (d) meetings (where ideas suggested by people from one group are ignored, but adopted later when suggested by someone 'more credible')
  (e) the receipt of praise and/or encouragement
  (f) inclusion in the informal groups and discussions that make or influence decisions

(g) differential access to resources, perks and power

(h) salary differences

(i) reactions by subordinates to leadership style (female managers who are mentees – with male subordinates)

(j) credibility and performance attributions

(k) feedback (women and people of colour often do not get the feedback they need when they are performing poorly).

For discrimination, intended or not, to occur there are at least two preconditions. One is that there must be an impact on the individual. 'My idea was attributed to someone else' is an impact, as is 'I felt discouraged from offering any further ideas'. 'I wasn't asked for my opinion' is not necessarily an impact, unless there is a specific negative condition, such as 'so the decision didn't take into account the issues I wanted to raise' – or 'so I felt excluded'. (The issue may not have warranted consultation, for example.)

The other precondition is that there must be an element of unfairness or inequality present. So a manager who took everyone's ideas for his own without due credit would not be discriminating – just very dysfunctional. A third possible precondition is that there must be prima facie evidence of an underlying negative stereotype about a particular group of persons. So if the manager appears to show favouritism to one black woman and disfavour to another, this is also not discrimination, unless it can be shown that some other stereotype is at work. (He may simply dislike people who appear to speak before their mind is 'in gear', or who have a particular personality type that clashes with his own.) Of course, it could be argued that all such clashes are the result, in part at least, of unconscious or conscious stereotypes – e.g. 'Never trust anyone whose eyes are too close together' – but the aim of diversity management is not to make everyone like each other and become great buddies. People will always associate most easily with those with whom they feel most comfortable and in greatest rapport.

A relevant issue here is the question of the rights of the group versus those of the individual. Any collection of people, who obtain benefit from associating, have a right to do so. Groups can be made up of dentists, people from the same religion, people who have an interest in debating, alumni of the same university or a group of relatively immature young men, who happen to work together. Just as a trade union or co-operative society (or a company, for that matter) is entitled to seek legitimate advantage for its members, so a group within a company has the right to network and mutually promote each other's interests. However, the individual also has rights, which include equal access to opportunity. Hence a mentoring programme that encourages sponsoring behaviours by mentors can be viewed as legitimate in the group context, but illegitimate in that it disadvantages people who are not in the group. The issues regarding affirmative action programmes are due in part to this conflict. Only if a specific group is seen as 'deserving' by others is there likely to be widespread acceptance of the group legitimacy.

If a group abuses its power and influence, or is seen as too dominant, then some form of corrective action may be needed and the structure and emphasis of the mentoring can provide part of that correcting mechanism – for example, by pairing the most disempowered mentees with the most influential mentors. But who defines 'abuse', or 'too dominant'? Intelligent people tend to dominate the executive floors of most large organizations; should we therefore encourage equal access for people of lesser intelligence, perhaps setting quotas for them? Of course, the idea is ridiculous (we hope!) but it illustrates the complex minefield the mentor has to negotiate in helping the mentee deal with issues of diversity or equal opportunity.

A sensitive issue here is that of complicity – to what extent and how might a mentee himself reinforce a stereotype, consciously or unconsciously? For example, failure to speak up when someone has something useful to say may originate in a feeling of being intimidated, but in may be interpreted by others as having a lack of ideas. Pushed too far, exploring complicity may simply make the mentee feel more culpable and inadequate, so a balance has to be struck between raising their level of behavioural self-awareness and bolstering their self-confidence. This is not always as easy as it sounds. A helpful guideline for the mentor is to let the mentee decide how deeply to probe the manner in which the latter's own behaviours and attitudes help sustain a stereotype.

Where there evidently is discrimination, mentor and mentee need to consider the options. Taking the issue up formally within the complaints structure of the organization is certainly an option, but one with multiple downsides. By its very name, any form of grievance procedure will create ill feeling and resentment. Moreover, it exposes the accused as much and sometimes more than the accuser. (Who wants to take a 'troublemaker' into their team?) In general, it is usually more productive, at least initially, to reserve the formal structures for complaints about structural discrimination (for example, an appraisal process that is biased against recent immigrants, or a child-care policy that discriminates against single fathers).

For most other instances of real or perceived discrimination, there is considerable value in helping mentees determine how to deal with the issue on their own, or with other members of their group. For example, a mentee working in a North European insurance company complained to the mentor that a very senior manager was making her and her colleagues work extremely long hours, to the extent that it was causing those who had small children serious domestic problems. While the men in the department were generally happy with the overtime pay, the women did not feel this was an adequate or appropriate compensation. The reward system and the working arrangements, said the mentee, had been designed around male lifestyles and responsibilities, with no thought to the needs of working mothers. She was afraid to take up the issue with the manager directly, for fear of being ridiculed and cast as a poor team player.

With the mentor's help, she identified a number of possible strategies for tackling the manager. In the end, she chose to arrange a meeting with him, at which a number of the women affected by the policy voiced their concerns. She also rehearsed with the mentor the case for a change, and some alternative ways the manager could achieve his objectives without harming their family lives. The group approach was too substantial for the manager to ignore. Some changes were agreed and the manager (who the mentee had expected to be defensive) asked the group to look in addition at a variety of other policies, to check that they, too, were not discriminatory. The mentor was less surprised at the manager's reaction. 'Very few people set out to discriminate or put other people down,' he explained. 'Most discrimination problems are the result of poor contextual awareness, not deliberate policy.' Note the mentor did not use the word 'ignorance', which has come in recent years to incorporate a sense of wilful not knowing.

When the mentee's inner stereotypes appear to limit their capability

The mentee's own stereotypes can be dysfunctional in two main ways. First, they may depress their levels of personal aspiration and performance. Second, they may cause the mentee to present himself or herself in a manner which other people will interpret negatively. To say that this requires greater self-awareness is true, but not particularly helpful. What does help is frequent analysis, with the mentor, of specific situations and interactions with other people. Some key questions include:

- How do you think your beliefs about (supervisors, single mothers, ex-offenders, librarians) might make it difficult to get on with such people?
- To what extent is your expectation of this group based on direct experience? Hearsay? Received wisdom? Some unknown origin?
- Supposing your son/sister/best friend married a Muslim? Would you feel the need to change your perceptions?
- If you did not have this stereotype, would it make it more or less difficult to do your job?
- Do you think these assumptions about a particular group apply to all its members: e.g. are all psychiatrists mad? Do all husbands dream of cheating on their wives? Or vice versa?
- What assumptions were you making about the other person's motivations and attitudes?
- What assumptions do you think he was making about you?
- Where do you think either of you could be making a false assumption?
- What might you have been doing to reinforce his false assumptions?
- What could each of you have done to suggest a different attitude and/or beliefs about each other?
- What is your motivation for trying to change the dynamics of such interactions in the future?
- What benefits would there be for the other person?
- How could you initiate a constructive dialogue to develop greater understanding on both sides?

Such questions, of course, can have equal value for the mentor in examining his or her own stereotypes!

When either party perceives that negative (or overpositive) stereotypes are occurring within the relationship

It takes relationship of very strong rapport for the mentee to challenge the mentor on real or apparent stereotyping, yet the willingness to give and receive such constructive challenge can be the most valuable (and valued) aspect of the relationship. Implicit assumptions, for example, that a younger mentee would want to follow the same broad career path as an older mentor, may be challenged from both sides.

A very confident mentor or mentee can recognize and seize opportunities for challenge as they occur. Others may need to create the specific environment to do so, by setting aside some specific time to discuss stereotyping as an issue. Making it an agenda item gives it legitimacy, allows both parties to prepare their thoughts and reduces the potential for resentment. Some useful questions, which work both ways, include:

- What would you like me to do more of? Less of?
- What do you particularly value about our discussions? What do you feel is least valuable?
- What makes you feel more confident? What, if anything, undermines your confidence?
- On what issues do you feel we have strongest agreement? Weakest agreement?

If the mentor and mentee cannot discuss these issues openly, they are likely to fester and reduce the impact of the relationship. Here is one of the occasions where the programme co-ordinator can play a valuable counselling role. In a few cases (we have never met one yet) it may be appropriate to dissolve the mentoring relationship.

Winding down

Given the special problems of creating dependency in cross-gender mentoring relationships (and possibly in cross-ethnic relationships, although there is less evidence for this), it is very important to manage the winding-down process. In many cases, this will be a matter of shifting gear from a formal to an informal relationship; in others, it will involve the mentor gradually fading from the picture, allowing the mentee to 'fly free'.

Where there is a clear time limit placed on the formal programme by the organization, it is relatively straightforward to plan in a gradual winding down. Many dyads find it helpful to celebrate the conclusion of the formal relationship with a dinner, and some companies do this as a group activity, bringing all mentors and mentees together. While the latter makes it more of a celebration, the one-on-one approach allows for more reflection on how (and whether) to manage the informal relationship.

Where there is no clear time limit, it may not be obvious when it is time to wind down. A useful checklist from *The Mentoring Diagnostic Kit* (Clutterbuck, Lickfold and Martin, 1998) is that it may be time to move on when:

- we have largely achieved all the goals we set for our relationship
- we cannot think of any significant new topics of objectives we need to cover at the present time
- we sometimes struggle during meetings to find new issues to talk about
- the mentee can now tackle most situations confidently, without needing the mentor's help
- the mentee has reached self-sufficiency, and could cope more than adequately if we ceased to meet
- we are in danger of getting dependent on each other for advice/guidance/ support
- the mentor quite often uses the mentee as a sounding board for his or her own issues/problems/opportunities
- the mentee can often predict what the mentor will say next.

Occasionally, a relationship will already have gone beyond rapport into dependency. Some signs of this may be a combination of:

- the absence of genuine dialogue and deep reflection
- strong feelings of loyalty
- an unwillingness on the part of the mentee to make decisions without consulting their mentor
- the main benefit to the mentor is the emotional high of being needed
- 'life' issues become more important topics of discussion than career or work issues
- mentor or mentee (or both) find it difficult to accept not being in the relationship
- neither party brings up the issue of when and how to move on
- the mentee shows few or no signs of establishing a broader network of developmental relationships.

Should the programme co-ordinator intervene in such circumstances? We cannot offer a blanket answer – each situation will be different, and very hard to assess from outside. However, it is in everyone's interests to encourage the mentee to become both more self-resourceful and better networked, so the most effective interventions may be to introduce the mentee (perhaps through their line manager) to other sources of mentoring help. The more the relationship is built around the power of the original mentor, however, the more difficult this may be.

The outcome of winding down will depend on a variety of factors – not least how positively mentor and mentee feel about each other and whether the winding-down process was managed or simply left to happen. Kram (1983) perceives the winding-down process as one that either evolves into a peer relationship or terminates completely. More common in my experience is that it becomes a different kind of relationship – less frequent, much less formal and with much less clarity of purpose (a combination of friendship and occasional sounding board).

The critical importance of dialogue

It is one of the truisms of our time that there is too much discussion and debate and too little dialogue. Switch on the television and it is very likely that you will find people engaged in dialogue. When an issue is discussed, whether between two people or with a large studio audience, the art of stagecraft demands that two protagonists with different views slug it out. When people agree, or try to understand each other's viewpoint, rather than to score debating points, it makes for much less interesting viewing. At school, too, there are debating societies, but not dialogue societies.

The difference between discussion, debate and dialogue is an important factor in organizations' inability to absorb diversity of thinking and perspective. Debate assumes at least two opposing views and an intent on both sides to win the argument; the expectation is that neither side will change its views significantly. Discussion implies a greater willingness to listen, but within the context of achieving one's goals through winning the other side over. Dialogue, on the other hand, assumes a sincere desire to understand and a willingness to modify opinions and perceptions as a result of the exchange.

For diversity mentoring, the mastery of dialogue by both mentor and mentee is essential. Wherever and whenever there are indications of a difference in perspective or a reaction by the mentee that seems out of proportion, there is an opportunity to increase understanding and to strengthen the relationship. There are many ways to embark upon reflective dialogue, but one of the most useful approaches in tackling diversity issues is 'Help me understand . . .'. This simple phrase contains a number of important signals:

- I suspect there is a difference here, which I cannot empathize with at the moment.
- I want to be able to empathize, but first I have to understand how it appears to you/how you think about the issue.
- If I can understand the difference in perspective, I can be more effective in helping you deal with the issue.
- I have something to learn here, too.

These are powerful messages and the ensuing dialogue will frequently open up as many mental doors for the mentor as for the mentee. Deborah Flick, an experienced teacher of dialogue for diversity, emphasizes the importance of being able to

> listen deeply to and seek to understand:
>
>> How they interpret events, people and their own circumstances
>> What is important to them, of value, and what is not
>> What they assume to be true or not about a given situation
>> The meaning they ascribe to circumstances. (Flick, 1998, pp.68–9).

This kind of active listening and mental framework is valuable for all mentors, but is essential in mentoring relationships, where the two people come from very different backgrounds. It requires patience and the internal discipline to suspend judgement as you attempt to view perhaps familiar situations through someone else's eyes and feel them through someone else's emotions. Difficult as it may seem, mentors, who have acquired these skills, often report that they are able to apply them beneficially in a range of circumstances outside the mentoring relationship.

Some practical tools and approaches

Helping mentees empower themselves

Although the word 'empowerment' has been much abused and discredited, the underlying concept of liberating people to achieve their potential is still very valid. Mentors can help mentees understand the environment in which they develop and manage career plans, in a variety of ways, but one we find particularly useful is the grid in Figure 4.3.

Separating out factors that help and hinder career progress in this way permits a detailed analysis and allows mentor and mentee to work together on designing creative ways of tackling each area. It also helps to overlay this dialogue with an understanding of the four key freedoms that are granted or denied in each of the four unshaded areas of the matrix. These freedoms are:

- the freedom to control your working environment (how, when and where you work)

EXTERNAL What you are permitted	Influence of external (other people's) perceptions and stereotypes	Restrictions imposed by context/authority
INTERNAL What you permit yourself	Influence of own perceptions and stereotypes	Restrictions imposed by personal capability

Figure 4.3 Personal empowerment

- the freedom to pursue opportunities (promotions, appointment to project teams, training programmes)
- the freedom to access resources (information, networks, financial support and the tools to do the job)
- the freedom to contribute where it matters and to be recognized for having contributed (having ideas acknowledged, equal pay, being noticed for what you have achieved).

The mentor can work with questions such as: how much freedom do you want in each of these areas, given that with freedom also comes responsibility? Where is your freedom constrained more than you feel it should be? Are you more constrained in those freedoms than colleagues and, if so, is that justifiable? How different are your desires for empowerment compared to those of other people here?

The benefit of such an analytical approach is that it takes much of the anger out of the mentee's perceptions of disenfranchisement or unfair treatment, by focusing instead on the nature of the interaction of the individual and his or her environment.

Circles of empowerment/disempowerment

Because people may be members of a variety of groups that give them influence and/or power, thinking of someone in just one context is not adequate to understand the issues, with which they have to cope. Obvious examples of multiple combinations might be being female, black and educationally disadvantaged. However, a person with membership of all of these low-power groups may also be a member of the predominant function within the organization (e.g. sales in a sales-driven company, finance in a highly controlled company), or member of a project group making significant change happen. A black American in a middle management position in an African subsidiary is likely to find more attention paid to his or her national origins than to racial factors. Being a woman is more of a disadvantage working in the Gulf States than, say, in Scandinavia.

In short, mapping the spectrum of advantage and disadvantage can help to put these multiple influences into perspective. A simple way to do so is to draw each definable grouping as a circle. Circles may be empowered or disempowered, vis-à-vis an organizational norm (typical the individual's peers) – illustrated by shading disadvantage and clear circles for advantage. They may also be large or small, to reflect the scale of disadvantage or advantage.

Mapping the individual's influence network in this way facilitates discussion around:

- what they can do to enlarge the clear circles
- what the organization can do to shrink the shaded circles
- what new clear circles the person can add to their map and how.

Separating out personal disadvantage and group disadvantage

Being a member of a group does not automatically mean that an individual is stereotyped in the same way that the group is. Individuals are often initially perceived on the basis of stereotypes associated with group membership, but when they behave in ways that conflict with those stereotypes, the stereotypes are often cast aside and perceivers are forced to view the individual as an individual rather than as a group member. There may still be times, however, when they are perceived to be part of the larger category – i.e. when the context obscures the scale of their difference from the stereotype, such as in a crowd at a football match.

Similarly, attitudes and behaviours that hold someone back at work may be culturally driven (i.e. they are common to most people from that cultural background) or personality driven (the product of individual preferences and context). Examples of the former would be the tendency of Finns to be almost brutally direct in their comments to others, or of English people to score themselves lower in appraisals than Americans. Examples of the latter might be learning styles, communication styles, innate levels of motivation and so on.

Within a multicultural organization, achieving flexibility of style and behaviour to accommodate a variety of group norms can be considered a key competence. Part of the role of the mentor, then, is to help the mentee identify those situations where disadvantage or disempowerment stems from a failure of flexibility on the mentee's part, and those where it is symptomatic of a broader malaise arising from inflexible stereotypes on the part of other parties and, in particular, on the part of those exercising power over the individual and/or the group within the organization. (It could be – and experience suggests that it is often the case – that both factors are present.)

This is not an easy dialogue to pursue, as all sorts of expectations and misperceptions about intentions (the mentee's, the mentor's and those of third parties) are likely to intervene. A simple, if imperfect, way to work through this is by analysing key situations where the mentee has either felt disadvantaged or has been given negative feedback.

Some key questions here are:

- What were you intending at the time? (What outcome did you want?)
- What was the other person intending? (What outcome did they want?)
- What was your attitude towards them?
- What was their attitude towards you?
- What did you *not* say (although you thought it)?
- What do you think they did *not* say (although they thought it)?
- How did you feel about the exchange?
- How do you think they felt about the exchange?
- Who was in charge of the exchange? If the other person, what prevented you taking charge?

- How would you have liked the script to have gone (being realistic about the situation that gave rise to it)?
- How could you and the other person rewrite the script next time?
- What responsibilities does that place on each of you?

Some situations will not involve any direct dialogue between the mentor and third parties – for example, when a minority employee is not considered for a promotion, for which they believe they are qualified (whether they are qualified or not does not matter). Modifications of the same questions will still work, however, especially if they focus on the long-term relationship which led up to the event, rather than on the event itself. One of the goals of this exercise is to equip the mentee with the confidence, tactics and language to manage the situation on their own. The mentor must take care, however, not to allow his or her own stereotypes to colour their perceptions.

Sharing values

Sharing values is an important part of building rapport within the developmental relationship. Yet many people feel awkward about approaching the issues and rely upon intuition and inference to understand each other's values.

The following are two ways of opening and continuing the dialogue in a more direct manner, with the aim of achieving a much more rapid exchange of values.

Questions to open dialogue on values: a checklist for mentor and mentee

1 What's important to your future career?
2 What are you most proud of having achieved?
3 What do you most value in a friend?
4 What do you most value in working colleagues?
5 What frustrates you most about your work?
6 What opportunity do you most regret not having seized?
7 What gives you status?
8 Why do you come to work?
9 How does your non-work life influence how you feel/think about your job?
10 How would you like to be remembered in this organization? As a person?
11 What do you think have been your biggest mistakes and what did you learn from them?
12 Who do you most admire and why?
13 Who have been your most useful role models and what did you learn from them?
14 How do you manage the balance between work and non-work?

15 What social changes do you think are necessary in modern society? What changes make you concerned?
16 Where's the fun for you?

Each question can be extended with requests for examples.

A language for discussing values

Values relate to self-image and public image, to your sense of responsibility towards others and your expectations of their responsibilities towards you. See the value matrix in Table 4.1.

Table 4.1 Values matrix

	Image	Responsibility
Self	Who you are Who you aspire to be What makes you feel good/bad about yourself	Your responsibility towards other people
Others	How you want others to perceive you	Your expectations of other people's responsibility towards you

It is best to use the values matrix as the basis to discuss real problems and issues, rather than for abstract discussion, i.e. how do you want others to perceive you in this situation? In this way, you open out a much wider spectrum of responses and self-awareness.

A question of appraisal

One of the most difficult areas, where stereotypes have an impact, is the formal performance appraisal. It takes a very aware manager accurately to assess people from diverse backgrounds in their leadership skills, independence of thought or degree of commitment, e.g. when those same characteristics may be expressed in very different ways. For example, is the organization's idea of a leader someone who is highly action oriented, or someone who achieves through consensus building? To overcome the influence of stereotypes, the organization and the managers within it need to establish a wider definition of leadership, which encompasses a variety of valid styles.

For the mentoring relationship, appraisals may provoke an examination of whether the mentee has been treated fairly. The role of the mentor includes helping the mentee to:

- understand how the organization views the characteristics, on which the mentee has been appraised
- plan how to demonstrate those qualities more clearly
- put their own capabilities and performance into context and 'market' themselves.

Mentors may also act together as a group to arbitrate between the organization and a minority group – for example, to legitimize different styles of leadership. A case in point is the multinational information technology (IT) outsourcing company, whose appraisal and reward system was based on the assumption that everyone should seek greater responsibility. So programmers and analysts became team leaders, then project leaders, then junior managers, and so on. As a result of a formal mentoring programme, mentors became aware for the first time of a significant minority – people whose ambition at this stage of their career was to become very good technicians and who did not want to manage anybody. This minority only came to light when mentors got together in a mutual support and programme review meeting. They took the issue on board and took it to senior management, along with cogent arguments about retention of these skilled employees. The result was a dual career path that recognized both management and technical competence.

The key requirement in all this is to achieve sufficient dialogue, in sufficient depth, to help the mentee understand the organization and its prevailing assumptions about behaviours that are valued and not valued.

And, finally, how *not* to do it

Whether a mentoring relationship is in a diversity context or not, there is ample evidence of the damage that poor mentors can inflict (Kizilos (1990). The following, only slightly tongue-in-cheek checklist covers some of the most common dysfunctional behaviours by mentors.

Twelve habits of the ineffective mentor

1 Start from the point of view that you – from your vast experience and broader perspective – know better than the mentee what is in his or her interest.
2 Be determined to share your wisdom with them – whether they want it or not – remind them frequently how much they still have to learn.
3 Decide what you and the mentee will talk about and when; change dates and themes frequently to prevent complacency sneaking in.
4 Do most of the talking; check frequently that they are paying attention.
5 Make sure they understand how trivial their concerns are compared to the weighty issues you have to deal with.
6 Remind the mentee how fortunate he or she is to have your undivided attention.

Table 4.2 Issues and comments

Issue	Comment
We don't seem to have anything to talk about/ We've run out of steam	*Is the purpose of the relationship sufficiently clear? What outcomes are you both expecting?* Many relationships founder because mentor and mentee assume they have to focus on problems, when actually the greatest value may come from *identifying opportunities*. Perhaps the relationship has run its normal course and it is time to move on
	Suggested solution(s): Explore mutual expectations of the relationship. Be prepared to help the mentee describe and find another mentor, if appropriate
My mentee doesn't respond	*Do they want to be there? Sometimes in formal mentoring schemes, the mentee (and sometimes the mentor) feel obliged to attend rather than are motivated to do so. Small wonder, then, if they do not participate.* Do they feel you are the wrong mentor for them?
	Suggested solution(s): Do not feel you have to fill the silence. Turn the tables, 'Before I can be any use to you, I need to learn about you . . .' Try to share good and bad experiences of learning, to build a common set of values. Use these experiences to draw out and examine expectations, as above Emphasize the value of learning from differences Demonstrate a genuine interest in the mentee's views and perceptions
We never get into depth on anything	*The most common causes here are failure to challenge sufficiently and giving too much direct advice*
	Suggested solution(s): Have the courage to challenge constructively more frequently. Help the mentee learn how to challenge for himself/herself Listen to how much talking you do – is it for less than 20 per cent of the time? Listen, too, for how often you use phrases, such as, 'I suggest', 'In my experience', etc.
My mentee feels the world is against him/ her	*Of course, it may be, and it is important for the mentor to recognize that perceptions of unfairness are usually based on some actuality. But equally, it may be that the mentee cannot cope with a series of barriers and problems.*
	Suggested solution(s): Do not be too hasty to decide whether discrimination is real or imagined. Accept the mentee's feelings and focus on how they can change the environment that makes them feel vulnerable

Table 4.2 Continued

Issue	Comment
	Help the mentee to scope the issues they face, both in number and type. What solutions could be applied across some or all of them? Which issues are the highest priority to resolve? Where can they get some quick wins that will make them feel more positive?
We never seem to meet	The two most common causes here are that the mentor keeps changing appointments, so the mentee feels the relationship is unimportant to the mentor, or the mentee is reluctant to take the time of someone so important and so obviously busy
	Suggested solution(s): Emphasize how useful you find the relationship to be and how important mentoring is to the organization's well-being Keep in touch between meetings, by telephone or e-mail. For example, send the mentee clippings or other information relevant to dialogue in previous meetings
My mentee is unrealistic in his/her ambitions	*Many great men and women have been seen as having little potential earlier in their careers. If the mentee appears overambitious, the mentor can still help them build a plan to achieve their goal; and be there to help and encourage, should they fail* Mentees, who appear underambitious, can be helped to raise their sights by, for example, putting them in touch with other people, from similar backgrounds who have achieved. In some cases, the mentee may be deliberately throttling back on career ambitions, because of domestic commitments. The mentor can help by exploring with them a wider range of work/career scenarios, with a view to identifying one with a higher element of win-win outcomes
My mentee ignores my advice	*Great! Whatever you feel about the wisdom of their decision, accept its legitimacy and help them to think through any implications this choice of action will have. The more they feel you are supportive of their decisions, the more they are likely to listen to you next time*
My mentee wants to pass his/her problems on to me to resolve	*Are you encouraging this expectation? Does the mentee need counselling rather than mentoring?* Suggested solution(s): Assuming you are not encouraging them to pass responsibility for their issues over to you, their desire to do so may stem from a high level of personal stress and inability to cope. That may be outside your competence to cope with, or outside the mentoring role, in which case, you should discuss with the mentee how to hand them on to a professional counsellor. Only in exceptional cases should you sort the problem out for the mentee

7 Neither show nor admit any personal weaknesses; expect to be their role model in all aspects of career development and personal values.

8 Never ask them what they should expect of you – how would they know anyway?

9 Demonstrate how important and well connected you are by sharing confidential information they do not need (or want) to know.

10 Discourage any signs of levity or humour – this is a serious business and should be treated as such.

11 Take them to task when they do not follow your advice.

12 Never, never admit that this could be a learning experience for you, too.

Troubleshooting the diversity-mentoring relationship

See Table 4.2.

References

Clutterbuck, D. (1985). *Everyone Needs a Mentor*. CIPD.

Clutterbuck, D. and Megginson, D. (1999). *Mentoring Executives and Directors*. Butterworth-Heinemann.

Clutterbuck, D., Lickfold, G. and Martin, D. (1998). *The Mentoring Diagnostic Kit*. Clutterbuck Associates.

Flick, D. (1998). *From Debate to Dialogue: Using the Understanding Process to Transform our Conversations*. Orchid.

Hampden-Turner, C. and Trompenaars, F. (2000). *Building Cross-Cultural Competence: How to Create Wealth from Conflicting Values*. Wiley.

Kandola, R. and Fullerton, J. (1998). *Diversity in Action: Managing the Mosaic*. 2nd edn. Institute of Personnel and Development.

Kizilos, P. (1990). Take my mentor please. *Training Magazine*, April, 49–55.

Kram, K. (1983). Phases of the mentoring relationship. *Academy of Management Journal*, **26**, 4.

Megginson, D. and Clutterbuck, D. (1995). *Mentoring in Action*. Kogan Page.

Rogers, C. R. (1994). *Client-Centred Therapy*. Constable.

Stewart, I. and Cohen, J. (1997). *Figments of Reality*. Cambridge University Press.

5

What every diversity mentor should know about stereotyping

David Clutterbuck

Stereotypes: oversimplified, rigid, and generalised beliefs about groups of people, in which all individuals from the same group are regarded as having the same set of leading characteristics. (Harre and Lamb, 1986)

The issue of stereotyping occurs and recurs throughout any discussion on diversity. The reality of human existence is that, to make sense of the world around us, we need to classify objects, people and any other phenomena our senses detect. In making such classifications – for example, that trees are tall green things with lots of leaves and branches, but one trunk – we inevitably simplify reality. Some trees are not green; green trees in temperate climates are sometimes green, at other times brown, or red or bare; horticulturalists have successfully bred dwarf trees (and Japanese *bonsai* art produces trees even smaller); and there are varieties of tree that have multiple shoots from the ground. Yet we usually have no difficulty in recognizing a tree when we see one.

This capacity to categorize develops quite early in childhood and is what enables us to cope with the complexity of the world around us. The generalized assumptions we make about a category usually operate at an unconscious level, so unless we meet with something or someone who does not quite fit with those assumptions, they tend to be unquestioned – especially if they are reinforced by continuing stimuli that fit the assumptions. So it takes a question such as, 'is asparagus a tree or a vegetable?' to make most people stop and examine their assumptions consciously.

We can describe these underlying assumptions as either *defining* or dependent. Defining assumptions relate to attributes that relate to the essence of the category – treeness, for example. Dependent assumptions relate to perceptions or beliefs that stem from defining assumptions. So, trees are good because they provide shade or because tigers are dangerous, you should never turn your back on them. The categorization process often ignores the situational context that may influence these second-order assumptions – broadly true is good enough for most situations.

When we deal with people, however, our lack of awareness of the assumptions, which we are drawing upon, often leads us into gross misunderstandings. We may see groups as much more different than they really are, or much more similar. Our assumptions create a framework of expectations, which can lead to self-fulfilling prophecies. Very often, behaviours based on stereotyped assumptions lead to 'collusion' – the white manager, who expects a black employee to be lazy will find that the employee complies with the stereotype, believing there is no point demonstrating that he can be as highly motivated as the next person. The adage 'behaviour breeds behaviour' is nowhere more valid than in dealing with stereotypes.

Second-order assumptions derive in large part from the group, to which we perceive ourselves to belong. In assessing people as 'good' or 'bad' managers, for example, the female manager may be at a disadvantage, because the stereotype of a good manager is based on the self-perceptions of the dominant, male, management group (Powell, 1990).

Whereas stereotyping concerns the group, similar processes are at work with regard to the individual. Typecasting is not something that just happens to actors. An employee's reputation within the workplace may be based on long-past, atypical incidents that colour other people's perceptions. 'Not a team worker', 'has poor judgement' or 'over-emotional' are the kind of comments that often appear in appraisals without current supporting evidence, but may have a severe impact on the employee's prospects. When stereotypes reinforce typecasting, it can be very difficult for the employee to succeed.

To add to the complexity of stereotyping, there is the issue of where stereotypical responses reside. While the individual may perceive his or her characterizations of other people as predominantly rational – i.e. based on a mixture of experience and received wisdom (the experience and observation of other members of 'our' group) – in practice, they are often emotionally driven. Distrust of differences is primarily a reaction of the limbic brain, rather than the neo-cortex. It evolves from the survival instinct to identify and be wary of anything that does not fit the 'normal' context. The same mechanism that tells us to fear unexpected rapid movement (it could be that tiger) tells us to be wary of someone whose behaviour, beliefs or appearance is different to our own.

Difference, of course, is only relative. Less than one-tenth of 1 per cent differs between any two humans in genetic terms, and not a great deal more between humans and other mammals, or even very distant genetic relatives such as goldfish or chickens. It is ironic that our fear of rats arises more from similarity than from difference. Because they are genetically similar, they are able to host diseases deadly to humans.

Like any mechanism, when overused our ability to categorize and identify minute differences can be deeply harmful, in the same way as an overactive immune system causes crippling disease. We need to be able to distinguish between individual humans, if only to ensure that we maintain the same family unit and recognize to whom we are talking (witness the appalling problems of Alzheimer's victims who lose this ability). But this ability becomes socially dysfunctional when it causes us to focus on differences between people rather than similarities. Some modern authorities on culture (Hampden-Turner and Trompenaars, 2000) emphasize that there is very little variation in the dilemmas societies have to cope with; the differences arise in how they approach those dilemmas and the pecking order of the values and assumptions they apply in resolving them.

The values and assumptions we apply are far from static and it is arguable that they now change more rapidly than at any other time in history. At one time, it was possible for several generations to pass without significant evolution in assumptions about relationships within a society, between societies, and between societies and their environment. There can be few middle-aged adults in the developed world, who have not had to adjust quite radically their assumptions in all three areas – in effect, become different people. Our assumptions about the environment, discrimination in the workplace, work–life balance and so on have changed substantially in the past twenty years alone. Proponents of 'The American Way' might be surprised how alien and strange their ancestors of a mere 100 years ago would seem in their thinking and behaviour.

Wanguri (1996) emphasizes the importance of liking and disliking in how we react to similarity and difference. Following West and Wicklund (1980), she relates diversity mentoring to two established social psychological theories:

- the *reinforcement-affect model* of attraction, which asserts that people like those who have similar attitudes to our own
- *social comparison theory*, built upon the observed tendency of people to compare our abilities and opinions with others, who we see as similar to ourselves.

In her review of the related literature, Wanguri highlights a variety of very subtle mechanisms, by which we discriminate against those we see as dissimilar to ourselves. For example, black workers often felt they had less access to information at work. They would only be given half the picture, while white colleagues would be given a fuller briefing. These 'micro-inequities' reinforce stereotypes in both parties – for example, if blacks have less complete information, they are less likely to perform as well as people who are better informed. The cycle of subtle suggestion is hard to recognize and hard to break.

Recent experiments by two scientists at the University of Victoria in British Columbia reinforce this message. (Gifford and Reynolds, 2001). They asked people to judge the intelligence of students, seen making presentations on video, on the basis of a number of clues, such as body language. Students who spoke rapidly, were easy to understand, or who had an extensive vocabulary were generally rated as more intelligent – and this correlated fairly well with actuality. However, intelligent students who hesitated, used slang or were fat, were usually scored much lower than they should have been. Where the judges only heard, rather than saw, the presentations, their assessments of these latter students were more accurate.

Being aware of one's own stereotypes and helping the mentee recognize and explore their own are essential elements of diversity mentoring. Many of the programmes in the case study chapters of this book include some element of diversity training, in recognition of this need. The approaches may vary considerably, but the objectives are the same:

● to enhance the effectiveness of the relationship by increasing the sensitivity of one or both parties to the influence of stereotypes
● to help people value and manage the differences between them.

This applies as much to mentoring programmes aimed at increasing general diversity as to those, which target specific equal opportunities issues.

Recognizing one's own stereotypes is not easy. When we see a behaviour that is contrary to our stereotypes, we often rationalize it away as 'the exception that proves the rule'. We do not expect to see a scruffy young person in the first-class compartment of a European train, so we assume that they are an interloper, who should be fined for illegally occupying a first-class seat. The idea that this was a successful and extremely well-paid musician on his way to a recording studio would not occur to us, unless there were other clues.

Here is an example of a stereotype one of the authors recognizes himself to hold – 'religious fundamentalists make poor employees'. Underneath this defining assumption are a number of dependent assumptions concerning the motives and trustworthiness of such people. The origin of this stereotype lies in childhood experience of religious fundamentalists – remembered in overwhelmingly negative terms. An element of selective deletion of memories may well have occurred in the intervening years. The stereotype has been reinforced by observation of a small number of employees, who were Christian fundamentalists and were found to be unconcerned about lying to customers. The rationalization behind the dependent assumptions is that the act of insisting something to be true against all rational evidence is a form of personal dishonesty, and that a dishonest self-image makes it more difficult to benchmark one's behaviour. It also suggests that such people are more likely to be humourless and poor team players.

The fact that the stereotype appears (at least from the author's perspective) to be well grounded does not mean, however, that it is *universally* true. The key to managing this stereotype has been to recognize that there is a spectrum of belief that extends from the highly irrational to the rational. While the stereotype may apply to people at the extreme irrational end of the spectrum, people at other points need to be assessed more generously.

Admitting to and accepting prejudices as stereotypes is undoubtedly helpful in dealing with them. There are at least four stages, in order:

1 Recognizing our stereotypes, where they come from, and what useful functions they perform.
2 Recognizing that a stereotype does not apply universally and may have negative functions, too.
3 Attempting to understand the thinking, behaviour and motives of the person(s) the stereotype applies to.
4 Learning to value both differences and similarities.

One way of analysing our beliefs to identify stereotypes is to examine our perception of groups of people is to think about them in terms of the following cascade:

All are.
All tend to be.
Most are.
Most tend to be.
Many are.
Many tend to be.
Some are.
Some tend to be.
A minority is.
A minority tends to be.

Forcing ourselves to categorize our perceptions in this way brings the categorization process from the subconscious to the conscious, where it can be reflected upon, analysed and discussed with others. Mentoring across the boundaries of difference provides a valuable opportunity to explore our understanding of other people's perceptions and beliefs, and to modify our own stereotypes and behaviour. They key to doing so is having the courage to engage in open dialogue about such issues.

Engaging in such dialogue opens up the possibilities of moving beyond stereotypes to genuine diversity management. In this context, it becomes practical – and useful – to explore what values different people apply to key business dilemmas and to ask the question: 'Could a different perspective, or a mix of perspectives help us create a better decision?' Multidimensional decisions are much more likely to fit with multidimensional problems.

The goal, we suggest, is to move from stereotyping, through stereo-vision, to stereo-action. By stereo-vision, we mean:

● seeing things from multiple perspectives
● tolerating ambiguity

- extrapolating between cultures, values and perspectives
- listening to and seeking out different perspectives
- multiperspective, multicultural networking.

By stereo-action, we mean:

- win-win resolution of cultural and gender conflict
- inclusive thinking and behaviour
- valuing differences in interpretation of shared values.

Figure 5.1 represents a useful tool for exploring perceptions, both conscious and unconscious, in relatively simple terms. As a template for mentor and mentee to explore specific incidents or relationships, it can help focus dialogue on understanding.

	Conscious stereotyping		Unconscious stereotyping	
	Positive	Negative	Positive	Negative
Mentee's perception				
Mentor's perception				
Third party perception				

Figure 5.1 Template for exploring conscious and unconscious perceptions

Three strategies (at least) are available for the mentee to tackle behaviour in others, which they perceive to be based on inaccurate stereotypes. These are:

1 Change their own behaviour to match the mental model of the other person. For example, becoming more proactive in suggesting alternative approaches to business problems can force someone who believes unconsciously that certain races are less creative than others, to reconsider their perceptions.
2 Confrontation – make the other person aware that their behaviour/view is unacceptable. This can lead to argument and procedural processes but may sometimes be the only way, where the other person is not willing to question their own assumptions.
3 Dialogue – help the other person recognize that there is a clash of perceptions. Through rational discussion, develop an understanding of each other's views.

The mentor can play a strong role here in helping the mentee plan which strategy to adopt, how and when.

Mentoring is only one part of creating organizations with these attributes. The quality of leadership, the effectiveness of training, the selection of diverse employee groups all play a role. However, the key to all of these is to develop dialogue that explores differences openly and with a distinct willingness to learn. The mentor, who approaches the relationship with a mentee as an opportunity to learn both about other perspectives and about himself or herself, is part of a much larger and more significant process of positive change.

If a competitive advantage for companies is to be flexible in the face of change, it helps to have a culture that is constantly evolving in directions that make it more efficient at understanding and responding to its environment. Diversity mentoring creates the circumstances, where this kind of recombinant evolution can take place to maximum effect. Not only is there an exchange and discussion of perceptions between the mentor and the mentee, but each interaction with other people the mentee brings up for the discussion adds to the complexity of the system. Mentor and mentee are changed by their understanding of each other; they in turn have an impact on other relationships in which they apply this learning (for example, the white mentor of a Sikh mentee modifying his or her behaviour towards other Sikhs, perhaps direct reports). Their heightened ability to recognize stereotype-driven behaviour in others generates further discussion, and so on. In short, providing the reflective space where this kind of dialogue can occur has at least the potential to make a hugely disproportional impact on the way the organization as a whole thinks and behaves.

References

Gifford, R. and Reynolds, D. (2001). *Personality and Social Psychology Bulletin*, **27**, 287.

Hampden-Turner, C. and Trompenaars, F. (2000). *Building Cross-Cultural Competence: How to Create Wealth from Conflicting Values*. Wiley.

Harre, R. and Lamb, R. (1986). *The Dictionary of Personality and Social Psychology*. Blackwell.

Powell, G. (1990). One more time: do female and male managers differ? *Academy of Management Executive*, August, 68–76.

Wanguri, D. G. (1996). Diversity, perceptions of equity, and communicative openness in the workplace. *Journal of Business Communication*, **4**, October, 443–57.

West, S. G. and Wicklund, R. A. A. (1980). *Primer of Social Psychological Theories*. Brooks/Cole.

6
Individual case studies

Sexual orientation and mentorship: the benefits of a gay mentor/gay protégé relationship

Brian Welle[1]

I entered my current organization – a non-profit women's advocacy organization that conducts research and provides consulting services to corporations – in 1998 as a research associate. As one of the few males in the organization, and the only male in my department at the time I was hired, I was a clearly 'visible' new employee. I stood apart from my colleagues not only in terms of my gender, but also because of my atypical work schedule: at the same time that I began my new job I was working to complete my doctoral studies in organizational psychology, so chose to work only a part-time schedule of three days per week. Finally, my identification as a gay man clearly distinguished me from a majority of employees in my organization.

Rachel, the woman who was to become my mentor, and I met formally after I requested an informational meeting with her. Because our organization does not have a formal programme in which new employees are matched with a mentor, I made a point of introducing myself to those individuals who were working on interesting projects and seemed to be well regarded within the organization. Rachel was one of those people. Upon our first meeting, we quickly started to develop an informal mentoring relationship.

Rachel was a senior research associate at the time that I joined the organization. She had about two years' tenure and, like me, was also working to complete the requirements for her PhD degree. Although in many ways she fitted the demographic profile of the 'typical' employee in our organization (young, Caucasian and well educated), she was atypical in that she self-identified as a lesbian.

To a large extent, the reason a mentoring relationship developed between us was because of our *similarities*, particularly our shared identity as gay people, our dual responsibilities as employees and students, and the similarity in our class background. I will discuss the impact of each of these in turn.

Similarity in sexual orientation was a major factor leading to our mentoring relationship. Both Rachel and I quickly realized the advantages of having a gay mentor. Through our personal experiences Rachel and I have found – as have many gay, lesbian and bisexual people – that the 'management' of our sexual identities can be a critical determinant of workplace experiences. Unfortunately, it is a fact of life in the USA that many people have moral and religious objections to homosexuality, and that these attitudes are often expressed as discriminatory treatment at work. Even in an ostensibly open-minded and liberal working environment such as that found in our current organization, it is still necessary to gauge the kinds of reactions certain people will have to the disclosure of a homosexual identity, and the ramifications for being open and honest about aspects of our lives that are influenced by our sexual orientation.

Finding a gay mentor meant benefiting from Rachel's accumulated knowledge and her awareness of the subtle cues to the openness, tolerance and support offered to gay employees of our organization. But apart from this 'functional' advantage of having a gay mentor, the comfort of finding someone in the workplace who was part of the gay 'subculture' and who was interested in the issues of importance to gays and lesbians helped to foster our mentoring relationship.

Our similar academic situations also helped bring about our mentoring relationship. Staying focused on the demands of a PhD programme while remaining committed to one's job is a difficult task. Rachel and I chose different tactics to achieve this balance, but our similar circumstances made it natural for a beneficial, two-way mentoring relationship to develop between us.

Other ways that we are similar to one another undoubtedly influenced our relationship, but their impact was more subtle. Most notably, we share a similar class background – one that was heavily influenced by a working-class heritage. We hold similar views about the value of working even while going to school, and we also have similar personal experiences of coming out (i.e. disclosing our sexual orientation) to our family and friends. Thus, our class background gave us a set of shared experiences and attitudes that led naturally to our mentoring relationship.

The structure of our meetings and mentoring activities has always been informal. We frequently visit each other's office when we find a short span of free time, regularly spend lunch together and, on occasion, meet during an after-hours event. This informal structure makes it possible for us to consult each other as issues come up rather than wait for an appointed meeting time. In this way, problems that can benefit from the other's experience can be resolved sooner. This arrangement is successful because we make the effort to be available to one another for a short period of time at least once each week. Without our willingness to have a flexible work schedule, the informal structure of our relationship would not have been effective.

Often the issues we discuss together are outside the other's experience. This was inevitable given the number of ways that Rachel and I are different from one another. First, of course, we are different because of our genders. Second, Rachel has a longer tenure within the organization, a more intensive workload and different kinds of work responsibilities. Finally, we are different in our sexual orientation 'management' strategies: while I had chosen to disclose my sexual orientation early on, Rachel had waited almost two years before beginning to tell her colleagues that she is gay. Given the number of ways that we are different from one another, our workplace experiences are often not shared ones. Nonetheless, we were often able to draw on our own observations to advise each other even on those situations that were unique.

For instance, my experiences involving co-worker reactions to my sexual orientation were surprisingly different from those of Rachel. While I perceived very little negativity from co-workers who learned that I was gay, Rachel's disclosure was sometimes met with subtle hostility. Some colleagues, for example, became very reluctant to talk with her about non-work-related topics – conversations that otherwise were commonplace in our organization (e.g. 'so what did *you* do this weekend?'). Rachel had a more difficult time than me for a number of reasons. First, her colleagues had assumed for a long time that she was heterosexual and were learning to come to terms with her new identity. Second, as a leader in the organization she was inherently more visible than I was. And third, some women in our organization may have felt more threatened by Rachel's sexual orientation than my own because Rachel is a woman. Despite these differences, I feel that I was able to help Rachel through this time by simply being available to listen, and by providing insights from my past experiences when appropriate.

Likewise, Rachel was able to assist me through some difficulties arising from my part-time work schedule. My three-day-per-week schedule was atypical for my organization, so I found that I was being excluded from important developmental opportunities due to scheduling conflicts. Because I raised these concerns with Rachel, she was willing to speak to others on my behalf. Eventually, after her promotion to director of research, she placed me on an influential committee. Our experiences as mentor/protégé led her to believe that my perspective would benefit the committee and, in the process, my own career advancement.

We have both enjoyed a number of positive outcomes from our mentoring relationship. Both of us have gained confidence in our ability to be open about our sexual orientation while maintaining positive relationships with co-workers and our credibility as objective researchers. We have also enjoyed the benefits of a dissertation support group that we organized along with other students working in the organization.

Individually, Rachel and I have benefited in unique ways from our mentoring relationship. The advice I was able to share from my earlier experiences as an openly gay employee of other organizations helped Rachel navigate her own coming out process at work. At the same time, her insight into the organizational culture and attitudes of key players in the organization helped me to do the same. My career and standing within the organization were definitely enhanced by Rachel's advice and, eventually, her sponsorship of me for key opportunities. Indeed, a significant benefit to me came from the 'traditional' mentoring role played by Rachel, through which she provided advice about networking with colleagues, gaining access to development opportunities and also taking advantage of high-visibility assignments.

This mentoring experience has convinced me that for gay, lesbian and bisexual employees, having a mentor that shares this identity can be invaluable. Until such time as all workplaces are bias-free and gay people have legal recourse for discriminatory behaviours, the special insight and support offered by fellow gay, lesbian and bisexual mentors are invaluable. It is important to keep in mind, however, that this opinion is culture specific, and based on experiences working within the USA. In cultures with less positive attitudes toward homosexuality it may be dangerous for gay people to associate with one another. In contrast, the sexual orientation of one's mentor may be entirely circumstantial with no special benefits or dispensations for people in cultures that are more tolerant than that of the USA. The very conceptualization of homosexuality varies across cultures, as does the prevailing attitude toward gay, lesbian and bisexual people. It is important for individuals and organizations to keep the national, social and cultural context in mind during the formation and maintenance of mentoring relationships.

Fiona, Bob and office politics: a case study of intimacy

Chris Bennetts[2]

This short case study is drawn from larger in-depth mentor research (Bennets, 1994) and addresses from the perspective of the learner, the impact of an intimate mentor relationship within a local government office in the UK. It takes a descriptive rather than critical stance and is presented where possible in the words of the learner, Fiona, who identified this relationship as a mentor alliance although it was not part of any organized formal programme.

Fiona was twenty-six when she decided to move from her job in teaching into a staff training post in local government. She was aware that Bob the Chief of Personnel saw her as 'new blood', and that although he was looking for a fresh approach within the organization, in some ways would have to 'mould' her to fit her new role. Bob was fifty-one, had reached the top of his profession and took a constructive approach to Fiona's lack of government experience. He had a strategic plan for Fiona's development within the office, and used an open approach to learning. She says:

> He'd say 'Go off and explore staff induction'. It was very constructive because he didn't say 'Come here and listen to me'. He'd allow you to go off and find out for yourself, then come back and talk it through with him. We'd follow that pattern as we came to various tasks.

Fiona felt that Bob had taken a risk in appointing her, and she wanted to meet his expectations of success. She knew that he recognized her energy, but was aware that she needed some shaping. They worked closely in that she took all her ideas to him, but she remained in control of her independence and was encouraged to look elsewhere for help and support.

> He would say 'You've got great ideas, but lets see how they're going to work in practice', or ' Let's have a look at how this can be approached'. He acted as a sounding board, there isn't a right and wrong. He'd say 'This approach could have this effect . . . that one that . . . , consider it, go away and find out this particular fact', or whatever. He was good at directing me to information or people who could help me.

The process of the relationship encouraged a shifting alliance as Fiona embarked on an MBA. Bob continued to provide mentoring support during her studies, despite being sometimes out of his depth in some areas of the course. 'He would still meet me to keep the process. . . . it's good to have someone who will keep you on the straight and narrow even if their role has changed from someone giving you resources to someone keeping a timetable check on you.'

For two years Bob gave freely of his time and expected Fiona to work hard towards high standards, but the development of their close relationship had not gone unnoticed in the office, and ultimately it caused jealousy among colleagues who engineered a situation in which Fiona made an error of judgement:

> my colleagues in the office had set me up, for want of a better word. It was difficult for him as Chief of Personnel because he was in a position where he had to act. The problem had been pointed out to him in a formal way by another member of staff who knew that Bob would have to act on it. I was given a written warning. It was very painful for both of us, and we spent a long time afterwards discussing the implications. There was bloodletting on all sides.

The fact that Bob and Fiona's relationship was innocent seemed of no importance to Fiona's workmates. They perceived that she and Bob enjoyed a relationship to which they were not party, that of an intimate, special alliance. For eight months Fiona tried to find a way of remaining within the office and working with her colleagues, and in this interlude the relationship with Bob became even deeper.

> Almost like a love really. Those discussions were much more fatherly, because it was his caring for me as an individual rather than my development as an employee. And that's when it got on to a much safer level. During that time I was emotionally hurt, very angry and almost vindictive, because I couldn't see a way out of working in a department with people I could no longer trust. He was having to cope with both sides and still be professional as my manager, but he also spent time nurturing me as an individual, caring for me as well. It was very constructive, but it took us eight months to work through.

It was at this stage of their relationship that Fiona felt the alliance became more of a peer relationship, with Bob starting to consider Fiona's way of thinking and working.

> He had been rules and regulations led. He was very thorough, had an excellent memory and was very strong on fairness. To meet someone like me who was much more of a questioner and explorer challenged him a bit as to why he thought the way he did. I was never more intelligent than him, but I did just shed a different vision on the knowledge and experience that he'd got.

Fiona and Bob never discussed the deepening of the emotional aspects of their relationship, and she thinks that this was because they both knew that it was too emotional for a professional relationship. She says that it manifested itself in tacit ways of communicating, and that they were more direct with each other, no longer requiring the 'opening gambits' of normal office conversation, but working in a more intuitive way. 'I liked the specialness of the relationship. I could see that he hadn't got that with other people. I felt in a star-like position and I enjoyed that obviously – but it was an absolute death-knell for me with the other people in the department.'

Fiona thinks that her colleagues noticed the 'non-verbal things', the amount of time she spent with him, her promotion and the time he devoted to helping her with her MBA. Since Fiona's disciplinary hearing, their time together had not lessened but doubled, and the jealousy from workmates became intolerable. Fiona was the main breadwinner in her marriage and she felt concerned that if she were set up again by colleagues, it could mean the end of her career in that department. 'I was very fearful. I enjoyed the special relationship and I enjoyed the MBA. I was exploring all the time and I enjoyed it a bit too much. I'm not the kind of person who can disguise it terribly well.'

Eventually the strain on Fiona became intolerable and she chose to leave her job and take a post a few miles away. Despite this the mentor relationship with

Bob continued. She envisages the relationship enduring but recognizes that it has once more changed and evolved. 'It is much safer, more fatherly, more genuinely concerned for me, rather than me developing for the benefit of the organization, because he doesn't have the need to do that now.'

She feels that Bob helped develop her professionally by sharing his standards and thoroughness in ways that were appropriate to the rules and regulations of local government. Although Fiona always thought of herself as a 'pond-skater', never going into things too deeply, she appreciates what Bob gave her, and why he felt it was necessary:

> For me as an individual it's much harder to be thorough and systematic because it's not in my nature anyway. But I do it now because of necessity, and I tend to set limits on people because my time is limited, or I have to set limits because of financial constraints. So it's a means to an end really, but it's an appreciation of the importance of that which I didn't have before.

Fiona has transferred the learning she experienced with Bob into her new role and anticipates acting as a mentor herself at some future date. She considers that to some extent she has modelled herself on Bob. 'It's a bit like an inheritance, but in a way that didn't railroad me, 'I've done it this way, you do it this way', it wasn't like that at all. That's why I think modelling is such a good term, you have your own form, but he was shaping that.'

The cost of this relationship was high, in terms of personal strain, and in Fiona's ultimate decision to leave her jealous colleagues. Bob, too, has now retired from his post and has taken up work elsewhere, in a similar role. Despite everything Fiona and Bob's relationship continues today, but is no longer visible to those with whom they work. They meet to share friendship and professional concerns. They have never shared a sexual relationship; they share a relationship of continuing potentiality and possibility, the mentor relationship.

Race, gender, and mentorship: going beneath the surface

Belinda Johnson White[3]

It gives me great pleasure to share my mentoring story with you. Please know that I do not believe that there exists a scientific procedure through which successful mentoring relationships can be dissected, analysed and placed into a formula from which other successful mentoring relationships can be guaranteed. However, I do believe that individuals who are truly committed to making a positive contribution to human development can gain insight and knowledge through exposure to diverse human interactions. It is with this goal in mind that I share one of my most enjoyable personal experiences, a cross-race, cross-gender mentoring relationship.

In September 1996, at the age of forty-two, I entered a PhD programme. I had previously worked for thirteen years in sales and marketing at the largest computer corporation in America, and was starting a second career as a business instructor at an undergraduate college. I was in the sixteenth year of my marriage and the mother of a thirteen-year-old son and eight-year-old daughter. I was described by friends and associates as a self-assured, competitive and determined African-American woman whose courage and initiative left her fearless in the face of any obstacle or experience. And prior to the PhD undertaking, I was in definite agreement with this assessment of my skills and abilities. But something about attempting to earn the highest and most prestigious academic credential in the land left me weak at the knees. How could I, a black woman, raised in Birmingham, Alabama, who came of age in America's Civil Rights' Movement of the 1960s, whose emotions and attitudes are shaped and scared by first-hand experiences of racism and sexism, survive the rigours of such a politically charged academic system, undoubtedly owned by white males? Competing was not my concern, being allowed to compete as who I am was the concern.

I chose to enter a PhD programme in higher education at a large, comprehensive commuter state university. The higher education faculty consisted of two full-time faculty members: John, a white male, and Mary, a black female. I was thrilled that a black female was a member of the staff. Of course, I thought, Mary would be assigned as my adviser and based on our race and gender match, we would share a special bond that would develop into a close, personal, one-on-one mentoring relationship. But instead, John was assigned as my adviser. My initial high hopes of a close mentoring relationship between my adviser and myself were quickly dimmed and replaced by thoughts of internal and external conflict and tension, based on race and gender differences. I did not believe a white male could provide the attention and direction needed to guide me through a PhD programme. Nor did I believe he would want to. So my initial assessment of the situation was that he had nothing to gain if the relationship was a success and I had everything to lose if the relationship was a disaster.

Fortunately, my initial impression of John was false. What I saw on the surface was a white male. But in going beneath the surface, I found a caring, professional educator and academician. In fact, our cross-mentoring relationship evolved into a successful experience for the both of us in the same manner as successful traditional mentoring relationships. As I reflect on our relationship, I can clearly see that our relationship, not unlike traditional mentoring relationships, had three distinct phases:

1 A beginning in which the mentor and protégée develop a willingness to participate.
2 A middle where the mentor and protégée develop a mutual level of trust and respect.

3 An end where the mentor and protégée see a realization of their individual goals. I will use these three phases as a framework for the telling of my mentoring story.

I am the first to admit that I was apprehensive about our relationship. I simply saw no similarities between us. In addition to my concern regarding our obvious differences, I figured John had no real interest in me and would treat me as just another one of the many students he was required to advise. But this cursive assessment of him was quickly revealed as erroneous. I found out early in our relationship that John and I actually shared common ground among our differences. We are only a few years apart in age, which means that we both came of age during America's racially charged era of the 1960s. I believe that somewhere in his Midwestern, middle-class background, he was sensitized to the injustices of racism and sexism, and became a champion for the underdog.

John says that the first phase was not a difficult one for him. In fact, he says that his first impression of me, based on his interview of me as a prospective doctoral student, was of someone he could work with. Unlike me, John had no reservations around the gender and race differences. John very candidly admits he is 'capable of disliking people regardless of colour'. Therefore he is willing to freely enter into a relationship with anyone, knowing that the relationship will only develop if there is a level of mutual trust and respect based on the person's character, not her characteristics. Because John quickly showed a genuine openness to me as a person, I became open to the possibility that we could have a successful mentoring relationship.

Once we both identified the fact that the potential for a successful mentoring relationship existed for us, we moved into the second phase, developing a mutual level of trust and respect. I developed trust and respect for John as a result of the way he listened and encouraged me. John demonstrates a tremendous amount of skill in this area. He says he 'listens to feel' as opposed to 'listening to hear'. He listened to how I constructed problems, how I asked questions, to what appeared confusing to me and to how I straighten out the confusion. An example of his skill in the area of listening and encouragement is around his treatment of race and gender, two topics he is not afraid to discuss.

The subject matter in the American higher education doctorate curriculum, to a large degree, focuses on the topic of access to education and the systematic denial of access to quality education for minorities and the disenfranchised. As a minority, this is a topic for which I am very passionate and strongly opinionated. John not only allowed me to voice my opinions on the subject matter, he encouraged me to explore at the deepest level my feelings on racism, sexism and classism both in my writings and during classroom discussions. Where I had been reluctant to express my thoughts on these topics due to the extreme feelings of hurt, anger and pain it often caused me, John's mentoring helped me instead to view my personal experiences around racism, sexism and classism from a different vantage point. I tended to focus on the negative aspects of racism and sexism, which caused a heavy burden in my life. John taught me to refocus my thoughts away from the actual experiences to an appreciation for the strength, courage and perseverance I acquired as a result of the experiences. Viewing the affects of racism and sexism in this manner was a major growth opportunity for me and an unexpected benefit of our mentoring relationship.

Similarly, John's level of trust and respect for me is based on my willingness to listen to his advice and direction, acceptance of his constructive criticisms of my work, and the consistent improvement of the quality of my programme performance. John says I brought a lot to the relationship – talent and motivation – and all he had to do was tap those sources of success. 'It's easy to mentor talented students', is how John summarizes our mentoring relationship. And from my viewpoint, being named the 2000 recipient of our department's annual award for the best dissertation prospectus was evidence of the level of trust and respect I had earned from John.

The third phase of a successful mentoring relationship centres on goals. Without the presence of mutual attainable goals, mentoring relationships would have no reason to exist. For me, the goal was clear, to complete the PhD programme in a timely manner. I am proud to say I accomplished my goal and was awarded the PhD degree in December 2000. Not as clear was John's goal.

There are several ways John could measure the success of our relationship. My completion of the programme is one; my progress in relation to his peers' advisees a second; third, by the development of a strong personal and professional relationship between us that would continue beyond my earning the PhD; and, finally, his growth in understanding African-American women. I am confident that John is pleased with my performance in the programme as well as my growth as an academician, and we both look forward to a continued personal and professional connection. But what could possibly be the greatest benefit to John from this relationship is the invaluable insight he has gained into a lifestyle that most white males are protected from – the lifestyle of an outsider. By assertively participating in a cross-gender, cross-race mentoring relationship, John saw, and to some degree experienced the frustrations of a minority trying to successfully navigate in a majority ruled organization. As a result of this relationship, John had the opportunity to become a better mentor, a better educator and a better person.

In summary, let me say I believe at the heart of successful mentoring relationships are two similar individuals. Because my traditional view of similarity centred on visual sameness, that is, same gender, same race, same ethnicity, same age, same religion or same socioeconomic class, the thought of a successful cross-mentoring relationship was foreign to me. How could a man–woman, black–white relationship work when the individuals are so obviously different? Based on this thought pattern, the likelihood of John and me developing a successful mentoring relationship was slim. However, by going beneath the surface, I found these two differences were not a negative but a positive consequence to us. Beneath the surface, I found our differences created an intersection of similarities within our life experiences from which we developed a mutually beneficial, personal and professional relationship built on mutual trust, respect, and genuine concern for the well-being of the other.

The obvious question is whether other cross-gender and cross-race mentoring relationships can utilize these same strategies and have equally successful relationships? My answer is unequivocally yes, if the individuals have the courage to overcome the internal and external hurdles of stereotypes, prejudices and biases that societies and cultures across the globe have methodologically placed in our lives. Once these hurdles are crossed, overwhelming benefits to the individuals in cross-mentoring relationships can be realized.

Working with Bob

Wendy Rose[4]

Bob works as a part-time administrator a volunteer for a community self-help organization that arranges social events, leisure activities and outings for people with mental illness. He had been referred to the project as a user of the services but it quickly became clear to him and the management committee that he had skills he could offer the organization on the administration and operational side.

I am a self-employed management development consultant with qualifications in facilitating individual and organizational change.

We came together as part of a project funded by the European Social Fund intended to build the capacity of the not for profit sector by developing the management skills of people working in such organizations.

I met Bob at the launch of the project; he was wearing cycling gear having cycled about 10 miles to the venue.

Bob was very upbeat and enthusiastic about the project, which also included more formal training days in addition to the mentoring. I noticed that he had a lot of 'buzzy' energy around him. Bob was brimming with enthusiasm and explained that he thought his organization was significantly underperforming and he was interested in the mentoring as a way of helping to implement the changes he thought were necessary. However, the specific aims of our work together changed several times during the relationship.

During the launch mentors were encouraged to talk to participants to find out is they were potential mentees. Bob said he was drawn to me because I was not doing 'a hard sell'. We talked generally. Bob spoke about his experiences of having bipolar disorder (which used to be known as manic depression) and explained that he was currently experiencing an 'up' mood (or manic phase) during which he always had masses of energy – hence the cycling. He said he often overcommitted himself during these phases. I explained that I had experiences of this through my father, who had been diagnosed with this illness while I was growing up.

Later I found that I had been paired to work with Bob in response to a request from him. He says that he had 'an early feeling that we could work well together'. Overall we met six times for two hours each at approximately monthly intervals, at the offices of the organization.

During our first meeting Bob was surprised when I clarified that the aim of the mentoring was not to facilitate change by working with the management committee. He had hoped that I would attend their meetings in order to implement change at an organizational level. I explained that the primary focus of the mentoring was his development – and through him the organization. Bob immediately accepted this and wanted to get started. He was very keen to make substantial changes to the overall management of the organization in addition to the way in which activities and events were organized. I encouraged him to consider what was realistic and within his sphere of influence. Bob admitted that much of what he wanted to change was not within the formal remit of his job description and he realized that he ran the risk of annoying the other people involved. However, he also thought this was a risk worth taking and that the means would justify the end.

At the beginning of the second session I learned that, as a result of a meeting with the chairman, Bob was feeling unappreciated and undervalued. The chairman had asked him to rein in his involvement and stick to those areas of work that were outlined in his job. Bob was extremely frustrated and said he was just 'going through the motions at work'. We drew an option tree, tracing all the options open to him; one of which involved leaving the organization and going somewhere where he imagined his energy and drive would be more appreciated.

According to Bob the organization was like a 'pig stuck in mud' whereas he was like a 'thoroughbred racing horse'. We developed this into a whole spectrum of animal analogies in terms of energy and activity which enabled Bob to express his feelings and perceptions about his current situation and gain clarity about what was happening in this obvious mismatch of expectations and ambitions. We discussed the possibility of both him and the organization being more like a 'fit dog' and meeting in the middle.

Afterwards I reflected that my primary task during the session was to keep Bob on track, point out when he went off on a tangent (which he knew he did) and ask him to slow his speech down. I left the early sessions with a thumping headache.

The third time we met, Bob said he felt like 'a hibernating dormouse'. His mood was very different. On the advice of his general practitioner and community psychiatric nurse he was taking six weeks off work; he was experiencing the 'down' side of his illness. Despite this Bob wanted to carry on meeting. We agreed that this would be possible if we renegotiated our contract so that the objective became to support him in getting back to work as soon as he felt able. In this way the organization would still benefit – an important consideration for the overall project, and also a change that I needed to clear with my mentors' co-ordinator.

I am also trained as a psychotherapist and have a clinical practice. Because of this I was aware of the importance of maintaining boundaries between therapy and mentoring. In addition to the issue of his current depression, Bob was concerned about a specific family relationship. I was clear with Bob about the difference between mentoring and psychotherapy, and what could be inside or outside our contracted work. On this basis we carried on, and I offered to help him find a counsellor if he decided that that was option he wanted to pursue.

We agreed that if our work focused on helping him manage his symptoms day to day and perhaps, then this would be of benefit to the organization by enabling Bob to return to work as soon as he was recovered. In the end, he was off work for eight weeks – coinciding with sessions three to five. Inevitably we talked about Bob's illness and how he had learned to cope in the past. I gained a huge amount of respect for Bob. He had struggled by himself for years after becoming ill and losing his job as a plumber, with no medical support. He had not known what was wrong with him and became a devotee of self-help psychology books; everything from cognitive mind-mapping to psychosynthesis visualizations.

Once Bob returned to work our focus again shifted to his direct relationship with the organization and how he could be most effective. He decided to apply for a new job, which would give greater positional power from which to make some more modest but still significant changes, and ones that were more realistic to achieve for him and the organization.

I think what I did that was helpful in this relationship was to be flexible about recontracting the objectives when we needed to. For his part Bob was immensely open to change, had good self-awareness and was very honest about himself.

It could be said that we were diverse in several ways such gender, education and socioeconomic background. However, I have experienced depression personally, I have had first-hand knowledge of living with someone with bipolar disorder, I have clinical experience that was useful and I have extensive experience of working with volunteer and community organizations in the not for profit sector. I do not remember that we talked about our differences or similarities after the launch of the project.

The most difficult thing for me was Bob's capacity for non-stop talking. One of the other metaphors we used likened him to a helium-filled balloon; I stood on the ground hanging on to the end of his string and every so often when I thought he was losing sight of the ground, I reeled him in by drawing attention to the process. In his evaluation Bob particularly highlighted this as something he appreciated: 'being tolerant towards my tendency to digress and go off at a tangent'. Overall Bob scored the mentoring as nine out of ten in having been a useful and positive experience, and his suggestions for improving the project were to double either the length or the number of sessions. He identified four specific learning outcomes for himself:

- 'I have become aware of the need to balance my activities.'
- 'Improving myself and my skills is an ongoing process.'
- 'I am hoping to have counselling for personal problems.'
- 'I am learning to focus on my actual job in [X organization].'

The project, as a whole, was met with enthusiasm. The mentoring phase was undoubtedly the most popular with those assigned a mentor, with managers commenting that this was a unique and very valuable opportunity. Work is now under way to submit a second bid to the European Social Fund to roll out the project to a further group of mentees. One of the eventual aims is to train mangers from within the sector to be mentors for each, rather than to rely on importing external 'experts'. All the mentors thought this would be a significant step in building the capacity within sector in a way that developed self-reliance and respected the potential mentoring qualities of the managers involved.

Mentoring and the lesbian connection – USA

Jude A. Rathburn[5] and E. Holly Buttner[6]

Background of participants

Jude Rathburn is a forty-two year old, Caucasian, lesbian woman who was born in Green Bay, Wisconsin. She earned a Bachelor of Arts degree in Psychology from Marquette University and then moved to Tempe, Arizona, where she earned a Master of Counseling degree (1985), an MBA (1988) and a PhD in Business Administration (1995) from Arizona State University. From 1993 to 1998 she was an assistant professor in the Bryan School of Business and Economics at the University of North Carolina in Greensboro (UNCG). She is currently a full-time lecturer and 'Teaching and Learning Scholar' in the School of Business Administration at the University of Wisconsin – Milwaukee, where she teaches undergraduate and graduate courses in management. Her area of expertise is strategic management.

Holly Buttner is forty-seven years old, Caucasian and also a lesbian. She was born in Baltimore, Maryland. She has a Bachelor of Arts in Economics from Hollins College, an MBA from the University of Pennsylvania and a PhD in Business Administration from the University of North Carolina at Chapel Hill, which she earned in 1986. Holly was awarded tenure and promoted to Associate Professor in 1991 at UNCG, where she continues to teach graduate and undergraduate courses in management. Her area of expertise is entrepreneurship. She served as Search Committee Chair for her department as it recruited for a position in Business Policy and Strategy, the position for which Jude was hired in 1993.

Jude's perspective

In August 1992 I was ready to hit the road in search of a faculty position in strategic management. My journey began amid the glitz and glamour of Las Vegas, Nevada, where the annual meeting of the Academy of Management was being held. One afternoon, a colleague and I were walking through the placement area in the headquarters hotel and I saw a woman, dressed in a business suit, looking through the résumé book in the job placement area. She was obviously a member of a recruiting effort, but I did not recognize who she was. What I did sense, however, was that she was 'family,' our shorthand for one who is a member of the lesbian or gay community. I turned to my colleague and said, 'That woman is a lesbian and I want to find out who she is and what school she is from'. I walked closer and got a glimpse of her nametag – it read Holly Buttner from the UNCG. Needless to say my curiosity was peaked, but I did not have room in my schedule to request a meeting with her.

A few weeks after the Academy meeting I got a letter in the mail from the UNCG. The letter was signed by the chair of the recruiting committee, who just happened to be the lesbian I had seen at the meeting – Holly Buttner. I was intrigued by the possibility of working in an environment that had another lesbian on the faculty, so I responded with interest to her letter and sent supporting documents. In mid-November, while on an interview trip to another school, I retrieved a voicemail message from Holly indicating that UNCG was inviting me for an interview. At that point, I was pretty certain that she was a lesbian, but Holly had no idea about my sexual orientation – all she knew about me were my credentials. I accepted her invitation to visit Greensboro in January 1993.

I must admit that one of the concerns in the back of my mind as I visited other campuses, was 'how could I survive as a feminist lesbian in this environment?' It was very important for me to find a place where I could be myself and still fit into the academic community. At that time in my life, as a single, thirty-something woman, being able to connect with the lesbian community was a much more important criterion in my job search, than the academic reputation of the school or the presence of a doctoral programme. As a matter of fact I turned down offers from other universities, because I did not feel 'safe' being a lesbian in the halls of their business schools.

I did not officially meet Holly until late in the afternoon on the day of my campus interview. She attended the seminar on my dissertation research and then took me on a tour of the campus during which Holly 'came out' to me. I think we both 'knew' as soon as we saw each other, but I was glad that Holly took the risk and told me she was a lesbian. We spent the rest of the campus tour talking about the lesbian community and her willingness to help me make connections and develop a social network. I do not recall if any of our conversation focused on research interests or opportunities for collaboration – at the time, what seemed most important to me was the 'lesbian connection'.

During the course of the next few months, from February until I moved to North Carolina in early August, Holly and I had a few phone conversations, as well as a face-to-face visit in March. I was attending a conference in Atlanta and after it was over, I drove up to Greensboro to look for a place to live and get a general feel for the place. Holly arranged a dinner gathering at a local restaurant where she introduced me to her partner as well as a few of her lesbian friends. They were all very friendly and shared Holly's excitement about having another lesbian in the business school at UNCG. Holly and I also spent some time during that visit talking about our research interests and the possibility of working on a strategic management related project with another colleague. At that point, my expectations of our relationship began to shift to include a professional dimension, as well as the personal one. When I finally moved to Greensboro, Holly and her partner hosted a party to introduce me to more women in the community. They also invited me to join them for dinner every once in awhile, and did their best to help me make connections and build friendships. Most of the lesbian women who became my friends were those I met through Holly.

Holly was also an advocate for me within the department and helped me get to know the 'lie of the land'. Our department had a rather informal mentoring programme that matched up tenured faculty with non-tenured faculty and focused on teaching. As part of that programme Holly was assigned to observe my teaching at least once a semester. So some of our conversations centred on teaching strategies and what we tried to accomplish in the classroom. Her feedback on my teaching was always quite helpful, and I felt as though she supported me in my efforts to be the best teacher I could be.

Once I got to UNCG and felt somewhat settled in the community, I hoped that Holly and I would begin to work on a research project together. I had presented a number of papers at conferences, but I had not had any success in getting any of my work published. So, in some respects, I was counting on Holly to help me get established professionally. I wanted us to work on an article together and, at first, she seemed interested in doing that as well. However, our research interests were in completely different areas – she was doing work on women as entrepreneurs, and I was completing my dissertation on managerial cognition. We talked about a few potential projects when I was still new to UNCG, but nothing materialized.

In retrospect I realized that having a lesbian connection and being 'out' to a number of people within and outside the business school were the most important factors in my decision to accept the job. However that connection and sense of safety were not enough to help me succeed as a member of the business school faculty at UNCG. At this point in my career I feel it is much more essential to have colleagues who appreciate diversity and with whom I share a scholarly connection, than it is to work with other lesbians or gay men.

Holly's perspective

Early in Jude's campus visit, I recognized that she might be a lesbian. While I was 'out' to my department head and some of my colleagues and felt accepted, I was delighted at the possibility of having a lesbian colleague in a traditional, predominantly male business school environment. I decided that, while there was some risk, I would 'come out' to her as an opportunity to move our interview conversation to a potentially deeper level. Jude's credentials were very strong and the department faculty was very impressed with her self-presentation. At the end of her campus visit we made her an offer that she accepted.

One of my objectives was to help her get settled in her new location and role, since I knew that the transition might be more difficult than for a new heterosexual colleague. I liked Jude when I met her and also hoped to bring her into my community of friends. As I thought about Jude, I imagined what it would be like for me as a lesbian to be moving to a medium-sized southern city where I did not know anyone. I hoped to ease her integration into the lesbian community so that she would feel at home more quickly. I thought she would be more comfortable at work if she felt comfortable in the larger community. In addition, Jude came across as well trained and highly competent, and I did not think she needed to be told the 'tricks of the trade'. So, in a sense, rather than providing tools and techniques that could enhance Jude's job performance, I focused on the larger picture.

As Jude and I have talked about our mutual experiences, I have become aware of the importance of clarifying the dual roles I can play as mentor, in both the personal and professional domains. It would be helpful to discuss with future mentees which of these forms of mentoring could facilitate their growth and success most effectively.

Summary and conclusion

It has been very interesting to look back and reflect upon the evolution of our relationship over the past seven years. In Table 6.1 we have summarized some of our observations about our initial expectations of our relationship, actions that helped and hindered the relationship's development, individual outcomes and the lessons we each learned from this experience.

There are also a couple of bits of advice that we would offer others who may be in a similar situation. We both realize that it would have been helpful if we had talked openly about our professional roles and expectations of each other at the beginning of our relationship, especially in terms of research activities. While it is difficult to balance the social and professional demands of being a lesbian in a new environment, lesbian and gay mentors can play a pivotal role and assist in the transition from student to professor. Furthermore, acclimatization of new lesbian or gay employees may involve dimensions of integration that differ from heterosexual employees. It might be helpful for organizations to be aware that gay employees may have concerns that go beyond learning about job expectations, like how 'out' to be and how to manage the interface between personal and professional dimensions of their lives.

At some point in time in every work relationship, lesbian or gay employees wrestle with the decision to disclose our sexual orientation. In some cases coming out leads to all sorts of negative consequences, ranging from loss of support, to harassment and even termination. Regardless of how 'safe' the work environment appears, coming out can be very risky and anxiety provoking. Consequently, disclosure decisions often occur on a case-by-case basis after basic levels of trust and rapport have developed. Straight colleagues

Table 6.1 Expectations, actions, outcomes, and lessons learned

Expectations of the mentoring relationship	Actions that helped/hindered the relationship	Outcomes of the mentoring relationship	Lessons learned from the mentoring relationship
Jude expected:	**Helpful actions:**	**Outcomes for Jude:**	**Lessons Jude learned:**
Connections with lesbian community	Holly came out to Jude early in the campus visit	Friendship, collegiality	Responsible for her own success
Friendship, collegial relationship	Jude supported and encouraged Holly in her research/book	Support and encouragement	Did not need to agree or always see the world from the same perspective in order to be friends and care about each other's happiness
Collaboration on research	Discussions about being more authentic teachers	Opportunity to discuss the work environment with another lesbian	Having a lesbian connection was necessary, but not sufficient for her to succeed as a business professor
Shared feminist vision of life in the business school	Joint decision that our friendship was most important	Common bond as lesbians	Had to decide which came first – personal relationship or professional goals
Advocacy within department and school	Connections with other lesbians in the community	Support and encouragement is a two-way street	
Honest communication		Shared understanding of our experiences as women/lesbians	

Holly expected:	Not so helpful actions:	Outcomes for Holly:	Lessons Holly learned:
Assist Jude in developing research agenda	Did not talk explicitly about:	Friendship, collegiality	Need for greater clarity about what is most important – role at work as mentor or personal dimensions of relationship with a colleague
Help Jude get oriented in teaching her courses	Our respective roles and expectations, particularly about research activities;	Opportunity to discuss our work environment with another woman/lesbian	It is okay to have a mentee who chooses a different route from the one she took
Friendship, collegial relationship	What was helpful in the relationship;	Shared understanding of our experiences as women/ lesbians	Helpful to have a feminist female colleague who can be supportive/empathetic
Share knowledge about UNCG	How to make the relationship more helpful	Opportunity to derive satisfaction from bringing a new young colleague along in the business school	
Shared values about contributions of women and gays in the business school			

can ease the burden by offering support, encouragement and clear messages that all dimensions of diversity are valued. We also hope that this short case inspires other gays and lesbians to come out and support one another at work.

My experience as a mentor on the University of Hertfordshire's 'Women Entrepreneurs' course – UK

Sandra Lawes[7]

How it all began

'I would like a mentor who will understand the difficulties of juggling home and business. I have four children – the youngest are three years and sixteen months old.' My heart sank as I read these words. I am divorced, I live on my own and I have never had children. What on earth could I offer in these circumstances? Fortunately, I had the good sense to ignore this kneejerk reaction and the relationship that developed was productive and highly enjoyable for both parties.

It all began at the thirtieth birthday party of Women in Management, of which I have been a member for many years. I sat next to Dr Judith Carlson and I quickly learned that she was Course Director for the University of Hertford-shire's Women Entrepreneurs' course. This leads to the Postgraduate Certificate in Small Business Management and many of the students are eligible for funding by the European Social Fund. This fund aims to secure reintegration into the labour market for those who have been undertaking care and home responsibilities and to address under representation in the market.

During the evening, Dr Carlson invited me to become a mentor on the course and I readily agreed.

How mentor and mentee came together

Within days, I attended the mentoring evening at the university. First there was a professionally facilitated session on the principles and mechanics of mentoring. Then the potential mentors filled in and circulated a mentor information form detailing their background and skills, and later made a short presentation of the key aspects to the assembled mentees. The mentees had previously completed a mentor request form, giving information about their business idea, their objectives/needs and, most importantly, their proposed contribution to the relationship. The two-way, 'give and take' nature of the partnership was emphasized from the very beginning.

Throughout the evening the mentors and mentees circulated and talked, an excellent way to sum each other up and decide on an appropriate partner. We quickly realized that mentor and mentee could be diverse in many aspects, providing the personal chemistry and the ability to work together were present. This key truth was reinforced continuously as time passed.

During the evening, I met several talented women, whom I would have been pleased to mentor, but one in particular made a strong impression on me. I was struck by her energy, determination and self-effacing manner. I found it easy to think of ways I could help her to realize her business ambitions. Imagine my surprise when I discovered that this was Elaine, whose details I had read earlier with such a heavy heart, believing that we would have no common ground and that my experience would be of no use to her. Within a few days, I had confirmation that Elaine had requested me as her mentor.

Our diversity

And so our relationship began. Strangely, although there were many points of difference – age, family situation, life-stage, marital status, educational background and work experience – the relationship quickly focused on the points of common interest and the shared objectives, rather than exposing the diversity.

There were also positive aspects to our diversity. I have worked almost all of my life in marketing in blue chip organizations, holding senior roles and recently consolidating my experience with an MBA. I was able to use this to help Elaine with her study techniques, to focus on priorities and to introduce her to the concept of networking. This last was particularly beneficial in that it enabled her to increase her circle of contacts, identify people with whom she can discuss business issues, find business leads and achieve her objectives.

Getting started

We began the process by independently completing a 'Mentoring Contract', on a pro forma provided by the university. This deceptively simple document set out each party's needs, objectives, details of where and when contact would be made, and formalized the issue of confidentiality. When finalized, the document was signed by both parties and a copy lodged with the Course Director.

Elaine and I used this document as the basis for our first meeting. Wearing business dress, we met at the local Business Link premises, determined to put the relationship on a professional footing from the beginning. We are both self-employed, working from offices at home and we agreed that a meeting in either home would not set the right tone. Ease of access and parking were also considerations.

That first meeting lasted some three hours, during which we sketched our individual backgrounds, clarified objectives and identified short- and long-term goals. We were aware that this process could have thrown up too many problem areas for us to work together and we discussed the possible need to withdraw with dignity. Fortunately this was not the case and we completed the 'Mentoring Contract', setting formal action plans, with deadlines. We agreed the details of our next meeting. We made rules for how and when we could contact each other, to respect individual privacy.

It is largely due to the thought and commitment we invested in the early stages that the objectives remain as clear and as relevant now as they were at the beginning.

The rewards

These stark mechanics, while important, belie the underlying spark, the thrill we both experienced on finding that two people from such different starting points could get such satisfaction and *fun* from working together and making progress towards clear objectives.

When the relationship was delivering results, we both felt a positive, energizing effect, a real buzz of achievement that is all too rare in today's downsized, impersonal corporate environments.

Making it work

The keynote to our success, we both agree, has been our willingness and ability to be completely honest with each other and to establish mutual trust. This refers to objectives, methods, concerns and hopes. Honesty does not have to mean brutality or thoughtlessness, but involves integrity and the courage to say difficult things, albeit in an appropriate way.

We continued to meet, at designated times on neutral, business-related ground, usually the Business Link, over the formal period of the relationship. Between these milestones, we corresponded on an ad hoc basis by phone or e-mail. We found e-mail particularly useful, as urgency could be indicated and a reply sent in an appropriate timescale. Telephone contact was reserved for high spots and low spots, where an exceptional success or a serious problem needed immediate attention.

My contributions as the mentor

I believe that my main contributions as mentor were (and Elaine has confirmed this):

- to introduce her to the concept and skills of co-operative networking (a two-way, semi-focused process of skilled listening and connecting people with others who may be able to assist/inform them)
- to give her access to my extensive network of contacts – something I do not do lightly as my own reputation depends on the calibre of the person I introduce
- to continue to ask probing, open-ended questions such as 'Why?', 'Why do you say that?', 'Is that what you really want?', 'Is that taking you where you want to go?', 'How do you feel about that?' until Elaine (not I) was happy with the answers
- to help Elaine to prioritize issues and reach the right answer from *her* point of view

- to focus her on the right actions in the right sequence to achieve her priorities
- to draw on my thirty years of experience of work in identifying issues and options for Elaine to consider.

Although I had initial concerns that my lack of knowledge of family life could cause problems, these proved unfounded. Elaine has these aspects of her life well organized and we simply added issues such as child care or her husband's new job into the 'mix' of matters to be considered and prioritized. I am not aware of anything I did or said that hindered the relationship. Elaine has confirmed this and (with our rules of honesty) I believe her!

Elaine's contributions as the mentee

As a mentee, Elaine's contributions included her application to the tasks and her energy, coping with a combination of demanding assignments, projects, builders extending her house and other family demands. She was willing to listen to my input and to make the effort necessary to build on her natural skills and develop her potential. She was proactive both in managing the mentoring relationship and in pursuing business objectives and the demanding requirements of her course.

Circumstances that hindered the mentoring process

Elaine did nothing to hinder the relationship but we were both affected by difficult circumstances completely outside her control. First, her husband succeeded in gaining promotion to a demanding new role in his company, requiring her support and understanding. Second, the major house extension, with builders virtually in residence over a period of months, proved a distraction. Finally and most tragically, just at the point of launching the business, Elaine's sister-in-law was fatally injured in a motorbike accident and, after spending some time in a coma, she died, leaving four young children to be cared for. Naturally, priorities had to be reassessed and plans redrawn. The methods we had established proved reliable and we applied objective reasoning to the mass of tasks and emotions raised by this awful event. I believe this helped Elaine to draw on inner strength and use her new-found confidence to deal with the many practical and emotional issues that beset her. I could only stand in the background, offering support, but she showed immense courage throughout. She also managed to adjust her plans to take account of the unforeseen situation without losing sight of her ultimate goals.

What did the mentee gain?

Looking back over the official stages of the mentoring, I can see that Elaine has achieved a clear view of her real objectives and the options open to her. She has built a firm foundation for her business venture, blending the learning from the course with sound practical experience and face-to-face market research. She has learned new skills including networking, which will benefit her for the rest of her life. Most importantly, she has grown in confidence – not an unrealistic arrogance but a true reflection of her skills, knowledge and personal characteristics, which greatly increases her chances of success.

And the mentor?

As a mentor, I have had the chance to formalize the techniques I used when managing staff in my own departments. I have gained confidence in my own skills and learned to value my contribution appropriately. I have new insights into business relationships and I have also improved my IT skills, thanks to Elaine's patient and common-sense approach. I also gained immense personal satisfaction from seeing Elaine make progress and use some of the ideas and suggestions I put forward, knowing that she was going where she wanted to go. Although we started out as mentor and mentee, we have now developed a special sort of rapport/friendship – focused on business, but respectful of personal issues.

Some words of wisdom

To anyone thinking of embarking on such a mentoring exercise, I would say this:

● Invest time setting up the relationship. It will bear fruit later.
● Set out the objectives of each party *in writing and in full.*
● Be totally honest with each other at all times but not in a harsh way. Be respectful of the other's dignity but also of his or her need and right to hear the truth.
● Review progress, objectives and issues regularly to make sure you are on track.
● Do not be put off if you are diverse in your circumstances and approach. Agreement on direction and respect for each other are far more important.
● The more you put into the relationship, the more you will get out of it. Mentoring is a unique opportunity to work with another human being and achieve something really worthwhile.

Intergroup diversity dynamics and mentoring – USA

Cliff Cheng[8]

I am a Chinese-American mentor writing about a formal mentoring relationship I had with an Asian-Indian American mentee. The mentoring relationship was sponsored by the Asian-Pacific Islander Support Group (APSG) (alumni/ae group) and administered by the Asian-Pacific-American Student

Services Department (APASS) of the University of Southern California's (USC), in Los Angeles, USA. I am an alumni of USC and have held teaching and research appointments at USC off and on over the years. I am also a consultant on diversity issues and an expert witness in discrimination cases. In my practice, I often recommend mentoring as an intervention. To preserve privacy, I have changed, and in some cases merged, names and identifying information in this case.

The mentoring programme collects information on incoming Asian-Pacific Islander American (APIA) undergraduate students and contacts them to see if they wish to participate. A key criterion for me in the selection of my protégé was that the protégé have a sincere interest in helping our (APIA) people. Evidence of this might be volunteer work within the community-based organizations in the APIA, or stating an intention to help our people gain the knowledge, skills, and abilities they need in college.

Suresh was my first mentee in the programme and the one I had the longest relationship with (three years). We met when he was a sophomore in my department; he sought me out after hearing about my Organizational Behavior course. Given his interest, I signed him up for our mentoring programme and became his mentor.

Suresh is an Asian-Indian American who was born in the USA. He spoke no language other than English, and knows little of his heritage culture. I am Chinese, born in Taiwan and living in America. I am of a refugee family, which fled the mainland of China to escape the communists. English is my second language (Chinese being the first). In terms of diversity, we are both able-bodied men, and I am ten years older than Suresh. I am a heterosexual. Though I do not recall sexual orientation specifically coming up in our conversations, I know that Suresh dated women. Neither one of us belongs to an organized religion.

We are both regarded by the dominant group in the USA as 'Asians'. This classification is actually 'pan-ethnic', in that the dominant group has forced us into this one group despite very significant differences in race, nationality, ethnicity and religion. In Asia these differences cause great divisiveness, and historically have led to hate crimes, civil wars, genocide and national wars.

The term 'pan-ethnic group' means two or more groups who regard themselves as distinct and autonomous, despite the fact that they are categorized by the dominant group, usually against their sovereignty, into one larger group. For example, there are subgroups within the broad APIA pan-ethnic groups who see themselves as 'Indians', and view themselves as having no similarity with the 'Chinese'. In fact, some subgroup members think if they accept a pan-ethnic identity such as APIA, they will lose their heritage culture. However, many APIAs realize that one can be *both* an APIA and a member of one's heritage group. Initially in APIA history some decried being lumped into one category. What later emerged was to turn the social circumstance of pan-ethnicity into an advantage. Only if the subgroups unite as one pan-ethnic group and work with other groups who have been discriminated against in America can these groups ever hope to gain equality.

Suresh is a member of the 'Asian-Indian American' subgroup. Having grown up in a small town in which there were few APIAs (none his age) and no other Asian-Indian Americans, Suresh did not have an APIA identity. He did have a 'racial uniform' of skin which is darker and height that is shorter than the 'standard' set by the dominant Euro-American group.

Suresh had a form of an 'Indian' self-identity, but it was in reference to what he was not, rather than what he was. His identity was not in reference to his heritage culture in India, or the APIA movement. All Suresh knew was he was not 'white'. 'Not white' as an identity is disorienting for it is negative and does not tell one who one is. Suresh knew his family and his friends but not his ancestors and co-ethnics. His experience in being an Asian-Indian American was gleaned through personal relationships rather than as a member of a collective.

Oddly enough, I knew more about Suresh's heritage culture than he did since I have studied the sacred texts of India, associated with Indians, and I am now living in an Indian-, Brazilian-, Arab-, Latin-American, immigrant and working-class Los Angeles neighbourhood, where I eat Indian food daily and have been practising and teaching yoga for a decade. As an example, when we went to an Indian restaurant I often frequent, they spoke Hindi to him and looked to him to take the order. He 'looked like' he 'fitted in' but did not have the culture and identity that reflected his racial uniform. He would have liked it if race did not matter, but the social reality is that it does.

A key incident that happened during our mentoring relationship was the Los Angeles Rebellion, a civil disturbance that occurred after the innocent verdicts of the four white police officers who were videotaped beating an unarmed black motorist. This event occurred around our campus. Suresh was trapped on campus in the dormitories during the street violence. I could not call him because the phone was cut off, and I could not bring him back to my home due to armed bands wandering that part of Los Angeles. Suresh saw on television that down the road from campus Korean-American merchants were being looted and burned out by African-Americans because of intergroup conflict. Suresh started to appreciate that the group one is categorized in has vast implications on one's life; he learned from live television that you can get killed if you have the wrong colour at the wrong place at the wrong time.

In terms of other diversity differences, I was not aware of any age issues between us. I think Suresh did things he liked to do with his age peers. To him, I may have represented a different way of being and a set of possibilities. I do not think age was a factor but being a faculty member was an issue initially. It took Suresh most of our first year to become comfortable calling me 'Cliff' rather than 'Dr or Professor Cheng.' It took a while but we gradually became friends.

A key diversity factor was the fact that we both are biological males. Suresh grew up in a single-parent household, where there was an absence of male role models in his life. The conventional idea is that a young man needs an older man to 'teach him how to be a *man*' – which usually means to be a provider and protector. I have no interest in reproducing that patriarchal sex role with Suresh or anyone else. He did not look explicitly to me as a male role model. I would not have accepted this role for, whenever possible, I actively reject and educate others about the oppressiveness of conventional sex and gender roles (Cheng, 1996; 1997; 1999). This level of diversity work involves developing individuation and authenticity rather than assuming conventional sex-gender and cultural roles.

Suresh was curious about the personal growth work I was doing at the time in the men's movement (a social movement in which men work to break out of their restrictive traditional hegemonically masculine sex and gender roles). We talked a lot about this. I tried to show him a path of authenticity made possible by respect, equality and compassion for yourself, others, especially women and those different from us (and nature). Unfortunately, we never did find a time that he could go with me to a men's group meeting, and he was not able to take advantage of the scholarship I had arranged for him to attend a men's workshop.

In the end, while I did not get to mentor the APIA community leader I had wanted, I am not disappointed in Suresh. The relationship made me re-examine my expectations to see if they were reasonable. To gain perspective, I looked around at other APIAs in this age group. In my community work I do occasionally see people as young as Suresh, but these young people are rare to find. They tend to have a different background than Suresh. Specifically, they tend to be from families that have a strong ethnic, if not pan-ethnic, APIA identity, and are themselves active in APIA community institutions. Suresh did not have this. What I think I did for Suresh was to expose him to and get him to start thinking about the importance of one's racial-ethnic-national group membership. I also helped him think through his values in relationships and what he hopes to accomplish in these relationships. More tangibly, I helped Suresh get an Asian-Pacific Islander Support Group scholarship, the same one I was awarded as a PhD student.

I hope one of the major things we accomplished in our mentoring relationship was to help him understand that he is categorized as an APIA whether he likes it or not. Another insight I hope he gained was that working within our APIAs community to improve our conditions is both practical and necessary. At the same time, I stressed that he has tremendous freedom to explore and live his life as an individual.

I lost contact with Suresh. He stopped returning my telephone calls in his last semester before graduating. Maybe he was overwhelmed with graduating, going to law school and moving. He e-mailed me from law school a few times but when I replied, he never e-mailed back. I would have liked to know what became of him. There was no formal closure to our relationship, other than my saying a prayer for him on the day of his graduation. Suresh, wherever you are, bless you. Cliff.

Mentoring through major career transition – UK

Glynis Rankin[9]

> We may not really have personal stories about the future, or at least if
> we do have them, they may be very fragmented. We may rely on a few
> ideals from our family, and from the media or our friends, but no one
> has given life to it. Our stories about the future tend to be materialistic,
> not about what will bring a real sense of fulfilment. We have not
> performed them or listened to them, so you could say that our stories
> about the future are repressed, which may be why people have an
> attraction to Creative Futures. It is filling a void that would not be there
> if we already talked about our futures in a different way. (Extract from
> a description of Creative Futures by a participant)

This case study looks at one participant in a process of career transition, written
from my own point of view as her mentor. It raises some important issues
about diversity, in both an international and a local context. The specific
approach to career transition, called Career Futures is one which people cannot
use without training. Yet the specific ways of working used here can be of
value in any mentoring context.

Creative Futures is a process designed for use in mentoring, when people
reach a transitional point in their life, or their career. It provides a context,
within which the participant can stand outside the whole of their life, if they
chose to do so – their working life and their personal life – to evaluate their
direction and to find a new way forward. It is typically used in times of career
crisis, when issues of work–life balance become overwhelming, or when
people are facing issues that fundamentally challenge the way in which they
are living their lives. Organizations use this approach to provide a positive
context within which individuals can resolve issues, freeing them to make a
greater contribution to the organization in the future.

The mentoring context

Several years ago, I was asked, as an external consultant, to evaluate the
potential of a group of senior executives in a UK-based business of a large
multinational. The chief executive (CE) intended to retire in the next three to
five years and wanted to ensure that there were potential successors, and that
these successors were given appropriate opportunities to develop. There was
one woman in the group of fifteen people that I was asked to see. All the
candidates were white and British, and all except one had spent most of their
working career within the organization.

Of this group, I identified four individuals who had the capability that the
organization needed in the CE role. Jane, the only female candidate, was one of

these four. The issues raised by my work had caused Jane to think deeply about her own future. After we had completed the initial diagnostic work, she asked me to work through the Creative Futures process with her.

Jane had spent all her working life in the same organization, and had always been on the fast track. However, unlike the other three potential candidates for the CE role, she had not developed the business experience that would be required to fulfil the role successfully. Although she been deputy to several senior positions, she had not run one of the smaller businesses, or played a high profile operational role in a larger business. These roles would have given her full exposure to a leadership role, full profit and loss accountability, and the opportunity to demonstrate that she could handle the complexities of a CE role in the future.

My contract with the organization was through the HR director, who was quite clear that he saw placing Jane in a business managing director (MD) role as a risk. When I asked about the nature of this risk, he found it hard to articulate. His reasons were given in terms of behaviours rather than concrete knowledge, skills and experience. His initial comments, 'We could give her a business I suppose, and see whether she sinks or swims', were more reflective of the culture of the organization, than of his own genuinely supportive stance. There was no culture of mentoring in the organization. Indeed to need a mentor, was often seen as a sign of weakness. However, the organization was committed to helping Jane come to the right career decision, and was prepared to finance the ongoing work involved.

Working with Jane

In the initiation of the mentoring relationship, there was a commitment on my own part to work with a person who, I felt, had enormous unrecognized potential, at a pivotal point in her career. Jane's objective for the mentoring relationship was clear – she wanted to make a decision about the 'next step' in her career, to catch up with her male colleagues who had not had career breaks to have children.

When we started working together Jane described herself as having a 'complete lack of insight' about her future at this point. The organization had changed so that 'it's values and direction are no longer clear', and the part of the business in which she was working was 'laddish, very sexist, rude and aggressive'. Part of her difficulty in thinking about her own future lay in not being able to see herself in this culture, and in her own view that the business decisions that the organization was making were fundamentally flawed.

The first part of the Creative Futures process looks at the past, present and future, as the person concerned sees it at that moment in time. The focus here was very much on Jane's current decision. When she began to talk about the future, this too was in terms of the decision – to stay where she was 'doing a job that most people would die for', or to move on, either within the organization or outside it. It was only as she broadened out her thinking about her longer-term future, thinking about the wider context of her family, her personal life and her leisure interests, that she began to take a different perspective. We used creative ways to look at what was important for her, her values, the contribution that she wanted to make and her personal interests. Through taking this broader perspective, the issue that we were discussing changed.

At the beginning of our third meeting, Jane made this clear:

> I am seeing the whole situation differently now. I started out by thinking about what job to take next, whether to move on and which role to aim for. I now see that this is really a matter of the rest of my career. Do I actually want to go for the top job in an organization like this, with all that that entails? Do I want to make the sacrifices that I would have to make to get there?

One of the issues for Jane was that of her own personal style, in relation to that which was predominant in her working environment. She was renowned for building effective relationships both within the organization and externally. She sat on boards and made a substantial contribution to the community outside her work. Yet, she was seen as 'somehow different', by her senior colleagues. This issue had come up in appraisal, but it had never been really clear what the issue was. As she talked, she came to the view that she had a very different style from that of her male colleagues. The organizational style was very formal. Meetings were often 'a farce' from her point of view. She went in prepared for an open discussion about issues that were vital to the future of the organization. 'These problems are not simple, they require all of us to work them through, to thrash out the issues, for the good of the organization', she said. Time after time though, the meeting was 'stitched up from the start'. The key decisions had been made behind the scenes. Jane was renowned for raising difficult issues.

Jane realized that she formed co-operative rather than competitive relationships, building networks of strong powerful allies because she was trusted. In some instances her honesty and openness were rejected by her colleagues – she was seen as 'naïve' at best, at worst foolish, particularly when she appeared to act against her personal interests, in the interests of the organization. Others, she felt, both envied and resented the style that she used so naturally and easily, on the whole to great effect.

It was these insights that were, for Jane pivotal in thinking about her own position. Having stepped back, through the mentoring relationship, to look at her situation from a future perspective, she saw the underlying issues, the relevant contexts, and the opportunities in a new way. She realized why she had felt uncomfortable about her own career progression. She could now think more clearly, about the strategies that she would adopt, if she wanted to go further. She also explored what she would look for if she did move on, and recognized her loyalty to the organization that she had worked with for so long.

This process gave me a broader perspective, not just about work but about the whole context of my life – and the tools to continue to address these issues in the future. It is as though we are living life without understanding what is pulling the strings. We make decisions based on a few surface issues or problems without seeing what the real issues are – what will make us happy in the longer term, and what contribution we can make.

Jane did not make any final decisions about her future career within the process itself. However she did take on a senior role several months later, heading up a major business, having negotiated the support that she would need from the company, including senior level mentoring, in order to do this successfully.

My own learning in this relationship

Jane's own sensitive exploration of the issues deepened my understanding about what it means to operate as a person who is somehow seen as 'different' within a dominant culture – and what is needed, on a personal and an organizational level, to address those issues.

I was also involved in discussions about the development, career progression and promotion of the group of individuals concerned. During these conversations, my awareness of the subtle interpretations, the shades of meaning that can be given to behaviours, comments and, often trivial, events, that together constitute a person as suitable or not suitable for a senior role, substantially increased. These comments were often subtly gender related in some way, but gender was not the only issue. In the wider group that I worked with, there were men, who, in our model, had the potential to take on some of the most senior roles, but who had not been given development opportunities. Their style was different. They were seen as 'not political' or as acting against the party line. The organizational bias was not recognized, in part at least, because these individuals were very different from one another. The common thread was not clear. Once the bias was highlighted, people began to see the choices that they were making, and to make decisions about development and promotion on quite different grounds.

The approach to mentoring

There are some ways of working within the Creative Futures process that were particularly helpful in this context, and which I have found to be invaluable in working with people from many different nationalities and backgrounds in many different countries.

First, there is the need for a clear contract about the purpose of the work, and the nature of the confidentiality involved. Setting this agreement creates the boundaries of trust, within which the relationship can develop. I am also clear about the style that we adopt within this process, which is facilitative and non-directive. This transparency about the process enables the mentee to make an informed decision about whether this is the right approach for them or not.

Second, the process provides a very particular context within which to work. The role of the mentor or practitioner is to provide a listening for the individual which is completely non-judgemental, and which does not evaluate or comment on their interpretations. Rather, it seeks to draw those interpretations out further, using open questioning. In this way, the individual can open up their own thinking, and explore their own issues, in their own way. The views and opinions of the mentor are not relevant in this process. The role of the mentor is rather to provide a context, in a highly skilled way. This affirms the mentee's confidence in his or her own judgement. It is after all, their own solutions about their own lives that they are developing. No framework or model is used to interpret what they say, and it is this lack of framework that leaves them free to create new perceptions and new ways forward.

The neutrality of this approach makes it valuable in working with diversity, and the issues of marginalization, that people experience in many working contexts. The process fundamentally affirms people *as they are*. It is this fundamental acceptance, independent of a person's background or the issues that they are addressing, that creates its power.

To refer back to the quotation at the beginning of this study, we, as a culture, may not create coherent stories about our future. When people are marginalized, it is often the case, that their stories about their past, or their present, are denied validity. It is their very diversity that leaves these stories unshared and untold, or misunderstood. The organizational environment and culture, may limit what is acceptable, and play its own part in the fragmentation of people's experience. Mentoring has a great deal to offer, in listening to and validating people as they are, in accepting their diversity and working with them to find a way to bring their unique contribution into the world.

> Once we have created these more coherent stories about the future – about the way in which we would like it to be, our stories about the past change too. We see ourselves in a different light, and as we can only process so much information at once, we start to filter in information that supports the story and makes it become possible. We find ways of making it work – even though at first it seemed impossible – and from where we were when we started we could not have thought about it at all. (Continuation of the quotation at the commencement of this case study)

Lloyds TSB plc – UK

The mentee's tale

This relationship was established in November 1999. The mentee is a senior manager (a woman) within the bank's commercial division, which deals with the mid-corporate market. The role encompasses direct responsibility for a portfolio of customers, assisted by a small team. The team is profit based, responsible for budgets and targets. The mentor is a managing director (a man) in a different but related division within the bank.

The organization has developed an agenda based around diversity and the mentoring programme formulated to support this objective. There is obvious diversity in the gender between the mentor and the mentee but this was more out of necessity than design. There are very few women within the bank who possess the necessary commercial experience to understand the current role and have the breadth of knowledge of the organization, an element also identified by the mentee as an objective.

The 'pairing' was arranged by the head of the mentoring programme who was aware of the mentee's desire to have access to somebody who could relate directly to the current role, but still offer this wider perspective.

The objectives identified by the mentee in seeking the relationship in the first instance included obtaining help in recognizing and realizing potential. A perceived lack of confidence by the mentee is in her opinion hindering her development in a new role, and support in this area was a prime driver. Access to confidential coaching and a better understanding of the organization and the opportunities available within it are also identified.

These objectives were identified in a short paper written by the mentee at the outset of the relationship, along with a brief review of what, from the mentee's perspective, is involved in the mentoring process.

What the mentor is seeking from the relationship has not actually been verbalized although it appears to the mentee to include helping an individual unlock his or her potential which at the same time will benefit the organization.

This relationship has, at the time of writing, been running for less than twelve months. To date the mentoring has revolved around the coaching element. The mentee views herself as particularly fortunate that the mentor has an in-depth knowledge of the new role that the mentee has recently taken up, indeed he was instrumental in the design of that role. This has proved invaluable when seeking guidance and reassurance. It is envisaged that over time this role will evolve and the emphasis will move away from the technical aspects of the job into the other areas identified.

Meetings are normally held in rather formal surroundings, the date and time dictated by the mentor's availability in London as he is normally based in Bristol. Demands on his time are extensive and meetings are prone to be rescheduled at short notice; however, this is viewed as a small price to pay by the mentee. Meetings are currently running at about one every four months, which is in line with expectations.

Contact between meetings has been limited, although a situation has not to date arisen where the mentee has felt the need to seek advice between meetings. This in part is attributed to the very supportive role of the mentee's line manager. There would, however, be no qualms about making that approach if it was deemed necessary. Certain tasks are set which are to be completed before the next meeting, and this helps retains the focus.

The mentor has helped significantly in refocusing on the current role, providing advice on how certain elements should be tackled. More importantly the mentor has focused on confidence-related issues which at one level impact on the day-to-day job but the influence spreads much wider. Issues such as risk-taking have been touched upon and the intention is that this element should be explored further.

To date the biggest benefit identified by the mentee is that, through joining the mentoring scheme, a mechanism is in place to keep objectives in focus. It is easy to write an action plan after being enthused on a training course, but it also easy for this plan to go to the bottom of the 'in tray'. A lack of discipline can mean that the actions are not followed through and much of the benefit is lost. The mentoring relationship is ongoing and therefore has the advantage that, as the identified objectives will be reviewed at the next meeting, they are kept at the top of the agenda in the interim. It adds to the discipline to complete identified tasks and keep reviewing the process. Ironically it is when things are going well that there is the greatest danger that reviewing objectives can be ignored, as they are no longer seen to be as necessary. This is viewed as a mistake because when the next problem arises and things are not going well is when a retained focus would pay dividends.

This relationship has been going for nine months and three meetings and certainly from the mentees' perspective feels as though it is still developing. This is more a reflection of the time in the relationship and of the personalities rather than any element related to diversity, i.e. gender. The enthusiasm of the mentor certainly can be said to inspire, but also can be a little intimidating. Goals are clearer, confidence is building and the whole experience is viewed as positive.

The nature of the relationship has over the time it has been running changed, but in ways that are to be expected, i.e. it has become more comfortable. It is, however, a little early for pivotal points to emerge other than an increase in self-esteem and an exposure to enthusiasm which can be infectious.

The mentee now acknowledges that she is learning that the mentoring relationship is about more than an hour a month. It is about putting identified objectives into action and reviewing progress on an ongoing relationship.

To anybody starting a mentoring relationship the mentee's message is to go in with an open mind. It is important to have some idea of the objectives with which mentoring can assist, but this is different from having preconceived ideas about the actual relationship, which will be unique. There should be no fear about going off at a tangent as mentoring is about the whole person not just the job.

In this case the mentee is now also a mentor and recognizes that it is important not to underestimate the value that mentor feels in fulfilling this side of the relationship.

Notes

1 Brian Welle is an advanced doctoral student in the Industrial/Organizational Psychology program at New York University. His research, which focuses on bias in organizational decision making, reflects his dual interests in stereotyping and organizational justice. He has presented the results of his work at a number of conferences including the Academy of Management and the Society for Industrial and Organizational Psychology. In addition to his academic work, he is a senior research associate at a national not-for-profit organization where he studies the experiences of women and minorities in business.

2 Christine Bennetts works as a Lecturer in Lifelong Learning at the University of Exeter's School of Education. Her MEd and PhD research inquiries were undertaken at the University of Sheffield, and explored the nature and structure of the traditional mentor relationship and its subsequent meaning in the lives of learners. She has given papers at national, European and international mentoring conferences, and maintains a keen interest in learning relationships.

3 Belinda Johnson White is an Assistant Professor of Business and Associate Director of the Leadership Center at Morehouse College. She created and designed the first course in leadership for the business programme at Morehouse College and is currently working to develop a leadership studies minor for the college. Her research interests lie in the area of leadership studies, international youth leadership development, mentoring and cultural diversity. Belinda earned Georgia State University College of Education departmental honours for her dissertation, 'A descriptive study into factors of the first job choice of African American male undergraduate business students at Morehouse College'.

4 Wendy Rose works in several different ways concerned with individual, group and organizational development, all within the broad description of helping people with change. Her main qualifications are in psychotherapy and an MSc in facilitating change in organizations. She blends these two together in her current work as a management and leadership development consultant. In her coaching practice she uses a combination of tools and models drawn from psychology, business, stress management and personal development. According to the situation and the client this might include, for example, the use of psychometric instruments, visualizations, drawing, dreams, cognitive re-framing, or 360° appraisals.

5 Jude A. Rathbun, PhD, is a Teaching and Learning Scholar and Lecturer in Management at the University of Wisconsin-Milwaukee. At the under-graduate level, she teaches an introductory business course as well as

strategic management, international business, and organizational behaviour. She also developed, and currently teaches, a graduate course in management, operations and marketing. Her research interests include mentoring, the role of managerial cognition in organizational success, and the impact of technology on learning. She earned masters degrees in counselling and business administration and her doctorate in business administration from Arizona State University.

6 E. Holly Buttner, PhD, is a Professor of Business Administration at the University of North Carolina at Greensboro. She teaches organizational behavior, business policy and strategy, and managerial assessment in UNCG's undergraduate and MBA programmes. Her research interests include female entrepreneurs' career issues, managerial assessment and development and the business school course review process. She is co-author of *Women Entrepreneurs: Moving Beyond the Glass Ceiling* and has published articles in the *Journal of Business Venturing, Sex Roles, Journal of Management Education, Journal of Business Ethics, Journal of Small Business Management* and other scholarly journals.

7 Sandra Lawes runs the consultancy, Marketing on Tap, which specializes in health-care related businesses. Originally a languages graduate from Manchester University, Sandra's marketing career spans three decades, during which she held senior roles in companies such as Thomas Cook, Smith and Nephew, and McCarthy and Stone. She was Director of Marketing in BMI Healthcare, a leading operator of private hospitals and was later headhunted into BUPA to work with the Hospital and Care Home divisions. She has also lectured on marketing and advertising. Sandra has an MBA from Henley Management College, where she specialized in strategic marketing and the study of customer satisfaction. She also holds the Postgraduate Diploma in Marketing and the award of Chartered Marketer from the Chartered Institute of Marketing.

8 Cliff Cheng, PhD, USC; Postdoc, UCLA, has a research program, based at the University of Southern California, that includes diversity, discrimination, and Asian Pacific Americans (APA) which has resulted in over 130 publications, papers and presentations in journals such as *Academy of Management Review, Leadership and Organizational Development, Journal of Management Inquiry* and *Journal of Organizational Change Management*. He applies the knowledge of his field to act as consultant, trainer and expert witness in discrimination cases. Cliff is also highly involved in applying the knowledge of his field to help the APA community, and a coalition of women's and minority groups which work to prevent hate crime.

9 Glynis Rankin is Director of Creative Futures, a consultancy that works in individual and organizational development. Glynis's recent work has involved advising a global charity on organizational structures, and individual development needs, to support its work in Central and Eastern Europe. She has also delivered a pilot project to evaluate succession management systems for an international organization that wishes to create equality of access for staff around the world to senior managerial roles. Prior

to setting up Creative Futures, Glynis was Executive Director of the Institute for Financial Education and Training at the University of Wales, Bangor. She is a Certified Member of the Institute of Management Consultants, an Associate Member of the Chartered Institute of Personnel and Development and a Member of the Institute of Directors. She is also an Associate of the Brunel Institute for Organization and Social Studies.

References

Bennetts, C. (1994). Mentors, mirrors and reflective practitioners' an inquiry into informal mentor/learner relationships. M.Ed. dissertation, DACE Library, University of Sheffield.

Cheng, C. (1997). Diversity at heart: guts, soul, and diversity teaching. In *Teaching Diversity, Listening to the Soul, Speaking from the Heart: Educators Talk about the Joys and Complexities of the Work*. (J. V. Gallos and V. J. Ramsey, eds), Jossey-Bass.

Cheng, C. (ed.) (1996). *Masculinities in Organizations*. Sage Series on Research on Men and Masculinity, 9, Sage.

Cheng, C. (ed.) (1999). Masculinities from margin to center: studies on gender, status, and representation. *Journal of Men's Studies*, **7**(3), special issue, spring.

7

Some further reflections by the mentor

Anne Stockdale

What is diversity? Is it working with anyone different from myself? When I think back about mentoring clients during the last two years I can see that I must, then, have worked with a lot of diversity – or have I? I wonder why I have not given this subject much real thought until learning about this book? Oh dear what have I been missing?

I am a self-employed consultant specializing in individual development carried out, one to one, in a variety of settings. I am white, female, English born, brought up near London. An analysis of my socioeconomic background would no doubt classify me as middle class and I suppose I am middle-aged (although I think I prefer 'middle-youth'). I am relatively fit and healthy physically and mentally, have had a high standard of education, and most of my needs are met.

If I take as a working definition of diversity people who are different from me (or me from them), then I have been working with diversity over the last couple of years. For example I have worked with clients:

- who had mental illness
- who was a permanent wheelchair-user
- who were a different gender
- who were a different nationality or colour (French-Algerian, Estonian, Czech, Polish, Canadian, Syrian, German, Dutch, Malaysian, Mexican, etc.)
- who had a very different career path from mine (senior and middle managers in global commercial organizations), where much of my background is in the cultural heritage, not-for-profit sector.

I have also worked with people with diametrically different personalities. Supposing I take, for example, the Myers Briggs Type Indicator (MBTI) as a well-known and well-understood way of describing personality difference. My preferences tend to be for Introversion, Intuition, Feeling, Perception (INFP) while it is usual for many of my clients to have preferences for Extraversion, Sensing, Thinking, Judging (ESTJ). This is a deep and fundamentally different way of being in and experiencing the world, as much (I would suggest) as gender, special needs or colour.

I am surprised when I list these many examples of my mentee and I being different. In which of these situations of difference have I been most aware of diversity? In reflecting on this I seem to have come up with more questions than answers for myself.

I wonder if some differences are more 'different' than others? Or maybe there is a critical mass of 'differences'. As a mentor, there are various 'aspects' of me; my background, nationality, language, personality, education, gender, etc. There are also 'layers' of me; the physical, mental, emotional and spiritual. How many of these need to be different from those of the mentee before I am aware of diversity – over and above the sense I have of difference, simply because the other is a separate being from me?

We all have differences; I am unique. I am also the same as others in many ways. Do we talk about working with sameness? Seen in this way, diversity is in-built and, given the number of aspects and layers we all have, there may be more ways in which I am unlike a mentee than like them. Am I like them because I have one aspect that is similar to one of theirs? Am I unlike them because I have one thing that is different? The differences with some mentees are the same aspects that are commonalities with others. Of course, this seems obvious to me now I have thought about it – quite a revelation in fact.

What about mentoring with sameness? What might this say about my assumptions about being 'the same as' a mentee. My experience of the world can never be the same as a mentee's, regardless of the extent to which we are alike in these aspects that define sameness or difference. My hypothesis is that some aspects are more important than others – and that this will vary from person to person.

One of my poorest evaluations came from a mentee who, it seemed, had many aspects that were similar to mine; colour, family and educational background, language, age and there were similarities in our MBTI types. After receiving the feedback I was shocked. What I realized was that I had looked at the similarities and been lazy, I had made assumptions that we would get on and that the work we did would be good. I learned from this that I cannot assume that sameness will create a bond from which creative and satisfying work results. On that occasion it did not.

If I am too much 'the same' as the other I may fail to see their lives with objectivity and ask naïve questions. We may together, if we recognize a certain level of sameness in each other, work within shared unconscious biases of 'being in the world' that are then not challenged by either of us, like fish being the last to notice the water.

However, if I am too different I may have difficulty 'walking in their shoes' and understanding their world sufficiently to make useful interventions. This links back to my thought that some differences are more 'different' or have more impact than others. One recent mentee was a wheelchair-user and often seemed to be in pain. Apart from this, we were very much 'the same' in most other aspects that I can think of. I noticed, at the time, that I was less challenging (for example, when he had not achieved something he had undertaken to do). In this instance I was aware of difference affecting the way in which I worked; I held back. This was reflected in his evaluation in which he wished that I had been firmer.

For me language can also create a feeling of difference – I feel separate from the other if we are not able to communicate fluently and deeply. I really struggled with a Mexican mentee. His English was infinitely better than my Spanish but, for me, the relationship was inhibited. So this is another step forward in my learning about diversity. Is this the point where diversity becomes a difficulty – if it inhibits the relationship?

I can notice a difference in the quality of my work if I am unable to make a connection with the other, or if the connection is a weak one. And yet, as I noted with 'sameness', when I was not mindful this also resulted in a weak connection – although I was not aware at the time. Perhaps mindfulness is the key; being mindful to differences and to similarities and not making assumptions about either.

I sit here thinking of examples: 'Oh yes, the connection with X was not strong, it must have been because this aspect of difference was present.' And yet almost at once I think of another situation where the same difference was present, and yet the connection was good, our work was effective and the feedback from the mentee was very positive. On checking back, some of my best work, according to mentees' evaluations, has been where there has been most diversity between us.

How do I make sense of this? I do not think I do at the moment, but I am now thinking about diversity in way that I have not before. Thank you for prompting it.

Anne Stockdale, an advocate of learning for over twenty years, is delighted to see the heightened national focus on learning for all. She takes an active role in Learning Partnerships and Learning and Skills Councils, as a strategic partner on workforce development and providing the link with the Chartered Institute of Personnel and Development where she chairs the North Yorkshire Branch. Anne's consultancy work takes her into complex organizations such as NHS Trusts, government departments and high growth plcs – she enjoys facilitating change through keen listening and joint resolution approaches.

8

Differences that make a difference: common themes in the individual case studies of diversified mentoring relationships

Belle Rose Ragins

The individual cases provide some interesting qualitative insights into dynamics that are unique to diversified mentoring relationships. While these cases certainly do not represent all diversified relationships, they do represent an interesting cross-section of diversified mentoring relationships. In particular, these cases came from both sides of the Atlantic Ocean, represent both formal and informal relationships, and were discussed from the mentor's and protégé's perspectives. The mentoring relationships were also quite diverse: pairs represented minority status relating to race, gender, sexual orientation, disability, nationality and socioeconomic class. Some of the relationships represent classic diversified mentoring relationships (i.e. Belinda and John's pairing as an African-American female protégée and a white male mentor), while other relationships involve members who share a common identity but struggled with diversity issues stemming from that identity (i.e. Holly and Jude's pairing as a white lesbian mentor and a white lesbian protégée).

What do these cases tell us about developing effective diversified mentoring relationships? In this chapter, I identify six themes underlying these individual cases. There were also some interesting interrelated aspects of these cases that have implications for both practitioners and academics. These themes and aspects are useful for practitioners interested in promoting effective diversified mentoring relationships, and may also fuel the development of future theory and research on diversified mentoring relationships.

Theme 1: Sharing values and discovering deep diversity

One of the most salient themes that emerged from these cases was the importance of shared values in the establishment of diversified mentoring relationships. Shared values are important in all types of mentoring relationships, but they are crucial in diversified relationships.

A good example of this can be found in Belinda and John's case. Belinda, an African-American woman, initially was apprehensive of entering a formal mentoring relationship with John, her white male mentor. Belinda did not believe that a white male mentor could understand the issues that she faced as an African-American woman, and she doubted that he could or would provide for her developmental needs. In essence, she questioned both his ability and motivation as a mentor. In spite of these issues and obstacles, this mentoring relationship emerged as one of the most effective relationships presented in this book. A key process that made this relationship effective was the pair's discovery of their similarities in values and background. On the surface, the mentor and protégé had little in common. Some mentoring relationships may end at this point, but Belinda and John's relationship moved from an acknowledgement of the limitations of surface diversity to an understanding of a deeper-level diversity. Belinda's description of the process by which the relationship evolved illustrates that mutual trust and commitment were instrumental in overcoming their initial reservations and moving their relationship to a more effective level. Belinda observed that both members were genuine in their approach to the relationship, and were open to discussing the effects of race and gender on their relationship and their lives. Belinda was able to trust John because he really listened and encouraged her, and because he did not shy away from discussing racism and sexism. As a white male, discussing race and gender may have made John vulnerable to 'stepping in it', but this vulnerability increased her trust in him and the ultimate cohesiveness of the relationship.

In contrast to Belinda and John, Cliff and Suresh shared group memberships related to both their race and gender. What makes this comparison particularly striking is that while Cliff and his protégé Suresh shared demographic group memberships, they differed significantly on the values relating to these memberships, and this difference appeared to cause friction and frustration in the relationship. An objective observer would view Cliff and Suresh as having an automatic advantage in their relationship over Belinda and John, since Cliff and Suresh were both Asian men. However, while Cliff and Suresh were both Asian, they differed on the values they ascribed to their identities and the way their identities shaped their lives, daily experiences and expectations of the mentoring relationship. Cliff observed that Suresh viewed his identity in terms of being what he was not (white) rather than what he was (Asian-Indian). As a Chinese-American, Cliff noted that he might have known more about Suresh's East Indian culture than Suresh, implying that Suresh had become assimilated and lost his cultural roots. Cliff was keenly aware of the differences in nationality and culture in India and China, and rejected the practice of grouping all Asians into one global pan-ethnic group. Preserving his specific cultural roots was clearly an important value to Cliff, and Cliff expressed some frustration with his attempts to get Suresh to understand and value his own specific cultural identity. Cliff wanted his protégé to become a community leader and diversity activist, but Suresh did not share these expectations or values. Consequentially, the relationship did not meet Cliff's needs or expectations, and it eventually drifted apart without a real sense of closure or accomplishment. This case emphasizes the importance of shared values in diversified mentoring relationships, and also leads to some interesting insights about expectations in diversified mentoring relationships.

Theme 2: Inflated expectations in minority relationships

While the Cliff and Suresh case illustrates the importance of shared values, it also raises another issue that may be unique to mentoring relationships involving mentors and protégés who are in the minority in organizations (i.e. gender, race, ethnicity, sexual orientation). Cliff may have expected Suresh to share his values because of the fact that they were both Asian and ostensibly shared the same social identity. As an extension of social identity theory, members of minority relationships may assume that because of their shared group memberships, their partners may also have similar backgrounds, experiences and values. This expectation of shared values and perspectives may not be conscious or explicit, and may not even be articulated or recognized until the relationship is well under way.

This perspective suggests that minority members of mentoring relationships may have different and perhaps greater expectations of their minority as compared to majority partners. There are two components of this 'inflated expectation hypothesis', reflecting inflated expectations of proteges' and mentors' performance. First, minority mentors may be more likely to expect a 'cloning' type of relationship from a minority than a majority protégé. Minority mentors may unconsciously expect that because of their shared group membership, their protégés have the same needs as them and should develop in the same way. In addition to this transference process, minority mentors may also expect more appreciation and receptivity from minority proteges because of the extra burden the mentor faces in being a minority and mentoring others. The mentor may also expect more appreciation because of the lack of availability of other minority mentors to fill this role, and because the mentor may not have received the mentoring they needed when they were young. In short, while minority mentors recognize the importance of their role, it may represent a burden and may evoke internal conflict if that they are asked to give something that they themselves needed but did not receive as a young adult. The minority mentor may also expect the protégé to learn from his or her 'mistakes' and may therefore try to protect the protégé from important learning lessons. In sum, while 'cloning' and transference are potential problems in any homogeneous mentoring relationship, these problems may become amplified in homogeneous relationships involving minority members.

The second component of the 'inflated expectation hypothesis' relates to the expectations of the mentor's performance. Minority protégés may expect minority mentors to provide more role-modelling, counselling and empathy than majority mentors. They may also be more likely to expect their minority mentors to go out on a limb for them, and provide special protection and buffering, even though the minority mentor may not have the resources or power to provide these functions. In a broader sense, minority mentors may be expected, either explicitly or implicitly, to 'give back' to their own group, irrespective of the mentor's resources, abilities or constraints. From an organizational perspective, minority managers are regularly expected to mentor younger minority employees, even if the minority protégé is not in the same demographic group as the mentor. Mentoring is often implicitly viewed as part of the minority manager's job, and therefore may not be recognized or rewarded in the organization. In contrast, for majority managers mentoring may be viewed as extra-role behaviour that reflects organizational citizenship, and majority mentors may therefore receive extra recognition for these behaviours because they are not viewed as part of their jobs. The mentoring stakes may also be greater for minority than majority mentors. Minority mentors may be more likely to be held accountable for the failure of their protégés; the failure of a minority protégé is often viewed as a direct shortcoming of the minority mentor's ability, and this failure is amplified by the increased visibility of the minority relationship. In essence, compared to their majority counterparts, minority mentors may face greater risks but receive fewer organizational rewards for mentoring minority protégés.

In sum, both minority proteges and others in the organization may have different and greater expectations of minority than majority mentors. Future research can test the hypotheses that:

1 Minority managers are more likely to be expected to be mentors than majority managers.
2 Mentoring is viewed as an extra-role activity for majority mentors and a required role activity for minority mentors.

From a practical perspective, this suggests that it is important for human resource management professionals to recognize mentoring behaviours in performance appraisals and reviews, and to be aware of the multiple and conflicting demands that are often faced by minority managers in organizations.

Another nuance of this 'inflated expectation hypothesis' can be found in Jude and Holly's mentoring case. Jude, a white lesbian, selected Holly as her mentor because they shared the same sexual orientation. While this 'lesbian connection' was necessary, it was not sufficient for meeting Jude's mentoring needs. As discussed later in this chapter, Jude needed to have the social support and acceptance that could be provided by a lesbian mentor, but Jude also needed help with her career as a researcher. Holly was able to provide the psychosocial support that Jude needed, but did not share the common research interests necessary to help Jude's career. Jude was somewhat disappointed by this relationship, and both she and her mentor later observed that they should have been more explicit about their expectations at the very start of their relationship. However, what they did not discuss or perhaps even recognize is that the diversity in the relationship may have affected their initial expectations. Did Jude expect more from Holly because they shared minority status in their sexual orientation and gender? To complicate this issue, Jude's expectations of her relationship with Holly may have been affected by her lack of other developmental relationships. Most of Jude's colleagues were male and heterosexual, and may not have been willing to mentor Jude or assist her career because of her gender and sexual orientation. Would she have been more satisfied in her relationship with Holly if she had some of her needs met by other mentors? In essence, minority protégés may not only have different expectations for minority, as compared to majority mentors, but minority proteges may also have different and greater developmental needs that are not easily met in other developmental relationships. From a practical perspective, it may be important for human resource management professionals to help minority protégés recognize their needs and expectations, and help these protégés recognize that they may need to develop multiple mentoring relationships with both minority and majority mentors in order to meet their diverse needs.

It would also be interesting to assess the type or combinations of minority group memberships that elicit inflated expectations in minority mentoring relationships. For example, are there different expectations associated with minority mentoring relationships involving sexual orientation as compared to race or gender? A key factor here may be the composition of the work group or organization. For example, a female protégé working in an all-female work group may have more realistic expectations of her female mentor, and different work-related needs, than a female protégé working in a male-dominated work environment. From a research perspective, it would be interesting to assess what types of expectations are held by minority mentors and protégés entering minority as compared to majority mentoring relationships. Perhaps a mentoring relationship involving a majority member is more satisfying because the expectations are lower or simply different than a relationship involving two minority members. However, as discussed below, mentoring relationships involving majority mentors and minority protégés face a unique set of challenges.

Theme 3: Empathy and insights

A key factor determining the effectiveness of relationships involving majority mentors and minority protégés is whether the mentor understands or at least empathizes with the experience of the protégé. This theme emerged in three of the cases. A key challenge faced in Wendy and Bob's relationship was the mentor's ability to deal with her protégé's disability of bipolar disorder. Wendy's personal experience living with someone who had bipolar disorder was instrumental in her ability to understand the challenges faced by her protégé. Wendy even shared her own experiences of depression, and perhaps used that experience as a way to further understand and empathize with her protégé's disability. Of course Wendy's background as a therapist provided her with important listening and empathy skills that were useful in that relationship.

Another example of the importance of empathy in diversified mentoring relationships emerged in John and Belinda's case. As discussed earlier, the white male mentor, John, did not have the experience of being an African-American woman, but he tried his best to understand and empathize with that experience. His protégée, Belinda, observed that he was sensitized to the effects of racism and sexism, and that he was a 'champion for the underdog'. Belinda observed that John's empathy and insights were key factors in the effectiveness of their diversified mentoring relationship.

Instead of ignoring or denying the challenges faced by their minority protégés, both of these majority mentors met the diversity issues in the relationship head on. We again find that truth and honesty in the relationship are critical for the establishment of empathy, and that in turn empathy further develops the trust and closeness in the relationship.

In contrast, Bob and Fiona's relationship suffered from the fact that the mentor did not recognize or understand the gender-related barriers faced by his female protégée. These barriers interfered with Fiona's performance as a protégée and, eventually, the mentoring relationship. In particular, the mentor, Bob, was unaware of the jealous and destructive reactions of Fiona's co-workers. Her co-workers perceived Bob and Fiona's relationship as intimate and sexual in nature. While the relationship was not sexual, the emotional intensity of the relationship, coupled with its heightened visibility due to its cross-gender composition, made their relationship susceptible to discrediting rumours and sabotage. It seemed that Bob lacked the ability to empathize or understand the gendered office politics faced by his protégée, and Fiona ended up leaving the organization as a partial consequence of his lack of awareness.

From a practical perspective, these cases point to the importance of communication skills and diversity training. Majority mentors need to have some idea about the organizational realities faced by their minority protégés, as well as the key cultural issues and challenges faced by minority groups in their organization and society. From a research perspective, we need to know more about the factors that facilitate empathy and diversity insights among majority mentors. For example, while we know that prior experiences in mentoring relationships are an important predictor for future mentoring relationships, we need to assess whether prior experiences in diversified relationships heightens member's empathy, sensitivity and motivation to develop future diversified relationships.

Theme 4: Meeting the needs of minority protégés

As alluded to earlier, the mentor's ability to provide for the unique needs of the minority protégé is a theme that was central to many of these cases. This theme is crystallized in the two cases involving gay protégés. Brian and Jude explicitly recognized the direct effects of their sexual orientation on their career needs and the development of their mentoring relationships. They both recognized that they did not want to hide their sexual orientation from their co-workers or mentors, and that they needed the special support that can be provided by a gay mentor. Having a gay mentor not only allowed them to share a critical aspect of their social identity with their mentor, but also gave them information on how to manage their sexual identity at work. As a gay mentor, Holly furnished social emotional support and introduced Jude to the local gay community. Holly recognized that Jude needed to have support not only at work, but also in her new residence. Jude noted that being able to be out at work was not only central in her job search, but was even more important in her job search than the prestige of the organization or the resources associated with the position. Similarly, Brian's choice of organizations and mentors were also related to his sexual orientation. Brian observed that similarity in sexual orientation was a major factor in the development of his mentoring relationship. For him, finding a gay mentor not only helped him develop strategies for managing his sexual identity at work, but also gave him support in a heterosexual workplace. In addition, he knew that his sexual orientation would not be an issue in a relationship with a gay mentor. This reflects the fact that many gay protégés are uncomfortable coming out to heterosexual mentors, and that many heterosexual mentors are not comfortable with having a gay protégé. It was also interesting that the fact that Brian's relationship was cross-gender was not particularly salient to him. One reason for this may be that the sexual issues involved in cross- and same-gender relationships are diametrically opposed in gay and heterosexual mentoring relationships. In addition, having a mentor who shares the experience of being male may simply not be as important to a gay male protégé as having a mentor who shares the experience of being gay. An interesting twist in this case is that although Brian worked in a women's advocacy organization and was a minority on the basis of his gender at work, having a heterosexual male mentor may not have met his needs as much as having a lesbian female mentor.

A hypothesis that can be gleaned from this discussion is that identification in mentoring relationships will be optimized when parties share stigmatized social identities. In other words, the greater the stigmatization of the protégé's social identity, the greater the role-modelling involved with having a mentor who shares that social identity. As these cases illustrate, the role-modelling and psychosocial needs of Brian and Jude related more to their sexual orientation than their other social identities. This may reflect the fact that their social isolation at work was centred on their sexual orientation, and that they needed more support and role-modelling in that life arena. One important implication of this perspective is that the organizational context affects minority protégé's needs in the mentoring relationship. For example, Brian may not have been as adamant on his choice of a gay mentor if he worked with primarily gay co-workers in a gay advocacy organization.

A review of the other cases underscores the idea that the unique needs of minority protégés may be more easily recognized and met by minority than majority mentors. For example, as a mentor Elaine recognized that her protégée Sandra had great potential but needed specific help in developing her self-confidence and networking skills. Similarly, in the same-gender relation-ship involving Glynis and Jane, Glynis recognized how the climate of the male-dominated organization devalued her female protégée, and was therefore able to help Jane cope with these issues and recognize the value of her contributions in the organization.

While minority mentors may more easily assess the special needs of minority protégés, majority mentors may bring a fresh and independent perspective to the relationship. The case involving John, the white male mentor, and Belinda, the African-American female protégée illustrates this point. Belinda observed that John helped her work through her anger related to racism and sexism in a way that provided unexpected growth and learning. Perhaps because John did not have the personal experience of being the target of racism and sexism, he was able to provide an objective perspective and did not project his own experiences, anger or history on her experiences or the relationship. In particular, Belinda noted that John helped her explore her deepest feelings regarding racism and sexism, without letting his own feelings and experiences interfere with her processing of the events. He helped her get to the other side of her anger and then helped her recognize that her strength and character were a result of these hardships and experiences. She observes that this provided her with major and unexpected growth in the mentoring relation-ship. A minority mentor may have understood Belinda's experiences more fully, but may also have had a more difficult time maintaining the emotional distance necessary to help Belinda process those experiences. As discussed earlier, a key factor underlying the success in this particular relationship was John's communication skills, interpersonal skills and self-insights. While majority mentors may face greater barriers to helping minority protégés with psychosocial issues than minority mentors, if they are truly skilled mentors, they may be able to offer unique and incredibly valuable insights in the relationship. Along similar lines, in order to increase their effectiveness, minority mentors may need to understand and work through their own issues and personal experiences with racism, sexism, heterosexism and other forms of discrimination. Future research could assess the experiences, skills and backgrounds associated with highly effective majority and minority mentors in diverse mentoring relationships.

Theme 5: Understanding the organizational context

Another key theme of effective diversified mentoring relationships was the mentor's ability to understand the effects of the organization on the protégé's performance. This theme incorporates the previously discussed theme of empathy and insights, but also moves beyond these skills to a broader understanding of the political reality faced by minorities in organizations.

The case that most clearly illustrates this theme involved Glynis and her protégée Jane. It was clear that Glynis gained an excellent understanding of the gender-related dynamics that Jane faced in her male-dominated organization. Jane worked in an organization that did not provide her with the experiences needed for advancement, and in fact viewed her advancement as a 'risk' that would be approached as a 'sink or swim' venture. Glynis observed that Jane's organizational culture was 'laddish, very sexist, rude and aggressive', and that politically aggressive and self-serving behaviours were valued in the organization. Glynis recognized that Jane's style of developing collaborative and honest work relationships was devalued in her organization, and that her practice of putting the organization's needs before her own personal needs was viewed as naïve, and ridiculed by some of her colleagues. Glynis helped Jane both recognize and value her differences, and gave her insight into how these differences were instrumental to the organization. In particular, she helped Jane recognize the importance of her development of collaborative work relationships that were both internal and external to the organization, and the value of her honest and forthright approach to these relationships. Glynis then helped Jane assess the gendered outcomes associated with her differences, as well as Jane's personal values underlying her behaviours. This clarified the trade-offs involved for various career choices and future action. A key conflict faced by many minority members is whether to give up their personal style and assimilate to the dominant organizational culture, or whether to maintain their style at the cost of continued isolation and devaluation. Glynis did not ignore the organizational realities faced by Jane, nor did she press Jane into assimilating into the dominant organizational culture. In fact, as part of a broader organizational development initiative, Glynis tried to help the organization change its culture and the way it deals with differences. The case had a happy ending, in that Jane moved into a senior role and gained the support necessary to succeed in her new position. Her mentor was able to help her understand the processes underlying key career decisions: whether to stay or leave an organization, whether to assimilate or maintain one's individual and social identity, and how to deal with a workplace that did not accept diversity.

The outcome of this case would have been markedly different had Glynis not recognized the organizational constraints and barriers faced by Jane on a daily basis. This may be a common problem, as many mentors may deny that differential treatment exists in their organization because such an admission would undermine their belief in a just and fair organizational world. In this alternate scenario, Jane would not have received the insights and support necessary to cope with her situation. Of greater importance is that a mentor's dismissal of her organizational reality may have eroded her self-confidence and led her to question her perceptions, judgement and competence.

Understanding the organizational context is a critical skill for mentors, but protégés may also develop this skill. In a sense, minority protégés may be at an advantage over majority protégés as they already recognize that organizations have multiple 'micro' climates, and that the climate for members of the majority is often different than the climate faced by minority members. An example of a protégé's recognition of differences in organizational context is found in the case of Brian and Rachel. As a gay male, Brian's strategy for managing his sexual identity at work was to be out to everyone in the workplace. However, he recognized that the organizational environment he faced as a gay male was different than the environment faced by his lesbian mentor, even though they worked in the same predominantly female organization. While Brian disclosed his sexual orientation early in his employment and received very little negativity from co-workers, Rachel waited almost two years before sharing her sexual orientation with her female colleagues, and her disclosure was met with subtle hostility. Brian showed a sense of awareness of environmental differences in that he recognized that the negative response to Rachel's disclosure of her sexual orientation was at least partly due to the fact that the women she worked with would be more threatened working with a lesbian than a gay male. Brian was able to use his insights about their work environment to help his mentor manage her sexual orientation in their workplace, and this reciprocity is discussed in the next section.

Theme 6: Reciprocity in the relationship

A final theme that was present in effective diversified mentoring relationships was the degree of reciprocity in the relationship. Effective diversified relationships were mutually beneficial to both mentors and protégés. Most mentoring relationships provide benefits for the mentor, but the benefits involved for mentors in diverse relationships may be different than the benefits obtained in other types of mentoring relationships.

For example, in the case of Belinda and John, Belinda noted that by sharing her experiences as an African-American woman, she was able to broaden John's awareness and his understanding of diversity issues, cultural differences and the minority experience. It was particularly revealing to note that John himself recognized and valued this benefit; which was aligned with his personal commitment to increasing his understanding and sensitivity to diversity issues in general.

Increased insights into diversity issues in organizations were also found in same-gender mentoring relationships. For example, Glynis observed that her protégée Jane's exploration of the issues deepened her understanding about what it means to be different in an organizational culture, and increased her awareness of what is needed to meet those challenges and change an organizational culture. This underscores the basic idea that although mentors may share the same demographic or social identity group status as their protégé, it does not necessarily mean that they share the same life experiences.

Cases involving minority mentors and protégés also revealed unique benefits for the minority mentor. Holly noted that her protégée, Jude, provided important social support as both a lesbian and a woman. As a lesbian in a primarily heterosexual and male workplace, Holly was very isolated, and a benefit she received from having a gay protégée was reduced isolation and increased support. Holly also identified some of the more typical benefits received by mentors, such as friendship and gaining a sense of satisfaction from helping a younger colleague. Nevertheless, Holly's minority status in her organization created a unique set of needs in her mentoring relationship that were met by her protégée.

Similar reciprocity was found in Brian and Rachel's relationship. As discussed earlier, Rachel had a more difficult time disclosing her sexual orientation in the workplace than her protégé, Brian. Brian noted that he helped Rachel manage her sexual identity at work by sharing his strategies of disclosure and by being a sounding board for her decisions. This is indeed a unique relationship that provides unique benefits and outcomes to its recipients.

Most of the research and theory on benefits accrued from mentoring relationships has focused on homogeneous relationships involving majority members. We know little about the unique benefits obtained by minority mentors with minority and majority protégés. Since no two mentoring relationships are alike, and mentoring relationships are derived to meet the specific needs of their members, it is reasonable to expect that diversified mentoring relationships have distinct processes and needs. The cases presented in this book give us some preliminary insights into some of these processes, but it is clear that more empirical research is needed in this area.

Conclusion

In conclusion, while diversity is a part of organizational life, we have not given it the attention it deserves when considering mentoring relationships. Diversified mentoring relationships share many of the same features as homogenous relationships involving majority members, but there are unique differences in diversified relationships that reflect the background, values, needs and organizational realities of its members. The cases discussed in this book provide a good starting point for understanding some of these unique processes, but they also represent just the tip of the diversity iceberg. We hope that the qualitative insights provided by these cases will stimulate future research and provide a foundation for sound organizational practice.

9
Organizational case studies

Diversity by accident: London Borough of Ealing

Marianne Ecker[1]

When the London Borough of Ealing launched its pilot mentoring scheme in 1999, it was not particularly focusing on any racial or gender group, although it has a wide mix of backgrounds among its 7500 staff. It simply wanted to establish twelve mentoring pairs, from whose experience it could learn how best to spread the approach more widely within the authority. In the event, all the applicants to be mentees were women, primarily from clerical areas, while the mentors were both men and women from various departments and ethnic origins.

Like most boroughs in the UK, Ealing deals with a spread of community responsibilities ranging from housing and education to parks and street cleaning. Some of these activities are managed directly by the borough; others are contracted out.

Launching the scheme

The pilot was managed by a team of three people, an operational manager and two people from corporate development and training, with the backing of senior managers. They launched the scheme with a poster campaign and articles in the staff newspaper, asking people to put themselves forward to be either mentors or mentees (or both). The benefits promoted to mentees were that they would have a flexible development opportunity to discuss career and personal development choices in a confidential and supportive environment. For mentors, the intended benefits related to being able to hone their developmental skills out of the normal working routine. The programme was linked directly to a policy that aims to give every employee at least twenty hours of development each year – mentoring was positioned as a practical means of delivering development to people.

To apply for the scheme, mentees had to complete a detailed application form that explored their motivations for wanting a mentor, their career ambitions and progress so far, and what other training and development they had been through. They were also asked to carry out a strengths, weaknesses, opportunities and threats (SWOT) analysis on themselves and their careers and to indicate any preferences for gender or race of their mentor. Finally, their application was accompanied by a supporting statement by their line manager.

Mentors were also given a questionnaire and asked to do a similar SWOT analysis of themselves. The questionnaire explored in particular whether they could provide sufficient time to build and sustain the mentoring relationship, how they would review progress and what benefits they saw arising from the programme. They were also asked about their own history of training and development.

To ensure that the programme design had the support of actual and potential participants, the co-ordinators ran a number of focus groups to explore issues such as confidentiality, matching and the respective roles and responsibilities of mentors and line managers.

Out of these discussions and advice based on experience in mentoring programmes in other organizations, a number of practical guidelines emerged. Relationships would last formally for twelve months, although they could continue informally thereafter. Meetings would meet once a month, with each meeting and its preparation taking about three hours in all.

Matching mentors and mentees

The matching process took into account people's wishes about race and gender, and about where they might like to work in the future (i.e. by providing a mentor with current knowledge or experience of that area). Some effort was also made to ensure that people's working styles were compatible. Some very senior potential mentors were turned down for the pilot on the grounds that there were too many hierarchical layers between them and the mentees – a maximum of three layers became the ground rule. However, most of these were offered the opportunity to participate in another programme of mentoring across local authorities.

Training

Both mentors and mentees attended one-day courses that explored the nature of mentoring and how to get the most out of their relationships. Line managers were also offered a half-day workshop to educate them in how to align their role with that of the mentor and to reassure them about the intent of the programme.

Evaluating the pilot

At the midpoint (July 2000) mentors and mentees were invited to discuss in group meetings how their relationships were progressing. All the mentors remained with the borough, although some relationships have ended because the mentee has left. Only one of the twelve relationships failed to get off the ground – the mentor was not actively available. Three other relationships had ended for more positive reasons; two people had obtained promotions to posts in other authorities and one was on maternity leave. However, all twelve participated in the review process, either in the group or through a one-to-one interview.

Mentors reported a good deal of satisfaction with the relationship and the speed with which the mentee was able to establish a clear sense of direction and personal objectives for career and personal development. The clearer the mentee was about their needs, the easier and more enjoyable the mentor found the sessions. Mentors found that the discussions with mentees caused them to reflect upon and review their own career position, and to review how they deal with their own direct reports. They also reported that the programme had helped reinforce their development skills in general and had added to their knowledge of other areas of the authority.

Mentees also felt positive about the meetings, with several reporting increased self-confidence to pitch for greater responsibility or for higher education opportunities. (This was identified at the beginning of the pilot as a key measure of success.) They found the mentors especially useful in making links and networking. Some mentors had suggested practical tasks for the mentee to attempt between meetings.

Problems surfaced during the review centred around those relationships where the mentee had not been able to define sufficiently closely what they wanted to achieve, or had been unable to break big, vague objectives into manageable steps. Some pairs had experienced minor problems in the relationship between line manager and mentor (for example, when it became apparent that one mentor and line manager were very close). The main lessons to come from the review process, however, were:

- the need for continuing support for both mentor and mentee. Mentors, in particular, can benefit from regular (two or three times a year) 'supervision' in the form of a group discussion of experiences, facilitated by an (external) expert

- the value of using current participants' experience to publicize mentoring more widely. (Ealing intends to start the next tranche of mentoring with a social event that brings the pilot volunteers together with people, who are interested in taking part in the future.)
- the possibility of using mentoring to support specific issues, such as National Vocational Qualifications.

Mentoring up at Procter & Gamble – USA

Reproduced by permission of Procter & Gamble

Introduction

Procter & Gamble's (P & G's) mentoring scheme within its marketing division aims to retain and advance female managers within the company. The scheme was initiated as part of the Advancement of Women Taskforce (AWTF) in response to a disproportionate lack of retention and advancement of female managers in the early 1990s.

Background

The stimulus for the project was a 'regretted loss' survey that P & G carried out in the early 1990s. The survey results showed that promising young female managers were not leaving for typical reasons, such as promotion and better pay, but because they were not feeling valued in their job.

> While a prime assignment, promotion or pay increase translates to men as a sign that the organization values their work, the same rewards don't always convey the same message to female managers. They want to be explicitly told of their value, to hear their contributions verbally acknowledged, to have their career options openly discussed

says Kristen Nostrand, a marketing director within P & G, who has had the responsibility of overseeing the mentoring up programme (Zielinski, 2000).

Mentoring up was developed as a tool to help educate upper management to these gender differences, thereby better meeting the needs of women. It gave them another opportunity to mix with the management and increase the amount of cross-gender communication taking place. This, in turn raised the ability of top mangers, both male and female (senior female managers are also given the opportunity to participate in the mentoring up scheme as mentees) to improve their personal skills in managing against issues specific to junior female managers.

While there was a traditional mentoring scheme in place in the marketing function to help *all* junior managers understand how to perform to gain promotion and also provide a degree of sponsorship, it was not designed or conducive to addressing gender differences. Arguably this course of action indirectly suggested that any 'problems' were with the women themselves rather than the organization and culture they worked within, which the regretted loss survey showed was not the case. Procter & Gamble enlisted the help of the AWTF to help develop a suitable mentoring scheme.

The AWTF is an enabling organization committed to understanding issues facing female managers and developing programmes to address these issues, thereby helping to improve the satisfaction, retention and advancement of women in US advertising. Because the loss of top performers is especially acute among women, our efforts will focus on them. However, we expect that most programmes will also be effective among men, and we will take that into consideration as we deploy programmes. We will track results against goals and will share successes for global reapplication.

The AWTF was founded in 1991 as the Retention of Women Taskforce (RTWF). It was subsequently reorganized in 1994 to facilitate greater line management involvement and ensure that all other business sectors, not just advertising were represented. After significant successes and progress in terms of retention, the focus was shifted in 1996–9 to encompass the advancement of women as well – Hence the *Advancement* of Women Taskforce. The taskforce has also developed links with the Minority Development Taskforce to facilitate strong cross-fertilization of learning and co-ordination of programmes. It is from this vast and varied experience base that P & G's 'Mentor Up' scheme was developed.

There are four main areas of action outlined by an AWTF programme:

- the creation of an environment in which all individuals can work to their full potential
- the improvement of advancement and retention results among minority women
- the improvement of recruiting efforts to bring talented women into an organization
- the creation of strong networking programmes to ensure connectedness within an organization.

The mentoring up programme at P & G was used to help the company take action upon these areas.

Mentoring Up

Mentoring Up's objectives were to:

- provide male managers with informal non-threatening feedback on how to manage issues specific to women
- provide male managers with a sounding board
- allow junior women to develop quality relationships with senior management.

Programme leadership

In order for the scheme to be a success it was important that leadership and steering should be sought from all the most effective areas. The senior managers agreed to provide support and drive the programme following an executive committee presentation, and the sponsorship from the AWTF was an excellent resource of know-how, experience and guidance. It was agreed that the programme should be executed on a sector basis and led by a line manager, ideally teamed with an HR manager. The overall programme is co-ordinated by a Mentor-Up Steering Team, which meets bi-monthly to discuss progress, issues, and improvements.

Establishing mentor pairs

Potential mentors were selected from the ranks of female junior and middle management. Mentees were selected from upper management. In the first instance participation was voluntary, but now all eligible male senior-level and female junior-level managers are expected to take part. The women are usually one to two management levels beneath their mentee. The mentors are expected to have a minimum of one year's good performance prior to starting in a mentoring relationship.

Great care was taken to ensure that the mentors and mentees were paired to create as successful relationships as possible and to steer clear of pairing a mentee with a mentor who has to report directly to him or her (Zielinski, 2000). A questionnaire was fielded to all participants to discover which pairings might prove to be the most compatible in terms of expectations, personality, and experience. There was also some extra input from Mentor Up programme administrators. It was decided that Mentor Up pairs should be monitored and changed if the relationships were not proving successful.

Characteristics of a good mentor

The definition of a Mentor Up mentor that P&G works with is as follows:

> A woman manager who acts as a trusted counsellor, sounding board, advisor, and teacher on women, workplace and life/balance issues to a more senior manager (man or woman) . . . They must understand the programme and be willing to take some risk in the role they play as mentors to senior management. They should represent the diversity of women in the organization.

The mentor is expected to provide a safe, non-threatening relationship in which the mentee can ask sensitive questions and candidly seek a thorough understanding of all pertinent issues. She should share her personal experiences in order to illustrate the issues that affect women and fully bring to life the implications from a female perspective. She should offer her own opinions freely, and make suggestions on new behaviour approaches.

She should not, however, divulge specific names or examples of women with issues. Nor should she offer solutions and opinions to every issue or provide the sole source of feedback to the mentee. It is important that although they offer as much information and perspective as possible they do not become solely accountable for the mentee's behaviour and growth in this area.

The characteristics of a good Mentor Up mentor, then, are the ability to create a trusting relationship with the mentee – in terms of the validation of the information that they give and the confidentiality of the information that flows both ways. The mentor must also be willing to spend as much time as is necessary to get their own points across and, perhaps more importantly, to listen to what the mentee has to say.

Characteristics of a good mentee

The mentee is expected to use the relationship to gain as much as possible from the experiences and perspective of the mentor. The mentee should proactively seek the mentor's feedback and to use the mentor to explore personal attitudes and behaviours. It is important that the mentor's input is seen to be valued and, so, listening and question asking is important to build confidence within the relationship. Sensitivity is a necessity, but it must not get in the way of asking pertinent questions, or challenging assumptions.

It is vital that the mentee does not participate in the programme unless he or she is truly committed to learning about the issues. Equally, if the mentee assumes full knowledge, then this undermines the essence of the programme. To say too little in a conversation with the mentor will also impair the relationship. The mentor will be made to feel uncomfortable and therefore not as willing to be as open, frank and honest as she should be.

The characteristics of a good mentee are very similar to those of the mentor. The ability to create a trusting relationship with the mentor is again paramount. Adherence to the principle of confidentiality is also an integral part of this, as is the resolve to spend the necessary time with the mentor and diligently to listen to what she has to say. Most importantly, a good mentee should be able to understand when they are being given advice and then go away and act upon this advice.

The programme

Kickoff meeting

In order for this reversal of roles to be a success for all parties involved there is a formal kickoff session, which helps build relationships between pairs and provides role clarity for them. Groups of up to sixty mentoring pairs participate in different activities to help prepare them for their mentoring partnership and shift to the mentality required for a reverse approach. For example, right-handed people were asked to write sentences with their left hand and vice versa.

The majority of the exercises take place in pairs, though there are some group activities like one of the most valuable parts of the kickoff which is a panel discussion where people who have already experienced Mentor Up talk about their experiences.

Finally, the mentor/mentee pairs meet up to discuss and confirm the parameters and expectations of their own relationships. They are encouraged to discuss previous mentoring experience and whether any benefits can be brought to bear on the current relationship. The structure of the scheme is deliberately left loose so that the pairings can mould it to their own individual needs. This means that the participants must impose their own structure firmly to ensure that the relationship and its' objectives do not suffer from drift.

Expectations

Partners have to agree upon the expectations and principles that will govern the pair function. They also define their individual roles within the relationship. Of equal importance is the decision as to how and when to give and get feedback. All of these agreements are documented as a mentoring contract, with a resolve to check adherence in six months' time.

When the mentoring programme gets going it is expected that pairs will meet bi-monthly, although this could be more often if both the mentee and the mentor wish to meet more frequently. In order to help maintain an informal feel the meetings should take place away from the office. In order to help facilitate discussions for the pairs as well, as to remind them to meet up Mentor Up administrators, hand out discussion guides every other month.

Discussion guides

Even though the pairs are not required to stick to the discussion guides, they are seen as critical for most pairs at the outset of the programme: however, once they have achieved a productive level of trust in discussing diversity topics, the guides become less central. Discussion guides are most effective when the content is provocative (as opposed to politically correct). The topics that are raised, and the responses from participants, unearth valuable areas of misconception and often lead to key issues.

Although it was found that the guides did not need to be long to be effective, they have included a variety of different discussion stimuli. One included short 'feeling valued' surveys where the mentor and mentee answer a series of questions to determine what makes/has made them feel valued in the workplace. The pair can then talk about their answers in order to discover differences in the ways in which genders and individuals like to be rewarded and reassured.

Pilot test

The scheme was test-piloted in two sectors. Survey results from this indicated positive improvement in awareness and quality relationships and that programme participants were supportive of expansion. The programme initially concentrated on improving the awareness of males of at least director level.

After a year it was identified that the mentoring up programme needed to be moved down to middle and first-line managers. There was some initial resistance from these male managers as they are mainly of the same generation, therefore closer in age to the female mentors and felt they were already aware of the issues for the women. However, it has been noted by Kristen Nostrand that mentoring up has been just as successful at this level.

Among the main issues that arose from the meetings within the mentoring up scheme were the difficulties that females experience in striking a balance between their personal life and work. The other was no surprise to P & G as it had already been highlighted by the 'regretted loss' survey. It was the difference in managerial and decision-making styles between men and women. Women felt that their way of solving problems, which they saw as more inclusive, was not held in the same regard as men's by P & G.

The commitment of line managers was also essential. It was discovered that while some mentor/mentee pairs were excellent and the two worked really positively together, others struggled. It had been agreed at the start of the programme to change pairs, if they were not working well together.

The positive outcomes

The ability of mentoring pairs to use one another as sounding boards, on a variety of different cross-gender work-based circumstances has proved to be one of the major acgievements of the programme. It has also proved an excellent opportunity for both parties to share challenges and success.

Some of the male manager mentees were capable of discussing issues with their mentors after difficult team meetings and received a different and more helpful point of view into why people might have spoken or behaved in a certain way.

It is not easy to measure the success of a sensitivity training programme within a company, but there has been some concrete evidence of what mentoring up has achieved at P & G. Most importantly, female 'regretted losses' for the past two years have fallen by 25 per cent and are now in line with those for male managers.

Mentoring up has also given junior female managers the opportunity to mix with top executives with whom they would otherwise have had little contact. Possibly the greatest benefit from mentoring up is the fact that P & G now recognizes the gender issues within the organization and actively involves staff in discussing them.

Male managers report that they frequently seek out their mentees after a contentious meeting, in search of insight into the behaviour or thinking of female colleagues. A small number of female executives have now joined the programme as mentees.

Mentoring to help women set up a business – UK

Monika Beutel[2]

> I know that my mentee feels that the course has 'changed her life' and given her the confidence she needs to try and put her business ideas into practice.[3]

This comment from a mentor on the Women Entrepreneurs scheme summarizes the experience of many participants. The programme is life-changing because it emphasizes gender diversity in business as a source of creativity, strength and solidarity. Mentoring is an essential element of the package of learning and support that the course provides. The mentors act as role models, practical guides and critical friends to the women on the programme.

As the name suggests, the Women Entrepreneurs scheme at the University of Hertfordshire recruits only women and offers them the opportunity of learning and developing the knowledge and skills necessary for setting up a small business. The six-month programme has been running since 1996 with financial help from the European Social Fund (ESF). In addition to mentoring, the programme also includes workshops for personal and management development as well as distance learning modules in Marketing, Finance, Business Planning and Human Resources. The programme offers the opportunity to gain a Postgraduate Certificate in Small Business Management. By October 2000 over 200 women from ten different intakes had followed the programme; two-thirds have gone on to set up a small business or are still at the business preparation stage.[4]

The course targets women because women are still under represented among new business start-ups: women represent about 25 per cent of the self-employed. Moreover, it is specifically for women who have been away from the labour market. When they start the programme most of our women entrepreneurs have been unemployed for at least six months or are returners to the labour market after a career break for family reasons. Most lack confidence and many also lack up-to-date marketable skills such as computing skills.

The Women Entrepreneurs course helps the women to rebuild their confidence and to develop the practical skills necessary for self-employment. The mentors – nearly all of whom are also female – have business and management experience which enables them to provide useful guidance on a one-to-one basis. The women entrepreneurs mentoring scheme thus combines a focus on gender diversity with issues of business practice. Mentoring makes this programme distinctive among other business start-up courses. Several participants have mentioned the opportunity to work with a mentor as their main reason for joining the programme (Carlson and Patterson, 2000; Coles, 1997; 2000; Deutsches Jugendinstitut, 1994).

Scheme objectives

The objective in designing the women entrepreneurs programme was to enable women who have a business idea to develop the knowledge and practical skills to run a small business successfully. The team that designed the Women Entrepreneurs programme was able to draw on previous experience in developing programmes for women (Beutel, 1994; Michaels, Headlam-Wells and Wolfing, 1995). Thanks to this track record the team knew of the importance of peer and mentor support in helping women achieve their career goals and this led to the inclusion of mentoring as one of the main pillars of the new programme. The team was also aware of the importance of induction training for mentors and of the desirability of giving mentees a say in the choice of their mentor thanks to the course director's previous experience of setting up a mentoring scheme (these points are emphasized in some of the mentoring literature: cf. Clutterbuck, 1991; Megginson and Clutterbuck, 1995).

The main objective of the Women Entrepreneurs mentoring programme is to provide each woman on the course with an 'ally' or 'critical friend' with whom the budding entrepreneur can bounce ideas around. The mentors' task is to listen, ask pertinent questions about the planned business start-up, facilitate access to relevant networks and, occasionally, give advice or counselling support. Very importantly, the mentor will provide the learner with a model of personal development and an example of how a small business may be managed. Mentoring occurs through face-to-face meetings between mentor and mentee. The personal contact may be supported or to some extent replaced by telephone calls and e-mail if the parties to the relationship find this helpful.

Mentoring is now used in many diverse contexts. (Schemes include learning mentors to support underachieving students in schools; mentors to support a programme of rehabilitation of offenders; mentors for nurses; mentors to support the job search activities of various groups of unemployed people – to mention just a few.) It was developed as a human resource strategy in organizations to 'bring on' promising junior people by giving them a mentor, who would 'show them the ropes' and open doors for them. The mentor was usually a senior person in the same organization. Some mentoring schemes were developed with the specific purpose of valuing diversity and enhancing the career development opportunities of diverse groups such as women and black and ethnic minority employees.

The Women Entrepreneurs scheme was influenced by the literature on mentoring for personal and career development for diverse groups (Alred, Garvey and Smith, 1998; Business in the Community, 1993; Carter, 1994; Clutterbuck, 1991; Deutsches Jugendinstitut, 1997; Hay, 1995; Megginson and Clutterbuck, 1995; Murray and Owen, 1991; Segerman-Peck, 1996). The scheme is an external mentoring scheme (i.e. not based in one organization and not drawing mentors from only one organization). It has both developmental and business or task-based objectives. It focuses on business objectives while fostering and valuing gender and other forms of diversity. The mentor is the senior person (in the sense of having been in business longer) who facilitates the budding woman entrepreneur's personal and business development.

The Women Entrepreneurs programme addresses gender diversity by catering specifically for women. It deals with issues of common concern to women in the business world and generates a high level of peer group support within the group. Other types of diversity – race/ethnicity, disability, social class, family situation, education, language and culture – have been important within the programme, too, and have influenced the choice of mentor and the nature of the mentoring relationship.

The Women Entrepreneurs scheme and diversity

The learners on the Women Entrepreneurs programme have some attributes and experiences in common: their often difficult or even discouraging experiences of trying to return to the labour market – in the recent Women Entrepreneurs survey 44.8 per cent said that they had experienced dis- advantages in the labour market due to discrimination – as well as their experience of being in a minority in the business world by virtue of their gender.

In many other ways, however, the women who join the course have very diverse backgrounds – with respect to their ethnic or social-class origins, their educational qualifications, their age, their marital status and family situations. The 1999–2000 intakes are indicative of the types of diversity found amongst participants: from a total of eighty-one women who started the programme in 1999–2000 25 per cent come from ethnic minority backgrounds, 17 per cent have a disability, 21 per cent are lone parents, 27.5 per cent are returners and 2.5 per are cent homeless (these figures are taken from annual monitoring returns to ESF). The educational qualifications and social class backgrounds of the women are also very diverse. According to the Women Entrepreneurs survey, some participants join the course with few or no formal qualifications (6.7 per cent) whereas others already have postgraduate qualifications (26.7 per cent); the majority are somewhere in between, possessing a range of educational and/or vocational qualifications. Social-class backgrounds range from professional to unskilled occupations. Fifteen per cent have a language other than English as their first language. The age range spans the early twenties through to state retirement age (almost one-half of the participants are in their forties). Some of the women are single, including a significant minority of lone parents, most are married or live with a partner (63.6 per cent); 59 per cent have children living with them and 9 per cent have parents of self or partner living with them. With such a diverse intake, experiences of social inclusion/exclusion have varied considerably between individuals in each group.

In line with the aims and title of the programme, 'Women Entrepreneurs', more explicit attention is given to gender diversity than to racial and ethnic diversity, age or disability. Thus, gender diversity in business is an underlying theme on the course; it underpins the mentoring relationship and is discussed in workshop sessions on labour market segregation and the 'glass ceiling'. These sessions are characterized by lively discussions when the women make the link between their own experiences and the literature on discrimination and diversity.

Within the Women Entrepreneurs programme diversity issues are discussed both as factors of potential discrimination and as factors of enriching diversity. The course encourages the women to see themselves as pioneers in helping to make the business world more diverse and in helping to set examples of a good work–life balance.

The scheme emphasizes what common challenges businesswomen have to face, while also acknowledging both individual differences and social diversity in its many facets. The way individual participants define their identities influences to some extent how difference and diversity are dealt with on the scheme. For example, there have been participants with non-visible disabilities who have not wanted their disability to be acknowledged; there have also been participants with a strong sense of ethnic identity who specifically asked for this to be acknowledged and valued. Within one intake participants were keen to distinguish differences in their marital statuses and family responsibilities.

Several women on the course have reported experiences of discrimination because of their family responsibilities, their race, their age or because of disability. Some have stated specifically that they are opting for self-employment because direct, indirect or institutionalized discrimination has made their return to employment difficult.

Such experiences are reflected in the following comment from one of the women from an ethnic minority background: 'My experience (is) of having to try three times as hard for things that some people take for granted as their just due.'

Diversity issues in the mentoring relationships

The mentoring scheme provides individual support to each woman in her plans for business start-up. The mentors act as role models and are willing to be available to give the forms of support that the women themselves see as most helpful.

When recruiting mentors to the scheme, attempts are made to reflect the gender, ethnic and age diversity of the course participants. The scheme explicitly tries to recruit women mentors but also takes care not to exclude men as mentors. It aims to reflect the ethnic diversity of the business community, but does not normally attempt to match individuals by ethnicity – unless a specific request for a mentor from a particular ethnic group is received. Over the years the scheme has succeeded in increasing the number of mentors from ethnic minority groups but there is still some way to go before the ethnic diversity of course participants is reflected in the ethnic diversity of mentors.

Diversity may influence the choice of mentor. Participants who have a strong awareness of social diversity may want support to express and affirm their difference and may want a mentor from their own backgrounds who is already successful in business. Charlotte (names of mentors and mentees have been changed in order to preserve anonymity), who was in her late fifties, had experienced age discrimination and this led to her to request to be matched with a mentor of similar age. Many mentees choose a woman mentor. Ethnic identity played an important part in Lisa's, Angela's and Pauline's requests for black mentors. Pauline asked for, 'a mentor that comes form a similar background – e.g. black (or any other racial minority) and working class. Does not have to be female'.

Evidence on the relative effectiveness of opposite gender and cross-race mentoring versus same-gender and same-race mentoring relationships is not clear-cut but seems to favour same gender and same race mentoring pairs (cf. the discussion in Kram and Hall, 1996). The Women Entrepreneurs scheme, too, has tended to favour same-gender relationships. Female mentors are more likely to provide good role models for the complex choices that most women have to make in order to manage their work and home lives effectively, a particularly pressing issue for many of the women entrepreneurs.

When same-race mentors are explicitly requested by mentees from ethnic minority backgrounds, such requests are met whenever possible. As there are relatively few ethnic minority mentors currently available to the scheme, the implication is that few white mentees have the opportunity of being mentored by someone from an ethnic minority background.

It has been suggested that cross-race mentoring is often awkward, because racial stereotypes and taboos make it difficult for even well-intentioned individuals to set up an effective mentoring relationship. Cross-race mentoring has however been found to be successful if both parties (tacitly) agree to pursue the same strategy with regard to the 'race' issue – either denial of the saliency of race and concentration instead on task-based issues, or alternatively by direct engagement with race questions (Thomas, 1989 and 1993, cited in Kram and Hall, 1996). So far there have been only a few examples of cross-race mentoring on the scheme and they have usually involved white mentors with black or Asian mentees. In only two cases have mentors from ethnic minority backgrounds mentored 'white' women. A few individuals who have been asked about their experience of cross-race mentoring relationships have simply said that 'it was not an issue' or that 'it did not come up in the mentoring meetings'. It is intended to follow up issues around race, ethnicity and mentoring in the context of in-depth interviews with a sample of the women entrepreneurs. (Pilot interviews as part of a qualitative comparative study of women entrepreneurs in Britain and Germany have been undertaken. Further interviews with women from this scheme are planned.)

The Women Entrepreneurs mentoring relationships are usually for only six months. This is a relatively short period and it is therefore important that there is good rapport between mentor and mentee to enable the relationship to progress quickly and achieve both task-based objectives and personal development goals. Good rapport may be most easily achieved with others whose backgrounds and cultures are similar to one's own. This is comfortable, but may serve to perpetuate stereotyped assumptions and may mean that opportunities are missed of learning to see things from a diversity perspective and of building supportive mentoring relationships in an increasingly diverse business environment.

The scheme deals with these complex issues on a case-by-case basis.

The gender emphasis in the scheme is reflected in the mentoring relationships that are set up. Most of the mentors are women. For many women on the programme being a mother may be the most important part of their gender identity and the women returners have tended to be particularly explicit in requesting mentors whose background is similar to their own: 'Someone who will understand the difficulties of juggling home and business.'

They may be looking for advice on 'how other women run successful businesses from home with family commitments'.

A clear statement of the need for gender diversity in business is contained within the quote from this mentee: 'I am looking for a good role model of someone who is successfully juggling business and life.'

Some of the women are careful to distinguish their identities as mothers from what they see as their separate (and possibly conflicting) identities as businesswomen. One mentee, a returner, specifically asked for a male mentor on the grounds that this would be a more accurate reflection of relationships in the business world.

The many requests for female mentors who have personal experience of managing families suggests a wish to bring these different parts of their identities into harmony with one another. Yet the juggling act itself tends to be seen by most participants as a woman's issue, not as a business or work life issue. Men have families, too, and may also want to balance work and family life – yet this has remained by and large unacknowledged by many women on the course.

The dilemmas of the successful highly achieving businesswoman who is also a mother are well summed up in the following quote: 'I want to be successful – give me my status and position that being a housewife and mother closed . . . but I don't want to work all hours – need flexibility and freedom of choice to meet family commitments.'

Diversity of educational qualifications may also be an issue in the mentoring relationship and may be expressed indirectly by potential mentees in terms of the need for an encouraging and understanding mentor,

'What I need is someone friendly, approachable, low-powered.'
'Someone to hold my hand, a counsellor.'
'An open minded mentor.'

In cases where a mentee has mentioned that they had experienced discrimination, particular care was taken to match her with a mentor who could help her regain confidence and focus on the enriching aspects of diversity in business.

One success story concerns Angela who has excellent qualifications and experience in her profession but felt that she had been the victim of racial discrimination because of her African background. She was matched with a white mentor who opened doors for her through networking. Angela is now able to use her professional skills and qualifications in her business and has been able to deal with her fear of racial discrimination. Before obtaining support from her mentor she had thought of setting up her business in a different field to the one in which she had experience overseas, a field for which no professional qualifications were required and where she thought she would therefore encounter less discrimination.

Diversity in mentoring relationships can at times erect barriers to successful communication between mentor and mentee, particularly when cultural assumptions come into play. One mentor said: 'It was interesting to compare my two mentees and realize the value of maturity, stable home life and personal family support.'

The mentor seemed to feel that the more mature women with a stable home life was more willing and able to accept guidance and would be more able to cope in a competitive business environment than the younger black homeless single parent, who apparently 'totally ignored all advice, confident in her own abilities – which was totally misplaced.'

Sandra, who had appeared confident in spite of her difficult situation, acknowledges that she had ignored the mentor's advice initially. She has since gone on to find a home for herself and her daughter, and to set up a successful business with employees and subcontractors. She involves her former mentor as one of the non-executive directors in her business, clearly now valuing the mentor's advice.

How does the scheme find suitable mentors?

How does the scheme find suitable mentors for the 'women entrepreneurs'? Personal recommendations followed up by letter and telephone calls have been the most effective ways of recruiting mentors to this scheme. Existing networks and contacts are used. For example, the course directors' membership or knowledge of various women's networks such as Women in Management (WIM), the Women Returners Network (WRN), British Association of Women Entrepreneurs (BAWE), Business Women's Network, ew-network, Professional Family Women's Network and others led to approaches to individual members of these organizations to ask them whether they would consider becoming mentors. The university's partnership in Hertfordshire Business Link also provided links to existing business networks (including a black and Asian business network) and to a mentors forum.

Additionally, leaflets about the Women Entrepreneurs programme and the mentoring scheme were distributed widely. The programme also has its own web page with a section specifically for potential mentors (www.herts.ac.uk/business/women/). Over time it has been possible to build up a database of suitable and willing mentors for the programme. Not every potential mentor on the database is called upon to mentor for every intake – and not all potential mentors are always available, although a few of the mentors have mentored several women on almost every intake. In practice, mentors are sought specifically to match the needs of each individual woman on the course. Thus the process of finding mentors has tended to be combined with the process of matching mentor and mentee. The group of potential mentors is large and fluctuating, and this in turn has made it difficult to provide the same level of training to all the mentors to the scheme.

Training and preparation for mentoring

Mentoring induction training is led and facilitated by an experienced mentor, and business consultant. The training is provided separately for both mentors and mentees, and separately for each intake to the course. For each intake a joint meeting is also arranged, which enables potential mentors and mentees to meet one another and gain first impressions.

The mentoring induction training for *mentees* focuses on what mentoring is and how to use a mentor wisely. The session also includes discussion of diversity issues in mentoring (Segerman-Peck, 1996; 2000a).

The induction sessions for *mentors* are usually well attended. The sessions are voluntary but strongly recommended. Geographical distance or the business commitments of some mentors make it impracticable to require all potential mentors to join the training sessions. The induction for mentors includes discussion of what mentoring is, the skills involved in successful mentoring, how to draw up a mentoring contract as well as who to contact when trouble shooting is required (the course director) or where to get support (from existing mentoring networks) (Segerman-Peck, 2000b).

After induction to the mentoring process, both parties, mentors and mentees, fill in an information sheet including details of their occupational and business backgrounds. They are also asked to specify what they want to gain from the mentoring relationship and to state what qualities, skills and experience they are bringing to the mentoring relationship. This information assists mentors and mentees to choose one another and helps the course director in suggesting particular matches. The matching process involves careful negotiations and occasionally has to include a process of managing unrealistic expectations.

Matching mentor and mentee

Mentees are encouraged to find and choose their own mentor. Sometimes this works very well. Mostly, however, the course director takes an active role in helping to match mentors and mentees. This may be because mentees do not know the potential mentors or have met them only once, or because they ask for a mentor with particular attributes, qualities or experiences not for a named person.

The matchmaking process tends to happen about two months into the Women Entrepreneurs programme. By this stage the women's business ideas have become focused, and their appreciation of their own strengths and weaknesses has become more grounded. For example, they will have become aware of their own preferred learning styles (Honey and Mumford, 1992; Mumford, 1998) and will have had a personal profile report based on Myers-Briggs Personality Inventory (Briggs Myers, 1980; Hirsh and Kummerow, 1990). Consequently many of the potential mentees describe their 'ideal' mentor in terms of personal qualities and facilitative or developmental skills, as is shown in the following quotes:

> I envisage my mentor being a sounding board for ideas who will be able to give me advice on skills development, help with problem-solving and guidance on networking.

> I would like my mentor to be a critical friend from whom I could develop 'personally' (role model).

> Feedback, advice and constructive criticism on various areas of setting up my business.

> An objective listener that gives feedback and acts as a troubleshooter.

> A critical friend; non-judgemental, compassionate to provide inspiration at appropriate times, focus on goals, advice on presentation skills.

Requests may make reference to negative experiences around diversity: 'Help with getting the contacts, particularly given my ethnic background'. Or requests may be accompanied by an acknowledgement of the individual's own perceived areas of weakness:

> Encouragement and help with selling self.

> De-clutter, get focus right.

> I would love support around 'finishing/completing' tasks.

> I would like a mentor who has had a problem in the past with self-discipline or has overcome some similar problem.

Many of the women want a mentor who can give guidance on specific business functions or processes:

> Ideally my mentor would have a sound knowledge of marketing and management. I am particularly inexperienced in the management of finance.

Practical help with business start-up especially contacting new clients and developing leads.

Support, encouragement, assistance, particularly with marketing.

Day-to-day small business management from start-up to staff recruitment, development, delegation.

I will not be seeking emotional support – just advice really. I definitely need help with networking.

Some of the women feel strongly that they need a mentor who can give very sector-specific guidance, but there may be no mentors with the appropriate experience on the database. For example, there are few potential mentors from a manufacturing background on the database. Most of the mentors to the programme have experience of the service sector and very few have product-based experience. (This is a reflection of the fact that women in business are concentrated in the service sector and that the scheme recruits mainly female mentors.) This is a problem for the scheme and one that is highlighted in the following quote: 'Someone who has designed, manufactured and sold *any* product would be of great help to me.'

A few potential mentees on the other hand may have unrealistic expectations of the mentoring relationship, confusing it with the role of an individual business consultant. They want to tap into particular types of expertise rather than seeing mentoring as a process of facilitating learning and development. The Women Entrepreneurs mentoring scheme was devised to support women's personal development and their development of generic business skills. Yet many of the mentees want very specific and detailed advice from someone in the same business field and see mentoring as an opportunity to obtain coaching in specific skills, or even as an opportunity to obtain business consultancy for free. Whereas it can be good to have someone in one's own field who can introduce the woman who is newly starting in business to relevant networks, there can also be a conflict of interest and roles, if this person is a potential competitor. There may be a risk that mentor and mentee would be too protective of their ideas and client contacts. Mentees are therefore encouraged to look for a mentor who is not too close to the field of the learner's proposed business.

Eventually, sometimes after prolonged negotiations, almost every course participant who wishes mentoring support is paired up with a mentor. Both mentor and mentee then agree a 'contract' which spells out specific objectives and general expectations including practical details such as frequency and place of meetings. The contract is for six months, which takes the mentee beyond the Women Entrepreneurs course towards their actual business start-up. Some mentoring pairs continue to meet after the six-months stage with mentors giving ongoing support to their mentees.

The scheme does provide some further support for mentors, too, although this tends to be on an ad hoc basis. For example, a mutual support and networking group has been facilitated and mentors are encouraged to join the Hertfordshire Mentors Forum. (Contacts with the Hertfordshire Mentoring Forum which has met monthly has proved useful for those mentors who live locally. As the Women Entrepreneurs scheme recruits both mentors and mentees nationally the Hertfordshire Mentoring Forum has not, however, been accessible to all mentors on the Women Entrepreneurs scheme. More scheme-specific training has therefore been requested by some of the mentors.)

Troubleshooting, monitoring and review

Troubleshooting has been necessary at times, either because expectations were not clearly negotiated by the parties to the mentoring relationship at the outset, or because some aspect of the agreement between the parties was not working. For example, most mentoring pairs agree that it is the mentee's responsibility to initiate meetings. In a few cases mentees did not follow through and failed to contact the mentor or cancelled meetings with the mentor at short notice. When this happens it is usually an indication that troubleshooting is required. Failure to contact the mentor may sometimes signal the need for other types of support – for example, the need for more tutoring from university staff rather than mentoring by a business person, or the need for counselling support. One mentor reported: 'I considered whether she would benefit from meetings on a one-to-one basis with a private personal development specialist.'

Course director and mentors communicate about mentees' progress while keeping confidentiality with respect to information obtained within the mentoring relationship.

There may be other issues that may prevent the mentee from moving forward to implement her business plan, for example: 'Juliet was considering another child . . . She said that the timing was not right for her and that she was putting the whole idea of the business back.'

Monitoring and review of the programme is usually undertaken once a year. Difficulties with the mentoring scheme are picked up at each of the monitoring and review stages and attempts have been made to improve the scheme to foster realistic expectations and manageable contracts. The main elements of the mentoring system, and its underlying rationale, have remained unchanged. The scheme has, however, evolved and improvements have been made following feedback from both mentors and mentees. For example, the 'mentoring contract' format has been improved. Lessons have also been learnt in relation to training. Training for mentors as well as mentees is important, and more training and mutual support sessions for mentors are planned for the future.

International perspective

In the process of review, the international relevance of the scheme was also considered. How relevant would the scheme be for budding women entrepreneurs in other countries and cultures? Some of the course *content* would have to be changed to reflect the legal, fiscal and general institutional context cf the other country or countries. The *format* of the programme however, with its combination of developmental support through mentors, tutors and peers, is relevant in many other cultures. The fact that the Women Entrepreneurs programme is provided specifically for women, is a useful model wherever women constitute a minority of the self-employed, or where many women are involved in family businesses without being acknowledged and without having a formal stake in that business (a situation that pertains in many countries both in Europe and in the Third World, particularly in economies with large agricultural and craft sectors).

The mentoring scheme provides a good example of how career relevant support can be provided in situations where individuals are not part of organizational hierarchies. The mentoring scheme could be adopted – with modifications – in other cultural contexts.

Modifications might be required because mentoring within the Women Entrepreneurs programme relies heavily on the goodwill of mentor and mentee. There is a 'mentoring contract' but it is quite informal and would be very difficult to enforce in a court of law. Also, the mentors do not have professional indemnity insurance. In a different context, with stronger traditions of legal regulation (as in Germany for instance) or with a litigious culture (as in the USA), the mentoring scheme might have to be made more formal and the areas of competence and responsibility of the mentor would have to be more clearly defined. In some countries business advice may only be provided by suitably licensed and accredited persons.

Women take the bulk of responsibilities in the domestic division of labour virtually everywhere, and hence the work–life balance issue is an international one. Many women on the Women Entrepreneurs programme wanted to be mentored by someone who is a role model in having successfully juggled home and business, and this may also be the case in other cultural context. On the other hand, it may be an issue that is 'taken for granted' in some countries, for example where there is a tradition of full-time employment for women and where there is publicly provided child care, such as in Sweden or France or in the transition countries in Eastern Europe.

Ethnic and racial diversity, too, may have a different significance in other contexts. Where a model of assimilation defines race relations, as is the case in many other European countries, cross-race mentoring may be most appropriate for giving developmental support to a mentee from an ethnic minority background. In countries that have adopted a model of multicultural development both same-race and cross-race mentoring will be appropriate, depending on the particular objectives for which mentoring is set up.

The mentoring model is appropriate in many different cultural contexts, but the objectives of the mentoring relationship need to be appropriate to the particular diversity situation in each country – the historical background, the legal and political framework, and the cultural expectations.

Outcomes

The outcomes of the Women Entrepreneurs scheme have been positive and encouraging. Course feedback forms and the Women Entrepreneurs survey results suggest that all respondents have benefited and have achieved some positive outcomes for themselves. It is not possible to separate outcomes that are specifically attributable to mentoring from the wider outcomes of the Women Entrepreneurs course. Mentoring relationships, peer group support, tutor-supported open learning and skills development workshops have all contributed to the programme's success, giving the women access to a range of developmental relationships.

Different participants have looked towards their mentors to provide different kinds of support. Most wanted both task-focused learning and person-centred support from their mentor, but some tended more in one or the other direction. Mentors appear to have helped the learners in a variety of ways but in general appear to have been particularly influential in giving the women entrepreneurs confidence and contacts that helped them make their first business deals.

The quantitative outcomes of the programme stand up very well in the context of other business start-up programmes. The Women Entrepreneurs survey found that 33.3 per cent of respondents are running their own business; a further 32.2 per cent are still preparing to start their business; 35.6 per cent are in full- or part-time employment (this includes some who are in employment while continuing their business start-up preparations) and 21.1 per cent are undertaking further training/education (in some cases further study is oundertaken as part of business start-up preparation). Only a very small proportion, 6.7 per cent, are unemployed, whereas when they first started the programme, nearly all course participants had been unemployed or where returning to the labour market after a career break. An increasing number of participants complete the course with a postgraduate qualification in Small Business Management (of the 1999–2000 intakes 65 per cent achieved the Postgraduate Certificate). These quantitative outcomes are evidence that the programme aims are being met.

From the point of view of the individual woman entrepreneur, more qualitative outcomes may be just as significant. Qualitative changes have included greater self-confidence, finding new directions, building business networks, making new friends and developing skills (e.g. spreadsheets on the computer, developing sales techniques, making presentations to clients, and many others).

The benefits, very importantly, also include the learning experience of how to build supportive relationships with those who come from different gender, disability, racial/ethnic and family backgrounds. Both mentors and mentees have enhanced their awareness of the way diversity can improve the quality of businesses.

A number of mentors have written to say how much they, too, have gained for their own professional and personal development. Here is a selection of their comments:

I found being a mentor rewarding; it gave an additional boost to my own experiences. It highlights a number of areas in which my own business was lacking . . . and gave me the encouragement to improve in certain areas.

I do feel that I have personally gained by taking part in the mentoring process . . . the challenge of assisting an individual to achieve a more clear sense of direction is always very fulfilling.

For me, it's been a joy to watch Pamela build in confidence and help her recognize that she does have the qualities needed for running a business (and importantly, being able to go out and get customers).

Positive outcomes from the point of view of the scheme become experiences of personal growth from the point of view of the individual and have potentially life-changing impact, as was indicated by the quote from a mentor with which this paper had started. By way of conclusion another quote from a mentor: 'I think that the programme that you developed is an excellent one, which will do a lot of good for a great number of women who need someone to hold their hand while they find their own feet.'

A diversity mentoring programme: advisory circles – USA

Ellen J. Wallach and LueRachelle Brim-Atkins[5]

A divisional vice-president of a large manufacturing company in the USA engaged our services to assist in designing and implementing an overall corporate diversity plan. We were asked to provide consulting and training services for 18 000 executives, managers, supervisors and union representatives.

Diversity for this organization was more than race and gender. It was generically defined as 'all the ways people differ', including visible (e.g. colour, size, appearance, etc.) and invisible differences (e.g. background, experiences, sexual orientation, job function, etc.). Part of the three-year effort included developing and delivering an eight-hour mandatory diversity awareness and skill-building course.

The vision for the diversity effort was to have a workplace that supported the development of all employees. Their goal was an inclusive, participative environment where the diverse thinking and ideas of the total workforce would assist the organization in attracting, developing, and retaining the best employees thereby providing the competitive edge needed to retain leadership status in its industry. To help achieve this vision, we created and facilitated an innovative diversity-mentoring programme that would support their overall diversity plan. We called the mentoring programme, Advisory Circles.

The structure and process

An advisory circle is a process for developing relationships among five to seven employees (called advisers) and a senior manager (a mentor or coach). Some organizations have established expectations for the role of a mentor, usually someone who shepherds hand-picked employees through their careers. Since this is not the expectation with advisory circles, we chose a name that was not as loaded in this organization. We used 'coach'.

Advisory circles were created to consider issues related to diversity and career success. The goals were to:

- help coaches improve their comfort level with diverse employees and ideas
- give coaches opportunities to help employees identify, plan and pursue desired career goals
- help advisers gain exposure to career fields outside their current area
- increase coaches' awareness of any barriers or impediments to inclusion and advancement in order to inform senior executives of the company
- enhance appreciation of differing perspectives, ideas and values in the workplace
- increase everyone's awareness of tools and processes that can be used to value diversity.

There were two components to this process. The first was a bi-monthly one-on-one meeting between the adviser and coach where the adviser was seeking career information and coaching. The second component involved a small group of advisers providing constructive suggestions to the coach on ways to develop a more open environment. This process formed a continuous feedback circle between the individual and the organization. As the individual is learning how to be successful within the organization, the organization is learning how to be more open and inclusive. Quarterly, all coaches met with the vice-president to discuss the progress of their circle and make recommendations for increasing inclusion in the organization and programme changes. See Table 9.1 for an overview of the advisory circles process.

Circles could choose to focus on one or more of the following:

- identification of barriers within each coach's organization for which the advisory circle could develop a situation/target/proposal (STP) for implementation by the coach
- proposals for possible division-wide implementation (e.g. diversity web site or calendar, etc.
- increased awareness of diversity issues, including improved perspectives of what it takes to achieve individual professional goals.

The pilot programme involved eighty-four advisers and twelve coaches.

Table 9.1 Advisory circles: an overview

	One-on one coaching meetings	Advisory circles
Frequency	1 hour every other month	2 hours per month 1st hour – advisers only 2nd hour coaches and advisers
Who initiates	Adviser	Coach initiates 1st meeting Secretary can schedule subsequent meetings
Who plans 1st meeting	Adviser	Coach Coach can set agenda or involve advisers. Circle decides who will set subsequent agendas, meeting schedule and structure
Who reports progress	Adviser informs diversity manager when meeting occurs	Coach informs diversity manager when meeting occurs
Where to begin	Coach initiates one-on-one meeting with each adviser before scheduling the 1st advisory circle meeting	
Feedback	Three feedback sessions during the year and at the programme's conclusion.	

Selecting coaches and advisers

At the encouragement of the vice-president, all of his direct reports elected to participate in the pool of coaches. All had completed the eight-hour Diversity Training Programme. Each perspective coach was asked to complete a Coach Profile Questionnaire and attach a résumé. Because each adviser had different coaching needs, this information enabled them to make appropriate coach selections. The questionnaire included job skills, related expertise, knowledge, skills and abilities the coach would like to share. Coaches were invited to include additional information that they felt would be helpful in assisting advisers in choosing a coach. The questionnaires and resumes were assembled into a loose-leaf book and each adviser received a copy during the eight-hour Advisory Circles workshop.

Advisers were invited to participate by human resources. Diversity of race and gender were a given. Because an additional benefit of the programme was to help participants expand their knowledge of and possible career options in the company, we also wanted heterogeneity by function. Before an employee could participate in any coaching programme they must have worked for the company for three or more years and in their current job for at least a year. A prerequisite to participation was completion of the eight-hour Diversity Training Programme.

The training programme and forming the circles

Coaches and advisers were trained separately. Although the content of both training programmes was similar, each group felt more comfortable asking questions and voicing concerns without the other present. Coaches' training was two hours in length and included opportunities to freely express apprehensions or concerns they had regarding participating in the programme. Advisers' training was held over two days for three hours each day. Training was divided into three content areas: Review of Valuing Diversity, The Career Management Process and The Advisory Circle Process. A separate meeting was held with advisers' supervisors for whom we described the programme in detail and addressed their questions and concerns.

The philosophical underpinning of the programme was that each individual is responsible for his or her own career. Therefore, adviser training was longer and included an overview of the career management process and a homework assignment to complete a self-assessment questionnaire of their motivation, skills, values, interests and goals. Having completed the self-assessment after the first session, participants discussed what kind of coaching they needed to reach their career goals.

Advisers were then given the Coach Profile Book and asked to select four possible coaches that best met their career needs. They were encouraged to select coaches who they did not know and who were in totally different areas of the organization. Circles were constructed based on adviser choices and all advisors were placed with one of their four choices.

In any mentoring programme, success is dependent upon clear definitions of roles and responsibilities to provide participants with structure and comfort. It is particularly important to focus not only on what a mentor/coach or advisor's role *is*, but also what it is *not*. The roles often overlap. Role definitions will vary dependent upon the goals of the effort. For this programme:

- A coach is a listener, an agent of change for valuing diversity, a reality check, an appraiser, a career adviser, a resource person and a person who values giving and receiving feedback.
- A coach is not a sponsor, a therapist, someone to complain to, a mind reader, a source of all information, always right or responsible for anyone's career except his or her own.
- An adviser is a listener, an agent of change for valuing diversity, a person who values giving and receiving constructive feedback, responsible for his or her own career, an information gatherer/sharer, and able to give the coach his or her perspective on 'life in the workplace' and suggestions for elimination of barriers to equity.

- An adviser is not a complainer, seeking a therapist, parent or sponsor, expecting an automatic promotion as a result of his or her participation or hesitant to gain exposure to career fields outside of her or his current area.

Advisory circle meetings

Circle meeting

Each circle met for two hours each month for a year. Specific goals and exercises were outlined for the first few meetings to provide initial structure. After that, circles were encouraged to set their own agendas and structure and work at their own pace. There was no prescribed amount of work to be done and no set amount of time to accomplish what the circle decided to undertake. The work of the circle would be determined solely by the amount of time and interest circle members could devote to their tasks.

The initial goals were to establish ground rules, get to know each other, brainstorm a collective vision of what valuing diversity might look like at the company, discuss concerns about the programme, and agree on a working relationship. Circles were encouraged to conduct a personal and process check at the conclusion of each meeting. It was suggested that they discuss two questions: what is working well? What can we do to be more effective?

Since circles were vehicles for sharing information, groups were encouraged to decide what kind of information members wanted to give and get. Group members told stories, shared experiences about current and past dilemmas and described which things worked well to enhance or inhibit inclusion of employees. Some groups decided to initiate specific projects including launching a diversity web site and designing a community mentoring programme for youth.

One-on-one coaching

Coaches met with each adviser in their circle for a minimum of one hour every other month. Keeping the principal that each person is responsible for his or her own career, advisers were responsible for the preparation, content and direction of each meeting. As with circles, we suggested structured guidelines for the first one-on-one meeting. The goals were to establish ground rules, get to know each other, share career histories, express and clarify concerns and personal goals, agree on a working relationship, and thank each other for support and commitment. Participants were provided with a one page information sheet on 'The Basics of a Coaching Meeting'.

Once the relationship was established, coaches and advisers were encouraged to design a structure and content which met their needs. Coaches and advisers read articles and discussed them, attended professional meetings, discussed difficult employee problems, shared perceptions of the organization's culture and discussed career options, etc.

Feedback meetings

Four feedback meetings were held during the year – one per quarter:

- an interim meeting with all circle members
- a Steering Team meeting with one representative from each circle (two meetings)
- a final meeting with all circle members.

Each circle was asked to respond to the following questions at the final meeting:

- What were your key lessons?
- Do you think the advisory circles programme should be implemented division-wide? Why or why not?
- Have you identified any specific changes in your attitude or overall outlook as a result of participating in advisory circles?
- Has this programme met your expectations? (Programme goals listed) Why or why not?
- Does your circle plan to continue any aspects of its work? If so, how?

Anticipating problems and solutions

As part of both the coach and adviser training we solicited participant concerns. As well as the usual mentoring programme concerns of trust, personal effectiveness and time usage, we found two concerns that bear directly on diversity issues and deserve mention.

The first was expressed by both coaches and advisers: 'What if we don't like each other and don't get along?' This concern was most strongly felt in anticipating the one-on-one relationship. We had already discussed this with our client and the initial organizational answer was, 'Yes'. Our answer was different.

We are all usually most comfortable with people like us. We select friends and make hiring selections based on who looks, acts and has experiences that are much like our own – all of which contributes to the dilemma people in organizations face when they are perceived to be 'different' than the majority. A major goal of this programme was to help expand individual comfort zones to open people to appreciate and include differences. This programme was designed to encourage people to move into their discomfort rather than avoid it, recognizing that the world is changing as are the people with whom we will work and do business in the future. Colleagues will not all act and look like similar and people all will be more effective professionals when they are more comfortable, appreciative and inclusive.

The second concern was expressed during the coaches' training. This group was totally male. They were concerned about coaching a female. The advisers group was half female. There was discomfort with developing a 'close' professional relationship, with concern about sexual harassment issues and making inappropriate mistakes. We discussed this at length to acknowledge their fears and encourage their participation.

We suggested that coaches initiate one-on-one meetings with each adviser before beginning their circle. The structured meeting guidelines would help both parties get to know each other and establish a more comfortable relationship before being in a group together. It would make the beginning circle meetings easier and more comfortable for all participants.

Lessons learned

In the final meeting of all circles and the vice-president, each circle reported their key lessons learned. The following is a compilation of their findings.

Learnings for future advisory circles

- Maintain a clear objective for the circles and communicate it to the entire organization and to prospective participants.
- Ensure that there is visible diversity within each circle.
- Be sure that all circle members are clear about their involvement and want to participate.
- Anticipate and provide needed information to circles. Maintain a continuous feedback loop.
- Consider circle members' geographic location for scheduling meetings.

Learnings by circle members

- Visible diversity is only a small piece; diversity issues are often in that uncomfortable area that we do not see and do not like to talk about. Circles provide one way of talking about the issues, including the tendency to coach people with similar backgrounds, culture, and experiences.
- Diversity brings a lot to the table, including new and broader perspectives that help us avoid groupthink.
- Diversity is not 'affirmative action' but rather is a new way of looking at things like promotion, succession planning, cross-functional training and inclusion/exclusion.
- Stereotyping exists in the work place and impacts most aspects of people's lives.
- Fear is the theme in 'reverse discrimination'.
- Every employee should feel that he or she has promotional opportunities, limited only by his or her own abilities and initiative.
- Every effort must be made to help employees become comfortable with each other's differences to perform as a team to get the job done more effectively.

- Eight-hour diversity training is critical and should be mandatory for 100 per cent of the employee population and should be included in basic supervisory training.
- Include diversity issues in regular employee publications.
- Continue and broaden advisory circles.

Organizational learnings

All circles felt that the Advisory Circles programme should be implemented division-wide based on the amount they had learned about themselves and about others with whom they would probably not have come in contact if not for the programme. Individual participants talked about specific changes in their attitudes and overall outlooks as a result of participating in the advisory circle. The programme met and in some cases exceeded expectations and they were anxious to help the division apply lessons learned to subsequent programme incarnations. Several circles planned to continue some of the aspects of their work, including the community mentoring and the diversity web site.

Participants in the advisory circles saw the following as necessary changes in organizational policy and practice if the organization was to achieve its diversity goals:

- Include diversity in all aspects of the organization including performance management, company rules and policies, management attributes, recruitment strategies, promotions and new employee orientation. Reward employees to get it right. Provide assistance to those who do not.
- Develop cross-functional assignments to all kinds of people, initially for circle participants, then throughout the organization.
- Continue to monitor visible and invisible diversity in all employee surveys.
- Increase community awareness of efforts of the organization to improve the perception of the company as a desirable place to work.

What happened next?

Six months after initiating the pilot programme, we began another round of circles with 16 coaches and 112 advisers. The pilot and second round were enormously popular with participants and exceeded the organization's expectations. The organization's original intent was for us to design and deliver two or three rounds and then train internal trainers to conduct the programme. Their hope was that this would encourage organizational ownership and further infuse diversity and mentoring into the culture.

The vice-president enthusiastically supported the programme. We believed that his championing this effort would ensure its continuation. Two issues arose that challenged this assumption.

While we designed the programme content, the implementation strategy was the work of an energetic internal committee headed by the vice-president. Unfortunately, after the pilot programme, a series of personnel changes occurred. The vice-president eventually delegated responsibility for the programme to an employee who was new to his division and who had not participated in the programme or its design. She arrived with very different ideas of how to proceed and began making significant changes. The vice-president continued to be an ardent supporter of the Diversity Mentoring Program, but his attention was focused elsewhere.

Business realities also prevented its continuation. With disappointing corporate earnings and continued production problems, the organization's focus shifted to manufacturing solutions. We were both involved with other diversity mentoring programmes within this organization. For these business realities and resulting changing focus, none of them continued.

As consultants with forty years' experience between us, we did all the 'right' things. We involved a core group in the design of the programme. We had support from the top for the design and implementation of the programme. During the pilot, we developed enthusiastic support from participants. We provided a quality programme and did continuous quality improvement checks with those who were involved. Despite this level of planning and implementation, change happens.

Conclusion

Although we completed only two rounds of advisory circles, 224 people participated as advisers or coaches. The vice-president, his leadership team and participants evaluated the training with top scores and highly recommended it as part of any overall diversity strategy. Although the project was suspended, the advisory circle design bears consideration if you are initiating a diversity mentoring effort. It provides substantially more than the usual diversity and mentoring programme benefits. Advisory circles provide:

- a process for people to discuss sensitive and difficult diversity issues and work them through as they complete projects that benefit the organization
- a forum that impacts larger numbers of participants than individual mentoring
- a feedback mechanism that explores inclusion at all levels of the organization that involves senior-level managers who have the power to make organizational changes.
- a procedure whereby many of the major issues raised in diversity training programmes can be impacted directly.

A case study from SAS – Sweden

Christina Jellbring Klang[6]

When SAS, the Scandinavian Airline, set out to create a mentoring programme, it did not have diversity issues as its highest priority. It simply wanted to support the development of leaders. Although the scheme soon evolved to include a strong measure of cross-gender mentoring, SAS perceives diversity in the wider sense of using the talents of people of different backgrounds.

The background of this initiative was a request from SAS top management in spring 1992, to 'investigate the possibility to establish a formal mentor programme in SAS, not only for the existing target group Management Trainees (which had mentorship in its development-programme since 1991), but also for other leaders'.

The purpose at this early point was that 'mentorship in SAS shall through a comprehensive professional and human way secure the continuous development of leaders in accordance with the goals and strategies of SAS'. When the mentor programme was established in 1994 a new formulation of purpose, which is still valid, was made, as follows:

- The leaders shall develop themselves, personally and professionally, towards a *supporting leadership* (SAS term).
- The leaders shall widen their networks outside the own division.
- The leaders shall deepen their knowledge about SAS.

Designing the programme

My colleague Robin Tamm-Buckle and I made about forty interviews, mostly with top management, partly to find out if the SAS environment was suitable for the programme and partly to create an understanding in the company that the programme was under preparation. A bonus at this stage was that the investigation also led to the finding of many presumptive, fitting and willing mentors.

Robin had previous experience of mentorship from his initiation of 'course mentors' in a programme for leadership development at the end of the 1980s. I started a formal mentor activity in connection with the management trainee programme, which I was responsible for at the time of the project. The purpose with the latter was to give these newly recruited, well-educated future leaders a guide into the company and support when they got their first position. The result of this activity was very positive – hence top management's decision to expand it to include more target groups. We had a theory, or perhaps it was more of a conviction, that people who meet and create a dialogue will develop a mutual confidence. This is the foundation on which the relation stands and from which it can be used, in various ways, for development.

Once we had acceptance of the programme in top management, a steering committee was set up to oversee the implementation. This committee consisted of leaders from Sweden, Norway and Denmark. Initially the support of the committee was not very strong. I participated in four meetings during the period March to September 1993, before the group reached an understanding of what we wanted to accomplish with 'Mentorship in SAS'. They expressed fear and suspicion concerning, for example: how the closest leader of the mentee would be affected, whether the loyalty of the mentor should be with the mentee or with the company and how one should deal with issues such as criminality (with the mentee). None of this type of question occurred later during our work with the programme. When the group finally decided to accept the suggested organization, it was time to involve the people within HR who worked with leadership development in the three countries. We had most success with the acceptance in Sweden and within the international management of expatriates. Slow progress was made in Norway and Denmark, where the route was not through HR, but through leaders who volunteered as mentors and who passed on their positive experiences.

It was a part of our strategy not to have a marketing campaign. We decided to start on a small scale, let the good examples talk for themselves and develop gradually through experience. This strategy proved successful and has been used since then.

The reason not to have a marketing campaign was that we did not want to risk a failure. We had seen some formal mentorship activity in big Swedish companies where one started up on a very large scale and received a lot of attention, but then failed to follow up with the individual pairs. Many of these relationships were not fulfilled, which disappointed the participants. We wanted the possibility of following up each mentor relationship as long as it was a part of our formal activity. We also wanted to avoid giving mentorship a bad reputation, by not being able satisfactorily to handle it .

Selecting mentors and mentees

Through making contacts with leaders who we considered potential mentors, we also made them interested in mentorship. We had great possibilities to meet leaders in different situations and those meetings came to function as a natural search for mentors, also from outside SAS. The interested leaders were asked if they would participate in a meeting to talk about mentorship, which all of them agreed to do. The purpose of the meeting was to get an idea about what this person knew about mentorship, to tell him or her how mentorship worked in SAS and establish if he or she had a genuine interest in becoming a mentor. We also wanted to get as much information as possible about the person, to be able to help with the matching at a later stage. If we found the leader fitting to our purposes, we concluded the meeting by asking if he or she was interested in becoming a formal mentor. But we also explained that we could not tell when the moment should arise, since the choice of mentor always depends on the needs of the mentee.

Initially the offer to have a mentor was given to particular target groups: management trainees, female first-time leaders, leaders in the international organization and leaders in the marketing and sales organization. The decision to focus on women first-time leaders was made by the steering-committee from a list of ten potential target groups. These people were informed that they could choose mentorship to develop their leadership skills. Soon the need of mentorship arose in other groups as well – for example, leaders at top-management level or leaders, who themselves had been mentees and who wanted to offer their colleagues the same possibility, independent of position. Because of this development, we have gradually abandoned the division into groups and instead we now try to meet whatever current needs people bring. In other words, we are not choosing who is going to have a mentor, but whoever feels the need for it turns to us or gets the offer from his or her own leader.

The matching process comes about in the following way: when the mentee has described his or her needs of mentorship and when I have got as much information as possible to get to know the person, we also discuss if there are any role models or even a particular person who could be seen as an attractive mentor. In other words, the matching is about finding a mentor who is able, as much as possible, to satisfy the needs of the mentee in question. Their specific needs can be very different from those other individuals. In situations, when the mentee has a suggestion of his or her own of a possible mentor, we carefully discuss, if this person really can meet the described needs. If not, there is always a good possibility that I can suggest one or two suitable people, since I already have had similar interviews with leaders interested in mentorship.

It is very important that none of the involved parties finds themselves forced to accept a suggestion that does not feel right. It is my task to justify why I believe that the suggested presumptive mentors are suitable for the mentee. If the mentee still has doubts, the search will continue until we have found someone we both believe in. The next step is to ask the suggested mentor, who has the right to decline both to be a mentor or to be a mentor for a particular person. This process, of course, is always handled with great discretion.

Diversity happens naturally

The age of the mentees has varied between twenty-five and fifty-one years and the age of the mentors has varied between thirty-two and fifty-nine years. We have rather many relationships where both parties are of the same age (it can be a difference of three to four years where the mentor can be both younger and older than the mentee). We also have examples of extremes where the mentor has been fifteen years younger than the mentree or where the mentor has been twenty-five years older.

There were seventy-one female and eighty-one male mentees (see Table 9.2).

Numbers of mentors : thirty-nine female and 113 male mentors.

Of the mentors 126 were internal and twenty-six were external.

The difference in position-levels differ from the level of group leader in a very operational activity to top management – which includes about 100 positions (where we have had ten mentees with usually external mentors). The target group has been leaders of all kinds but we have also had a number of specialists (nine) as mentees. Each mentor has had the position of a leader.

When asked for their preference of same or different gender mentors, most people say that it does not matter – they just want to have a 'good' mentor. *If*

Table 9.2 Numbers of female/male mentees in relationship to numbers of female/male mentors

Female mentees with		Male mentees with	
Male mentor	44	Male mentor	69
Female mentor	27	Female mentor	12

Numbers of relationships where the Scandinavian nationality is different between mentor/mentee (Swedish, Danish or Norwegian) = 43

Numbers of relationships where other nationality is different between mentor/mentee (Japanese, English, Australian, Finnish, Estonian, Belgian) = 7 mentorees

they say something, it is more common that they ask for a female mentor because they want to have a role model to help them to manage and gain from the experiences of a woman who also is leader and mother (10 per cent of the cases). Male mentees sometimes ask for female mentors, because they have experienced that it is easier to talk to a woman about sensitive issues (5 per cent of the cases).

Since our mentorship activity is founded on the individual needs of the mentee, it was already from the beginning understood that the relationships would differ in many ways. What surprised us was the great diversity of the initial needs and how those needs changed during the different phases the mentee went through during the relationship. For example, a mentee's principal need could be to discuss the future, be challenged, and have mental stimulation. But if the mentee during this period gets a new, more challenging leadership job, his or her needs would change to discussions about current leadership tasks. Another example could be someone who has the same initial needs as described above, but who during the period leaves the company. In all, twenty-nine mentorees (about 20 per cent) left SAS during or shortly after their participation in the mentor programme. This has not necessarily got anything to do with the mentor relationship, but is a high proportion in relation to SAS employees in general.

To sum up, diversity in needs could be about someone wishing for advice and inspiration, experience and wisdom, to someone who listens, has new impulses, needs support in choice of career or help to get another perspective on daily work. Some mentees need all this and others want to concentrate on one specific area.

Preparing for the relationship?

The preparation for both mentor and mentee starts with the initial conversation regarding their own ideas about the meaning of mentorship, what kind of previous experiences they have and, concerning the mentee, what different needs affected the decision to get a mentor. Then I tell them about the history of mentorship in SAS, how we have organized what we call 'form for mentorship' and 'framework for mentorship'. A description of the basic values of mentorship in SAS is also included. After these initial conversations, both parties should be fully aware that both the decision to get a mentor and to become a mentor is based on one's own free will and that the relationship is directed by the needs of the mentee. The discussion takes about two hours and takes place on different occasions for the mentor and the mentee. The next step after the matching process is to bring the mentor and mentee together for an introductory meeting, during which both can clarify their respective expectations on the relationship. This discussion leads to their personal 'framework'. Here is also an opportunity for me to share my experiences from other mentor relationships, anonymously, and to answer questions they both might have before their coming relation. The main intention is to not serve up too much or to give directives, but to let the individuals create their own relationship. It is now their responsibility to develop and deepen this relationship and also to handle it if it does not work.

Feedback from participants indicates that:

- Where we have had mentoring across nationalities, (Norwegian, Danish, Swedish), they have often found that it helped them to understand different ways of thinking and acting which have been useful in their own work situation. On the other hand, sometimes the mentee asks for a mentor of the same nationality because they want to use their mother tongue. For example, a male mentee was happy to have an English-speaking mentor because although he was Swedish, he had grown up in a country where he used English more than Swedish and he felt it more natural to speak English.
- Male mentees have gained a better understanding of their female employees when 'using' a female mentor.
- A younger mentor (fifteen years difference) learned from the mentee a lot about life conditions for younger people today which was useful in her work.
- A male pilot (who also is a leader) had got a female, external mentor (a businesswoman) to gain a better understanding of how to manage the business he has been responsible for.
- Some 95 per cent of all the mentorship relationships have seen the usefulness of having a mentor with a different background. It has given them a very dynamic relationship and it has sustained the interest of both the mentor and the mentee.
- There have been very few difficulties in managing differences, because the difference was something they wanted in choosing a mentor.

I have, however, encountered a number of stereotypes, that needed to be changed. For example:

- How can a *younger* mentor be useful?
- How can a mentor from a different professional discipline understand my problems?

- Does a retired mentor still understand the business?
- What use is a mentor from an operational area such as ground handling or catering, when I come from the commercial end of the business?

In each case, once we discussed the issues with the mentee, they accepted the value of the difference and committed to making it a positive aspect of the relationship.

Managing the programme

Most expectations of the relationship come from the participants. I have given them, however, an expectation regarding my presence and support in case of problems. I may also have given them my own strong belief in mentorship and what it can generate provided that the relation develops in appropriate ways.

Mentors and mentees are together called to two meetings, after four and eight months, to follow up the relationship. They also come to a meeting to finish the relationship. If a need for support arises at any stage of the relationship, they can ask for it.

The nature of this support varied considerably. In some cases help to 'finish' the relationship is required – for example, if the mentoree is transferred to a position close to his or her mentor, or if the mentee feels that there is no driving force in the relationship, or that they have met too infrequently. I may also at a follow-up meeting have been able to inspire them to use the relationship in a more effective way. On one occasion the mentor needed support because they felt inadequate for the mentee. The mentee tended to use the mentor more like a therapist, which is not part of the mentor role. Another mentor needed guidance on how deeply involved one should be in a conflict between the mentee and his or her leader.

Since the needs of the mentees have varied greatly, it is hard to point out specific outcomes here. But one big and important outcome (which has been stated by most mentees) is the unique access to a person, who has promised to be available for a whole year for the sake of one's development.

For the mentor the main outcomes have been the satisfaction to give, to learn new things about another person and about the company, and to realize that the development has been mutual. It has also been a great experience for many to realize that it is neither necessary to be a man to become a mentor, nor to have a higher position or to be older than the mentee. It can work out perfectly well if you are a woman, younger or with a lower position than your mentee. Once again everything is about what you want to achieve with the relationship.

The mentorship programme has given many SAS leaders more security in their roles. It has helped them to make decisive choices (which in the long run is positive for SAS) and it has inspired them to become mentors themselves or to offer their colleagues the opportunity to have a mentor. I would say that for many, mentorship is today a part of the SAS culture.

Concerning outcomes for the community, I believe that it must be positive that I have been asked on so many different occasions to tell others about my nine-year experience of mentorship. Hopefully it can lead to inspiration and introduction of mentorship in other environments.

Lessons learnt

I learned not to avoid differences but search after them when it comes to creating a dynamic mentoring relationship. How is it possible to develop if two people have the same opinions, the same backgrounds, the same experiences and the same conceptions of the future? New perspectives provide the mentoring relationship with energy. Furthermore, I have learned that I should not tell others how to develop their relationship, since that will limit them. Instead they should take the responsibility themselves and my role is to give my support, if it is needed. If you avoid making differences an issue, you also make it possible for more individuals to participate in the mentoring programme. One should make things easy!

We have applied those lessons in other programmes by showing great respect for other people's wishes and abilities, and listening very carefully to how they want to organize their relationships. In other words, if one offers others tools for their development when they have not asked for them, it has to be done with great humility and sensibility. Recognizing that there is never just one way to do things, avoids stereotyping.

A lot of work may be needed to adapt our approach to some cultures, such as facilitating in Germany and Japan, which are more authoritarian and therefore may limit the possibilities of diversity. But because of the simplicity of the programme there should be a good possibility to apply it to other cultures. The main thing is the meeting of two people, built initially on one person's need for development, and to keep in mind that mentorship is *not* about getting a faster-track career through an influential mentor.

Mentoring teen parents: fostering individual and community resilience – USA

Margi Waller[7]

Introduction

This case study describes an ongoing inner-city community volunteer mentoring programme for at-risk pregnant teenagers in the north-eastern USA. This community volunteer mentoring programme was developed over a three-year period by an urban community health centre where more than 50 per cent of the women receiving pre-natal care were between fifteen and eighteen years of age. Funding for the programme was secured in the second year and renewed in the third year. Over the first three years, the programme used forty-five volunteer mentors and served fifty teens, all of whom were unmarried. The programme has the dual objective of promoting positive outcomes for at-risk pregnant teenagers while, at the same time, providing the community with a cost-effective strategy for addressing a pressing social problem. In addition, the mentoring experience provides caring adults with a means of making a positive contribution to their community. The authors provide detailed information related to community education; recruitment, training, and ongoing support and supervision of mentors, funding requirements and programme evaluation.

Background

The taboo against early, out-of-wedlock pregnancy runs deep in US society. Current punitive social policies related to teen pregnancy reflect this taboo and are indicative of a community that has failed to understand and protect its most vulnerable members. Young, poor, pregnant women are failed not only by policy-makers, but by every other social institution in their communities as well. Inside religious institutions, schools, social service agencies and within their own families, young mothers are judged and shunned by the very adults who might give them the support and hope they so desperately need to meet life's challenges, care for their children and fulfil their own potential. One cost-effective alternative is to establish volunteer mentoring programmes that connect pregnant teenagers with adults in the community who can provide them with nurturing, guidance and hope.

Mentoring and pregnant teens

The most important benefit of mentoring programmes for pregnant teens is social support, a key factor in positive adaptational outcomes. Many of the bio-psychosocial risk factors associated with both early pregnancy and child maltreatment may be significantly altered by the social support that mentoring relationships provide (Buchholz and Korn-Bursztyn, 1993). For example, social support during pregnancy, including encouragement to maintain good nutrition and regular pre-natal care (Combs-Orme, 1993; Hayes, 1987) is associated with healthy birth outcomes (Nuckolls, Cassell and Kaplan, 1972; Turner, Grindstaff and Phillips, 1990). Encouragement to continue with education can break the cycle of poverty. Emotional support is associated with reduced stress levels in young mothers (Coletta and Hunter Gregg, 1981), and education about child development and parenting skills seems to reduce the incidence of child maltreatment (Buchholz and Korn-Bursztyn, 1993; Haskett, Johnson and Miller, 1994; Phipps-Yonas, 1980; Rickel, 1989). Just as social isolation is a risk factor for young mothers and their children, the social support that mentoring relationships provide can lead to positive outcomes.

Programme description

Initial recruitment of mentors

We recruit mentors through newspaper articles and advertisements, local bulletins, word-of-mouth referrals, and presentations to religious and other community organizations. In each case, we highlight the issues confronting pregnant teens. The personal stories of teens in need of mentors (altered to protect confidentiality) are a particularly powerful means of engaging the interest of potential mentors. Community members who express an interest in becoming mentors are invited to an introductory orientation at the community health centre where the mentoring programme is based.

Introductory mentor orientation

In this orientation we provide additional information about teen pregnancy, describe mentor roles (e.g. educator, friend, coach, liaison and broker) and present profiles of mentees. We specify the fourteen-month time commitment for the programme, which includes seven, weekly two-hour training sessions, monthly mentor support meetings, weekly supervision with the programme co-ordinator and two hours per week for one year in direct contact with the pregnant teen. Following the orientation, participants who wish to continue, sign up for an individual pre-training interview with the programme co-ordinator.

Individual pre-training interview

The pre-training interview focuses on the prospective mentors' motivations for mentoring, family experiences, views on teen pregnancy, beliefs about raising children, and remaining concerns and questions. This interview allows for mutual evaluation of the 'goodness of fit' between the prospective mentor and the mentoring programme.

Given the fact that teen pregnancy typically occurs in the context of multiple pre-existing psychosocial risk factors, many pregnant teens have had negative experiences in their lives which result not only in difficulty intrusting, but also in a tendency to repeat negative patterns in their current relationships. Because relationship-building and positive change can be slow processes, endurance and unflagging optimism are essential qualities for mentors. Additional criteria include interpersonal skills, cultural sensitivity, motivation, reliability and experience as a parent.

Selection of teens

Like the mentors, young women needing mentors participate in the mentoring programme on a voluntary basis. The only stipulation is that the young women agree to keep appointments with their mentors. The programme is most likely to benefit pregnant teens who fall into a moderate-risk category. Moderate risk is indicated by conditions such as social isolation, childhood history of abuse, lack of knowledge and experience related to parenting, prior involvement with child protective services, multiple life stressors and unwanted pregnancy. Young women who fall into the high-risk category because of serious mental health issues, criminal histories or active substance abuse problems have needs that are beyond the scope of a community volunteer mentor programme.

The training programme

Overview

The training consists of seven, weekly, two-hour sessions led by the mentor programme co-ordinator and attended by a group of seven to ten mentor trainees. Trainees gain a knowledge and skill base in pre-natal care, labour and delivery, child development, child management, family violence, stress management, coping skills, interpersonal skills, problem-solving skills and accessing community resources. The training uses a multi-modal approach that combines didactic information, group discussion, role play, audiovisual material and presentations by health-care professionals and representatives of community agencies.

Fostering genuine empathy for the young parents is a critical element of the training. The group anticipates expectable difficulties related to establishing trust and rapport and engages in problem-solving together. Experiential exercises and discussion of case narratives help mentors understand the subjective experiences underlying teens' overt behaviours as well as the tensions that are expectable in the mentoring relationship.

We have found that the process aspect of the mentor training programme is as important as the content aspect. The relationship between the co-ordinator and the prospective mentors mirrors the mentor relationship, in that the programme co-ordinator models the qualities and values required of mentors. For example, the programme co-ordinator highlights the strengths and potential of each trainee, listens actively and empathically, validates trainees' experiences, and encourages independent problem-solving.

The seven-week time frame of the training programme offers an opportunity for relationship-building between the programme co-ordinator and pro-spective mentors. This relationship with each prospective mentor gives the programme co-ordinator a basis for making the eventual matches between mentors and mentees. It also increases the trainees' confidence in the programme co-ordinator, to whom they will turn for ongoing supervision and support. The group format of the mentor training has the additional benefit of establishing a network of supportive relationships among mentors.

The curriculum

The first training session focuses on defining the roles that mentors play, clarifying the parameters of each of these roles and using an experiential learning approach to cultivating trainees' empathy for young parents. For example, trainees discuss personal experiences that might parallel teens' experiences.

The second training session employs both didactic presentation and experiential exercises to teach mentors strategies for establishing rapport and bolstering teens' self-esteem. The characteristics of both successful and unsuccessful mentoring relationships are delineated and discussed.

The third session provides an overview of pregnancy, labour and delivery. Didactic and audiovisual presentations inform mentors about pre-natal care, danger signs during pregnancy and symptoms of pre-term labour.

The fourth session covers child development and parenting skills. Mentors learn strategies for teaching young parents about child behaviours that are normative at each developmental stage as well as age-appropriate and behaviour-appropriate disciplinary strategies.

The fifth session deals with family violence, with an emphasis on the dynamics of domestic abuse and child maltreatment. Mentors learn about prevention strategies, particularly stress management techniques. They also learn about accessing resources for victims of domestic violence, including obtaining restraining orders and emergency shelter. They learn about child-abuse reporting laws and receive guidelines about the limits of the mentoring role and how to recognize when supervisory intervention is appropriate.

The sixth session begins the process of matching mentors with mentees. Based on direct knowledge of mentors and information about teens provided by their case workers, the programme co-ordinator determines which pairs will work well together. Mentors learn about mentees, are given guidelines for first contacts and discuss their concerns. Seasoned mentors are invited to this session. Their first-hand accounts of the mentoring experience serve to generate excitement and allay anxiety among the trainees.

In the seventh and final training session, mentors learn about the full range of local resources and learn strategies for helping teens create and sustain linkages with the resources they need. For example, the teen may need linkage to material supports such as food, clothing and shelter; she may need counselling or educational resources; she may need child care; or she may need to expand her social support network. In preparation for this session, each mentor researches a particular community resource. She presents information about this resource to the group and provides each group member with accompanying materials. These presentations and materials provide mentors with the beginnings of a resource file to which they can refer as needed. The programme co-ordinator supplements the information presented with additional resource materials and reminds mentors of the availability of ongoing consultation.

The initial meeting between mentor and mentee

Careful preparation for the initial meeting is critical to an auspicious beginning of the mentoring relationship. Prior to the meeting, both mentor and teen are provided information about one another and both have input into when and how their first meeting will occur. The objectives of this initial meeting are to establish a positive connection, to clarify mutual roles and responsibilities, and for the mentor to identify and begin to respond to the mentee's most pressing concerns. If the teen has a strong connection with her case worker at the community health centre, the case worker can be present to facilitate this initial meeting between the teen and her mentor, and to clarify the differences between the roles of social worker and mentor. It is important for the case worker to make sure that the teen understands that she will continue to have the support of the case worker, but will now have the support of the mentor as well.

Ongoing support and supervision: celebrating successes and problem-solving

Monthly mentor meetings

After the mentors have completed their training and are matched with teens, the mentor group continues to meet with the programme co-ordinator on a monthly basis. The group provides members with continuing peer support and professional supervision, and serves as a buffer to mediate stress related to the inevitable frustrations and difficulties that are part of the mentoring experience. Mentors also celebrate one another's achievements. As the mentors gain experience, they become valuable resources to one another and the programme co-ordinator's role typically shifts from leader and teacher to group facilitator.

Relationship issues that were addressed theoretically in training now become a reality to be discussed in the monthly meetings. Earlier discussions of establishing rapport take on an immediacy in the context of the new relationships. The issue of limit-setting typically emerges early, as it is not unusual for mentors to have difficulty knowing when and how to set limits. For example, mentors initially may want to be available whenever their teens call. Since pregnant and parenting teens have many needs (concrete and emotional), they may push the limits of the relationship. Not only can this lead to a feeling of resentment or overload on the part of the mentor, but it may cause the teen to become overly dependent on the mentor. Feedback from the group helps members to recognize such boundary problems and to set appropriate limits. For example, if a mentor begins to feel like a taxi service, the mentor group might coach her to help the teenager learn to use public transportation rather than providing the transportation. This not only solves the transportation problem, but also teaches a skill that fosters independence.

Some teens seem to stretch the limits, some ask for too little from the relationship. For example, a young woman who frequently misses appointments may be anticipating being let down by her mentor and may prefer not to be home at the appointment time rather than suffer disappointment if her mentor does not keep their appointment. Such relationships can be the most difficult for mentors. Mentors may feel rejected or blame themselves. The group is helpful in providing perspective and support in these situations. For example, the group may remind a mentor that difficulty with engaging does not reflect a deficit on her part, but is to be expected when building relationships with adolescents who have had negative relationship experiences. In some cases, the mentor is unable to establish a relationship, and needs to be reassigned. In these situations the group can support the mentor through the transition.

The monthly mentor meetings also provide mentors with corrective feedback when their expectations are unrealistic. For example, an enthusiastic mentor may impose her own agenda or timetable. In this situation, the group may remind the mentor of the importance of self-determination, particularly how empowering it is for the teen to learn to set her own goals and meet them.

Individual supervision

The programme co-ordinator provides additional support and supervision to individual mentors on a weekly basis either by telephone or face-to-face contact. The weekly contact sustains the relationship between the programme co-ordinator and each mentor, and provides the mentor with a continuing model for the mentoring relationship. Weekly contact also keeps the programme co-ordinator informed and gives her the opportunity to provide support and intervene before difficulties develop. In addition to the regularly scheduled contact between the programme co-ordinator and mentors, the programme co-ordinator or her appointee is available on a twenty-four hour basis in case of emergency.

Mentors receive additional support and information from the community health centre multidisciplinary team that provides health and social services to mentees. Mentors get to know health centre staff when staff members make presentations during mentor training. Mentors visit the health centre regularly to attend mentor meetings, to consult with the programme co-ordinator and when they accompany mentees to medical appointments. During these visits, mentors are encouraged to consult with health care providers and case workers.

Future directions: evaluation of outcomes

Two strategies for evaluation of outcomes that will be utilized by this community health centre mentoring programme are also applicable to mentoring programmes across settings. The first strategy evaluates the effectiveness of the mentoring programme in terms of the impact on the children born to the teen parents in the mentoring programme. This strategy will involve tracking birth outcomes as well as abuse and neglect reports during the infants' first year of life.

The second strategy for measuring outcomes will evaluate the effectiveness of the mentoring programme in terms of the impact on the teen parents. Given that social support is recognized as an important buffer against the bio-psychosocial risk factors associated with early pregnancy (Buchholz and Korn-Brusztyn, 1993), social support is a critical construct to assess in evaluating the effectiveness of a mentoring program. Social support will be measured by the Perceived Social Support Scale (Procidano and Heller, 1983). It will be administered before a mentor has been assigned, and again one year later.

Conclusions

In the volunteer community mentoring programme described here, the key ingredients included:

- community education
- effective strategies for recruitment, selection, and matching of mentors and teens needing mentors
- a training programme that provides mentors with a knowledge base related to teen pregnancy and mentoring
- ongoing support and supervision for mentors, including weekly super-vision, monthly mentor meetings, and establishing linkages between mentors and multidisciplinary treatment teams
- agency investment and support, including funding for a programme co-ordinator for a minimum of ten hours per week.

Punitive legislation, attitudes and practices towards pregnant and parenting teens are costly and ineffective reactions to the problem of teen pregnancy. Community volunteer mentoring programmes are a creative response to teen pregnancy that is cost effective, provides community members with an opportunity to take positive action, and can lead to improved biological, psychological, social and economic outcomes for teen parents and their children.

Mentoring for disability in the Civil Service – UK

Introduction

Mentoring forms an important part of the Civil Service's bursary scheme, which helps employees with disabilities with their personal and career development. The aim of the scheme, which includes the provision of a mentor from the senior Civil Service, is to give disabled employees the tools with which they can compete more effectively for jobs at higher levels.

The Cabinet Office, which champions and organizes the Civil Service's bursary scheme for employees with disabilities, has two main roles in government. These are to help the Prime Minister and Cabinet reach well-informed decisions on policy and presentation, and to promote measures to modernize and improve the workings of government and Civil Service.

Nurturing disabled talent

The Bursary Scheme for Civil Servants with Disabilities was set up in April 1997 as a response to a report published two years earlier on equal opportunities in the Civil Service. Subsequently, the scheme has been given impetus by the Modernizing Government White Paper which has set targets for improving the under representation of people with disabilities in the senior Civil Service. The scheme is run in partnership with the Leadership Consortium, a project founded by the Prince of Wales' Advisory Group on Disability.

The Leadership Consortium's objective is to expand the UK's pool of talent 'by developing the cream of Britain's six million disabled people'. To this end, it offers bursary holders management training and a mentor to offer 'advice and assistance on career development and choice of training'. The Cabinet Office is one of ten bodies that support the consortium: others include BT, J. Sainsbury and Barclays Bank.

Training bursaries

The scheme provides bursary holders with £10 000 over two years to fund up to thirty-five days of training and the provision of a senior mentor. Training is meant to cover longer-term development issues rather than work-based instruction, which is the responsibility of the employing department or agency.

The scheme also offers networking opportunities with other disabled employees from both the public and private sector. Bursaries are funded either by Civil Service departments or centrally by the Cabinet Office. Applicants to the scheme who are not awarded bursaries may still be allocated mentors.

The bursary scheme is designed to give employees with disabilities the tools to equip them to compete more effectively for higher positions in the Civil Service. Currently the percentage of disabled staff is lower in the upper levels of the service than in the junior grades. Bursary holders and mentees are generally selected from the first rung of the Civil Service management ladder – normally from the first-line or middle managers – with the intention that they develop into suitable candidates for more senior positions.

Choosing mentors

Mentors are chosen from the top 3000 managers – i.e. the senior Civil Service (grade 5 and above). Managers interested in putting themselves forwards as mentors are asked to provide 'pen pictures' of themselves and attend a briefing day organized by the Cabinet Office and Leadership Consortium.

The Cabinet Office has drawn up a number of criteria that potential mentors should fulfil. It asks managers to volunteer as mentors if they believe they have the following personal profile:

- I am interested in playing a part in developing the next generation of talent.
- I like exercising the development role.

- I wish to gain some space and time to reflect on the framework of the values which shape the way I work.
- I wish to develop my coaching and mentoring skills.
- I get a buzz out of seeing other people grow and develop.
- I want to understand more about the issues that affect staff with disabilities.

Four briefing days are held each year, with places for ten mentors on each. The briefings cover the theory of mentoring, how mentoring works in practice and disability awareness. At the end of the briefing day, participants are asked why they want to take on board this type of commitment. Once signed up to the scheme, mentors also attend supporting seminars throughout their participation in it.

Selecting mentees

Similarly, the Cabinet Office has constructed a profile of an ideal bursary mentee. The eligibility criteria are as follows:

- I have a disability as defined by the Disability Discrimination Act 1995.
- I am a permanent member of the Civil Service.
- I have the support of my division/unit.
- I am able to demonstrate the ability to reach a senior management position within the Civil Service – at least grade 7 or equivalent.
- I am prepared to develop my career.
- I am prepared to take advantage of all opportunities provided by the programme.
- I am results driven.

Potential bursary holders are asked to complete an application form. They are then assessed against similar criteria to those shown above for mentees. Those short-listed are asked to attend an interview, which is carried out by either the Cabinet Office or the Civil Service department sponsoring the bursary.

The Leadership Consortium assists the Cabinet Office in selecting mentors and mentees, provides mentor training and runs the mentee induction days (see below). It is also the first point of contact for any questions or problems bursary holders may have about the scheme. The scheme for non-bursary holding mentees, however, is administered directly by the Cabinet Office.

Since its inception the scheme has grown. In 1999 thirteen bursaries were awarded, compared with seven in 1998 and three in the scheme's first year in 1997. It is planned that a further twenty bursaries will be awarded in 2000, while a further fifteen non-bursary holders will be allocated mentors.

The mentoring relationship

Mentors are allocated using five criteria:

- the needs of the mentee
- geographical location so that mentor and mentee can meet easily, although telephone mentoring is allowed
- the mentee's preference for a mentor in a particular department or area of work
- the personal characteristics of both mentor and mentee
- simple intuition or 'gut instinct'.

Mentors are first matched to bursary holders, with the remainder then allocated to the non-bursary holding mentees.

Induction day

Mentees attend a half-day training course where they learn about mentoring and what it can help them achieve. Training also covers the possible problem areas such as issues of confidentiality between the menteee and their mentor and line manager. When the training is completed, mentors break for lunch and this is when they meet their mentor for the first time.

Ground rules

At their first meeting after the induction day, the mentee and mentor set goals and agree on what they expect to achieve out of the relationship. This is essentially a mentoring contract.

No hard and fast rules are set on how subsequent meetings should be arranged, but the Cabinet Office does offer some guidelines. Ideally it recommends that mentor and mentee should meet every six to eight weeks and that meetings should normally last for two hours. It also advises that meetings should not be held at each other's desks, where discussions may be interrupted and where it might be difficult for the mentee to talk openly.

Evaluating the scheme

The bursary lasts for two years, although mentoring relationships can and do continue. At the end of the two years, mentees complete a questionnaire which covers, among other things, the helpfulness of the mentor in identifying and evaluating training courses, the number and content of mentor meetings, the perceived benefits of mentoring and any ways in which the mentoring relationship could have been made more effective. Mentors and Civil Service departments also receive similar questionnaires.

The benefits of mentoring

The Cabinet Office believes mentors gain because the experience of mentoring offers them the opportunity to examine their own values as they explain to the mentee 'how they think, why they think that way, and what matters to them'. It adds that the mentors' critical thinking and insight into the organization is sharpened as discussions with the mentee about workplace issues develop.

Mentees gain generally from contact with a senior civil servant who takes a personal interest in their development. Specifically, the Civil Service believes the following benefits can be realized:

- advice and support on career development
- increased confidence through access to senior managers
- speedier and easier insight into the formal and informal culture of the organization
- personal support to learn new strategies and how to take calculated risks
- an opportunity to observe a role model close up
- advice on how to improve certain areas of work
- an overview of the Civil Service outside their parent department.

The Cabinet Office has recently processed the questionnaires it sent to the mentors on the 1997 and 1998 mentor schemes. The results show that mentoring and training were the most highly rated parts of the bursary scheme. Mentees found the mentoring relationship to be a positive experience that had given them a wider perspective on their employment prospects. None reported a poor relationship with their mentor.

Future plans

From the feedback it has received from the mentors and mentees, the Cabinet Office is planning a couple of minor revisions to the mentoring aspects of the bursary scheme. First, it will make more effort to ensure that the mentor is best placed – i.e. from the same Civil Service department or agency and with a similar working background – to assist the mentee's development. Second, it plans to encourage an increase in the frequency of meetings to every four to six weeks.

Government departments will be encouraged to use mentoring more generally. The newly launched Civil Service Reform Programme provides departments with a number of initiatives to bring on and develop talented people, and mentoring will underpin many of these programmes.

Embracing diversity at Sheffield Hallam University – UK

Jill Nanson[8]

Background to the project

Our mentoring initiative was funded by Yorkshire Forward, the Yorkshire and Humber Regional Development Agency, an organization which strives to 'make a positive difference to our people, our business and our environment' (http://www.yorkshire-forward.com). Aiming to prepare students for graduate employment, our objectives reflected Sheffield Hallam University's ongoing commitment to enhancing its students' employability. We hoped to achieve this by charging our mentors with sharing their knowledge, skills and experience with our students, and by doing this to equip their mentees with the confidence and ability to secure suitable jobs. By focusing on promoting the under-utilized employment opportunities in small and medium-sized enterprises (SMEs – an SME is an organization that employs fewer than 250 people), so enabling graduates to work in the local area, the project also supported the university's role in promoting sustainable regional development.

The stages of our programme

The project, which had around sixty participants, began in September 1999 and formally concluded with an award ceremony and evaluation event in June 2000. The project team worked with a consultant to design the programme, with the intention of building capacity within our department. During the autumn, publicity material and application forms were sent out to potential participants and preparation took place to provide induction and support, and to carry out monitoring and evaluation. In January 2000 the selection and matching processes were carried out, prior to an induction workshop at the end of that month.

Embracing diversity

Embracing and celebrating diversity was central to this initiative. Within this context we aimed to recruit students from groups that face particular difficulties in securing appropriate graduate employment. We targeted students from ethnic minority groups and students with disabilities and decided to also work with students specializing in art, craft and cultural studies. This decision was informed by research which showed that the median starting salary for these students is considerably lower than the university average. Although clearly a positive action measure, the overriding aim was to provide a highly student-centred programme, with participants choosing how to take forward the opportunities presented to them.

The demographic composition of the mentors' group did not reflect that of the mentees. In fact, very few of our mentors stated that they belonged to an ethnic minority group, or that they had a disability. We felt that it was more important that their professional and personal attributes reflected the needs of our mentees. Just over half of our mentors worked for SMEs, a large proportion of which represented the cultural industries. Others were drawn from large companies and organizations, including HSBC, the Benefits Agency and the university itself. Many group members, although new to mentoring, were experienced managers with a particular interest in staff development. Others were involved in teaching and training, while a few were committed to related work in the voluntary sector. The commitment, skills and experience of the group were highly compatible with our objectives and proved to be key to the success of the project.

Selecting and matching our participants

In order to facilitate the selection and matching processes, both mentees and mentors were asked to complete application forms that provided us with detailed information. Mentees were selected mainly on the basis of their personal objectives. They were also asked to describe how they could contribute to the programme. The mentors were required to record their skills and experience, and to give their reasons for applying to the programme. The project team found selection a straightforward exercise, with a similar numbers of people wishing to be mentors and to be mentored. More importantly, a very high proportion of applicants appeared to be well suited to the programme. This could be partly due to the way in which the project was promoted, in that we targeted people who were likely to identify with the aims of the programme. The need for some, if not all, students to enhance their employability is a key concern within the higher education sector. Similarly, all those we approached to be mentors had had prior contact with the university, either as a past student or through involvement in another project.

Our priority during matching was to find each mentee a mentor who worked in the sector in which the mentee was interested. Where this was not possible we looked for mentors who were able to offer appropriate skills development. In a few cases a strongly similar area of interest outside study or work provided the basis for a partnership. Despite making attempts to manage their expectations, mentee feedback at the induction session showed that some students were disappointed not to be matched with a mentor from their preferred vocational area. In response we tried to show the value of being paired with someone from an unfamiliar area and, interestingly, feedback at the evaluation event did not reiterate these initial concerns.

The induction workshop

As part of our client-driven strategy, participants were asked to identify issues that were important to them. Their comments informed the topics that were discussed at the induction workshop. Students were asked, on their application forms, to identify any perceived barriers to finding suitable graduate employment. Interestingly, only four of the twenty-nine students cited prejudice as a potential problem, while concerns about limited work experience, a lack of self-confidence, inadequate skills and uncertainty regarding career choice were far more prominent. As a result ethnicity and disability issues were not raised explicitly; instead it was stressed that the personalities, experiences and objectives of those involved would produce a set of highly individual mentoring relationships. This focus was the thread that linked together a number of workshop activities.

The first workshop activity was designed to highlight that mentoring can take many, equally valid, forms, but that success depends on factors such as mutual respect, objectivity and open-mindedness. By sharing their experiences of occasions when they had received guidance, support or practical help, the group was able to identify a set of characteristics that they felt would be common to any effective mentoring relationship. These included being non-judgemental, providing constructive feedback, giving encouragement and respecting the need for appropriate levels of confidentiality. During the second part of the session participants were asked to record their personal objectives. Once again this demonstrated the importance of recognizing the uniqueness of the individuals in each partnership.

The final section of the workshop explained what support was available to those taking part. Participants were encouraged to contact the programme manager if they encountered any difficulties, and other sources of help were also outlined. Guidelines for working with students with dyslexia and hearing impairments were given to relevant mentors. The group was then asked to describe any problems they thought they might face, and to work together to find possible solutions. As well as putting forward practical and proactive strategies, the mentees' comments revealed their commitment to taking responsibility for their own progress. Their comments included: 'Give as much as you take', 'Be keen and willing to learn new skills', 'Let your mentor know what you would like to achieve, and ask for their help in doing so'. The mentors' contributions reiterated the characteristics already identified as being necessary for a successful partnership.

Improving training and support

Those attending the evaluation event were asked for feedback on the induction workshop. Almost all of the mentors and mentees who responded said that the induction they received was useful. Their comments, however, suggested that there was room for improvement in this part of the programme. Although it was good to hear that over three-quarters of the mentors said that they had understood their role, only half went on to agree that their mentoring experience was as they had expected. That almost half of the mentors felt that they would have liked further training was also a cause for concern. Furthermore, feedback from some of the mentors suggested that their mentees could have been better prepared for their mentoring relationship. This is perhaps reflected by the fact that fewer than half of the mentees felt that they had understood their role as a mentee, or that their experience was as they had expected. Interestingly only a small proportion of this group said that they would have liked more training. Another issue was also highlighted. A number of participants reported that although their relationship began strongly, they found maintenance more difficult, especially once the initial areas for development had been addressed. This could be because many objectives focused of specific tasks, for example, writing curriculum vitae or taking part in mock interviews. Goals which necessitated in-depth discussion of more intangible issues, such as building self-confidence, were much less common.

To summarize, it seems that a lack of clarity about their role, and appropriate activities to be undertaken, caused problems for some of our group members. Paradoxically it could be argued that too much emphasis was placed on the individuality of relationships, and that this treatment of diversity left some of our participants without a clear framework in which to operate. The task this year will be to provide more guidance without losing sight of the broad and varied scope of mentoring. Two strategies will be piloted in our next programme. First, it will be possible, with their agreement, to provide case studies about our first cohort of mentors and mentees. In addition, a number of mentors are keen to take part again this year, and some of our mentees have offered to talk about their experiences to the new group. Changes will also be made to the content of the workshop with the aim of providing more practical support and therefore opening up a greater range of activities to participants. We hope that this will help our new group to tackle issues that might not be apparent at the beginning of their relationships, for example, the need to increase the mentee's motivation. Alred, Garvey and Smith (1998, pp. 32–46) provide a useful illustration of how this might be done. Their mentoring process model is based around three phases: exploration, new understanding and action planning. Helpful techniques for both mentors and mentees to use at each stage are described, and examples of possible questions and comments are given. The project team intends to develop a participative exercise based on this model. This will hopefully help to provide a practical focus to the more general discussions that predominated last year.

In addition to the support outlined in the section about the induction workshop, the team tried to make telephone contact with each participant at least once during the programme. We decided not to contact participants more frequently as we were concerned about intruding in the mentoring relationships and hindering their development. In hindsight it appears we might have been overly cautious, and although almost all of the mentors and mentees attending the evaluation event felt they had received sufficient assistance from the programme manager, we hope more proactively to support the members of our next programme. This is because we suspect that the development of a closer relationship between the project team and the programme participants might be beneficial. Although some trouble-shooting did take place last year, this was mainly around time management and finding places for people to meet. Problems of a more sensitive nature were not reported and none of our participants mentioned issues related to diversity. Of course, it is possible that no serious problems arose, but it is also possible that people did face difficulties but did not feel comfortable asking for help. Furthermore, if we successfully encourage participants to discuss more complicated, and potentially challenging, issues, rather than just carrying out task-based activities, it will be important to offer appropriate levels of support.

The outcomes of our programme

The evaluation exercise also considered outcomes in relation to the personal objectives that were agreed at the induction workshop. A brainstorming exercise revealed that the mentees had a wide variety of goals which can be categorized as professional development (e.g. gaining work experience and acquiring insights into the expectations of employers), skills development (e.g. report writing and time management) and personal development (e.g. improving self-confidence and increasing motivation). The mentors reported a narrower range of objectives. By far the most common aim here was to support and help students in both their personal and professional development. Other objectives included their own professional development and building more positive links between business and education.

The results of the evaluation exercise strongly indicated the existence of effective relationships, with over half of the mentors feeling that they had met their objectives, and the rest of the sample stating that they had partly achieved their goals. Similarly, all of the mentees felt that they at least partly met their objectives. Comments made by the mentees reveal more about the value of the programme. They included: 'I was encouraged to believe in myself', 'I was given the impetus to succeed and find my niche', 'It helped me build my confidence', 'I found someone who supported me ... a friend as well as a mentor'. Their mentors also reported valuable experiences: 'I would recommend the programme to others, and plan to take part again next year', 'I achieved my goal of helping my mentee with her personal and professional development', 'I improved my communication skills and self-confidence', 'Taking part gave me a sense of achievement'.

In conclusion, we felt very positive about the outcomes of our programme. As a result we intend to run it again, implementing the improvements discussed in this case study, during the 2000–1 academic session.

The Probation Service: a congruent mentoring network – UK

Coral Gardiner[9]

Background

Beginning Employment and Training (BEAT) was the first mentoring scheme for people in the UK Criminal Justice System. Developed in 1993, it helped offenders to move from punishment to prevention. When considering the research, the message was then, and remains stark: unemployment is a significant cause of crime, particularly among those people who already have a criminal record. Moreover, the position is more acute for those from minority ethnic backgrounds who are often likely to be unemployed and to feature disproportionately within the Criminal Justice System. As a result, these cohorts are particularly prone to finding themselves on an 'unemployment-crime-imprisonment-reoffending' helter-skelter.

The West Midlands Probation Service initiated BEAT as a multicultural mentoring programme, which proved highly successful in its aims to help offenders access Employment, Training and Education.

An evaluation of BEAT carried out in 1997 by Paul Tilsley found:

> One is therefore left with an impression of a young person with learning difficulties who has had a very poor experience of school, very little knowledge of employment routine, probably suffered from social exclusion, having very low self esteem. These issues are important, as without a network of contacts, their life is very limited to those young people who are in the same situation as they themselves are. The temptations to criminal activity are therefore greater due to lack of a structured routine and to peer pressure.

This statement suggests there is a need for continuing support to individuals through the mentoring process to help them to move on.

Funding constraints and other factors gave way to the loss of BEAT in 1998. This offered an opportunity to build a new sustainable mentoring structure, integral to the Probation Service and with commitment from the top. The system had to operate in a climate of collaboration and co-operation with other similar organizations.

Like all things, the Criminal Justice System is undergoing change and the Probation Service has developed a 'congruent mentoring network' in response to these changes.

Its aims are:

- to enable every offender who requires the support of a mentor to have one
- to provide a service that is responsive to the needs of the offenders it serves

- to enable offenders to achieve their goals of Employment, Training and/or Education (ETE).

This new model translates the best working practices of the BEAT project to a multiagency networking partnership which builds on those lessons learned from BEAT. It is fundamentally different in its structure and operates on a network of small satellites linked to organizations with an interest in supporting the client group.

Programme design

The programme was designed against a backdrop of change in the provision of Criminal Justices Services. The Crime and Disorder Act 1998 introduced the Criminal Justice System to some underlying themes. These call upon the police and the local authority with the whole community to establish a local partnership to cut crime. In addition, the local authorities and other public bodies must consider the crime and disorder implications of all their decision making.

To support these themes, the Home Office Secretary's priorities for the Probation Service are expressed as the following goals:

1 Reducing crime and supervising offenders effectively.
2 Providing high-quality information, assessment and related services to the courts and other users of the service.
3 Providing value for money while maintaining fairness and high standards of service delivery.

Shortly after these goals were offered, the following statement was made:
Youth Justice Reforms will use mentoring to help 'nip youth offending in the bud' (Boateng, 1999).

Further statistics were provided from an evaluation of BEAT by Tilsley in 1997. From a study of sixty-one individuals and of the forty-two who had used the scheme, he found that, of those mentored:

- 60 per cent had not committed further offences
  15 per cent had reoffended
  10 per cent were receiving support while in custody.

Of the ETE outcomes:

- 46 per cent were involved in training.
  17 per cent have found employment
- 37 per cent were unemployed, but some were waiting for college courses to begin.

Within its time and context BEAT was able to prove that mentoring contributes significantly to reducing crime.

The Probation Service's responsibilities include the promotion of an understanding of the Criminal Justice System among Employment Service staff and other participating agencies. The purpose of this is to provide offenders with high-quality information. This new system uses mentoring as a strategy for meeting the goals by engaging mentors in a pivotal role.

Goal 3 relates to value for money. Comparative costs for BEAT and the congruent network mean a saving of almost two-thirds in real costs. This is achieved by entering into contractual arrangements with partner organizations willing to support the network aims.

In the context of the Crime and Disorder Act and the plethora of research studies, it is known that the main constraints to obtaining employment for offenders in the community are:

- limited experience and qualifications
- poor literacy and numerical skills
- employers' discrimination
- not enough of the right sort of jobs.

This information, supported by the statistics, strengthens the case for effective support of offenders through a mentoring network with a multi-agency, multiethnic approach.

The professional friendship

In a paper prepared for the Fourth European Mentoring Conference, 1997, the nature of mentoring as a special relationship was examined as a 'professional friendship' based on previous research findings by Gardiner (1994). Here 'friendship' is identified as a significant factor in what makes a mentoring relationship successful. The first consideration of the mentee was that they wanted 'someone' to help sort out their lives. Through a diagnostic questionnaire, individuals were able to use a checklist construction of the make-up of their mentor. They chose criteria and ownership of their requirements which include ethnicity and gender. Alongside this, the mentors were trained to work holistically and in a 'person-centred' manner. This approach to diversity highlights the BEAT project as a good quality model of working with equality with offenders. Mentees are members of the community who have offended and are supported by community mentors. These community mentors being individuals drawn from all walks of life within their own community who are prepared to act in the role of Professional Friend.

The BEAT as a model of community mentoring was constructed from David Clutterbuck's (1991) business model translated into the Criminal Justice System in 1993.

The principles of the community mentoring system

Community mentoring is established on the basis of the following principles:

1 It is a *one*-to-*one* activity base.
2 It has a *purpose*.
3 It works to set *goals* through an *action plan*.
4 It is about *empowering* the *parties*.
5 It is about *learning* and *change*.
6 It is usually a *voluntary* activity.
7 It is about *mutuality*.
8 It requires a *contract*.
9 It is a process which is *reviewed* and *evaluated*.

Mentors are recruited from all walks of life. In the network model the selection, recruitment, training, development and ongoing support for mentors is undertaken by the all partner organizations. This is achieved by working jointly to provide community role models for offenders.

In this system the mentors take on roles at the request of the mentee. These can be wide ranging (despite what can often appear to be minor distinctions); for example:

● befriending
● supporting
● guiding
● advising
● counselling
● coaching
● tutoring
● networking
● co-ordinating
● facilitating
● teaching
● listening.

They must offer themselves as a confidante, role model and advocate.

The attitudes demonstrated by good mentors in their roles can also be varied. The mentor must be non-judgemental, non-directive, open-minded, approachable, responsive and optimistic. They must demonstrate unconditional acceptance, confidence (both in themselves and the mentee), sincerity, reliability and a holistic approach.

The mentoring system takes responsibility for dealing with the ongoing issues which occur between mentors and mentees. Some of the most frequently dealt with issues within the relationship were:

● trust
● confidentiality
● the 'unpowered relationship'

- the effects of communication (verbal and non-verbal, body language and eye contact).

Equally common is the issue of the usage and effect of verbal language.

The mentoring network

The mentoring network forms a coalition of organizations coming together in a strategic alliance to meet the needs of the recipients.
The aims of the network are:

- to act as a steering group for the West Midlands Probation Mentoring Service (WMPS)
- to assist the partners to provide mentoring support for offenders on their path to employment, training and education.

The objectives of the network are:

- to monitor and evaluate the quality and development of the provision
- to identify issues as they arise
- to build on good practices.

The purpose of the network is to enable greater resourcing to be made available where it is most needed. This approach is integral to the Community Justice System and is achieved through collaborative working. For example, training venues are shared as are the take-up of training places. On a rota basis the organization offers a date and venue, and a total number of places for participants. This means there is flexibility for sharing resources such as mentors. As a result there is greater mobility among mentors to meet the needs of individuals in their location. There were teething problems at first as all the partners strove to find a way of working co-operatively together. Competitiveness was a central issue at first. The partners came to trust each other in a climate of mutual support. Although individuals moved on, the cultural values encouraged collaboration.

The partnership

Partnership took two forms – internal and external. In considering the structure at design stage we looked at the remit of the ETE unit with approximately fourteen employment and training specialists namely (employment liaison officers and probation service officers) who have day-to-day contact with offenders in their employment surgeries. These specialists were provided with numbers of mentors for matching to mentees (offenders). As the internal partner, ETE provides Community Justice training to mentors and works with the other partner organizations through a strategy group.

Partner organizations receive Probation Service Partnership money to provide services, which include the recruitment, selection and training of mentors to standards in mentoring.

There are several organizations currently working service-level agreements/ arrangements with WMPS across the West Midlands. In Birmingham, agreements are either paid or unpaid depending on the arrangements for partnership working. For the Walsall, Wolverhampton, Dudley and Sandwell areas the partner organization is a charity. In the Solihull and Coventry areas, there is a charity, a careers service and a youth offending team (YOT).

How the system works

The network is steered by the Mentoring Strategy group whose core membership includes all of the contract holders plus others by invitation. The group acts as a learning set coming together to find solutions to problems. Another of its main roles is to monitor the quality and development of the network.

The purpose of the network is to create support systems at all levels so that no person or party operates in isolation. The strategy group evaluates the effectiveness of this.

As a collective body the network organizations are providing a good practice model of high quality which is cost-effective and offers opportunities for organizational development.

Within the network there are opportunities for several initial mentoring pilots in the following areas:

- woman to woman
- ethnic minority mentoring for Afro-Caribbean males
- parenting skills
- drugs
- youth offending teams
- probation officer pilot.

In this way the network will be able to make local responses to local needs within the community where it is operating. The network in practice provides a massive collective resource to support probation offenders towards their holistic goals. The strategy group focuses on matters of coherence, training, monitoring and evaluation, resourcing, standards and quality.

Code of practice

Members of the strategy group commit to a code of practice in the Community Mentoring Model:

- To respect each other's differences. We are all at different stages of personal/ self-awareness.

- To be supportive of each other.
- To listen to each other.
- To be open and honest (with sensitivity).
- To challenge the issue not the person.
- To respect institutional confidentiality.
- To be willing to learn from each other.
- To share knowledge and resources.
- To actively participate.
- To create a safe, friendly, happy environment.
- To give time to each other, allow each to finish.

Mentor training

Community Justice mentors are trained in the generic skills of mentoring and receive training which includes:

- The history of the Criminal Justice System and the Probation Service.
- The work of the Probation Service and the role of the mentor in relation to that work.
- The roles and responsibilities of probation officers and employment liaison officers.
- Institutional confidentiality.
- Disclosure.
- Rehabilitation of Offenders Act.
- ETE issues in the criminal justice field in relation to public protection.
- Risk assessment.
- Child protection issues
- Familiarization with the WMPS diversity and anti-oppressive practice.

The mentoring relationship

Within the mentor/mentee relationship a code of practice similar to that used by the strategy group is operated as a contract. It expects a similar way of behaving from both mentor and mentee. Both parties are required to sign up to the contractual obligations of their relationship.

Partners bring their own unique experience of working with mentoring, but need to learn to adapt to a previously alien environment – one where they have to work collaboratively and collectively rather than competitively.

Ethical issues

There are a number of ethical issues that have to be considered within the network by the partners. Among these are:

- confidentiality
- disclosure

- openness
- responsibility
- valuing
- respecting
- integrity
- competence
- trust
- honesty
- individual freedom to be who we are
- goodness and rightness
- justice
- fairness.

Overall there is the principle that individual values should not be imposed on the network.

A huge range of issues have impacted on the BEAT mentoring model, some of which have served as lessons for the benefit of the congruent network model.

The lessons learned from beat

Diversity issue

BEAT was set up as a good practice model because of its open-door policy, under which no one was turned away. There were ethnic and gender mixes and matches dependent on the availability of mentors. It also offered diversity training for mentors. BEAT became established, assumptions were made that the matching process depended on well-trained mentors for the quality of the relationship. The selection process was improved by using a diagnostic questionnaire.

In one case, we found that a female mentor was matched to a sexist mentee. The female mentor patiently nurtured the mentee's attitude to become more positive. One of BEAT's greatest success stories was of a mixed heritage/black female grandmother, who mentored a nineteen-year-old, white offender because she was the only mentor who was not in a current relationship. A previous relationship she had concluded was with an Afro-Caribbean male.

Two-thirds of the mentors on BEAT were female and 50 per cent of the mentees were from ethnic minority backgrounds, while 90 per cent of all the mentors were from ethnic minority backgrounds.

The project found that maturity in individuals was not an issue of age. A cross-gender peer mentoring relationship of the same cultural heritage found itself with problems when the male mentee fell in love with the female mentor. When she found herself the subject of his affections, she turned to the co-ordinator for support. Mentoring relationships are complex and can be complicated by the variables of gender and ethnic diversity.

Management issues

The BEAT project's overall effectiveness depended upon the competence of the co-ordinator. The network is not dependent upon any one individual co-ordinating a mentoring system, but rather a group or body of devolved functions which can be carried out in co-operation with each other. For example the mentoring development officer organizes and delivers the Community Justice training. The partner organization recruits, selects, holds references, insures and jointly police-checks mentors. Also, the support for mentors, which is ongoing, is delivered jointly by a variety of involved organizations. In this way there is a shared responsibility and support for the achievement of the end goal.

It is important to continue the good practices in mentoring models which demonstrate success, through rigorous monitoring and evaluation methods. BEAT used robust recording systems and participant feedback.

Barriers to learning

Barriers to learning can paralyse offenders, and mentors need to be aware the need to help them move on. Mentoring can be said to be about learning and change. For offenders that can mean learning how to change within the safe confines of a positive mentoring relationship. Removing barriers to learning is challenging, not least because there may be so many of them. Some of the most common we identified were:

- lack of confidence
- very poor experience of institutions
- severely disrupted education
- problems relating to drug/alcohol/substance abuse
- problems with relationships/family
- debt/financial problems
- homelessness.

The most important of barriers in the lives of offenders are relationships. This is because without having positive stable relationships with family and friends they feel paralysed with the fear of not knowing who to turn to for help to find accommodation, work and other basic needs. Among the issues we identified here were:

- rigid course structures
- lack of flexible/open learning
- lack of guidance/counselling
- intimidating environment
- course fees.

Institutions are very intimidating environments to offenders, who often prefer informal/flexible modes of learning. Again, there are numerous barriers, including:

- lack of adequate accommodation
- discrimination against offenders
- seeking employment
- stigmatism
- fear of and awareness of negative attitudes from others,
- fear of falling back into offending or being accused of reoffending.

However, the single biggest social barrier facing offenders is the discrimination against them when seeking employment.

Potential barriers to the mentoring relationship

We identified a wide range of real and potential barriers to initiating and sustaining a useful mentoring relationship. Some of the most critical were:

- *communications*: inarticulacy, negative body language, lack of openness, etc.
- *immaturity*: for example, lack of emotional stability by the mentee
- *time/commitment*: failure to give the relationship the priority it deserves
- *lack of goals*: mentee not knowing what they want to achieve
- *mentor attitudes*: particularly being judgemental, failing to show confidence in the mentee, and conscious or unconscious stereotyping (by either or both parties)
- *supportiveness*: the mentor simply is not there for the mentee when needed.

Sometimes, barriers block the development of the relationship. For example, regardless of race or gender, dependency can occur. This can happen on the part of the mentor or the mentee. It is an important barrier because it can also cause other problems to appear, i.e. a lack of emotional stability, perceived lack of power, loss of goal orientation, imposing or deferring in the relationship, lack of openness.

When a mentee asks for a mentor of the same cultural background where there is none available it may lead to insuperable barriers. However, often an offender can accept differences in a mentoring relationship, because they see that the mentor is making strenuous efforts to overcome perceived barriers.

Taking the two sets of barriers as compounding together, the task of making a successful relationship within the Community Justice context is formidable. Yet it happens for the very reason given. If people are willing to accept each other for who and what they are and they can respect each other's differences, then they are able to have empowering relationships.

Conclusion

Mentoring in the Criminal Justice arena is challenging, but it can also be said to find mentoring at its most powerful. It brings support to those who are most vulnerable in our society. The BEAT project 'has demonstrated that those taking part in the mentoring process are less likely to fail and are more likely to succeed. Records indicate that they are not known to be re-offending' (Megginson and Clutterbuck, 1995).

This statement still holds true to Paul Tilsley's evaluation of BEAT in 1997. We are now taking the lessons learned to a new way of working in mentoring that may prove to be yet more appropriate for the future of Community Justice Mentoring.

Employers perceive offenders as people who are not to be trusted. In mentoring we depend on trust for success. The experience of cross-cultural and cross-gender relationships are of acceptance and respecting. Building trust in this way encourages employers to take risks on people and allows ex-offenders to trust in turn.

Mentoring the many faces of diversity – UK

William A. Gray and Marilynne Miles Gray[10]

Since 1978, our guiding principle, when developing each mentoring programme, has always been: while a mentoring programme is designed for a targeted *group* of protégés, it is important to remember that within the group are *individuals*, with different backgrounds, needs, goals and dreams within a unique corporate context. The programme must be designed to accommodate the individual differences within the same programme, and at the same time not lose sight of satisfying corporate needs and goals. Upfront planning and design – using a collaborative approach – ensures that the programme addresses everybody's diversity issues, as well as common issues.

While it is customary to focus on the visual differences, such as gender and race, we have also included the unseen differences that could potentially hinder or help a working relationship. We do not assume, for example, that diversity issues automatically arise from differences in race or gender. Indeed, these issues may stem from different working styles. Or from their different designations, such as labour, management, technical and non-technical. In sum, we have learned, over the years, to address diversity issues very broadly and to stress the teaching of many kinds of diversity so that programme participants are enabled to more accurately deal with the differences when they arise in the workplace.

The following five brief case studies illustrate how we have provided different Corporate Mentoring Solutions™ for the many faces of diversity.

Mentoring to facilitate silo-busting at CSX Transportation

Like most organizations that have been around for over twenty years, CSX Transportation is hierarchically structured and has departments that were created to carry out specific functions. Add to this, CSX's history as a railroad with often severe management–labour conflicts. Under CEO Pete Carpenter's leadership, in the early 1990s CSX began to transform itself into a high-performing organization with a threefold purpose: serving customers better, enabling salaried and exempt employees at all levels to develop themselves, and increasing stock market value for shareholders.

In 1992, an Associate Development Programme was launched, in which employees from all levels, from management and labour, and from all departments could participate. Its primary purpose was to enable employees to develop themselves so they could pursue career options in new directions, such as moving from labour to management, from one department to another and/or relocating into new positions, etc. By allowing everybody to participate in the mentoring programme, CSX combated another diversity issue: silo-busting.

Silo-busting occurs when the 'silos,' or different departments within the organization, are broken down. A culture of teamwork is fostered, rather than one of compartmentalization. Employees get a chance to understand the importance of each other's roles within the company, and learn from people that they may not usually have a chance to interact with. Working relationships that were previously antagonistic, due to misunderstanding a person's function or lack of communication, are smoothed over. People learn that each department is unique and is a vital part of the larger organization. They learn to work together for an essential business reason: to attract and keep valued customers.

One of the things that has made this mentoring programme so effective since 1992, is the Oversight Committee. This volunteer group puts more time into interviewing, selecting and matching mentor–protégé partners – and providing ongoing monitoring and support for each mentoring relationship – than any other company we've worked with. Another key to success is the Corporate Mentoring Solution™ we provide: a two-day training session at CSX's rural retreat centre in Welaka. This remote location and the time frame greatly reduces job distractions and enables mentor–protégé partners to focus on getting to know each other and on planning how they will work together to achieve major protégé goals. This arrangement also fosters silo-busting, by allowing participants to network and, through informal dialogue, realize the importance of all job functions and discuss how to work together more co-operatively to serve customers better. For example, one mentor–protégé pair learned about auditing and sales from each other, and then made presentations to each other's department; this fostered appreciation and co-operation between the departments.

Is the ninety-minute drive to Waleka and the time spent away from work really worth it? Participants think so. The programme has consistently been rated 4.3 out of 5 for eight years. CSX definitely thinks so. It has sponsored thirteen phases (groups) and plans to sponsor more. A senior executive has made the three-hour round-trip to Waleka to address each phase, emphasizing how this mentoring programme fosters the silo-busting necessary to achieve CSX's threefold strategic purpose as a high-performance organization.

Mentoring professional transformation at Exxon

Mentoring can often help people make professional transformations – literally shifting their style or way of functioning – enabling them to be more successful.

The sales division of Exxon had actively recruited women and visible minorities to meet Equal Employment Opportunity Programme (EEO) goals. Close tracking revealed that after five years, these valued salespeople were not performing at a high enough level to justify promotion. Upon realizing this, many females and black males left Exxon. In contrast, white males had higher performance ratings and were getting promoted because they had received informal mentoring.

Our Corporate Mentoring Solution™ for Exxon uncovered another reason for the high turnover rate of females and black males: they were having difficulty making the transformation from being just technically oriented to becoming more people oriented – an essential competency for sales.

The EEO data revealed that supervisors were providing adequate supervision to orient all new hires during the first year. The performance differences began to occur in the second year, when the females and black males were not getting any informal mentoring.

We carefully designed a more formalized mentoring programme to ensure that females and black males (and white males) received the systematic mentoring needed to become competent salespeople.

At the end of the year-long relationship, quantitative surveys revealed that some protégé's needs were not met as expected (due to long-distance relationships that hindered getting together with the mentor). Qualitative evaluation (structured interviews) revealed that every protégé felt valued and optimistic about their future with Exxon. All recommended that Exxon slightly reduce the job functions of mentors so that they had more time to assist protégés. This was done and the net result was significantly greater retention of Exxon's highly valued diversified workforce, which saved money and, in turn, increased sales, which made money!

Reciprocal mentoring overcame the generation gap at Varian Associates

The diversity issue for the Radiation Division of Varian Associates was the generation gap between recently hired personnel, most of whom had master's degrees, and veterans who did not. Although the newer hirers knew how to use the latest technology and software programs, they lacked the practical know-how and business acumen that the veterans had gained from years on the job. Due to animosity between the generations, we thought it best to allow protégés to nominate mentors, who were then asked if they would like to work with that protégé. In many instances, a protégé chose a mentor that he or she had difficulty working with. When asked why this mentor was nominated, the answer was – 'I want to see if we learn how to work together in a formalized relationship'.

Each mentor–protégé pair worked on a six-month Mentor-Assisted Project™ (MAP) in the mentor's area of expertise (expertise that the protégé wanted to acquire.) Was this beneficial? Yes. Every protégé completed a MAP in an area of professional interest. For example, one mentor was chosen for his expertise in project management. This mentor identified how to quickly prepare a future project manager. This was significant because the Radiation Division had no formal training courses on project management, yet most of the work they did involved working on project teams. After the MAP ended, this mentor and protégé developed a training programme that greatly improved the competencies of all future project managers.

A number of the mentor–protégé pairs engaged in reciprocal mentoring. The protégé taught the latest in software know-how and the mentor taught practical know-how. The pilot programme was so successful that it was expanded each year. By the fifth year, the Radiation Division had moved from the bottom of twenty-three divisions to become a profit centre.

Bottom-up mentoring at AT&T Global Communication Systems

Mentoring is generally thought to follow the hierarchical structure of the organization: going from someone higher ranking to someone lower ranking. However, when we worked with AT&T Global Business Communication Systems, our initial Mentoring Solution™ was bottom up. After top-level management mandated that everyone would receive diversity training, the group representing the diversified workforce approached the decision-makers and offered to mentor them. This lower-ranking group helped these corporate leaders understand the frustrations of being different and the unique contribution that diversity could bring to the organization. For example, leaders decided to target minority small businesses – something they had never previously thought of. They now had direct access to people who represented the diversified workforce and could contribute to these new initiatives. As a result of this unique approach, the decision-making process became more collaborative.

To add value to the initial mentoring initiative, we suggested reciprocal mentoring relationships be established. Corporate leaders continued to receive mentoring about diversity issues from the diversified workforce, which, in turn, now received mentoring to guide career development.

Mentoring teams improve management–labour relations at C&O Railroad

Management–labour conflicts have historically plagued many corporations, especially the railroad industry. The Chesapeake and Ohio Railroad (C&O Railroad) was no exception. General manager, Al Crown, wanted to resolve this age-old conflict. We guided the development of a mentoring programme with five-person mentoring teams comprising management and labour co-mentors for three protégés. On each team, the three protégés had common work experience.

For example, one group of protégés had all been working as computer programmers. They did such a good job technically that this qualified them to supervise other people doing these same jobs. Their diversity challenge entailed dramatically changing their style of work to become less detail oriented and better able to see the 'bigger picture,' as well as becoming more people oriented. A second group had earned promotions from the operations side of railroading (which required assertive decisions and actions to keep the trains rolling out of the yard on time). Now, they were learning to supervise other operations workers, and needed to become more people oriented and motivating.

The co-mentors were willing to work together to help the protégés make this major style-shift transformation. Was this of value? Absolutely. During the mentoring process, the protégés were able to observe the role model of co-operation between the co-mentors, which furthered C&O's initiative to improve management–labour relations.

The preceding examples illustrate that each mentoring programme must be thoughtfully designed to meet the diverse needs of participants and their organizations. For over twenty years, we have provided a wide variety of Corporate Mentoring Solutions™ based on this guiding principle: 'Different strokes for different folks'. Diversity is more than what you see.

The Pakistani Mentoring Partnership, an Excellence in Cities Learning Mentor in Birmingham – UK

Asif Mukhtar[11]

Pakistanis in Birmingham

Pakistanis are now an integral part of a multiethnic Britain. They are the third largest ethnic minority group in this country and their number is estimated at 609,543. The estimated number of Pakistanis in Birmingham is 66,085, which makes 6.9 per cent of the total number of residents in the city.

Fifty-one per cent of the Pakistani population in Birmingham was born in the UK , and many more that came here from Pakistan as small children and have grown up in the city.

The Pakistani communities' current socioeconomic position has largely been determined by its history of early settlement in this country. Pakistanis have largely settled in areas where there was a high demand for a migrant labour force prepared to accept low-waged, and low-status jobs. Due to the advancement in technology the Pakistani community has experienced mass unemployment.

The Pakistani community is one of the poorest communities in Britain. They have the highest unemployment, low educational achievement, and live in economically and socially deprived conditions. In order to improve this, Pakistanis need to work closely together to overcome some of these problems.

It is well documented that in Birmingham Local Education Authority (LEA) maintained schools on the whole, with the exception of Afro-Caribbean boys, Pakistani-background pupils' performance was not good compared particularly to whites and Indians. Further work needs to be undertaken to find out whether these poor results of Pakistani pupils are due to racial disadvantage and racial discrimination, direct or indirect, that they face in schools. Could it be the socioeconomic status of their parents or the poor expectations of their teachers?

As a result of this, the Pakistani Mentoring Partnership, was set up to see if mentoring could combat this negative effect.

Pakistani Mentoring Partnership

Pakistani Voluntary Mentoring Scheme

The purpose of my role is to recruit, train and support a team of voluntary mentors particularly from the Pakistani community, who will support young people who are experiencing difficulty in school. There are five schools currently involved in the project.

The main tasks for these mentors would be to divert pupils from a downward spiral that starts with truancy and exclusion, and ends with low educational achievements, unemployment and crime.

In the schools where the mentoring takes place the majority of the pupils are Pakistani, however, this is not reflected in the make-up of the teaching staff. I am not stating that this is having a negative effect on the pupils, but the only professionals these pupils come in contact with are their teachers. So bringing in a Pakistani professional, whether they be a doctor or an undergraduate, is just another tool, which could be used to motivate the young Pakistanis, therefore highlighting that there are positive role models from within their own community.

The mentoring is expected to last for a full school academic year. Even though it is primarily targeted at the underachieving pupils, it is open to anyone who wishes to see a mentor. I have had instances of pupils from all the other communities, including the white community, asking to see a Pakistani mentor.

A common question I am asked is what, if any, is the difference between mentoring a Pakistani young person and a similarly troubled youngster from another community? It all depends on the needs and requirements of the person. For example, if a young person is not concentrating in school because of bullying then any mentor, regardless of their race, would make a positive impact on the young person's life just as long as they are caring and supportive. If a Pakistani young person were having problems due to his identity, then a Pakistani mentor would be the most beneficial.

The secret is in the matching of mentors and mentees.

Birmingham Mentoring Consortium

The Birmingham Mentoring Consortium (BMC) is a mentoring scheme, which enables degree-level students to apply for Millennium Awards worth £2000 each. The students act as mentors for young people who are underachieving or at risk of school exclusion. They also design and carry out a one-year project in a local West Midlands community.

Each mentor supports two or three young people, together with four hours a week on the community project. Most of the mentees are supported by mentors from the same ethnic background as themselves.

The BMC is an intercultural mentoring organization, currently embracing the Hindu, African-Caribbean, Bangladeshi and Sikh communities as well as people from white and ethnically mixed backgrounds; the Pakistani community at present is not involved. Each of these groups have twenty-one Millennium Awards to distribute over a three-year period. The scheme at present is in its second year.

Because of the success of the above mentioned voluntary Pakistani Voluntary Mentoring Scheme, we have been successful in obtaining money from the Millennium Commission for twenty-one Awards for Pakistani degree students as from September 2001.

Recruitment and retention of mentors is a problem for most mentoring schemes. Without paying mentors it is difficult to get the long-term continuity that is so vital. In the BMC scheme, all the mentors who started the year were still there at the end.

Learning mentor

I am a mentor myself. I am employed part time as a learning mentor in a Birmingham inner-city school. The pupils speak to me openly about academic and general issues. I discuss the challenges facing them highlighting potential solutions.

Mentee

Sajad is an eleven-year-old boy. Since the start of school he has been late over fifty times. He has been suspended for bringing a knife into school. He has spent three weeks in the base. He has continually been on report and he has to report to the year head every day. The parents of Sajad have been into school a few times, but nothing has changed.

Mentoring sessions

I am going to briefly describe the mentoring sessions I have been having with Sajad.

First meeting:

- Introduced myself, what I do, explained to him what a learning mentor is.
- Explained why he is seeing me.
- Explained the aims and objectives of this and future mentoring sessions.
- How they are going to progress and monitored.

Feedback from Sajad:

- Why me?
- I know boys who are more naughty than me, and they do not have to see you.
- You are a friend of the teachers. I can't trust you.

Second meeting:

- Not as formal as the first meeting.
- Told mentee about myself, in more detail, hobbies, interests, etc.
- Clarified the difference between me and a teacher.
- Put him at ease, told a few jokes.
- Asked what he wanted from these sessions.

Feedback from Sajad:

- I am OK, I am able to speak the same language as him.
- His opinions of the school and specific teachers.
- He understood why he was always in trouble.
- He wanted to change, but was afraid of peer pressure.
- Asked me for advice on how to stay away from some conflicting situations.

Third meeting:

- Drew up an action plan together.
- Used SMART principle.
- Discussed about what had happened in the past week, if he was late etc.

Feedback from Sajad:

- Was happy for me to talk to his teachers.
- Was sitting on his own for some lessons.

Future meetings:

- Continue to monitor Action Plan.

Feedback from Sajad:

- Wanted instant access to me for advice.
- Told his friends about me, they wanted someone as well to talk to.
- His punctuality is improving.
- The school is going to consider taking him off report.

Concluding remark:

Sajad lives in Birmingham's inner city. He has been brought up in a family environment were both parents have been unemployed and have not had any formal education. Peer pressure has had an enormous influence on him. Education is not seen as important to him or his friends. He is not interested in a career, nor has he any ambition or drive to succeed in life.

This scenario is becoming increasingly common in today's Pakistani youth. I have only described one example of how mentoring has had a positive impact on the life of a young boy.

Sajad was considered by the school to be a failure. But mentoring was able to give him an opportunity to discuss issues he was facing that were having a detrimental impact on him.

Transco women's mentoring programme – UK

Will Large[12]

Introduction

Transco (part of BG plc) is the regulated national gas transmission company formed from British Gas in March 1994. The organization has experience of providing mentoring programmes for its employees gained through the provision of mentoring programmes for its 1997 and 1998 graduate intake. In 1998, following an equality and diversity review undertaken by the company, Transco agreed an action plan which included piloting a mentoring programme for seventeen mentees, designed to tackle the issue of the 'glass ceiling' which affects women at some levels within the Transco grading structure. At a workshop last year a number of women managers expressed a strong wish to be trained as mentors to assist in this process.

The model for the women's programme was to establish a mentoring relationship that is supportive of personal development, offering both support and challenge to the mentee with the mentor–mentee relationship being built around objectives defined by the mentee. As this is a pilot programme, part of the design is to evaluate it with the participants help, which includes anonymous questionnaires, review meetings – mentee session, mentor session, a mentee and mentor session, and some tracking of upwards, sideways or outwards moves.

Programme purpose

The purpose of the equality and diversity mentoring for women programme is to:

- overcome one 'glass ceiling' barrier identified (the grade below the recognized manager level)
- provide the opportunity to set realistic personal career goals
- facilitate the sharing of skills and experiences of female Transco managers.

Overview

Senior line managers were written to, asking if they had suitable women nominees for the mentoring programme and, if they did, to ask their nominee(s) to confirm their interest together with some information about why they think they will benefit from a mentoring relationship, given in writing to the programme manager. This information was used by the programme manager to prioritize participants for the pilot. Selected women managers were also written to, asking if they were interested in becoming a mentor in the pilot programme. Two separate training workshops were then run, using a trainer from Clutterbuck Associates, which consisted of one day for mentees and two days for mentors. Subsequently, a one-day network and review meeting took place which formed part of the evaluation of the pilot.

Thirteen of the seventeen relationships were still operating after a six-month period. Several of the women mentees achieved a managerial-level position and decided to stay in the relationship as they moved through the transition into their new operating level. Two women who achieved promotion finished their mentoring relationships.

Lessons from the pilot learnt to date

- Geography needs to be taken into consideration when matching mentors and mentees. For the relationship to be effective they need to be near each other.
- There needs to be a short timescale between the end of the training and the first contact between mentor and mentee.

- The first meeting of mentor and mentee should be arranged as soon as possible after the training and matching.
- The mentors need to be experienced managers.

Programme design

To determine the design for the programme, the experience of two graduate mentoring programmes that had been very successfully established in 1997 and 1998 was used.

Transco's mentoring definition is: a non-judgemental relationship, outside the normal manager/subordinate relationship, where a more skilled or experienced person (the mentor) can help another (the mentee) to enhance their learning and development.

The philosophy for mentoring programmes in Transco is that these are formal programmes that progress towards informality once established, and that mentoring is based around the European model of mentoring. The following principles are incorporated into mentoring programmes design:

- voluntary (both mentees and mentors)
- confidential relationship between mentors and mentees
- programme managed
- supported by participants' line managers
- formal programme duration established at the beginning
- ongoing informal relationships can continue beyond formal programme end date by mutual agreement between mentor and mentee
- meetings should take place regularly e.g. every four to six weeks
- mentors to be off-line managers at a more senior level
- option always available to change the mentor if the relationship is not working without blame or fault
- expectation that mentees will progressively manage their mentor and the mentor will facilitate this
- midpoint review meeting with mentees and mentors groups to share experiences and receive further mentoring skills development (outputs can also form part of programme evaluation process)
- invitation to mentors and mentees to contribute information to facilitate the matching process.

The attributes that are sought in a mentor include:

- being a good listener
- having a strong interest in their own growth and development
- natural positive outlook, yet able to be very realistic
- interested in helping to develop people
- able to share experiences in a non directive way
- willing to provide quality time to meet with the person they are mentoring regularly over the period of the programme
- prepared to provide a profile of their experience

- offer themselves to be selected by a mentee
- sufficiently self-assured to both give and receive challenge and constructive criticism.

Lessons learnt from mentoring programmes

The following list is a summary of the lessons learnt from the mentoring programmes that have been established in Transco and were incorporated into the design of the women's programme.

1 There is great value in selecting or establishing a definition of mentoring, and a clearly defined purpose, which are universally understood by all the stakeholders.
2 To be effective, the design of the mentoring scheme needs to fit with the culture of the organization.
3 If possible, all stakeholders should be involved in the programme in some way.
4 A formal scheme seems to work better if it has a defined duration.
5 Making participation voluntary is more likely to lead to enhanced commitment and buy-in from both mentees and mentors, which will help with achieving a successful relationship.
6 Ideally training/briefing should be an essential ingredient for both mentee and mentor groups. The training should reinforce the purpose of the programme, and help mentees and mentors understand their responsibilities within it.
7 Where possible the mentees should be involved as much as possible in the matching process, and should be strongly encouraged to manage the relationship with their mentors.
8 Everything practically possible should be done to help with the building of effective relationships between the mentees and their mentors. The programme manager should plan on bringing the relationship to an end and starting another with a new mentor if the relationships are not working.
9 There should be a plan to review progress, and share experiences of mentees and mentors at least at the halfway point of the programme.
10 The mentee should be encouraged take on the primary responsibility for managing the relationship, i.e. establishing their objectives and expectations for the programme (mentoring is their agenda).
11 Two mentees to one mentor is all that Transco managers felt they could take on during a mentoring programme.
12 Mentors and mentees should be encouraged to discuss their own and their partner's expectations, and the relationship objectives, early on (i.e. during their first or second meeting).

The above experience and learning have become principles which are used for new mentoring programmes in Transco. As new lessons are learnt they form part of a continuous improvement process for mentoring programme design and implementation.

International perspective

Although the Transco programmes are designed to fit with Transco culture and purposes, it is believed that many of the principles define or utilize existing good practice. It is believed that informal mentoring programmes can work very well in organizations, but that there is sometimes a need for initial structure to help establish the programme and mentoring relationships, to get them off to a good start. Often there is also a need to demonstrate to the sponsoring organization that the mentoring programme has been well designed, is being well managed, and will meet expectations and provide tangible business benefits. The mentoring programme has been designed to fit with Transco and British culture, and may not be appropriate for use in some European and Middle Eastern countries. The American mentoring model uses a different definition of mentoring which, if adopted, will likely necessitate a different design of programme. However, these programmes have worked well for Transco and should be suitable for other organizations with similar cultures, with some modification to fit with specific purposes, requirements and challenges.

Disabled writers' mentoring scheme – UK

Jonathan Meth[13]

Introduction

This case study reflects on a pilot scheme undertaken during 1999 to offer learning and professional development to nine disabled writers writing for performance.

Why a mentoring scheme for disabled writers?

In response to the lack of work for the stage being produced by disabled writers in 1994–5, New Playwrights Trust (working with disabled researcher, Sally Ree, disabled writer, Yvonne Lynch, with support from the Paul Hamlyn Foundation and BBC Equal Opportunities) undertook research for the London Arts Board (LAB) to map existing provision and identify priorities.

Out of this research there emerged a need for a supply of basic information to assist disabled writers in navigating their way through the system. This has resulted in the publication by the LAB of *Theatre Writing: A Guide for Disabled Writers*.

It also became apparent that there was both a need to change the attitudes that encouraged the development of disabled writers' work and a need to explore alternative ways to proactively support their careers. This was demonstrated very practically when writernet was subsequently approached by Graeae (the UK's premier theatre company of actors with physical or sensory disabilities) to try to address the lack of good quality scripts emerging from disabled writers. So that they could place a greater emphasis on the commissioning, development and production of new work.

The fact that disabled writers write poetry and fiction much more readily than theatre pointed to a series of access issues. In consultation over many years with a range of disabled theatre practitioners, mentoring was identified as the most appropriate strategy for exploring and overcoming some of these issues. One of the recommendations from the New Playwrights Trust's (NPT's) Women Writers Mentoring Scheme was that, where possible, mentoring should take place with access to a producing company. This led to writernet's partnership with Graeae. The proposed venture was discussed with Claire Malcolm, Director of New Writing North – the UK's only regional development agency working to support writers across media – she was very keen that we incorporate a specifically Northern aspect into our plans, leading to the association with New Writing North.

The aims of the scheme

The primary aim of this scheme was to provide disabled dramatists with the opportunity to draw upon the experience and wisdom of their more established counterparts – to develop them as writers and increase their chances of production. The emphases ranged from developing confidence and purpose in the professional work of the mentee to generating producible scripts.

This was within the context that Graeae had a new artistic director and had established a long-term commitment to the nurturing, development and production of new work, and enhancing opportunities to produce and commission.

It was also expected that disabled writers would subsequently form relationships with Soho Theatre Company, Theatre Royal Stratford East and other new writing companies, so as not to be 'ghettoized'.

Background to the scheme

Throughout 1993 and into 1994, NPT set up an ongoing series of meetings with key individuals and representatives of organizations concerned with writing by women. This panel developed the idea of a mentoring scheme for women writers. In 1994 NPT was successful in raising funds for the scheme from the Baring Foundation and private donations. The scheme ran from August 1995 to August 1996 with five pairings of mentors and mentees reflecting a diverse range and level of experience. A report was published and circulated to stimulate interest in mentoring. This scheme proved a successful first step. Mentoring writers as a developmental methodology is now being taken up widely.

The selection process

Recruitment

The scheme was widely advertised in theatre and disability arts publications. Careful attention was given to accessing potential candidates. Mentees were selected for the scheme according to a process agreed by the steering panel and described below. Not all mentees needed to have been writing for theatre (some may have been poetry or fiction writers), although all had to demonstrate a desire to do so. Mentors who were suitable matches were sought following the selection of mentees.

Fifty writers applied to the scheme, with a short list of twelve interviewed before the final selection of seven was agreed. A separate but allied process was sought for the additional two writers on the scheme from the north of England, who were identified by New Writing North.

Successful candidates were then invited, in consultation with the steering panel, to recommend appropriate writers to be mentors:

> The benefits of the scheme began when I saw it advertised in the Writers Guild newsletter. I was at a low point in my illness, feeling isolated and out of touch. Indeed the challenge of applying for the scheme nearly defeated me. But once I'd applied I found myself galvanised, as the process kickstarted me into facing my artistic and social predicament. (Mentee's journal)

Applications

The scheme was open to writers at any level: beginners, those whose who had some experience and those who would consider themselves experienced – and to anyone who defined themselves as disabled. As a guide the SHAPE definition of disability was used:

'People with physical, mental or sensory disabilities, with hidden disabilities, such as psoriasis, epilepsy, heart, chest conditions; people with disabilities linked to ageing; people suffering from mental illness.'

Applicants were invited to submit between one and three ideas of less than 250 words, or a scene less than ten pages of double-spaced text or lasting less than ten minutes of stage time, and a curriculum vitae and letter outlining what they hoped to achieve from the scheme. Sample ideas and information about the partner organizations were enclosed with details of the scheme for those interested in applying.

Applications were welcomed in any format including the option to e-mail.

Interviews

Applicants were asked:

- How would you aim to progress the ideas or sample scene that you submitted?

- How do you think mentoring might work successfully for you?
- What are your access needs and how might they be ideally met?
- What kind of skills and experience would you look for in a mentor? Do you have anyone in mind?
- Where would you like your writing to be in three years' time?
- Do you have anything you would like to ask us?

The steering panel used the interviews:

- to clarify the nature of the scheme, its parameters, what was expected of both mentors and mentees and the roles of writernet and Graeae.
- to identify access needs and consider appropriate strategies to meet them
- to identify ways in which those needs might be met by a mentoring relationship, and how the relationship might be best focused to enable this to happen
- to identify possible suitable mentors either from those who had already put themselves forward, from the suggestions of those wishing to be mentored, and from the panel's own knowledge
- to make selections.

Originally the scheme had been designed for six writers, but with successful fundraising it became possible to increase this to nine.

> Once I'd been short-listed for the scheme I was worried I'd be left out because I was too ill to attend the interview. I braced myself for the customary ritual of having to apologise for my uselessness and miss yet another creative opportunity. In fact, for once, the opposite was true. (The Project Director) arranged for the interview to be held by phone, and I realised that this was going to be an initiative run for the benefit of its mentees. The interview furthered my belief. Instead of having to cover for my condition, and minimise its impact (as I must whenever else I'm working, or directors/producers tend to panic over deadlines and rewrites) I found the interviewing panel were sensitive to my problems, as well as interested in my creative ideas. Whether or not I was selected for the scheme, this feedback was of considerable benefit. (Mentee's journal)

The matching process

Role of the mentor

Depending on the requirements of the mentee, mentors were encouraged to operate:

- as a *networker/facilitator* – providing information and opening doors to further opportunity

- as a *sounding board* – for ideas and approaches that the mentee may need more encouragement to pursue
- as *a role model* – giving confidence to the mentee
- as a *constructive critic* – providing feedback
- and as a *dramaturg*, offering detailed skills development.

These roles of course involved certain skills, and the balance and focus of each relationship needed to be carefully negotiated in each case.

Selection and approach

There are obvious difficulties in trying to lay down a firm structure for any mentor–mentee relationship which should primarily be built on trust and a willingness on the part of the mentor to pass on the benefits of their experience. Nevertheless it was important to establish clear parameters and to ensure that these and the pairings themselves were defined by the individual mentee's needs and the mentor's own individual experience.

With advice from the steering panel, on the basis of the needs that had been identified at interview, short lists of potential mentors were drawn up for each selected mentee and discussed with them. A potential mentor would only be approached once it had been checked with the mentee that this selection was (still) appropriate.

Each potential mentor was made aware of the basic principles behind the scheme. They were sent further details of what was required from them and asked to make assessments of their strengths and abilities which they might be able to bring to a relationship, as well as aspects they feel might need more support from writernet/Graeae as co-ordinators of the project. Prior to any consideration of any proposed mentees, prospective mentors were asked to consider the following questions:

- How do you think mentoring might be able to help a writer?
- What overall skills and experience do you think you could bring to being a mentor?
- What sort of specific help do you think you would be most able to give to a mentee?
- What sort of help do you think it would not be appropriate for you to be asked to provide (please note that you will not be asked to provide general counselling)?
- What are the ideas, approaches or styles that you would be most interested in developing in a mentee?
- Would you find disability awareness training useful?
- In what ways do you think mentoring another writer could develop you?

Mentors also needed to be open to the concept of the *mentee* driving the relationship according to agreed aims. After this the specifics of each relationship would be clarified in an agreement.

While informal mentoring is widespread practice, the formal nature of the scheme did not appeal to all writers approached and, as a result, some invitations were declined. Although flexibility was central to the scheme's aims, compromising the formality of the relationship from the start may or may not have jeopardized the partnership, but it would certainly have made it much more difficult to track and evaluate. Even with agreement to formal requirements it was anticipated that in practice formal adherence would be patchy.

The scheme

In each case, the relationship between mentor and mentee lasted over the course of a year interspersed by six two-hour meetings. The relationship and focus for each meeting was agreed between them in a 'mentoring agreement' outlined at the first proper encounter. Draft agreements had been sent to each mentee prior to this as examples. Each agreement set aims for the relationship and was both a means of reviewing each relationship at the halfway stage and assessing overall effectiveness at the end of the scheme.

The midway mentee review

While six meetings were originally budgeted for between each mentee and mentor, many of whom attended the launch at the Royal National Theatre, there was initially no provision for the mentees to meet together to share their experiences prior to the end of project gathering. Reflection-in-action had been identified through research as a very positive mentoring model.[13]

A day was facilitated by Jenny Sealey at Graeae and the project director to concentrate on creating an environment in which the mentees felt free to voice strengths and weaknesses of their learning to date. By scheduling the day at the midway point in the process, the mentees had an opportunity to practically implement positive developments yielded from the day.

Key notes that emerged from the meeting were:

- the sense of isolation felt by many of the mentees
- finances
- need for advice
- networking
- mentee/mentor matching
- ownership/participation
- the review process
- an exit strategy for the scheme.

A commitment was made to facilitate a final mentee meeting, once the formal relationships were complete and material had been submitted, to reflect back on the scheme as a whole and make recommendations for the future.

Steering panel midway meeting

The steering panel also met to evaluate confidential mentor feedback, which had been gathered by the project director. This highlighted the following issues for mentors/mentees:

- time management
- exit strategy
- following the submission of material
- report on the scheme.

Mentors and mentees were again reminded of the need to keep a record, in either diary or report form, of the process(es) during the scheme to feed into this report and also help the steering panel to evaluate the scheme. In compiling this material, both mentors and mentees would be asked to mark what from their material was confidential to the internal evaluation process and what they were happy for a wider public to see. The deadline for this submission was also set.

Reflection on the mentoring process (mentees)

The mentees took differing approaches to tracking their experience of the programme. Some kept diaries as they went along, others wrote up their reflections only once they had completed their work on scripting.

Their reflections were presented under the following headings:

- mentoring for disabled writers
- writing 'disabled content'
- the challenges of turning ideas into drama
- writing time and deadlines
- acculturation to theatre practice
- about writing practice
- the value(s) of the scheme.

Reflection on the mentoring process (mentors)

The material submitted by mentors during the scheme perhaps inevitably focused much more on implications for the ongoing management of individual relationships. In this context the project director operated as a sounding board to agree specific next steps or angles of approach. Some material has therefore remained for evaluation purposes rather than publication.

While mentees were positively pressurized towards delivering their reflections, as well as their scripts, less emphasis was placed on persuading mentors to contribute formal responses, as their function (and remuneration) was primarily linked to delivering the appropriate mentoring.

Final steering panel meeting

The panel had read all the mentees' material submitted by the December deadline and met to make recommendations as to next steps. These included a combination of script reports, rehearsed readings and workshops, as well as encouragement to complete drafts by the end of March where this had been the goal and scripts were still incomplete. The panel also offered brief reflections on particular individual needs and questions for the mentees regarding what *they* might now really want for their writing. Where appropriate these recommendations were checked with mentors before being fed back to the mentees.

Individual feedback was given to all the mentees before they gathered to share final reflections on the scheme as a whole.

Final mentee meeting and recommendations

This meeting concentrated on focusing recommendations for the readers of the report. Key headings here were:

● writing about disability
● the burden of representation
● learning and social inclusion.

Lessons learnt

Successes

● We originally planned six mentoring partnerships. Successful fundraising enabled us to achieve nine (including four from London).
● We hoped to use the scheme, in part, to increase the *chances* of the mentees writing producible material. We did not dare hope that we would actually yield a script that could be produced. Although not yet confirmed, Graeae are very seriously considering producing one of the pieces in spring 2001.
● Soho Theatre, Theatre Centre, Theatre Royal Stratford East and BBC Radio have all expressed interest in writers developed during the scheme.
● By keeping Channel 4 informed of the progress of the scheme, their disability officer, Alison Walsh, is talking to us both about our future plans and whether any of the writers on the scheme might usefully be linked in.
● On the whole the scheme was well funded, well guided and well managed.

Problems

● One of the mentoring partnerships was not carefully enough monitored and was allowed to drift. Not everyone is naturally suited to the formal processes required of mentoring but, if informality takes over, it must be linked to clear, mutually agreed objectives, to have a chance of succeeding. The mentee in question slipped, rather, between the partner organizations and her mentor. Although the danger signs were spotted at the midway review, collective 'eyes were taken off the ball'.

- Because of the dearth of other opportunities for disabled writers, one other mentee felt she might have wasted her mentor's time as she needed more rudimentary support than that which the scheme was ideally set up to provide.

Key learning for the future

- The value of creating clear partnerships – so we will very carefully look for both national and regional counterparts.
- The importance of taking the time to get certain critical things right (in this case the matching between mentees and mentors)
- The importance of a central figure (in this case the project director), who possesses the requisite combination of management, communication and art-form skills to provide pivotal support, facilitate flexibility and maintain an overview to guard against drift, negotiate obstacles and so drive towards completion. This is not currently recognized by many funding bodies as an essential criterion for success, possibly because it is expensive.
- Managing projects, which have sufficient resources to allow flexibility, substantially increases the chances for success.
- Sometimes the needs most easily missed are those closest to home. Nothing can be taken for granted – so we will self-audit at the start of each project to ensure that we maximize what we *already* have to offer.
- People frequently need to be given the chance to engage with the same information more than once for it to be meaningful – so while this increases the managerial workload, it is worth reflecting on how the recipient might best engage.

Plans to continue the project

Graeae and writernet are currently developing four separate strands of work complementary to this area:

1 Graeae's Year of the Artist project: millennium monologues, designed to provide an opportunity for six writers to create monologues to be performed in unusual settings. London Transport is a key partner.
2 Collaboration, possibly with the Arvon Foundation, to create two-week long residential workshops exclusively tailored for disabled writers who require very focused input to move their work forward.
3 Placements for three or four of the most advanced writers with Soho Theatre, the BBC and Channel 4.
4 Graeae has now commissioned one of the writers for production in spring 2001.

Mentoring for diversity or conformity: rhetoric and reality – UK

Heather Piper and John Piper[14]

Introduction

With few exceptions, particular social practices cannot be judged as good or bad, or effective or ineffective without reference to the context in which they are deployed. This discussion will not consider the absolute or intrinsic value of mentoring as an intervention to achieve personal or professional develop-ment. Rather it will raise a number of concerns about the increasingly varied social, political and economic contexts in which mentoring is now practised. It also suggests some implications and issues which should give pause for thought as the mentoring bandwagon rolls on.

In recent years, to suggest that there may be limits to the successes that could be achieved through mentoring, or that there might be real problems attached to its use in many contexts, has been to invite exclusion from mainstream debate. However, in the face of a mass of supportive, if largely ephemeral and anecdotal (Harris et al., 1997, p. 16) publications and official approbation for mentoring initiatives, a number of contributions have asked serious questions about the emperor's new clothes and why so much has been invested in them (Gay and Stephenson, 1998; Gulam and Zulfiquar, 1998; Piper and Piper, 1999; 2000). Drawing on these sources as well as on relevant theory and research, questions can be raised about the way in which mentoring is being deployed in social contexts far removed from its natural habitat. Wholehearted support for the achievement of a society characterized by both diversity and social justice does not entail acceptance that mentoring is likely to make a significant contribution to such a goal. On the contrary, it is suggested that the practice of mentoring in contexts of social diversity may have negative implications that have remained largely unacknowledged and unresearched.

Mentoring is a developmental approach pioneered in organizational and professional contexts, where interests and values tend to be agreed. Transplant-ing it into complex and contested situations, where diversity may involve extreme disjunctures in the economic and social capital of the mentor and the mentee, should not be treated as unproblematic. Defining someone as needing a mentor, usually on the basis of a negative label (disaffected, young single mother, school truant), is to impose an individualistic and pathological approach to a problem which is also structural. The potential mentee is stigmatized and implicitly told that they are responsible for their condition. The mentor will then seek to change and improve the mentee. At the immediate level it may be suggested that such initiatives are unlikely to be effective. Beyond that, the approach serves to mask structural inequalities and through its ubiquitous rhetoric obscure issues of social justice. Even where mentoring projects are successful (and positive evaluations by those anxious to justify funding are to be expected), in reality their principal effect can only be the reallocation of disadvantage.

In order to substantiate this jaundiced account, a number of related claims will briefly be considered. Contrary to the apparent belief that mentoring in the context of social diversity can be seen as a universally welcome panacea, questions may be asked about its:

- application and portability
- perceived value for money
- reliance on common sense over analysis
- lack of economic and/or structural awareness
- tendency towards pathology and disempowerment.

To argue these points is not to question the personal integrity of individuals involved in mentoring projects with the best of intentions, but to suggest the need for more research and more critically informed discussion than has been apparent to date.

Application and portability

Although mentoring is a proven and widely applicable approach, and successful mentors are characterized by generic awareness and capability, it does not follow that the practice can be inserted into any or every social context. The practice evolved in organizational and professional settings where an experienced individual supports the development of a less experienced colleague so that the difference between them is reduced over time. However, helping someone become a competent teacher, parish priest or gas fitter is a less complex process than employing mentoring in situations of significant social or economic disadvantage. The mentoring relationship has normally been an unequal one, with the inequality reduced through mutual effort and the improving influence of the mentor. This is unexceptional when the extent of inequality is limited, when there is a real consensus on the relevant values and goals, and when neither party is coerced into participation. But these conditions do not apply in many of the contexts of social diversity where mentoring is now deployed.

Mentoring practice originating in the developmental relationship of one individual with another has now been structured and redefined to meet complex and contested expectations. The potential problems arising from this are apparent (Gay and Stephenson, 1998). While in any situation mentoring is likely to have some degree of success, because people respond positively to individual attention, empathy and encouragement (Atkinson and Pollard, 1999; Banks and Davies, 1990; Hepworth and Capelin, 1986), such success is less likely in contexts of significant diversity. Indeed, mentoring at its most successful may be presented as a process of induction or modelling towards conformity. Such an assumption is inappropriate in situations of significant and manifold disadvantage, status difference or varying aspirations. In such settings, it is questionable whether the approach being applied is really mentoring and whether the term has ceased to have real meaning.

Perceived value for money

The mentor role has been exhaustively dissected. Summarizing the literature, Roberts (1998, pp.19–20) provides references for sixteen distinct and demanding dimensions, stressing that the list is not exclusive. Others describe the role as 'humane and civilising' (Smith and Aldred, 1993, p.10) and situate it at the 'highest and most complex level of functioning in the people related hierarchy of skills' (Alleman et al., 1984, p. 27). Finding appropriate people to perform such a daunting role in specific organizational or professional contexts is not always easy but, as mentoring has migrated into diverse and challenging social situations, issues of quality and cost have become more apparent.

As mentoring is seen as an appropriate response to more and more problems, the potential client numbers make using fully trained professionals (social workers, youth workers, careers officers, health visitors, etc.) highly expensive. Volunteer mentors represent a cheaper alternative. It could be argued that in some cases 'mentor' is simply a new word for 'volunteer', serving to mask the change in funding and status. Removed from the professional context, defining the personal characteristics and knowledge base for volunteer mentors to work in stressful and contested situations becomes problematic. So, too, does the responsibility for ensuring appropriate and ethical practice with potentially vulnerable mentees. The apparent assumption that most responsible adults can be an effective mentor, with a little training and some ongoing support, is dubious and should give cause for concern.

For all such worries there is little doubt that in some circumstances volunteer mentors can be effective, but the three most common problems in mentoring projects identified by Phillip-Jones (1989) are the assumption that anyone can be a mentor, the shortage of qualified mentors and inadequate preparation. Others have echoed the need for quality assurance, monitoring and evaluation in mentoring practice (Beattie and Holden, 1994). If the attraction of mass mentoring is the low cost of reaching large numbers of clients in a wide range of contexts, the assumed value for money may be illusory. The fact that many schemes produce their own next generation of mentors from the more successful mentees (just as many progress from 'client' to 'counsellor') might be claimed as evidence for good value. However, it should also suggest questions about the difference between activity for its own sake and the achievement of real progress.

Common sense over analysis

The high degree of public enthusiasm and support for mentoring activity in diverse contexts has seldom been matched by careful or appropriate prior categorization. Indeed, the focus on such activity has encouraged over-generalized and demeaning classification and, as a result, effective intervention appears unlikely. Thus, mentoring projects aimed at young people have been reported to employ indicators based on school truancy, school phobia or underachievement, mental illness, emotional and behavioural difficulties, illiteracy, pregnancy, being in or just leaving care, homelessness, offending or ex-offending behaviour, solvent or drug abuse, unemployment, single parent-hood, family-related personal crisis, area of residence, the absence of vocational maturity and the rejection of training opportunities (DfEE, 1997b; NICEC/ICG, 1998; QCSL, 1995). To justify the application of a single method of intervention in such diverse contexts might seem a tall order, but it appears to be made easier by the assumption that such varied groups of young people can all be considered 'disaffected' and thus suitable cases for mentoring (DfEE, 1997a; Piper and Piper, 1998). The unreflective and uncritical use of mentoring, in projects designed in part to match the assumptions of funders, is in symbiotic relationship with the application of over-generalized and pejorative labels to large numbers of young people. As a result, a swathe of current practice is conceptually incoherent, arguably unethical and probably ineffective. In worst case scenarios it may well be damaging.

The dependence of many mentoring projects on short-term funding, secured through successful bidding and extended only by demonstrating success, may explain the emphasis on activity over careful analysis. The reliance on taken-for-granted assumptions, the appeal to 'common sense' and an indifference towards theory or conceptual clarity may explain the consistent governmental favour enjoyed by mentoring both before and after the 1997 general election. However, this characteristic also means that mentoring is a generalized discourse and in practice may mean different things to different people. In particular, few authoritative discussions of mentoring have offered any prioritization between social control, social care or social liberation. Key concepts and principles are left implicit even though their practical implications could be significant, and could be contested on ideological grounds.

In considering mentoring in contexts of diversity, these concerns are not merely theoretical or academic. Obviously, potential mentees are likely to have a wide range of assumptions and priorities. While key concepts remain unexplored, this will remain true also for mentors or project organizers. Is society basically good and harmonious, so that problems are the result of individual failings? Is society oppressive to some and in need of deliberate structural change? Is mentoring an educative or liberative process, properly determined by the mentee? Is mentoring about normative behaviour modification towards desired outcomes determined by the mentor? These are non-trivial questions and the wide range of possible answers are linked to fundamental differences of ideology and perspective. They go to the heart of what mentoring in and for diversity may be about and what it might achieve.

Because such issues have been studiously ignored by the cheerleaders and organizers of mass mentoring, it is fair to suggest that many projects are operating with both a false premise and prospectus. Some mentors will perceive their practice as concerned with social cleansing or effective human resource allocation. Others will participate fired by charitable missionary zeal, and others will conceive their involvement as an opportunity for liberating personal and political education. In the challenging and contested environments in which mentoring is now deployed, such a lack of focus and clarity offers few grounds for confidence as to its real success.

Economic and structural awareness

A review of the Mentoring Action Project, co-ordinated by the Institute of Careers Guidance and funded by the European Social Fund's Employment Community Initiative, affirms that 'mentoring can help to free many young people from "disaffection"' (NICEC/ICG, 1998, p. 2). However, it also notes a key implication of the characteristics of the young people involved:

> A high percentage . . . in some areas over 50 per cent . . . were care leavers. The vast majority were from broken or unstable home backgrounds . . . Many lacked access to a caring adult . . . Most have low self-confidence and negative self esteem. Considerable and sometimes acute-poverty was . . . common . . . making progression from the state of disaffection difficult without access to additional funding. (NICEC/ICG, 1998, p. 2)

This partial recognition that there are limits to the scale of personal and social problems which can be resolved by mentoring should be welcomed. However, a more frequent strategy has been to define targets which can be achieved by mentoring and to assume that such superficial or limited success solves the underlying general problem. Thus mentoring towards a very limited range of outcomes (entry into education, training or work) has been presented as a proper response to the extremely diverse range of presenting problems referred to previously. Beyond the conceptual crudity of prescribing a single solution for such a varied set of problems, the approach demonstrates a worrying absence of economic and structural awareness.

Since the 1970s, successive governments have tended to emphasise training and education rather than job creation as the proper response to youth unemployment (Brown, 1997). At the same time, the economic and structural pressures which have fractured young peoples transition into work and adult status have been manifest (Battagliola, 1995; Coles, 1995; Jones, 1995; 1996; Kiernan, 1992; Williamson, 1993). Mentoring has been championed as a solution to these problems, in spite of the structural forces involved. While there will be many individual success stories, this reliance on individual achievement may be naive or disingenuous. The energy that unemployed people put into seeking jobs is directly related to their perceived availability (Quint and Kopelman, 1995; White and Lakey, 1992) so the success of particular mentoring projects will depend to a large extent on the local economic environment. In a situation where desirable jobs are in short supply, such success for some can only reinforce the failure and disadvantage of others.

Further, to assume that mentoring represents an appropriate policy response to severe and longstanding social and economic problems is to underestimate the oppositional environments which these engender. Mentoring appears an inadequate response in communities where prolonged adverse structural conditions have created a culture 'which sees "straight" people with (low paid) jobs as fools who are exploited victims' (Williamson and Middlemiss, 1999, p. 16). In such cultures, which are not uncommon (Bentley et al., 1999) 'evading participation (in projects) becomes a valued skill' (Williamson and Middlemiss, 1999, p. 19). Thus, any project, including those based on mentoring, needs to start from 'a realistic, rather than aspirational, appraisal of the condition and attitudes of the young people to whom it is directed' (Williamson and Middlemiss, 1999, p. 16). If an individualistic practice like mentoring is to be used to combat problems which are evidently structural and collective, it may require a more collective and economically and politically informed input than is currently apparent (Gulam and Zulfiquar, 1998). This would constitute a challenging departure from most current mentoring practice, and would require that the mentee should be offered a broad account of the rights of citizenship as well as its responsibilities.

Pathology and disempowerment

A junior minister at the Department of Education and Employment told a meeting of the National Mentoring Network (1998) that mentoring is increasingly being used to support the delivery of government policies on education, training and employment, and that a 'mentoring culture' would be good for our society. Although many mentoring initiatives are undertaken outside the direct control of government, this statement suggests the need to carefully reflect on the practice of mentoring and the dominant discourse which supports it. Contrary to common belief it is not ideologically neutral. It can be situated within a particular perspective on society and politics, and risks inviting damaging ways of thinking about those members of society to whom it is applied.

It may be suggested that (beyond the professional confines in which current mentoring practice originated) the taken-for-granted difference or inequality between mentor and mentee is transformed into something intrinsically pathological. There is something wrong with or missing from the mentee, and it is their responsibility to put it right through working with the mentor. The negative interpretation of this damaging and individualistic approach, and the intrinsic power relationship, can be illustrated by reference to empowerment, a frequently claimed goal of mentoring. Empowerment, as a concept like the practice of mentoring, may be argued to be a means by which those with power pre-empt the capacity of others to interpret their own needs and problems. Thus 'the empowerment discourse could be seen as part of the "civilising" process and a cure for the diseases of poverty and criminality. While appearing emancipatory, it could be behaviourist, intrusive and provide public service workers with the right to invade and colonise clients inner worlds' (Morley, 1995, p. 5). It highlights personal development and draws attention from structural issues (Barry, 1996). This facilitates its effectiveness as an 'aerosol, covering up the disturbing smell of conflict and division' (Mullender and Ward, 1991, p. 1). This process is far from neutral since 'by focussing attention on individual agency, rather than on structures, empowerment could be seen as an extension of the New Right's commitment to self sufficiency; one which ignores social formations' (Morley, 1995, p. 2).

This reference to the New Right is not far fetched. Charles Murray, the principal author of the underclass thesis, stresses the value of decentralized local initiatives by community and voluntary organizations acting independently of the state which, from his neo-liberal free-market viewpoint, he distrusts (Deakin, 1996). Mentoring projects, semi-detached from government, match the general tendency since the 1970s for citizenship to be redefined through an emphasis on individual responsibilities and obligations rather than on individual rights and the responsibility of the state (France, 1996; France and Wiles, 1997). This development has had unfortunate results during a period when the unwillingness of some young people to accept responsibility in employment or the community is less than surprising (France, 1998).

Thus it may be argued that current high-powered support for the widespread deployment of mentoring is part of a ubiquitous and individualistic rhetoric of social integration and inclusion. This obscures issues of structural and economic inequality, downplays the role of the state and stresses the responsibility of individuals and communities (Levitas, 1996). While this dominant discourse has been increasingly associated with the communitarianism espoused by New Labour, its hegemony in the UK predates the 1997 general election and is echoed in key tenets of the previous neo-liberal Conservative administration.

It has been argued that the underclass thesis serves to 'diminish the scale and complexity of the problem facing society in combating poverty, and encourages the belief that comparatively simple and inexpensive policies can be effective . . . it allows poverty to be acknowledged but does not imply that we should feel guilty about it' (Walker, 1996, p. 73). It is no exaggeration to suggest that the same argument can be made in relation to the apparent belief that mentoring can make a significant contribution to resolving substantial structural problems in society, in the absence of less individualistic and more politically challenging initiatives.

Conclusion

In this discussion, arguments have been briefly presented to support a sceptical interpretation of the idea of mentoring in or for diversity. These arguments are seriously made but should not be misunderstood as a critique of mentoring in all situations, of the principles of diversity and social justice or of the integrity of the many excellent individuals engaged in mentoring. However, it is hard to conclude other than that mentoring has more to do with conformity than with diversity. Indeed, for the many mentors working in projects which need to meet targets and demonstrate results in order to secure continued support and funding, we suggest a neat motivational motto: 'Be more like me – I'm on PRP.

BT Ethnic Minority Network Mentoring Programme – UK

Zulfiqar Hussain[15]

Background

The BT Ethnic Minority Network (EMN), is a proactive, employee-based, self-help group which is run by a small group of dedicated people over and above their very busy 'day jobs'. The EMN has grown into one of the largest company sponsored networks of its kind in the world, since its inception seven years ago, with thousands of members worldwide.

The EMN was established to encourage greater diversity throughout BT and help bring significant commercial, community and individual benefits to BT and its people. The network has a key role to play in persuading, advising and guiding individuals of the effective promotion of racial equality. The network contributes to the creation of a level playing field for all BT's people and influences decisions in the areas of recruitment policy, personal development and training. Its vision is to become the leading company sponsored network in the world. Its mission is to develop and encourage BT's ethnic community to achieve their full potential, while supporting BT in the pursuit of its global aspirations.

Key achievements

The EMN has grown to become the leading employee development organization since its inception. It has helped BT provide opportunities at all levels for its people and has become a role model for the business world. It has achieved successes at all levels, both internally to BT and externally on a global scale.

Internal successes include:

- Winning support from the BT board and aligning the network's objectives with BT's global aspirations.
- Establishing strong links with the Race for Opportunity (RFO) campaign and presenting to RFO member companies regularly on employment and community initiatives.
- Developing customized Employee Development Programmes for its members

- Producing a quality magazine called *Aequalis* (Latin for equal) which is read by well over 5000 BT people including the BT board and key members of a number of external organizations.
- Introducing divisional diversity awards.
- Launching a highly successful mentoring programme.

External successes include:

- The network has received numerous prestigious external awards and has notably been British Diversity Award winner for several years.
- It continues to help other organizations launch similar EMNs and has provided professional advice and consultancy to various government departments including, the Home Office, the Metropolitan Police, the Cabinet Office and the Inland Revenue. It also continues to help numerous organizations in the private and voluntary sectors to emulate its success.
- The EMN web site won a Bronze Award in the 'Good Practice in Knowledge Management – Web Awards 2000'.
- It received the Partnership Award at the prestigious Windrush Achievements Awards in June 2000.

The EMN Mentoring Programme

The EMN Mentoring Programme was set up to develop individuals and help them discover their capabilities, understand the culture of the organization, remove barriers, break the glass ceiling, enhance their careers and achieve their full potential.

The programme also helped develop a diverse pool of talent from the ethnic minority employees from which BT could choose its future managers and leaders.

Initially the more experienced members of the network were asked to care for and train the less experienced, in a non-judgemental manner, by coaching, counselling and imparting knowledge.

Over the years the Mentoring Programme has grown significantly with mentors being recruited from across the organization with varying knowledge, experience and cultural backgrounds. The net result has been the production of numerous role models, higher aspirations, increased motivation, better cultural awareness and improved attainment.

The role of the mentors

The mentors have acted as advisers/guides by listening, motivating, supporting and acting as a link to the world and work. They have used their abilities to communicate effectively, acted as positive role models and have been prepared to listen and relate to their mentees in order to help them realize their full potential.

They have also opened the eyes of mentees to opportunities out side their normal area of work and have helped these individuals develop new skills and break down perceived barriers, in order to take full advantage of these new found opportunities.

The following quotes have come from some of the current mentors:

> From my personal perspective, I believe, the mentoring relationship contributes significantly in increasing the motivation, achievement and personal growth of the mentee whilst enhancing the skills of the mentor at the same time. It also provides major benefits to the organization by producing highly developed professional people who are its 'life blood' for a successful future.

> There is nothing more satisfying than to help people reach their full potential and make a difference in their personal and professional lives. I would like to take this opportunity to recommend and invite all of those people reading this case study to become mentors and help make a real difference!

> Mentoring offers you a great opportunity to develop others to their full potential while enhancing your own skills at the same time.

> A good analogy, to mentoring is the 'life cycle' of an acorn. If you visualize an acorn as the mentee, which is given the right quantities of coaching, counselling, and feedback in a healthy non-judgemental environment, it will take solid roots and start to blossom until it reaches maturity of a great tree. It will then go on, to produce lots more acorns, which will in turn, continue to repeat the cycle.

The role of mentees

The mentees who have joined the programme make up a diverse group encompassing all the different business units across BT. They are all at different stages of their careers but have a common goal to be more successful and achieve more in their personal and professional lives.

The following quotes have come from some of the current mentees:

> The programme has opened my eyes to new opportunities across the business.

> I now have a better understanding of senior management decision making and strategic approach.

> I have received continued help, advice and guidance on how to develop new skills.

> I can now objectively look at my strengths and weaknesses.

Benefits of the programme

The programme has provided considerable benefits for the mentees, mentors and BT.

The benefits to the mentees have included improved self-confidence, learning to cope with the formal and informal structure of the company, receipt of career advice, extensive networking opportunities and of course managerial tutelage.

The mentors have also gained from the mentoring relationship. Benefits have included improved job satisfaction, a greater insight into their own level of knowledge, a new perspective on BT and the business case for diversity (provided by the mentee).

There is no doubt that BT has gained by having a workforce with improved motivation, improved communications and a leadership development programme that not only develops participants but also ensures that key cultural values are passed on.

Programme management

A work-package owner plus three helpers manage the programme on a voluntary basis. They do this over and above their busy day jobs.

The four individuals work as a team but do have agreed individual responsibilities such as a database management, promotion, recruitment and matching. The team generally use audio-conferencing to hold meetings but occasionally meet face to face to discuss and resolve any issues and/or make improvements to the programme.

Promotion and publicity

To attract new mentors and mentees and celebrate the periodic successes of the Mentoring Programme, the scheme is advertised and promoted in a number of ways, e.g. leaflets, flyers, EMN web site, BT intranet, internal publications, at EMN open days which are held around the country, and at the EMN annual conference.

Recruitment of mentors and mentees

Mentors and mentees are recruited in a number of different ways. These include face-to-face presentations, personal contacts, adverts in internal publications, via the intranet and through divisional campaigns organized by the various business units.

Those wishing to become mentors, mentees and/or both complete an application form online on the EMN web site. The form asks for their contact details, grade, training/qualifications, achievements in last two years, hobbies/interests, their area of business interest and the type of person they wished to be matched up with.

Training and support

Support is provided for mentors and mentees on an ongoing basis by the mentoring team.

A formal training workshop is also organized on a regular basis. The frequency of the workshop is currently under review.

Matching process

Matching takes place on a regular basis. The frequency varies, depending on how many new people have registered on the programme and/or how many existing members require a new match.

The matching takes the form of a paper exercise where the mentor and mentee forms are examined and evaluated to get a best match based on grade, location, shared hobbies/interests, career aspirations and development needs.

Once a match has been found, a letter of introduction is sent via e-mail to both the mentor and mentee notifying them of the match and asking them arrange a meeting to meet each other at a mutually convenient time.

Mentor and mentee are also encouraged to prepare for the first meeting to enable the ground rules of the relationship along with the aims and objectives to be agreed.

Ending the mentoring relationship

Both mentor and mentee are encouraged to achieve closure – particularly if a mentoring relationship should break down. The reason for this is to avoid damaging the enthusiasm and commitment of both parties by such an occurrence.

Monitoring the mentoring process

The main aim of monitoring is to keep abreast of what is going on, to make changes in areas of difficulty that have been brought up by the participants, and to evaluate the scheme on a continual basis using anecdotal feedback, verbal/written reports and annual survey/questionnaire.

A comprehensive online guide is provided for both mentors and mentees as a reference for the monitoring of the relationship.

Statistics are regular compiled and analysed to measure the performance of the programme. A close eye is also kept on the number of matched and unmatched participants, e.g. there are currently 125 matched mentor–mentee pairs, five unmatched mentors and eleven unmatched mentees. The unmatched people currently on the database will only be matched once suitable matches are found.

Rewarding mentors and mentees

There is no formal reward but mentors and mentees are recognized for their work by having their details published on the Success Gallery, which is part of the EMN web site. Their success and achievements are also celebrated in internal publications and at the EMN annual conference.

Lessons learnt to date

A number of lessons have been learnt to date including:

- There is a need for robust end to end processes with clear roles and responsibilities defined.
- Continual cleansing of the database is an absolute must.
- Expectations particularly of mentees need to be managed very carefully to avoid disappointment.
- The matching process needs to be slick and efficient to maintain momentum.
- Every opportunity must be used to promote the programme and recruit new mentors and mentees.
- Progression of mentors and mentees through the organization should be tracked to help evaluate the effectiveness of the programme.

Conclusions

The EMN Mentoring Programme has been very successful to date. It has helped countless number of people over the years develop their careers and progress up the corporate ladder. It has also been instrumental in promoting cross-cultural communications, raising cultural awareness across BT and breaking down barriers.

The scheme is highly respected within BT and is recognized as a leader in its field externally by other organizations that are actively trying to emulate similar schemes with the help and guidance of the EMN.

There is clear evidence of mutual learning for the mentors and mentees and the development of a knowledge-sharing environment for individuals and the business.

Future plans

There are three key objectives for the future.

1 Introduce an e-mentoring scheme to help overcome the distance barrier and also enable global reach for the Mentoring Programme. A pilot scheme is already under way and the initial results and feedback have been very positive. Plans are currently being drawn up to formally launch the EMN E-Mentoring Programme. Mentors and mentees will span the globe and will be made up of people from BT, its joint ventures and strategic global partners.

2 Develop links with external mentoring organizations to carry out a benchmarking exercise and share best practice.
3 Gain a recognized accreditation for the programme.

Zulfi Hussain can be contacted at zulfi@admnet.org or at zulfi.hussain@bt.com or by telephone on 0113 246 6730 or mobile telephone on 07802 920642.

Building a mentoring culture – the World Bank experience

Elizabeth Lopez[16]

The World Bank mentoring programme officially began in 1997. Although long-service staff recall that there used to be mentoring on a very informal basis in the bank before its reorganization in 1987, between 1987 and 1997 mentoring was hardly carried out at all in the organization. In September of 1997 the bank launched a programme called the Asia Pilot Mentoring Program, for professional women from developing countries and working mainly in two parts of the world – East Asia and South Asia. This programme involved fifty pairs of mentors and mentees.

From the success of that programme a whole mentoring movement has evolved in the bank. There are presently sixteen programmes and four more planned. These mentoring programmes are all different in certain aspects and alike in others. Our goal is to take the organization to the point where everyone who wants a mentor can have access to one. Already we have 1000 pairs working together.

The World Bank's main mission is the alleviation of poverty. This includes a whole array of different programmes being carried out in many of the developing countries. We have staff of around 10,000 people – 161 nationalities working together in a very diversified workforce. The bank is divided into five regions, after a recent reorganization changed its management structure to a matrix. All these factors together have created an organization that was greatly in need of mentoring programmes.

Mentoring in the World Bank is more experienced staff helping less experienced staff, taking into consideration that they do not have a reporting relationship. They can work on career issues, they can work on technical issues and, sometimes, we understand that mentors and mentees are now working on personal issues.

Programme co-ordination

Sixteen programmes are run independently. There is still a central co-ordination function but it does not have a supervisory role. Instead, it provides consulting services to any group within the organization on how to implement a mentoring programme. Lately, we have also been providing consulting to other organizations, which are interested in our programme and which have been benchmarking their programme against ours.

Another part of the co-ordinator's role is quality control. Even though there are no supervisory aspects of this co-ordination, there is great interest in ensuring the programmes will be as productive as possible. We also help develop project leadership for these programmes and support them with articles, books, workshops and a mentor database. For the hundreds of mentors in this database, we have information regarding the fields they work in, how long they have been with the bank, their nationality and gender, everything that we could need in order to make a good match. Also, as part of the central co-ordinator's role, we have meetings with other programme co-ordinators in order to learn from each other. The chair of the mentoring programme co-ordinators' group is one of the project co-ordinators.

These programmes are demand driven and they usually come from the grass roots up. Groups come to the co-ordinator's office to find out how to implement a mentoring programme. We provide guidelines on how to implement successful mentoring programmes and how to meet the needs of their targeted groups. Each programme is financed separately by the vice-presidency that wants the mentoring programme. Each programme has a co-ordinator chosen by the given group and also a steering committee made up of six to eight people. The members are selected by the sponsors of the programme within that group. Usually they involve staff members from all levels that the programme is going to cover. Some programmes only address the needs of a specific professional group and some programmes include all the staff, for example those who are working within a region.

We start with the purpose for the programme. Is there a real need? It is important that top management or sponsors at top management level are part of the programme and that they also take part in the design, along with line managers and mentees. These three groups work together in a steering committee to achieve the best results for each mentoring programme. They also have to find the financial resources.

The process begins with a meeting of mentees. A needs assessment is made using a form that is designed to take all the mentees' needs into consideration. Another form is also given to the mentors to find out what they want to mentor on (i.e. mentors' competencies). Then the programmes are launched, usually in a ceremony led by the vice-president. Other speakers may include a mentor and a mentee who have been successful in another programme.

The next step in the programme design is to select and match mentors and mentees. Mentees and mentors apply voluntarily. It is always emphasized in these programmes that they are not remedial in nature. The organization has other means to deal with remedial issues. Training of the mentors and mentees takes into consideration the level of commitment among top management, line managers and mentees, and how the mentors are going to be supported (i.e. how their contribution is going to be reinforced).

The programmes are also monitored in order to ensure that they sustainable. Assessment and review of the process is continuous and followed at the end by a final evaluation. It is being strongly recommended now that this final evaluation be done by an outside company and we are getting very impressive results from the evaluations, which provide the stimulus for more programmes to be implemented.

Benefits of the mentoring programme for the World Bank Group

In no particular order of priority the most frequently observed benefits of the programme are:

- Staff feel more welcome. The organization has in the past three years recruited 3000 new staff members. Mentoring helps them to gain a better understanding of the organization and to feel valued.
- Staff develop greater professionalism and contribute more to the institution.
- Highly qualified staff are retained.
- Professional knowledge is transferred from experienced staff to less experienced staff. (This does not necessarily mean older to younger!)
- Practical reinforcement of knowledge acquired elsewhere (e.g. in classroom learning).
- The organizational culture is preserved. The World Bank is made up of people from all over the world, so it is very important that all mentees are aware of the cultural similarities and differences that they will encounter. Mentoring is effective in teaching less experienced staff what this organizational culture is and how to make the best of it. In theory at least, this has a positive impact on productivity.
- An increasing sense of trust is being reported by mentees towards the organization, reversing a trend observed in recent years.
- A community of learning is arising. The bank is becoming more of a learning organization as people begin to share their knowledge
- A culture of mentoring is gradually developing in the organization.

Benefits for the mentee

The benefits are not all for the organization. There are also benefits for the mentee and the mentor. The mentees, through the various mentoring programmes, have an opportunity to acquire technical and organizational knowledge, and to improve their interpersonal skills. They also are being helped with career guidance and development from staff who have been in the organization for longer. They also benefit from developing a sense of trust. Perhaps the most important aspect is that mentoring offers to the mentee a personal reflective space, where the mentor and mentee have the opportunity to exchange ideas and points of view outside any reporting relationship. Mentoring is an ideal opportunity for a mentee to reflect and gain insight into his or her own professional development and behaviours.

It is important to mention here that the benefits to the mentee do not include sponsorship. Mentees at the World Bank are clearly informed in their training programmes that participating in a mentoring programme is not going to be a sponsoring relationship and that they should not expect to get promoted. If they get promoted, it is because they have come to the point where their career and technical skills deserve a promotion. They must go through the usual processes to be considered for more senior roles.

Benefits for the mentor

Through the evaluation of the programme mentors report that they:

- are developing better developmental skills, which they find useful in carrying out their management relationships
- gain insight into the perspectives of new staff
- have an opportunity to understand what new recruits or less experienced staff members have to deal with in their work
- enjoy the generativity efforts. Most mentors are at an age at which they really feel the psychosocial need to give back to society – to give to new generations some of the knowledge and experience that they have gained during the years that they have been at the organization and in their professional field. That provides them with a great sense of satisfaction, from the awareness that they are leaving a legacy to these mentees
- are challenged by the mentees in a way that involves a lot of inner thinking and reframing of some of the mentors' points of view or previous impressions
- include their mentoring activities in their overall performance management, as one of the developmental activities they do throughout the year.

We also educate mentors to ensure they do not expect mentees to be an extra pair of hands. This is a relationship in which the sharing and the giving will become the most important activity.

Selecting mentees and mentors for the different World Bank mentoring programmes

We apply a several-step process. Mentees are invited to participate; they fill in a form in which they indicate that they want to be considered as a mentee and on this form they also mark the areas, in which they want to be mentored. The mentors are also invited to participate and to indicate to the steering committee those areas that they feel most comfortable mentoring in. Once we have the mentors and mentees on our database and we have information on them – not only what their needs are but also information about their previous career development and educational experience – then we begin the matching process.

We have very clear guidelines on the matching process. The first and foremost parameter is that there is no reporting relationship between mentor and mentee. In cases, where there is a mentee who clearly specifies that they want a specific mentor, that is considered and if the other criteria are fine, we let the match proceed. Other characteristics that form part of the guidelines are:

- There has to be at least one grade level difference but hopefully not more than two. Also taken into consideration is the previous education background of both mentors and mentees.
- How does the career development of the mentors match the career ambitions of the mentees?
- The express needs of the mentee versus those of the mentor
- Cultural differences (when we know there are cultural differences that could hinder the relationship we do not match those pairs, but in other cases their differences may enhance the relationship).
- Gender considerations. Will the mentee benefit more by being mentored by a mentor from the same gender?

We look at these factors one by one. Many members of the steering committee have a pretty good knowledge of the different mentees and mentors, so, using the guidelines, they have a good track record of successful matching.

The next step is training mentors and mentees. The programme includes managing their expectations and giving them basic information about mentoring. We also use an instrument (FiroB) which helps mentor and mentee find more about each other's personality and ways of communicating. Also we talk about their concerns and try to address them. Finally, they go through a practice session to anchor the skills required as mentor or mentee.

Sustaining the programme

The programme is constantly monitored by the co-ordinators. First, the co-ordinator makes a special effort to interview, two months after the programme has begun, all the mentees (or at least a representative sample) in order to find out how the relationship is going for them. We assume that if the relationship is going fine for the mentee, it is also working for the mentor. Other evaluations take place periodically, in some cases often once a quarter and culminating in a final evaluation of relationships/the programme after one to two years. The central office provides assistance on the design of forms and information about conducting offline evaluations.

Some programmes check mentors and mentees, to see how it is going for both groups. We also have social gatherings, which meet once a month or every two months, over breakfast or lunch, where they bring speakers to talk to them on different kinds of topics. These may be technical issues, or mentoring issues such as how to improve their relationships, or any other topic the steering committee may consider important.

There is also a recognition programme for mentors. For example, some vice-presidents send communications to the mentors in appreciation of the work they have been doing. It has a very good effect on the programme if top management keeps involved and demonstrates interest by coming to social gatherings and by publicly recognizing mentors.

The co-ordinator role is key to the success of the programme. The co-ordinator has to be committed to learning and has to keep the process going after the enthusiasm from the launch of the programme has died down. The quality and quantity of sustained attention to the programme seems to have a direct correlation with the quality of the programme itself. Relationships have to be reinforced in order to stop them unfolding, at least at the beginning.

If mentors want to get in touch with mentees, that is perfectly okay. However, we have made it very clear in our programmes that the responsibility to keep the relationship going lies with the mentee.

Over the three years that the programme has been running, we have learnt some useful lessons. Among the most important of these is the importance of a good, solid steering committee. The steering committee plays a key role in helping implement and launch the programme, gives recognition to mentors and mentees, helps with the matching process and also helps in sustaining the programme. Another lesson learned is that the mentee has a higher responsibility in making the relationship work than the mentor. All programmes should have a budget for training and for speakers, either in-house or externally resourced (training people in house meant that the costs of the programmes were substantially reduced).

The mentoring co-ordinators' group is another successful innovation, the group has a lot of energy and is capable of making the whole mentoring culture more forward-looking. We are learning day by day. The immense size of the organization and the cultural diversity within it provide a constant stream of information about what works best in each of the programmes. One area of best practice that we have found is to use a participatory approach; the more people participating in the programme the greater the chances of success it has. Sometimes the tasks are divided among the steering committee. For instance, some members do the launching and some are in charge of participating in the matching process. The programmes that have 'drowned' in our organization have been mainly those that did not have a participatory approach. Those programmes that divide the tasks move forward much more fluently.

Programmes that have high top management involvement also have greater chances of success. Where all staff levels are involved, everyone feels part of the mentoring culture. Moreover, people not in the programme are less likely to feel left out or to feel that other groups are getting better opportunities than they are. Planning ahead in each of the mentoring programmes speeds up the implementation of the programme and increases the chances of both a successful launch and sustaining the programme. When planning steps are not followed logically, there is a much greater chance the programme may fail.

Our future plans include that every staff member, who would like to have mentoring, should have access to a mentor. Another goal is to be able to expand mentoring to the other country offices, making this a distinctive characteristic of the World Bank culture all around the world. Another future plan is that mentees will become mentors as they become more knowledgeable and more experienced. In short, we aim to continue to evaluate and improve our mentoring efforts with a view to building an enduring mentoring culture.

For more information contact elopez@worldbank.org.

Notes

1 After graduating from the London School of Economics Marianne Ecker worked for a few years in the voluntary sector. From the mid 1980s she began to specialize in learning and development. From 1993–2000 she worked as Training and Development Policy Advisor for the London Borough of Ealing, where she led the development of their first mentoring scheme. Marianne now works as Organizational Development Manager for the London Borough of Brent.

2 This section was written in consultation with Judith Carlson. Monika Beutel and Judith Carlson are past course directors to the 'Women Entrepreneurs' programme at the University of Hertfordshire. Monika Beutel was course director until 1998. She first set up the programme and designed the mentoring scheme. Judith Carlson further developed and improved the programme since 1998. The programme will continue to be offered subject to continuing EU Social Fund funding support.

Monika Beutel works as a freelance researcher, policy consultant and trainer. She is also a mentor and a community mediator. Previously she worked as a lecturer in social sciences with appointments at higher education institutions in Britain, Canada and Germany. Most of her university career was spent at the University of Hertfordshire, where she held academic management posts as Head of Department and Associate Dean. She also took on responsibility for courses to promote women's management and business development and for the university's relationship with Business Link. She initiated mentoring schemes with local businesses and local schools. Her contribution to *Mentoring for Diversity* describes her experience of setting up a women entrepreneurs course with mentor support. Monika is currently carrying out a comparative research project on women entrepreneurs in Britain and Germany.

Judith Carlson worked as a lecturer in Social Policy at the University of Hertfordshire. She took over from Monika as Course Director for Women Entrepreneurs and continued to develop the mentoring scheme in conjunction with the Mentor's Forum at Herts TEC. Judith is currently working as a local government officer in the field of urban regeneration.

3 The quotes in this section have been taken from 'Women Entrepreneurs' mentoring records – namely Mentoring Contracts, Mentor Requests and Mentor Report Forms. The quotes have not been attributed in order to preserve confidentiality and maintain anonymity of participants to the mentoring scheme. Names have been changed for the same reason.

4 A recent survey has been undertaken of 'women entrepreneurs' participants (population 165 and 90 respondents (further replies are still coming
in). Several references are made to the findings from this survey. Analysis of
the survey results is continuing. Two-thirds of respondents had started or
were preparing to start a business. During 1999–2000 there were eighty-one
participants or four intakes and of these 65 per cent achieved the
Postgraduate Certificate in Small Business Management.

5 Ellen J. Wallach is a consultant, speaker, writer and film-maker specializing
in career and organizational development. She works with public and
private organizational clients to find ways to keep employees happy and
productive. Ellen designs mentoring systems and programmes to develop
and retain the best employees. She is interested in motivation, effectiveness
and success. Ellen has developed four training films for the American
Management Association and is a frequent contributor to popular publications and professional journals. Most recently her work has appeared in the
Wall Street Journal's *National Business Employment Weekly*. She is the co-
author of *The Job Search Companion*, an organizer and motivator for job
seekers, now in its sixth printing.

LueRachelle Brim-Atkins is a consultant, keynote speaker and trainer
specializing in diversity and organizational development. She works with
clients in the public, private and non-profit organizations to help people
connect to their hearts, minds and spirits as they connect to each other.
LueRachelle provides training and consulting services that help organizations find, retain and develop great people to do great work. She frequently
writes articles on diversity for professional publications and helps
managers develop mentoring programmes as a logical way to enhance the
value for diversity in workplaces. She is a popular workshop leader and
conference keynote speaker, and is currently finishing a book on honouring
heart and spirit in the workplace.

6 Christina Jellbring Klang is a psychologist with an extensive career in line
management and leadership development in the airline industry. At SAS,
which she left in September 2000, she led the company's mentoring
programme. She is now a consultant working with 'Trygghetsrådet', the
employment security council in Sweden.

7 Margaret Waller, PhD is an associate professor at the Arizona State
University, School of Social Work, and has been a family therapist since
1982. She teaches human behaviour, cultural diversity, and clinical practice
with families. Her research and writing centres on intercultural understanding and resilience in individuals, families and communities, with
particular emphasis on indigenous peoples.

8 Jill Nanson works for the Student Services Centre at Sheffield Hallam
University. Based in the Careers and Employment Team, she manages a
broad range of projects related to graduate employability and employment.
Recently her team has focused on mentoring initiatives, the first of which,
SESSAME, is described in this article. A new programme will commence in
2001, and will once again involve local companies and organizations. This

time the students taking part will be from the University's School of Environment and Development.

9 Coral Gardiner's (MCIPD, DipEd, MEd) extensive and longstanding involvement in mentoring includes the initiation and establishment of the renowned BEAT Project and the Congruent Mentoring Network for the West Midlands Probation Service. Her current role examines all aspects of educational mentoring structure, systems and development on the government-sponsored Excellence in Cities Learning Mentor strand for Birmingham Education Service.

10 Copyright William A. Gray and Marilynne Miles Gray 2000. Since 1978, William A. Gray and Marilynne Miles Gray have been pioneers in the development of planned mentoring programmes which meet the needs of individual participants and their sponsoring organizations. While developing over 120 very different programmes and training over 14 000 participants, they have created a wide variety of print materials. These have been converted into web-based Online Mentoring Solutions (OMS) for identifying suitable programme applicants, matching compatible mentor–protégé partners, identifying their preferred mentoring styles, tracking each protégé's progress and evaluating benefits gained. The OMS system permits more people to participate, consistent with diversity initiatives, while saving time and money.

11 Asif Mukhtar BSc (Hons), MSc is the Project Co-ordinator for the Pakistani Mentoring Partnership, an Excellence in Cities Learning Mentor in Birmingham, and Secretary of the charity West Midlands Mentoring Network which is affiliated to the National Mentoring Network. He has successfully obtained twenty-one Millennium Awards from the Millennium Commission to offer Pakistani undergraduates for mentoring in schools.

12 Will Large is the Management Development Adviser for Transco (now part of the Lattice Group). He holds a teacher's certificate in further education, and a masters degree in management learning. He has twenty-five years experience of training and organizational development, and was responsible for establishing and managing mentoring programmes in Transco since 1997.

13 Jonathan Meth is director of writernet – an organization which provides writers working in performance mediums with information, advice, guidance and training. He trained as a theatre director at the Bristol Old Vic Theatre School. He is also Adviser on research to Metier, the National Training Organization for the Arts, Adviser to the London Arts Board, New Writing Working Group, Adviser on Creative Writing in Higher Education, to the Arts Council of England Literature Department, a Board Member of the Actors Touring Company, External Assessor for the New Opportunities Fund Lottery Programme, Vice-Chair of the London Arts Alliance and a Fellow of the Royal Society for the Arts.

14 Heather Piper and John Piper work at Manchester Metropolitan University. Heather Piper has experience in research and social work education (including some involvement of mentoring projects). John Piper's experience is in quality management and teacher education. Their interest in

mentoring is essentially academic, and focuses on issues that arise when a practice is translated into settings quite distinct from those where it was successfully developed, and the way this can mask structural and economic realities. The implication is that mentoring is not always value-free, but can be significantly ideological.

15 Zulfiqar Hussain is a respected Management and IT professional. He has a track record of delivering complex business critical solutions. Zulfi has received awards for his achievements in his personal and professional life, and also for his contribution to the community in the pursuit of helping others realize their full potential. Zulfi has become a key contributor in the areas of Mentoring, Equality and Diversity, Social Inclusion, Cultural Awareness and Religious Tolerance. Zulfi holds a BSc in Engineering Systems and Control, Certificate in Management Studies (CMS), Diploma in Management Studies (DMS) and the Masters in Business Administration (MBA). Zulfi is currently employed by BT Ignite Solutions with responsibility for its security and business continuity of the network infrastructure used by a major international bank. He is also a member of the government's National Minority Ethnic Advisory Group for New Deal and a member BT's Ethnic Minority Network strategy team with full responsibility for the EMN mentoring programme.

16 Elizabeth Lopez is a Senior Human Resources Counsellor at the World Bank, with over twenty years' experience in developing staff. She has coordinated the mentoring programme of the organization since it began in 1998.

References

Alred, G., Garvey, B. and Smith, R. (1998). *The Mentoring Pocketbook*. Alresford, Management Pocketbooks.

Alleman, E., Cochran, J., Doverspike, J. and Newman, I. (1984). Enriching mentoring relationships. *Personnel and Guidance Journal*, **62**(6), 329–32.

Atkinson, J. and Pollard, E. (1997). *Jobsearch: A Review of the UK Literature Prior to the Jobseeker's Allowance*. Institute for Employment Studies, University of Sussex.

Banks, M. H. and Davies, J. B. (1990). *Motivation, Unemployment and Employment Department Programmes*. Department of Employment, Research Paper 80. DfEE Publications.

Barry, M. (1996). The empowerment process: leading from behind? *Youth and Policy*, **54**, 1–12.

Battagliola, F. (1995). The social rejection of young people without qualifications. *Prospects*, **25**(3), 407–20.

Beattie, A. and Holden, B. (1994). Young person mentoring in schools: the Doncaster experience. *Education and Training*, **36**(5), 8–15.

Bentley, T., Oakley, K., Gibson, S. and Kilgow, K. (1999). *The Real Deal – What Young People Really Think about Government, Politics and Social Exclusion*. Demos.

Beutel, M. (1994). Training for women returners. In *Crossing the Frontiers* (Mee Foong Lee et al., eds), Council of Europe.

Boeteng, P. (1999). Eighth National Mentoring Conference, 5 May.

Briggs Myers, I. (1980). *Gifts Differing*. Consulting Psychologists Press.

Brown, R. K. (1997). Unemployment, youth and the employment relationship. *Youth and Policy*, **55**, 28–39.

Buchholz, E. S. and Korn-Bursztyn, C. (1993). Children of adolescent mothers: are they at risk for abuse? *Adolescence*, **28**, 361–78.

Business in the Community (1993). *An Introduction to Mentoring*. BIC.

Carlson, J. and Paterson, B. (2000). Success through mentoring. *Better Business*, **74**, March.

Carter, S. (1994). *An Essential Guide to Mentoring*. Institute of Management Foundation.

Clutterbuck, D. (1991). *Everyone Needs a Mentor: Fostering Talent at Work*. 2nd edn. IPM.

Clutterbuck, D. and Snow, D. (1994). *BEAT Beginning Employment and Training: An Evaluation*. European Mentoring Centre.

Coles, B. (1995). *Youth and Social Policy*. UCL Press.

Coles, M. (1997). Women help women succeed. *Sunday Times*, 2 February.

Coles, M. (2000). Women make the grade in business. *Sunday Times*, 9 January.

Coletta, N. D. and Hunter Gregg, M. A. (1981). Adolescent mothers' vulnerability to stress. *Journal of Nervous and Mental Disease*, **162**, 50–3.

Combs-Orme, T. (1993). Health effects of adolescent pregnancy: implications for social workers. *Families in Society: The Journal of Contemporary Human Services*, **74**, 344–53.

Deakin, N. (1996). Mister Murray's ark. *Charles Murray and the Underclass*. Institute of Economic Affairs, pp. 74–80.

Deutsches Jugendinstitut (1997). *Mentoring for Women in Europe*. DJI.

DfEE (1997a). *Survey of Careers Service Work with Disaffected Young People*. DfEE.

DfEE (1997b). *Directory of Careers Service Work with Disaffected Young People*. DFEE.

France, A. (1996). Youth and citizenship in the 1990s. *Youth and Policy*, **53**, 28–43.

France, A. (1998). Why should we care? Young people, citizenship and questions of social responsibility. *Journal of Youth Studies*, **1**(1), 97–111.

France, A. and Wiles, P. (1997). Dangerous futures; social exclusion and youth work in late modernity. *Social Policy and Administration*, **31**(5), 59–78.

Gardiner, C. (1994). *BEAT Beginning Employment and Training: An initiative to Help Young Offenders into Employment and Training*. West Midlands Probation Service.

Gay, B. and Stephenson, J. (1998) The mentoring dilemma: guidance and/or direction? *Mentoring and Tutoring*, **6**(1/2), 43–55.

Gulam, W. and Zulfiquar, M. (1998). Mentoring – Dr Plum's elixir and the alchemist's stone. *Mentoring and Tutoring*, **5**(3/1), 39–45.

Harris, A., Jamieson, I., Pearce, D. and Russ, J. (1997). *Equipping Young People for Working Life: Effective Teaching and Learning in Work Related Contexts*. DfEE Research Studies RS46. Stationery Office.

Haskett, M. E., Johnson, C. A. and Miller, J. W. (1994). Individual differences in risk of child abuse by adolescent mothers: assessment in the perinatal period. *Journal of Child Psychology and Psychiatry and Allied Disciplines*, **35**, 461–74.

Hay, J. (1995). *Transformational Mentoring*. McGraw-Hill.

Hayes, C. (ed.) (1987). *Risking the Future*. National Academy Press.

Hepworth S. and Capelin, H. (1986). *A Review of the UK Literature on the Benefits of Occupational Advice and Guidance*. Psychological Services Report 204. Manpower Services Commission.

Hirsh, S. K. and Kummerow, J. M. (1990). *Introduction to Type in Organisations*. 2nd edn. Oxford Psychologists Press.

Honey, P. and Mumford, A. (1992). *The Manual of Learning Styles*. 3rd edn. P. Honey.

Jones, G. (1995). *Leaving Home*. Open University Press.

Jones, G. (1996). Deferred citizenship – a coherent policy of exclusion? *Young People Now*, March, 27.

Kiernan, K. (1992). The impact of family disruption in childhood on transitions made in young adult life, *Population Studies*, **46**, 213–34.

Kram, K. E. and Hall, D, T. (1996). Mentoring in a context of diversity and turbulence. In *Managing Diversity* (E. E. Kossek and S. A. Lobel, eds), Blackwell.

Levitas, R. (1996). The concept of social exclusion and the new Durkheimian hegemony. *Critical Social Policy*, **16**, 5–20.

Megginson, D. and Clutterbuck, D. (1995). *Mentoring in Action: A Practical Guide for Managers*. Kogan Page.

Michaels, R., Headlam-Wells, J. and Wolfing, D. (1995). *Professional Women's Re-entry into the Labour Market*.WRN.

Morley, L. (1995). Empowerment and the New Right. *Youth and Policy*, **51**, 1–10.

Mullender, A. and Ward, D. (1991). *Self Directed Group Work: Users Take Action For Empowerment*. Whiting and Birch.

Mumford, A. (1998). Styles of mentoring. *Management Skills and Development*, June, 12–16.

Murray, M. and Owen, M. (1991). *Beyond the Myths and Magic of Mentoring*. Jossey-Bass.

National Mentoring Network (1998). *Mentoring News*, **6**, June.

NICEC/ICG (1998). *Briefing: Career Guidance and Mentoring for Disengaged Young People*. Institute of Careers Guidance.

Nuckolls, K. B., Cassell, J. and Kaplan, C. (1972). Psychosocial assets, life crisis, and the prognosis of pregnancy. *American Journal of Epidemiology*, **95**, 431–41.

Phillip-Jones, L. (1989). Common problems in planned mentoring programmes. *Mentoring International*, **3**(1), 36–40.

Phipps-Yonas, S. (1980). Teenage pregnancy and motherhood: a review of the literature. *American Journal of Orthopsychiatry*, **50**, 403–26.

Piper, H. and Piper, J. (1998). Disaffected youth; a wicked issue: a worse label. *Youth and Policy*, **62**, 32–43.

Piper, H. and Piper, J. (1999). Young people: problems for mentoring. *Mentoring and Tutoring*, **7**(2), 121–30.

Piper, H. and Piper, J. (2000). Disaffected young people as the problem. Mentoring as the solution. Education and work as the goal. *Education and Work*, **13**(2).

Procidano, M. E. and Heller, K. (1983). Measures of perceived social support from friends and from family: three validation studies. *American Journal of Community Psychology*, **11**, 1–24.

Quality Careers Services Limited (QCSL) (1995). *Reaching the Unreached*. QCSL.

Quint, E. D. and Kopelman, R. E. (1995). The effects of jobsearch behaviour and vocational self-concept crystallisation on job acquisition: is there an interaction? *Journal of Employment Counselling*, **32**(2), 88–96.

Rickel, A. (1989). *Teen Pregnancy and Parenting*. Hemisphere.

Roberts, A. (1998). The androgynous mentor: bridging stereotypes in mentoring. *Mentoring and* Tutoring, **6**(1/2), 18–30.

Russell, P. (1997). The use of mentoring projects for offenders. Paper presented to conference of 'Support Systems for Adult Learners'.

Segerman-Peck, L. (1996). *Networking and Mentoring: A Woman's Guide*. Piatkus.

Segerman-Peck, L. (2000a). *Essentials of: Using your Mentor Wisely*. Segerman-Peck Publishing.

Segerman-Peck, L. (2000b). *Essentials of: Being a Better Mentor*. Segerman-Peck Publishing.

Smith, R. and Aldred, G. (1993). The impersonation of wisdom. In *Mentoring – Perspectives on School Based Education* (D. MacIntyre, H. Hagger and M. Wilkin, eds), Kogan Page.

Thomas, D. A. (1989). Mentoring and irrationality: the role of racial taboos. *Human Resources Management*, **28**(2), 279–90.

Thomas, D. A. (1993). Racial dynamics in cross-race developmental relationships. *Administrative Sciences Quarterly*, **38**(3), 169–94.

Tilsley, P. (1997). *An Evaluation of West Midlands Probation Service B.E.A.T. Project*.

Turner, R. J., Grindstaff, C. F. and Phillips, N. (1990). Social support and outcome in teenage pregnancy. *Journal of Health and Social Behavior*, **31**, 43–57.

Walker, A. (1996). *Blaming the Victims, Charles Murray and the Underclass*. Institute of Economic Affairs, pp. 66–74.

White, M. and Lakey, J. (1992). *Restart Effect*. Policy Studies Institute.

Williamson, H. (1993). Youth policy in the UK and the marginalisation of young people. *Youth and Policy*, **40**, 33–48.

Williamson, H. and Middlemiss, R. (1999). The emperor has no clothes: cycles of delusion in community interventions with 'disaffected' young men. *Youth and Policy*, **63**, 13–24.

Zielinski, D. (2000). Mentoring up. *Training*, October.

10

Some key issues for diversity mentoring

David Clutterbuck

In this chapter, I extract a number of themes from the case studies and, where appropriate, offer further observation upon them. The cases represent a wide variety of applications of mentoring, on behalf of a wide variety of audiences. Diversity issues are sometimes at the core of the relationship; at other times just one aspect of it. In short, we have great diversity to draw upon.

The themes I have extracted are as follows.

Power in the relationship

The expectations regarding power and the actual application of power and influence in our cases illustrate well the difference between sponsorship-oriented mentoring and developmental mentoring. In several of the cases – for example, Welle's case of a gay mentoring pair, the expectation and practice of sponsorship was an important part of the relationship. Power of knowledge was also an important element in some programmes – for example, help in navigating the complexities of the theatre system in England was a core activity for the disabled writers' programme. In the case of Fiona and Bob, sponsorship was a key part of the mutual expectation.

By contrast, at Ealing Council, very senior people were excluded from the scheme in part because they were too powerful. Another interesting spin on the issue is Procter & Gamble's deliberate reversal of the power structure, which opened up extensive learning opportunities for both mentors and mentees. Exerting their own authority as mentors to people much more senior than themselves provided an unusual opportunity to develop leadership skills and to become comfortable in dealing with powerful people.

It is interesting that one of the key areas, in which a mentor's power is exercised – opening doors – was particularly useful in one of the programmes where mentor and mentee are not linked by an organizational hierarchy. Monika Beutel's description of mentoring to help women set up small businesses emphasizes the value of opening doors through networking. Again, there appears to be a very different emphasis between networking in sponsorship mentoring (I know just the person to introduce you to) and developmental mentoring (let me help you think through how you can build the networks you need). Both approaches appear valid, but the nature of the relationship is likely to determine which predominates.

Culture change

A number of organizations, including Procter & Gamble, saw diversity mentoring as an opportunity to change their culture, by changing people's perspectives. They recognized a link between that greater sensitivity to the perceptions and values of people within the organization and greater sensitivity towards customers and the customer environment; or they perceived the intrinsic value of a working environment that recognizes and values difference.

The Advisory Circles concept reported by Wallach and Brim-Atkins takes the concept of diversity along the lines of a potential competitive advantage. Defining diversity as 'all the ways people differ, both visible and invisible', it encouraged people to find coaches/mentors they did not know and to expand their comfort zones to include people with very substantial differences to themselves. Diversity issues, it emphasizes, 'are often in that uncomfortable area we don't see and don't like to talk about'.

One issue that deserves greater exploration is whether diversity mentoring approaches adapt to organizational culture, and if so how. For example, are relationships in a generally open culture more likely to focus on valuing difference than on overcoming disadvantage? Defining what is meant by an open culture may prove difficult, and establishing valid measures that would apply to different organizations in different contexts even more so.

A potentially useful matrix in this context would be that shown in Figure 10.1.

A broadly based relationship in an open culture is likely to receive more support than one in a closed culture. If the latter is to thrive, it may have to operate relatively clandestinely, working in effect against the system. If the objective is to change the culture, both indirect and direct support will be needed from those in positions of power. A narrowly focused relationship, conversely, might be expected to thrive in a closed culture, where the goals and

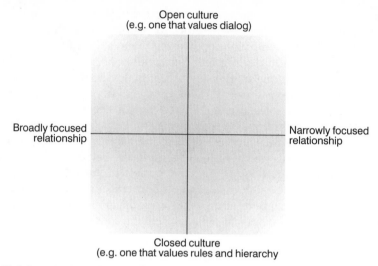

Figure 10.1 Organization culture matrix

outcomes are more clearly defined. In an open culture, the probability is high that the learner will find many sources of support and learning, and will be less reliant on one specific mentoring relationship. These observations, we stress, are conjecture at this stage. However, they appear to fit in well with anecdotal data and are at least a starting point for further research.

A pragmatic starting point for assessing the influence of organizational culture on mentoring may be to use the organization's own stated (published) values and assign each a valence according to how employees and others perceive the organization to put the value into practice. In one organization, for example, the disparity between the stated value of work–life balance and the experience/perception of employees (you only progress if you are prepared to sacrifice most of your free time) has tended to focus mentoring discussions either on career decisions or work problems, or both. However, educating mentors and mentees that this is a legitimate topic for discussion is raising the profile of this clash between the real and the published culture. The more it is discussed between mentor and mentee, the more pressure on the organization to change the culture.

A similar situation arose in the European operations of a major US computer software company a while ago. The stated culture was one that valued people's individual aspirations; the reality was that people were expected to conform to a career model of steady progression through team member, team leader, project leader and beyond. When the newly established mentor group met to compare notes, they quickly identified that there was a hitherto unrecognized group of employees, who perceived themselves to be disadvantaged by the cultural norms. These employees had no desire to take on managerial or supervisory responsibilities. On the contrary, their model of success was to develop their technical competence, becoming specialists. The mentors were able to make representations as a group, persuading the organization of the value of diversity in career paths and changing the culture so that the specialists felt more valued and were better able to contribute.

A recognition of the role national culture plays in mentoring approaches is also appropriate. The SAS case raises the issue of more authoritarian cultures, such as Germany or Japan, and how mentors and mentees from these backgrounds will differ in their expectations from the relationship. As indicated in an earlier chapter, field experience of one of the authors suggests the importance of being prepared to negotiate the relationship norms within the context of both national culture and organizational culture – and of equipping mentors and mentees to do so.

Training

The importance of training – particularly for mentors – is emphasized in many of the organizational cases, for example, the teen mothers' programme, Ealing Council, the Cabinet Office programme for disabled people and Wallach and Brim-Atkins. An initial 'sheep-dip' is generally seen as inadequate and it is notable that, in some cases – for example, the Sheffield programme for disadvantaged students – the mentors themselves have requested further training. This appears to be related to their own desire to learn and expectation of achieving learning through the relationship. The teen parents programme requires mentors to attend training sessions spread over seven weeks and includes continued weekly supervision by the programme co-ordinator.

Training in most cases has two facets – an understanding of mentoring per se and an appreciation of the issues facing the target group of mentees. How programme co-ordinators integrate these two facets is another area, in which additional research would be useful.

In helping people understand diversity, Procter & Gamble's technique of helping people to think about different approaches (e.g. asking them to write with the other hand) is a very practical way of reinforcing the general message that different is not necessarily better or worse. However, the programmes generally felt the need to provide much greater specific awareness of diversity issues. Mentors to the Sheffield students, for example, were given guidelines on working with people who have dyslexia or hearing difficulties. The teen parents programme provides insights into the problems this group has, building in the mentors an understanding and empathy essential for creating deep rapport.

Setting goals

Mentees often find it difficult to set personal development goals. For example, the Sheffield students needed help in defining less tangible goals, such as building self-confidence.

Figure 10.2 Building self-awareness

A contributory factor here may be a relatively low level of self-awareness (see Figure 10.2). If nothing else, the model in Figure 10.2 helps open up some of the hidden boxes in the Johari window!

An important debate here is whether low self-awareness is the result of low motivation to explore the inner self (disinterest), or high motivation to avoid such exploration, or simply an inability to make complex emotional and rational connections (in which case there may be physiological aspects to consider as well). The approach in helping someone develop self-awareness will be different in each case and is likely to be least effective in bringing about personal change.

Belinda Johnson White talks of encouraging discussion of personal feelings, of refocusing from experiences to what has been learned from them. This introspection will inevitably lead, in most cases, to an increased self-awareness and may help the mentee become clearer about their personal goals, the extent of the opportunities available to them and the nature of the barriers, which lie between them and their goals.

A useful approach applied by one of the authors is to work with the mentee to establish as precisely as possible their definition of success. Generically, we can talk about success as *achieving what you value*. At a greater level of detail, the mentee can be asked to consider the relative importance to them of, say, monetary reward, career progression, job satisfaction and work–life balance. By understanding their own motivations and feelings about each of these areas, the mentee can begin to map out personal priorities.

The impact of stereotyping and/or prejudice

In our cases, mentees' experience of stereotyping or prejudice was almost always indirect – an observation that challenges conventional wisdom. For the Sheffield students, prejudice and racial bias were not significant barriers to employment, but relevant experience and skills were.

One of the few overt examples of stereotype driven bias concerns the attitudes of a sexist young mentee in the BEAT scheme. The mentor worked with the young man to help him develop a different perspective. This was a situation where the (female) mentor could easily have withdrawn from the relationship, on the grounds that it would be difficult to build rapport with someone, who had such different values. Seeing the task as a mutual learning opportunity is a more constructive – but much more challenging – option.

Setting boundaries

Mentors and mentees were not always sure where to set the boundaries of the relationship and what topics were admissible. In the teen parent programme, a boundary issue was how available the mentor would be to the mentee – what was reasonable to expect on both sides? In the case of the mentee with bipolar disorder, the mentor had to exercise discretion about when Charlie's needs had crossed over into psychotherapy or, in the case of some domestic issues, into family counselling.

A broad conclusion from the cases and from observation elsewhere is that boundaries need to be set initially as general programme guidelines, which are discussed and modified as needed by each mentoring pair.

Acknowledging the source of disadvantage

This is an issue which has not been widely explored in the mentoring literature. However, a study by David Thomas (1993) at Harvard into mentoring across racial boundaries found that pairs adopted one of two distinct strategies to manage the difference. One strategy, adopted mainly by people who were relatively close in age to each other, was to discuss race openly and view the cross-cultural dynamics as a strength of the relationship (direct engagement). The other, favoured by pairs with a greater age difference, was to ignore the race issue completely, or discuss it only at a very superficial level (denial and suppression). The strategy people adopted was also influenced by previous experiences at work.

Thomas established that alignment between mentor and mentee was key to the success of the relationship – both needed to adopt the same strategy. If they agreed to ignore the racial issue, the mentee often sought another relationship to compensate for the psychosocial elements and the relationship focused primarily on sponsorship.

In our cases, Gray and Gray make the overall point that diversity issues do not automatically arise from differences in race or gender – they may arise from a host of causes, including working styles.

Monika Beutel's case study illustrates an approach that allows people to decide for themselves whether and how their disability or differences should be acknowledged. Widening the definition of diversity and emphasizing the common challenges business women fact allowed a more positive agenda to emerge.

Procter & Gamble's feeling valued surveys are an innovative method of helping people acknowledge difference and place it in the context of experience.

In the end, the core message of almost all the cases is the value to both the individual and the organization of what Glynis Rankin describes in her case study as 'fundamentally affirming people as they are'.

Acknowledging the value of difference

The issue of how similar or different the mentee and mentor needed to be arose in many of the cases. Interestingly, the expectation that mentor and mentee should share the same background seems to be more common with some sources of disadvantage (gender and race) than others (e.g. physical ability). Belinda Johnson White showed initial concern as to whether a cross-race, cross-gender relationship would work – only to find that valuing each others' differences greatly strengthened the relationship. SAS has found it relatively easy to convince mentees of the value of having someone from a different background and many of these relationships seem to have flourished on the differences. Similarly, where the Sheffield students could not be matched with someone from the employment sector they were interested in, they generally accepted that a mentor from elsewhere could still have a useful helping role to play.

SAS, which perceives diversity as using the talents of people with different backgrounds, has made a virtue of seeking differences out, rather than avoiding them. It reports that 95 per cent of mentees see the value of having a mentor with a different background and observes that male mentees gain a better understanding of their own female direct reports when they have a female mentee. The whole area of male mentee/female mentor is remarkably unexplored – most studies focusing on male mentor/female mentee or same-sex relationships. Again, this is an issue on which we would like to see further research.

Brian Welle's account of a gay mentor/mentee relationship stresses the value of having a perceived disadvantage in common. Mentor and mentee had interests and experiences in common that helped establish rapport and legitimize the supporting role. In this case, the fact that both were working class also provided some commonality of experience, on which practical discussions could be based.

Mukhtar's account of mentoring Pakistani schoolchildren also suggests that having someone from the same community is important in gaining acceptance and trust within the relationship.

In short, our cases tell us that the issue of where to seek similarity and where to focus on difference is highly situation dependent.

Confidence

Many of our cases refer to the mentoring relationship in one way or another as a safe environment to explore difficult issues. Helping the mentee develop confidence was a recurring theme throughout the individual and organizational cases.

Intensity of the relationship

'I often left sessions with a thumping headache', says the mentor to Charlie, the mentee who suffers from bipolar disorder. While the level of intensity of discussion in this relationship was especially high, it illustrates the fact that effective mentoring is hard work. The mentee in the CIPD scheme reflects upon how her mentor was stretched and made to think on her feet.

Evolution of the relationship

Ever since Kram's analysis of the phases of a mentoring relationship, there has been a broad consensus that we largely understand this aspect of mentoring. Our case studies suggest that within the broad evolutionary framework, relationships follow their own developmental paths, in tune with the evolving needs of the mentee. In the Lloyds TSB case, the relationship initially emphasized coaching behaviours and the building of confidence. Thereafter, it was able to progress to broader issues. In the lesbian connection case, the initial meetings concentrated on helping the mentee fit into the particular academic environment and only gradually evolved into a concentration on how to stretch the mentee academically.

Field observation suggests that many relationships – particularly those that last for a relatively long time – progress through an agenda that focuses initially on practical, relatively immediate issues (including, for example, setting a career plan). As confidence between the two grows and the mentee better understands the potential of the relationship, the focus shifts to wider horizons and the deliberate seeking out of opportunities, by which the mentee can stretch himself or herself. Eventually, they enter what might be called 'the philosophical phase', where even broader issues of personal discovery emerge and the dialogue between mentor and mentee may take them both into uncharted territory. During this journey, the mentee may learn to rely less upon the mentor to provide the discipline and focus (as in the Lloyds TSB example) and more on their own inner strengths.

Creating clear expectations

One of the cases that particularly illustrates the value of having clear expectations is that of Charlie, the mentee with bipolar disorder. An initial expectation that the mentor would sort out Charlie's management committee (acting as a cross between a White Knight and a management consultant) gave way after discussion with the mentor to a greater understanding of what he should and could do for himself.

Reviewing progress

Transco, the disabled writers' mentoring scheme and most other developmental mentoring cases included some form of review or feedback about the progress of relationships and the programme as a whole. This contributed both to troubleshooting individual relationships, if they needed it, and to improving the operation of the programme, particular in terms of support provided.

Adapting the selection and matching system to take account of diversity issues

The disabled writers' mentoring scheme illustrates the importance for programme co-ordinators of understanding as deeply as possible the context, in which mentees put themselves forward. Expecting people to come for interview would be the norm in most contexts. Recognizing that some candidates might find this difficult, if not daunting, the organizers of this programme introduced the option of being interviewed by telephone.

Even in those programmes, which focused on people, who had made a mess of their lives so far, such as BEAT, the importance of involving the mentee in selecting their mentor comes across as a strong theme. Mentees in this scheme chose from a range of characteristics people who they felt could best 'help them sort out their lives'. By contrast, however, Transco adopted a process, by which senior managers nominated women managers, who they felt would benefit from having a mentor. It is important contextually here to recognize, however, that this particular programme was part of a much broader mentoring initiative aimed at a wider audience.

The story of Fiona and Bob provides a cautionary tale of the problems that arise when cross-gender mentor occurs between people, in a boss–direct report relationship. We would go so far as to say, based on this and numerous other cases, that mentoring in this context should be actively discouraged by organizations, because of the disruption and disharmony it can cause. Very rarely does the situation occur, where a mentor cannot be found outside the line. The manager, who feels that a direct report (of different or same gender) would benefit from having a mentor, must understand that attempting to take on the role himself or herself has a whole raft of negative consequences.

Programme management

Several programmes emphasize the importance of the relationship between the mentors and the programme co-ordinator. Once again, this is an aspect of mentoring, which is little explored – yet it clearly has a significant impact. The roles co-ordinators can play in supporting mentoring relationships can range from the merely administrative, through supervision, to a professional friend and adviser (mentor to the mentors). All these roles are illustrated in one or more of our cases.

The SAS case illustrates how rapidly a programme aimed at one group (in this case, women leaders) can expand to a much wider audience. This appears to be a significant trend, from the evidence of the authors' consulting work with organizations.

Summary

The issues selected here are simply those that stood out to the authors as recurring themes, but there are many more within the cases. It is a source of amazement that such a widely researched issue as mentoring contains so many largely unexplored facets. We hope that further research will illuminate some of these.

Reference

Thomas, D. (1993). Racial dynamics in cross-race developmental relationships. *Administrative Science Quarterly*, **38**, 169–94.

Index